PENGUIN CLASSICS

THE HISTORIES

TACITUS, born in about AD 56 in southern Gaul (modern Provence) under the emperor Nero, was probably the son of an equestrian. He was in Rome by 75, training as an orator. As Tacitus himself concedes at the opening of the *Histories*, his own political career flourished under the Flavian emperors, Vespasian (69–79), Titus (79–81) and Domitian (81–96). It was not until after the dynasty had ended that Tacitus set in motion his career as a writer. In quick succession, he published the *Agricola* (a biography of his father-in-law) and the *Germania* (an ethnographical study of the peoples of Germany), both in 98. There followed (some time early in the second century) his *Dialogue about Orators*. Today Tacitus is best known as a historian. His debut in the genre, *The Histories*, is a gripping narrative of turbulent events from Galba's accession in 69 until Domitian's assassination in 96. His next work, *The Annals*, moves further back in time to cover the Julio-Claudian emperors from Tiberius (14–37) to Nero (54–68). Neither narrative survives complete, but both preserve Tacitus' uniquely compelling historical voice and offer a chilling denunciation of the corrupting force of power in the Roman empire. His strong moralizing ethos, together with brilliant techniques of literary artistry, combine to create a powerful and enduring portrait of imperial Rome at its best and its worst. The culmination of Tacitus' public career was when he won the prestigious post of proconsul of Asia (112/13). He died at some point after 115 and probably lived into the reign of Hadrian (117–38), but there is no evidence for his later life or the date of his death.

KENNETH WELLESLEY was, until 1981, Reader in Humanity (Latin) at the University of Edinburgh. He contributed a number of papers to learned journals on various aspects of Roman history and literature and was also engaged in a textual, literary and historical study of the *Histories* of Tacitus. Most of the sites mentioned in the *Histories* were familiar to him from personal knowledge, and he was co-editor of the standard Teubner text of Tacitus (Leipzig). He died in 1995.

RHIANNON ASH is Fellow and Tutor in Classics at Merton College, Oxford. After taking an MA in Medieval Latin at the University of Toronto, she returned from Canada to Oxford, where she wrote a doctorate on Tacitus' *Histories*. Her publications include *Ordering Anarchy: Leaders and Armies in Tacitus' Histories* (1999) and a commentary, *Tacitus Histories Book II* (2007), in the Cambridge Greek and Latin Classics series. She has also written articles on Naevius, Pliny the Younger, Pliny the Elder, Suetonius and Plutarch.

TACITUS

The Histories

Translated by KENNETH WELLESLEY
Revised with a new Introduction by RHIANNON ASH

PENGUIN BOOKS

PENGUIN CLASSICS

Published by the Penguin Group
Penguin Books Ltd, 80 Strand, London WC2R ORL, England
Penguin Group (USA) Inc., 375 Hudson Street, New York, New York 10014, USA
Penguin Group (Canada), 90 Eglinton Avenue East, Suite 700, Toronto, Ontario, Canada M4P 2Y3
(a division of Pearson Penguin Canada Inc.)
Penguin Ireland, 25 St Stephen's Green, Dublin 2, Ireland
(a division of Penguin Books Ltd)
Penguin Group (Australia), 250 Camberwell Road, Camberwell, Victoria 3124, Australia
(a division of Pearson Australia Group Pty Ltd)
Penguin Books India Pvt Ltd, 11 Community Centre, Panchsheel Park, New Delhi – 110 017, India
Penguin Group (NZ), 67 Apollo Drive, Rosedale, North Shore 0632, New Zealand
(a division of Pearson New Zealand Ltd)
Penguin Books (South Africa) (Pty) Ltd, 24 Sturdee Avenue, Rosebank, Johannesburg 2196, South Africa

Penguin Books Ltd, Registered Offices: 80 Strand, London WC2R ORL, England

www.penguin.com

This translation first published 1964
Reprinted with revisions 1972, 1975, 1986, 1990, 1991, 1992, 1993, 1995
This revised edition first published in Penguin Classics 2009

010

Translation copyright © Kenneth Wellesley, 1964, 1972, 1975, 1986, 1990, 1991, 1992, 1993, 1995
Revisions to the translation, Introduction and editorial material copyright © Rhiannon Ash, 2009
All rights reserved

The moral right of the translator and editor has been asserted

Set in 10.25/12.25 pt PostScript Adobe Sabon
Typeset by Rowland Phototypesetting Ltd, Bury St Edmunds, Suffolk
Printed in England by Clays Ltd, St Ives plc

ISBN: 978-0-140-44964-8

www.greenpenguin.co.uk

Contents

Chronology

Tacitus' *Histories* and the parallel tradition offer a wealth of information about the detailed chronology of the civil wars, but some dates are more secure than others, and critics still debate points of detail. A helpful study of this whole topic is C. L. Murison, *Galba, Otho and Vitellius: Careers and Controversies, Spudasmata* 52 (Hildesheim, Zurich, New York 1993), some references to which are cited below. What follows here is intended to offer some guidance, but inevitably absolute certainty is impossible. References to the relevant sections of Tacitus' *Histories* are included (where possible) in brackets. You will notice that the real chronological order of events does not always cohere with Tacitus' presentation of the material in the narrative and the differences are often instructive about his historiographical techniques.

Events of the Civil War

AD 68

April (early) Galba, governor of Hispania Tarraconensis, sets himself up as a challenger to the emperor Nero.

May (middle) At Vesontio in central Gaul, Verginius Rufus, governor of Upper Germany, successfully puts down the revolt of Vindex, governor of Gallia Lugdunensis, though he later claims that his troops acted spontaneously (1.16, 1.51).

9 or 11 June Nero commits suicide (1.4).

16 June Galba is declared emperor in Spain.

July (middle) Galba sets off from Spain across the Pyrenees, through southern Gaul, across the Cottian Alps and down to Rome (1.6).

September (early) Fonteius Capito, governor of Lower Germany, allegedly rebels and is murdered by the legionary commanders, Cornelius Aquinus and Fabius Valens (1.7).

September (late) or October Galba arrives in Rome after massacring troops at the Milvian Bridge (1.6).

November (end) Vitellius, appointed by Galba, arrives in Lower Germany as governor (1.9, 1.52).

AD 69

1 January The troops in Upper Germany revolt (1.12, 1.55–6).

2–3 January The troops in Upper and Lower Germany go over to Vitellius (1.57).

c. 9 January A letter arrives in Rome from the procurator of Belgica, Pompeius Propinquus, to inform the emperor Galba that the legions of Upper Germany have broken their oath of allegiance (1.12).

10 January Galba adopts Piso as his successor (1.18).

12/13 January Vitellius' general Fabius Valens sets off southwards from Colonia Agrippinensium on his mission to cross the Alps (1.62–6; Murison, pp. 86–90).

15 January Otho is declared emperor in Rome and recognized by the praetorian guard (1.27–35). Galba, Piso and Vinius are murdered (1.41–3); Otho is recognized as emperor by the senate (1.47).

January (end) Vespasian's son Titus, having left Judaea, reaches Corinth in Greece, hears that Galba is dead and so aborts his mission to offer congratulations (2.1).

c. 28 January Vitellius' general Alienus Caecina sets off from Germany to cross the Alps (1.67–70).

February (middle) Vespasian's son Titus returns to Judaea, and Vespasian, governor of Judaea, and Mucianus, governor of Syria, begin to consider an imperial challenge from the East (2.6–7).

c. 8 March Vitellius' general Caecina and his troops reach

Augusta Praetoria at the Italian end of the Great St Bernard Pass (1.89, 2.11).

March (early) The emperor Otho sends off troops under Annius Gallus and Vestricius Spurinna, as well as a fleet, in order to confront the Vitellian armies (1.87, 2.11; Murison, pp. 96–9).

c. 10–11 March Vitellius' general Valens hears the initial news of the Othonian counter-attacks before he has a chance to cross the Cottian Alps (2.14; Murison, p. 89).

14 March Otho leaves Rome to confront Vitellius' armies in the north, handing the day-to-day administration of the empire to his brother, Salvius Titianus (1.90).

c. 30–31 March Vitellius' general Caecina carries out an unsuccessful assault on Placentia in northern Italy (2.20–23; Murison, p. 108).

c. 5 April Caecina and his soldiers unsuccessfully try to ambush the Othonians at Castores (2.24–7).

c. 6 April Vitellius' general Valens and his troops reach Ticinum in northern Italy after being delayed in crossing the Alps by Otho's fleet and diversionary raids (2.27; Murison, p. 87).

c. 7 April The Vitellians combine forces as Valens joins Caecina at Cremona (2.30; Murison, p. 110).

c. 8 April Otho reaches Brixellum in northern Italy (Murison, pp. 95, 107).

c. 10 April The Othonians hold a council of war at Bedriacum (2.31–3; Murison, p. 95).

14 April Vitellian and Othonian forces engage unexpectedly and fight the first battle of Bedriacum. The Othonians are defeated (2.41–5).

15 April The defeated Othonian troops surrender (2.45).

16 April (early morning) The emperor Otho commits suicide at Brixellum in northern Italy (2.49).

18 April The news of Otho's suicide reaches Rome with amazing speed (2.55).

19 April Vitellius is recognized as emperor by the senate (2.55).

c. 20 April Vitellius in Germany only now learns of his victory (2.57; Murison, p. 144).

April (late)/May (early) The new emperor Vitellius reaches Lugdunum (Lyons) in southern France (2.59).

c. 23 May Vitellius reaches Cremona and inspects the gruesome site of the battlefield (2.70).

June–July (early) Vitellius progresses slowly towards Rome (2.71, 87–8).

1 July Vespasian, governor of Judaea, is proclaimed emperor in Alexandria in Egypt (2.79).

3 July Vespasian is proclaimed emperor at Caesarea (2.79).

June (end)–before 18 July The emperor Vitellius arrives in Rome (2.89).

July (late)–August Vespasian's main supporter, Licinius Mucianus, leaves Syria and makes preparations for heading westwards towards Rome via Asia Minor, Moesia, Dalmatia and northern Italy (2.82–4).

August (late) The supporters of Vespasian hold a council of war at Poetovio in Pannonia. Vespasian and Mucianus are not present, but one general, Antonius Primus, emerges as a dynamic supporter of the Flavian cause (3.1–6).

August (late)–September (early) The rebel Julius Civilis receives a letter from the self-proclaimed Flavian general Antonius Primus (based in Pannonia) and starts to plan his revolt in Germany (4.13), taking up the tribe of the Canninefates as allies (4.15–16).

September (early) The Flavian general Antonius Primus occupies Aquileia, Opitergium, Altinum and Patavium in northern Italy (3.6).

c. 10 September News reaches Rome that Antonius Primus is invading northern Italy (2.99).

c. 17 September Vitellius' general Caecina leaves Rome to confront the Flavians (2.99–100).

c. 19 September Vespasian's general Antonius Primus surprises a Vitellian detachment at Forum Alieni in northern Italy (3.6).

c. 23 September The Flavian legions from Pannonia, hurrying to reach Antonius Primus, arrive at Patavium in northern Italy (3.7).

c. 25 September Vitellius' general Valens leaves Rome to confront the Flavians (3.36).

September (late)/October (early) The rebel Julius Civilis defeats the Roman armies near Vetera in Germany (4.18) and enlists the Batavian auxiliaries to join his revolt (4.19).

c. 1–4 October The Flavian general Antonius Primus leaves Patavium and reaches Verona in northern Italy, chosen as a base for the war (3.8).

c. 4–10 October Antonius Primus clashes with some Vitellian troops (3.9).

c. 10 October Vitellius' general Caecina and his troops arrive at Hostilia in northern Italy (3.9).

c. 12 October The fleet at Ravenna in northern Italy revolts from Vitellius (3.12).

October (middle) The rebel Julius Civilis attacks the legionary camp at Vetera in Germany (4.21–3) and Hordeonius Flaccus, the governor of Upper Germany, sends troops from Mogontiacum to intervene (4.24).

c. 17 October The Flavian legions from Moesia reach Antonius Primus' base at Verona (3.10).

18 October Vitellius' general Caecina, while at Hostilia in northern Italy, opts for treachery and tries to get his men to swear an oath to Vespasian, which leads them to imprison him (3.13–14).

24–25 October The Flavians under Antonius Primus defeat the Vitellians in the second battle of Bedriacum (3.16–31).

26–29 October The victorious Flavians under Antonius Primus sack the city of Cremona in northern Italy (3.32–4).

c. 30 October The emperor's brother Lucius Vitellius denounces the treacherous general Caecina at a meeting of the senate (3.37).

October (end) The rebel Julius Civilis besieges the legionary camp at Vetera in Germany (4.28–30). Vitellius' general Valens hears about the defeat at Bedriacum and makes plans to raise support in Gaul (3.41).

31 October Rosius Regulus holds the consulship for a single day after the treacherous Caecina is demoted from office in his absence (3.37).

c. 1 November Vitellius' remaining general Valens sends troops to occupy Ariminum in northern Italy (3.41).

November (early) The German legions reluctantly swear an oath of allegiance to Vespasian (4.31).

c. 9 November The Flavian general Antonius Primus starts to move south to Rome (3.50).

c. 19 November Vitellian troops, after setting off from Rome, try to hold the Apennines at Mevania in central Italy, and Vitellius himself leaves Rome a few days later to join them (3.55).

c. 28 November The fleet at Misenum mutinies and abandons Vitellius, who decides to return to Rome (3.56).

November (late) Vitellius' general Valens is captured on the Stoechades islands off the coast of southern Gaul (3.43).

c. 4 December The remaining Vitellian troops retreat to Narnia (3.58).

c. 7 December The Flavian general Antonius Primus reaches Carsulae, 60 miles from Rome (3.60).

c. 10 December Vitellius' general Valens is executed at Urvinum and his severed head is displayed to the Vitellians (3.62).

c. 15 December The Vitellian troops at Narnia surrender (3.63).

16 December Antonius Primus reaches Ocriculum, 45 miles away from Rome (3.78).

c. 17 December Vitellius' brother Lucius Vitellius captures Tarracina in central Italy (a final moment of success for the Vitellians), but he fails to march his victorious soldiers to Rome (3.77).

17–18 December The Flavian troops with Antonius Primus celebrate the Saturnalia holiday at Ocriculum (3.78).

18 December The emperor Vitellius in Rome attempts unsuccessfully to abdicate (3.67–8).

19 December The temple of Capitoline Jupiter is destroyed by fire while Vitellians and Flavians fight it out on the Capitoline hill (3.71–2) and Vespasian's brother, Flavius Sabinus, is captured and killed (3.73–4).

20 December The Flavian general Antonius Primus enters Rome (3.82) and Vitellius is killed (3.85).

c. 21 December Vespasian is recognized as emperor by the senate in Rome (4.3).

December (end) Vespasian's colleague Licinius Mucianus reaches Rome (4.11). The Roman legionaries at Novaesium in Germany initiate a mutiny, kill Hordeonius Flaccus, the governor of Upper Germany, and set up statues of Vitellius, even though the emperor was by now dead (4.36–7).

AD 70

1 January There is a meeting of the senate in Rome (4.39).

9 January At the next meeting of the senate in Rome, there are reprisals against those who engaged in prosecutions under Nero (4.40–43).

15 January The move against Neronian prosecutors in the senate is terminated (4.44–5).

January (first half) Lucius Piso, governor of Africa, is murdered (4.48–50). Civilis' rebellion gains momentum as Classicus, Tutor and Sabinus join (4.55–6).

February/March The general Dillius Vocula advances towards the legionary camp at Vetera, held by the rebels, but he is killed by a Roman deserter (4.56–9); the legionaries at Vetera and on the upper Rhine swear allegiance to the Gallic Empire (4.59–60).

April/May (early) Vespasian's son Titus sets up camp before Jerusalem (5.1).

21 June There is a ceremony to begin restoring the Capitoline temple (4.53).

July/August The Roman general Petilius Cerialis arrives at Mogontiacum in Germany (4.71), captures Augusta Trevirorum and the rebel camp (4.72–8). Petilius Cerialis successfully defeats Julius Civilis near Vetera, and the remnants of the rebels withdraw to the Island of the Batavians (5.14–19).

August/September Vespasian leaves Alexandria and sets off for Rome.

2 September Titus overruns Jerusalem and destroys the Temple (although the fortress of Masada will hold out until April 73).

September (end) The rebel Julius Civilis surrenders (5.24–6).

Tacitus' Life

AD 54 Claudius dies and Nero becomes emperor.

c. 56 Tacitus born, probably in Narbonese Gaul.

68 Nero commits suicide and Galba becomes emperor.

69 Year of the four emperors, culminating in Vespasian becoming emperor.

75 Dramatic date of the *Dialogue about Orators*.

77 Tacitus marries the daughter of Julius Agricola.

79 Vespasian dies and Titus becomes emperor.

81 Titus dies and Domitian becomes emperor.

81/82 Tacitus becomes quaestor.

85 Tacitus probably becomes tribune of the plebs.

88 Tacitus becomes praetor and organizes the secular games. He holds a prestigious position as a priest.

89/90–93 Tacitus is absent from Rome on military service.

93 Agricola, Tacitus' father-in-law, dies.

96 Domitian is assassinated and Nerva becomes emperor.

97 Tacitus becomes suffect consul and delivers the funeral oration for Verginius Rufus.

98 Nerva dies and Trajan becomes emperor. Tacitus publishes his first work, the *Agricola*, and, soon afterwards, his second work, the *Germania*.

c. 100–105 Tacitus publishes the *Dialogue about Orators*. The exact date is uncertain, although some have argued for 102.

106/7 Tacitus is working on the *Histories*.

c. 109 Tacitus publishes the *Histories*.

112–13 Tacitus becomes proconsul of Asia.

c. 114 Tacitus is working on the *Annals*. We do not know exactly when it was published, nor when Tacitus died, but probably after 115.

117 Trajan dies and Hadrian becomes emperor.

Introduction

Tacitus and his Audience in Context

Without Tacitus, our picture of Roman imperial history would be frustratingly patchy. His seminal historical narratives, the *Histories* and the *Annals*, have done more between them to shape modern perceptions about the workings of empire and Roman politics than any other surviving texts from the ancient world. It is no coincidence that, where the accidents of manuscript survival have left holes in the fabric of Tacitus' continuous narrative (for example over the entire principate of Caligula and the last troubled months of Nero's life), modern scholars have struggled hard to impose meaning on the surviving pockets of other material and to integrate relatively isolated facts in a broader context. Of course, the distinctive nature of ancient, as opposed to modern, historiography certainly means that we must approach Tacitus' version of events with sensitivity towards the moralizing and rhetorical tendencies of the genre, but even so, the value of the hard evidence that he preserves is extraordinary. So too is the sheer emotional power and vividness of his narratives. Here, corruption, injustice and abuse of power are ruthlessly laid bare by an author who uses the very structure and syntax of the Latin language to shed light on protagonists' hypocrisy and on the location and nature of real power.

Tacitus certainly lived in interesting times. Born in about 56* when Nero was emperor, Tacitus may have been the son of Cornelius Tacitus, the equestrian procurator of Gallia Belgica. Pliny the Elder names this man as the father of a mentally

---

* All dates are AD unless specified otherwise.

impaired and short-lived dwarf child (*Natural History* 7.76), who would have been Tacitus' sibling. Although Tacitus may have grown up either in Transpadane Italy or Narbonese Gaul, he was in Rome by 75, training as an orator and listening to court cases being conducted by prominent barristers. He engaged in such activities with great passion and refers to his youthful ardour during this time (*iuuenilis ardor*, *Dialogue* 2.1). This soon bore fruit when the emperor Vespasian awarded him the *latus clauus*, permission to sport the broad purple stripe on his tunic which allowed him to stand for senatorial office (*Histories* 1.1). After this, he probably held a minor magistracy of some sort and a military appointment as a tribune *laticlauius*. We know that in 77, Tacitus married the daughter of Agricola (*Agricola* 9.6), a military man from Forum Julii in Narbonese Gaul, who was suffect consul at this time. This wedding reflects and reinforces local connections between two prominent provincial families. Probably in 81, Tacitus reached the quaestorship, and if we accept that a fragmentary inscription (*Corpus Inscriptionum Latinarum* VI.41106) is indeed a posthumous record of Tacitus' public career, he became tribune of the plebs in 84 or 85. By 88, he had risen to the praetorship and was holding a senior priesthood, since he was one of the *quidecimuiri sacris faciundis* responsible for organizing Domitian's secular games (*Annals* 11.11). Those who had served as praetor usually then went on to hold a military command abroad, and indeed Tacitus was out of Italy when his father-in-law Agricola died in 93 (*Agricola* 45.5). We can see from references in the *Agricola* and the *Histories* that Tacitus was obviously hostile to Domitian, but there is no doubt that his public career had flourished under this emperor, as he concedes at *Histories* 1.1. After Domitian's assassination in 96, Tacitus remained close to the centre of power, becoming suffect consul himself in 97 under the short-lived emperor Nerva and delivering the funeral oration in honour of Verginius Rufus (one of the protagonists in the *Histories*). He continued to be involved in legal cases, collaborating with Pliny the Younger, for example, in prosecuting Marius Priscus, the proconsul of Africa, who was condemned in 100 and exiled (Pliny, *Epistles* 2.11). The culmination of his public career was when he was awarded the prestigious post of proconsul of Asia (112/113). The precise date of his death is uncertain, but it was probably at some point after 115.

The *Histories* is Tacitus' first full-scale historical narrative, published around 109. It followed his literary debut, the *Agricola*, purportedly a biography of his father-in-law, and the *Germania*, an ethnographical study of various Germanic tribes (both published in 98). In addition, Tacitus also wrote the *Dialogue*, a debate about the reasons for the declining state of contemporary oratory, which probably appeared after the *Agricola* and the *Germania*, but before the *Histories*. Against this backdrop, what drove him to write history? And why did he choose this particular period (69–96) for his historiographical debut? His earlier works, especially the *Agricola*, certainly contain individual scenes, such as the battle of Mons Graupius (*Agricola* 29–38), which could easily have featured in a continuous historical narrative. Yet Tacitus chose to reserve the genre of history for a relatively late stage in his literary career. One explanation lies in the hierarchy of genres in ancient literature, where historiography and epic were perceived as being especially prestigious. We can see broad parallels with the literary trajectory of Virgil, whose *Eclogues* and *Georgics*, located in the relatively minor genres of pastoral and didactic poetry, form the precursor to his mature work in the grand genre of epic, the *Aeneid*. Ancient authors had to earn their spurs, progressing from lesser to loftier genres, if they were to be taken seriously, and the trajectory of Tacitus' literary career coheres with broader patterns.

Yet Tacitus' contemporary historical context is central to his vision of history and to the literary techniques that he used to shape his narrative. We can see from the powerful prologue and epilogue to the *Agricola* that Tacitus regarded the assassination of the emperor Domitian and the demise of the Flavian dynasty in 96 as a watershed. So, a work that purports to be a biography of his father-in-law actually sets up a series of emotive polarities between the principate of Domitian (oppressive, bleak, fear-ridden, dark) and the principate of Trajan (liberating, robust, open-minded, light). By postponing the publication of the *Agricola* until Trajan's principate, Tacitus persuasively bolsters this polarization. In many ways, Tacitus' vision, articulating extreme ideological contrasts, sets up an attractive prism through which to view the period. Yet Trajan's principate did not directly follow Domitian's: in between came the elderly *princeps*, Nerva (96–8), who renders such reassuring contrasts between a tyrannical Domitian and an enlightened Trajan much murkier. Precise details of what actually happened after Domitian's assassination (September 96) until Trajan's adoption and accession to the principate (January 98) are contested and rendered problematic by the relative paucity of evidence. It is clear, however, that the failure of Domitian's assassins to put in place a clear plan for what would happen after removing the *princeps* caused problems. Their actions could have triggered civil wars on a huge scale, as potential candidates took their chances and competed with one another for power. At a crucial juncture, Nerva stepped in and prevented that eventuality by adopting Trajan, a strong military man. Yet events could so easily have unfolded very differently. Romans of Tacitus' generation had already seen one devastating set of civil wars in 69, the 'year of the four emperors' (the main focus of the surviving portion of the *Histories*). Tacitus, perhaps already thinking about writing a historical work, saw the contemporary relevance of choosing 1 January 69 as a starting point for his narrative and realized the huge potential of this period for seeing earlier protagonists (such as Galba) in terms of later ones (such as Nerva).

Indeed, Tacitus' version of Galba's adoption speech to Piso (*Histories* 1.15–16) is packed with resonances recalling Nerva's adoption of Trajan, prompting readers to compare the two situations. As Galba says, 'Now that the dynasty of the Julii and Claudii has come to an end, the process of adoption will find the best man for the job' (1.16). That description, 'the best man' (*optimum quemque*), naturally calls to mind Trajan, the 'best *princeps*' (*optimus princeps*); but it also raises fundamental questions: Galba's speech is addressed to Piso, who never became emperor because he was brutally beheaded in the forum soon after this speech. What if he *had* become emperor though? Tacitus presents Piso as a man whose qualifications to rule (or at least to meet the needs of the empire at this particular moment) are open to question. Adoption may sound ideal, but there are practical difficulties with its implementation, and its viability depends on the right candidate being available in the first place and on the willingness of that candidate to become emperor. Thus, as so often in Roman historiography, a speech which apparently addresses the particular circumstances unfolding at a particular moment in time actually has a much wider sphere of reference.

Audiences for Roman historical texts were in any case predisposed to make sense of contemporary events by seeing one character or situation in terms of an earlier one, often – paradoxically – better known to them from their extensive historical and rhetorical education. So, Tiberius' right-hand man and *éminence grise*, Sejanus, could be expressively portrayed by Tacitus in Sallustian language recalling the republican conspirator Catiline (*Annals* 4.1). Similarly, when a disastrous fire broke out in Rome in 64, contemporary observers quickly made comparisons with the attack on the city by the Gauls early in the fourth century BC (*Annals* 15.41). Such meaningful deployment of examples from the past, bridging wide chronological gulfs, is increasingly alien to modern audiences, versed as we are in up-to-the-minute electronic media, which tend to condense the time spans in which we operate. Yet for the Romans, their past was very much a living tradition. In addition, ancient audiences were naturally inclined to think in terms of counterfactuals and to be fully alive to the possibilities of viewing historical events in terms of 'what if?'. A good example is Livy's famous digression on the question of how history could have developed differently if Alexander the Great had directed his campaigns not eastwards, but westwards, to face the men of Italy (Livy, *From the Foundation of the City* 9.17–19). Such techniques of conceptualizing historical events meant that Tacitus' subject matter for the *Histories* (the civil wars after the death of Nero, the last Julio-Claudian emperor, and the subsequent principates of Vespasian, Titus and Domitian) would have resonated powerfully with his contemporaries, primed and ready to filter the events of 69–96 through the dominant protagonists of their own day.

The Nature of Ancient Historiography

In order to understand the *Histories*, or indeed any ancient historical narrative, it is crucial to appreciate the salient differences between ancient and modern historiography. Roman historical writing did not exist in a vacuum, and Tacitus, whose *Histories* and *Annals* represent the acme of achievement in the genre, laid his writing on creative foundations that stretched back over many centuries. As in so many areas, it was the Greeks who developed the fundamental building blocks of the genre, with the historians Herodotus (who lived from the 480s to the 420s BC) and Thucydides (*c.* 460 to after 404 BC) being the most important practitioners of historiography whose works have survived – always an important proviso. Their individual techniques were rather different from one another's: Herodotus is generally perceived as being anthropological in his interests and not obviously driven by a need to impose a rigid structure on his narrative, while Thucydides is often seen as a rationalist, albeit as one fully alive to the power of tragic historical patterning. Yet they were both linked by a common aim to establish why incidents happened as they did and to investigate the impact of human nature and individual character on wider historical events.

Some of the methodological techniques of Herodotus and Thucydides would certainly not satisfy the standards of modern historiography. A notorious example is the inclusion of speeches which were not accurate records of what was said on a particular occasion but creative representations of what the historian judged was called for by each situation. This distinctive aspect of Greek historiography retained in its Roman counterpart an important function as a tool for dramatizing the main issues of the narrative, for revealing crucial aspects of a speaker's character, and for foreshadowing and developing central themes. Tacitus in the *Histories* regularly deploys such

speeches at key moments. We have already considered Galba's
adoption speech, but there are many other examples, including
Otho's address to the mutinous soldiers in Rome (1.83–4).
This speech eloquently dramatizes the difficulty of a former
pretender trying to stop precisely the sort of disorder which he
himself had so recently exacerbated to secure the principate; or
there is Mucianus' speech to the hesitant imperial candidate
Vespasian (2.76–7), which sets up the paradox that Mucianus
has many more of the manipulative qualities necessary to succeed in the murky contemporary political world than Vespasian
himself does.

Such speeches also have the advantage of suspending the fast,
often dizzying, pace of the military narrative and allowing
readers to reflect on the moral issues. Ancient readers seemed
to enjoy this process, as we can see from the fact that Pliny
the Younger presents himself as busily excerpting from the
monumental narrative of Livy during the early stages of the
eruption of Mount Vesuvius (*Epistle* 6.20.5). Speeches would
have been ripe for this sort of selective treatment. Ancient
historians also expected sophisticated readers of their works to
be familiar with previous practitioners of the genre, and they
self-consciously echoed earlier speeches. For instance, Dillius
Vocula's appeal to his armies (*Histories* 4.58) is actively
modelled on Livy's version of a speech delivered by the republican general Scipio to his mutinous soldiers (Livy, *From the
Foundation of the City* 28.27–9). Such allusions remind us that
reading ancient historical narratives is a collaborative effort,
with practitioners expecting informed responses to their
material from well-educated audiences. In fact, creative engagement with the historical material was generally regarded as even
better than the real thing. So, a particularly expressive indication
of the imaginative freedom of ancient historians in composing
their speeches can be seen in the fact that even when a 'real' speech
survives, such as the emperor Claudius' speech about whether to
extend membership of the senate to the Gauls (this has come
down to us in an inscription), the historiographical version
(*Annals* 11.24) does not feel rigidly bound by the presentation
of ideas and arguments as laid down in the 'original'.

Rhetorical practice was firmly embedded in every aspect of Roman historiography, not just in the speeches. The first historian to write in Latin, Cato the Elder (234–149 BC), was the foremost orator of his age, and we know that in his *Origins* he included at least two of his own speeches, and that he also extended his rhetorical tricks of the trade to the surrounding narrative. In one surviving fragment, he eloquently expresses dissatisfaction with historians who turned out bare unadorned lists of information, the sort of thing that could be found among the priestly records. Sempronius Asellio (late second century BC), another historian, makes a similar complaint: 'As far as I am concerned, it is not enough to proclaim what was done, but one must also show with what purpose and for what reason actions were taken' (Fragment 1). Such sentiments meant that the historical narratives of the second and first centuries BC were often increasingly expansive, as writers drew on their rhetorical skills to flesh out the skeletal records that they found in their sources. Perhaps the most obvious culmination of this tendency is the monumental narrative of the Augustan historian Livy, whose (now fragmentary) *From the Foundation of the City* originally ran to 142 books. We are lucky enough to have a pair of passages that vividly show the extent and manner of the embellishment. Claudius Quadrigarius wrote an annalistic history (now fragmentary) in the early first century BC, including an account of a single combat between a huge Gaul and a Roman, Manlius Torquatus (preserved at Aulus Gellius 9.13), but we also have Livy's rendition of the same encounter (7.9), which expands and elaborates the archaic simplicity of his predecessor's version.

In ancient historical works, there were particular types of scene which lent themselves especially well to the rhetorical embellishment at which these writers excelled. Narratives of battles certainly allowed scope for emotive description, regardless of what actually happened on the day itself. So too did set-pieces such as the capture of cities, which could also be inspired by other genres, such as epic. In addition, historical narratives could be further expanded by ethnographical descriptions of foreign peoples, particularly if the work involved recounting a war away from Rome. What these practices meant in the long term was that writers inevitably had to resort to increasingly imaginative techniques to retain the interest of audiences who were well versed in the topoi of the genre. Tacitus was simultaneously faced with the creative opportunities afforded by a rich historiographical tradition and the challenge of engaging in an innovative fashion with audiences who were in danger of having seen it all before. One of his most effective weapons in this respect is his cynical, biting, neo-Sallustian language, whose economy and pungency ruthlessly unmasks his protagonists for our benefit. There are many examples of his verbal dexterity, including when Galba, after Otho had been hailed emperor, continued to sacrifice and 'importune the gods of an empire no longer his' (*Histories* 1.29). So, often, it is impossible for an English translation to convey Tacitus' meaning without using many more words.

One aspect of the ancient historiographical tradition before Tacitus is crucial: these narratives had a strong moralizing agenda, which permeates individual episodes and indeed whole works. We can trace this characteristic back to Cato the Elder, the founder of the genre in Latin, who had played many public roles, including his tenure as censor. This meant that he was publicly responsible, among other things, for regulating Roman aristocratic morals. Indeed, his concern with ethics and correct behaviour is reflected in his (now fragmentary) writings and is further developed by his literary successors. The historian who most directly follows Cato's moralizing lead is Sallust (86–35 BC), whose pithy Latin style recalls Cato. Sallust's practice was considered perverse and striking at the time, but it was designed to reflect the ideology of an earlier, better era. In a similar spirit, Tacitus deliberately writes Latin that evokes Cato the Elder and Sallust, thereby also aligning himself with them in moral and ideological terms. Particular sections of Tacitus' narrative are heavily Sallustian in tone, such as his digression at *Histories* 2.38, where the clash between Otho and Vitellius is seen as part of a repeating historical pattern: the comparison is made in language evocative of Sallust, which reinforces Tacitus' basic point.

Yet these historians are not just rooted in an idealized past. Sallust, for example, regularly strives to articulate the contemporary usefulness of his history, especially in the prefaces to his two surviving monographs, the *Catiline* and *Jugurtha*. These arresting narratives are shot through with notions of contemporary moral decline, but they are also alive to the possibility that audiences could learn valuable lessons from reading history and apply them constructively to their own lives. Livy too in his preface emphasizes the practical benefits for his own contemporaries of reading his monumental narrative, which offers them the chance to see positive and negative examples from the past and to choose what to imitate and what to avoid. Whether a historical narrative takes the form of a monograph devoted to a specific subject or annalistic history with its year-by-year structure measured out according to who the consuls were, exemplarity is an intrinsic part of Roman historiography. The *Histories* is no exception. Tacitus includes some conspicuous instances, such as the Ligurian woman who impressively resists torture by the Othonian soldiers to protect her son (2.13) and the Flavian soldier who kills his brother, fighting for the other side, and then shockingly demands a reward (3.51). Times of crisis, such as civil war, traditionally generated rich exemplary material. In the preface Tacitus flags as an enticement the positive examples that are to come (1.3), although in the bleak surviving narrative these are outweighed by the number of negative paradigms.

The Four Emperors

In the *Histories*, Tacitus constructs a complex narrative of a complex period, imposing meaning on confusing events and artfully juggling multiple spheres of action as pretenders rise – sometimes almost simultaneously at opposite ends of the empire – and emperors fall. There is no doubt that what survives of the text, especially *Histories* 1–3, is highly unusual, even within the Tacitean corpus. For example, Tacitus narrates the actions of three days in Rome in about the same amount of text that he uses to present a whole year in the *Annals* (*Histories* 3.67–86 for 18–20 December 69; cf. *Annals* 15.33–47 for the year 64). This lavish scale was probably unusual even in comparison with the later, missing books of the *Histories*, which unfortunately breaks off at 5.26, but where Tacitus originally narrated the principates of Vespasian (70–79), Titus (79–81) and Domitian (81–96) in a year-by-year annalistic format, more familiar to us from the *Annals*. Indeed, if we assume that the *Histories* originally had twelve books (St Jerome says that the *Histories* and the *Annals* together had thirty books), then about a quarter of the whole work (three books) focused on the events of a single year, while the remaining three-quarters (nine books) had to incorporate all the events of twenty-six years, including potential 'purple passages' about dramatic incidents such as the eruption of Vesuvius in 79 and the assassination of Domitian in 96.

Given this top-heavy chronological arrangement of the *Histories* and the wealth of detail Tacitus supplies, particularly about the civil wars, it was crucial for him to organize his material in the clearest possible way. Ancient historians could of course elaborate or condense particular events in their narratives at will, depending on the significance of the material; and, in dealing with chronologically unanchored events, it was always possible to locate a particular incident in the continuous narrative at a point which allowed suggestive juxtaposition with another event (whether or not they had happened at exactly the same time in reality). For the sake of clarity, it was also desirable for historians to postpone the start of a particular sequence of events until a previous section was complete, even if there was some chronological overlap. We can see an instance of this when Tacitus only begins his sequence about the rise of Vitellius at *Histories* 1.51 (see next page): in strictly chronological terms, Tacitus could have focused on Vitellius earlier than this, but he clearly wanted to complete his version of the struggle between Galba and Otho first and to avoid confusing his audience unnecessarily.

As well as aiming for clarity, Tacitus also wanted to create a gripping narrative. This may be one of several reasons why he chooses to begin the *Histories* on 1 January 69, a provocative starting point, given that Nero had killed himself in June 68, so most of the events of Galba's short principate are passed over. Arguably, however, the most important point about Galba is indeed the manner of his death, rather than any lasting contribution made by his administration (such as it was). Although death is often a traditional closural device in ancient literature, Tacitus paradoxically begins his account with the chain of events which will quickly lead to Galba's decapitation in the forum at Rome on 15 January 69. Using a technique which will become a hallmark of the *Annals*, Tacitus manipulates the annalistic structure for his own artistic and historiographical purposes, swiftly drawing in his readers and setting up for them an exciting narrative.

How then does Tacitus go about constructing a narrative which is both clear and exciting? A broad overview of his strategy may be helpful. The opening of the *Histories* (1.1–50), devoted to the demise of Galba and the rise of Otho, takes place largely in Rome, although there are some flashbacks and foreshadowings as Tacitus sets the scene. Only when we have seen Galba's decapitation in the forum does Tacitus direct our attention to the origins of Vitellius' challenge in Lower Germany (1.51–70) and to Otho's response to the threat in Rome (1.71–90). By postponing any extensive narrative of Vitellius' uprising until after his account of Galba's murder, Tacitus favours clarity of presentation over a strict chronological sequence. Vitellius had been hailed as emperor by the armies of Germany on 2–3 January 69 (1.57), so he was rebelling initially against Galba, not Otho. Tacitus, however, is careful not to overwhelm readers with too much information.

At the opening of the next book, we see a sharp geographical shift as our attention is directed eastwards towards the first stages of the Flavian challenge (2.1–9). Tacitus thereby asserts his independence as a historian, since pro-Flavian accounts of Vespasian's rise to power judiciously tended to post-date his challenge as the only possible response to the 'decadent' Vitellius. Yet Tacitus makes it clear that Otho was still in power when the first plans were made by Vespasian's supporters. This narrative arrangement casts a shadow over the whole account of the clash between the Othonian and Vitellian armies at Bedriacum in northern Italy (2.10–45), suggesting the futility of Vitellius' victory and Otho's moving suicide (2.46–50). After presenting the consequences of the battle for Italy (2.51–73), Tacitus turns again to Vespasian, to whom the eastern armies pledge their loyalty at the start of July, and introduces the dynamic Flavian general, Antonius Primus (2.74–86). The prospects now do not look good for the Vitellians, revelling in their victory in Rome and losing their military edge (2.87–101).

The third book is dominated by the Flavian campaign engineered by the highly competent Antonius Primus, a second battle, fought between the Flavian and Vitellian armies, at Bedriacum (3.1–35), the repercussions around the empire (3.36–48) and the disastrous fighting in the streets of Rome herself, which culminates in the Capitoline temple burning down and Vitellius' murder (3.49–86). Vespasian is out of Italy throughout this chaotic fighting, which will conveniently enable him to distance himself from taking direct responsibility for the destruction. The end of the fighting, however, does not necessarily signal the beginning of peace, as the turbulent events in Rome outlined in the fourth book demonstrate (4.1–11, 38–47). There are problems further away, too, especially in Germany, where Julius Civilis, a Batavian who had served as a Roman auxiliary leader, was organizing an opportunistic revolt (4.12–37, 54–79, 5.14–26), and in Judaea, where Vespasian's son Titus had undertaken to finish off the Jewish war (5.1–13). Vespasian, meanwhile, is in Alexandria, waiting for the sea to become calm and engaging in miracle cures (4.81–6). The manuscript of the *Histories* unfortunately runs out at a dramatic moment (5.26), when the rebel leader Julius Civilis and the Roman general Petilius Cerialis are standing on opposite ends of a broken bridge over the River Nabalia and engaging in negotiations.

What about the cast of characters? Tacitus' account offers us a range of vivid portraits, incorporating not just the four emperors, but also their various generals and advisers. Galba's cronies include Cornelius Laco, prefect of the praetorian guard, Icelus, a freedman, and the noble Piso Licinianus, adopted by the emperor as his son for a brief spell. Since Galba swiftly disappears from the narrative, these figures remain relatively unelaborated (apart from Piso). Yet they do introduce important themes and character types: these include manipulative advisers, who are apparently loyal to their emperor but really have their own ambitions at heart, and low-ranking individuals such as the arrogant freedmen, who are problematically elevated to positions far above their usual social status. Otho's entourage has rather more scope to emerge from the narrative as individuals with distinctive personalities. Apart from the freedman Onomastus, instrumental in the early stages of Otho's imperial challenge, there is the senior high-ranking general, the self-important Suetonius Paulinus (who crushed Boudicca's rebellion in Britain), Licinius Proculus (a close friend of Otho and chosen as prefect of the praetorian guard by the soldiers themselves), Annius Gallus (whose capacity to contribute meaningfully to the campaign was abruptly curtailed after a fall from his horse), Otho's brother, Salvius Titianus (whose most disturbing characteristic is perhaps how elusive and shadowy he remains, despite his close family relationship to the emperor), and Galerius Trachalus (Otho's speech-writer and spin-doctor in Rome). Some of these men are not untalented, but there are so many of them that they spend more energy clashing with one another than protecting Otho's interests.

The next emperor, Vitellius, is at first much luckier in his supporters. Two energetic legionary commanders spontaneously materialize from the German armies to fight for his cause. Fabius Valens, a hedonistic equestrian who had relied on his wit to survive under Nero, and Alienus Caecina, physically imposing and ruthless, manage initially to cooperate in making Vitellius emperor, despite their different personalities. Also involved in the process is Vitellius' brother, Lucius, alert but highly manipulative, and an ostentatious freedman, Asiaticus. Yet Vitellius' cause founders since, when the crisis comes, his two main generals, Caecina and Valens, are unable to sustain a fragile bond which was originally formed for mercenary reasons. Valens stays loyal, although he has lost his edge after the sprawling victory progression from northern Italy to

Rome, while Caecina, with his eye on the main chance, betrays Vitellius.

Vespasian's entourage is the most competent, although it lacks capacity for long-term cohesion, and fault lines begin to emerge soon after the final victory. The silver-tongued and politically astute Licinius Mucianus, governor of Syria, is the catalyst for Vespasian's imperial challenge, but the unscrupulous and talented general, Antonius Primus, is its military architect. This man manages to galvanize the soldiers as nobody else has done, undertaking a lightning invasion of Italy which is diametrically opposed to Vespasian's dishonourable plan of starving his enemies into submission (3.8). Vespasian can also call upon the resources of his two adult sons, Titus and Domitian. There are underlying tensions in this family's relationships (which Tacitus would certainly have developed in the missing part of the *Histories*), but in 69 Vespasian's two sons are invaluable as a propaganda device and as a way of indicating publicly that Vespasian will establish a secure dynasty at the end of the civil wars.

The Parallel Tradition

We are extremely fortunate that the extant portion of Tacitus' *Histories* coincides with other surviving accounts of the same events and characters. What this means in practice is that we can compare Tacitus' narrative with the parallel tradition (and vice versa) in order to shed light on what is distinctive and unique about his selection, presentation and arrangement of events. Indeed, the year of the four emperors is almost unparalleled in the richness and diversity of the surviving narratives from the ancient world that cover it.

There is, for example, a particularly fruitful crop of biographies. The prolific Greek writer Plutarch (*c.* 50–120) wrote a series of imperial lives from Augustus to Vitellius, of which we now only have the *Galba* and *Otho*, while the Latin writer Suetonius (*c.* 70–130) wrote twelve biographies, running from Julius Caesar to Domitian, all of which survive. Plutarch's *Galba* and *Otho* pre-date Tacitus' *Histories*, while Suetonius may well have executed his project at the same time that Tacitus was gathering material for his narrative, even if he had a very different agenda. The beauty of ancient biography as a genre is that it often preserves intriguing details that, for reasons of taste, usually lie outside the more austere realm of ancient historiography. For instance, where Tacitus talks in general terms of the emperor Vitellius' insatiable lust for banquets (*Histories* 2.62), Suetonius gives all the ingredients for a particularly extravagant dish concocted by the emperor and known as Minerva's Shield (*Vitellius* 13). We are clearly meant to revel in the sheer prodigality of a recipe that includes scar-fish livers, peacock brains, flamingo tongues and lampreys' guts. The disadvantage of ancient biography is that material tends to be ordered thematically, rather than in strict chronological sequence, which can sometimes leave particular incidents difficult to pin down. That said, these works can still offer crucial information to supplement or question Tacitus' account. We can see this when, for example, Tacitus tells us that a centurion named Julius Agrestis actually killed himself in front of the emperor Vitellius in order to make him believe the news that his troops had been defeated by the Flavians (*Histories* 3.54). This is indeed a dramatic story, vividly underscoring Vitellius' capacity to ignore a crisis. Yet if we compare the parallel tradition (Plutarch, *Otho* 15, Suetonius, *Otho* 10, Cassius Dio *Roman History* 64.11), all the other accounts unanimously locate the story under the emperor Otho. Tacitus, wilfully or otherwise, appears to have shifted an anecdote from Otho's principate and applied it to Vitellius, for whom he perhaps found it to be a more expressive story. All of these accounts taken together enable us to gain a remarkably detailed picture of events, even if some discrepancies remain.

As well as these biographies, we also have access to the account of Josephus (born *c.* 37/8), whose *Jewish War*, written in Greek, appeared between 75 and 79. Its main focus does not relate primarily to events in Rome and Italy, but it still touches upon relevant incidents. The credibility of Josephus' narrative has often been questioned because he owed his life to the Flavian dynasty (*Jewish War* 3.396–7, 5.541), but even a partisan account is not without its value as a point of comparison. Tacitus himself is acutely sensitive to the pitfalls of pro-Flavian bias in his own sources (*Histories* 2.101), but even so, a few modern critics accuse him of partiality in some areas, although if we consider his narrative technique sensitively, we can usually challenge such views. As well as Josephus, we have the later annalistic narrative of the Greek historian Cassius Dio (*c.* 164– post 229), although this is a problematic source, since unfortunately the material about the year of the four emperors is preserved only in later epitomes. Cassius Dio's *Roman History* was originally a meticulously well-researched account, written by a man who spent his professional life working under the emperors, and there are still some useful nuggets of information in what remains of his text.

Reception of the Histories

The greatest proportion of the surviving narrative focuses on the centripetal events of the civil war, but it is in fact Tacitus' account of cultures at the empire's margins that has drawn most attention in terms of the later reception of the *Histories*. Tacitus' memorable portrait of the Romanized leader of the Batavian revolt, Julius Civilis, in *Histories* 4 and 5, has a particularly lively afterlife. Although Tacitus casts him as a devious chameleon, who plays up his barbarian characteristics to drum up support for his rebellion – which in some ways can be seen as an extension of the civil wars – nevertheless, such ambiguities were later brushed under the carpet by Dutch historiography. These writers wanted to formulate a collective historical identity for the Dutch people and saw Tacitus' historical account of Batavian freedom-fighters as a useful weapon. From 1568, when the Dutch revolt against the Spanish Habsburg Empire broke out, the one-eyed leader Civilis was taken up as a source of inspiration and became a national hero, whose fight against the Roman oppressors served as a model for the Dutch struggle against Spain. Civilis became a role model for William of Orange and images of the one-eyed Batavian leader began to proliferate in books, dramas and paintings. One of Tacitus' important early editors, Justus Lipsius, appointed as professor of history and law at the University of Leiden in 1579, commented directly and patriotically in his edition of Tacitus on Civilis' role as a defender of public liberty. Such moments were also celebrated in the visual media: particularly memorable is Rembrandt's dramatic depiction of Civilis and his associates swearing an oath of allegiance (1661). Tacitus' Civilis and his Batavians thus became an emotive focal point in the turbulent political scene of sixteenth- and seventeenth-century Europe. The presence of the myth was even felt at the margins of Dutch colonial territory. Thus, in 1619, when the Dutch under Jan Pieterszoon Coen conquered Djakarta in Indonesia, the city was obliged to change its name to Batavia, upon instructions from the directors of the Dutch East India Company. It is striking that Civilis remains virtually invisible in other ancient accounts, so that Tacitus' memorable portrait offered a goldmine for those in search of a cohesive Dutch national identity.

One of the most contentious portions of Tacitus' work in its reception is his infamous ethnographical excursus on the Jews, outlining their history, customs and religious practices in terms of the 'other' (*Histories* 5.2–13). Jewish culture is presented as an inversion of everything that a Roman reader would regard as normal, and the tone is, at best, perplexed, and, at worst, hostile. Jewish exclusivity, monotheism, burial practices and so forth are described by Tacitus for Roman consumption in language that is starkly polarizing and often pejorative. This section of the *Histories*, perhaps more than any other, tends to make modern readers uneasy. Yet the context is important. Tacitus is here constructing his narrative against the established ancient literary backdrop of ethnography, a way of writing which tended to exaggerate and to simplify the collective characteristics of a group, partly to entertain and partly to reinforce what was distinctive about the writer's own culture. Ethnography could be formulated as a separate monograph, such as Tacitus' own *Germania*, or as a distinct section embedded within a continuous narrative, such as Sallust on Africa (*Jugurtha* 17–19) or Tacitus on Britain (*Agricola* 10–12). Ancient readers were familiar with the device, and there were

certain set introductory formulae, which would reassuringly
signal their entry into an ethnographical segment, whetting
their appetites for the entertaining or shocking ethnographical
details to come.

Moreover, it is a mistake to take Tacitus' excursus on the
Jews out of context, no matter how clearly it is compartmental-
ized by the author himself. The narrative of the Jewish war,
to which this excursus forms an introduction, has a crucial
transitional role to play within the internal dynamics of the
Histories. It is a section in which the Roman state makes the
leap from self-destructive civil wars to a foreign campaign.
Now, domestic and external national identities are once again
contrasted and the differences between opposing sides are
(finally) more prominent than the disturbing similarities that
had characterized the protagonists of those successive conflicts
in which Roman fought Roman. This 'restorative' function of
the excursus is, however, masked by the fact that the *Histories*
breaks off at 5.26, leaving so much of the Jewish war still to be
narrated. In fact, the striking point about *Histories* 4–5 is not
that Tacitus devoted so much attention to the Jews, but that
he treated the Batavian revolt, almost ignored by our other
sources, so extensively. The more reassuring character of the
Jewish war – signalled by the formal ethnographical excursus
– is in sharp contrast with the much more murky world exem-
plified by the shifting identities of Julius Civilis and his Batavians. So, we can partly explain the distinctive nature of the
excursus on the Jews as reflecting a wider narrative movement
whereby Tacitus gradually reconstructs collective Roman
national character after the self-destructive civil wars docu-
mented in *Histories* 1–3. Yet the original context mattered
little for those who subsequently turned to Tacitus' excursus in
search of evidence to endorse their anti-Semitic viewpoints,
particularly in the Nazi period when the material was eagerly
taken up for negative propaganda. The reception of *Histories*
5.2–13 (as opposed to the rest of the *Histories*) is so rich and
involved that it has received a book-length study in its own
right by R. S. Bloch, *Antike Vorstellungen vom Judentum: der
Judenexkurs des Tacitus im Rahmen der griechisch-römischen*

Ethnographie (Stuttgart 2002). No doubt the excursus on the Jews will continue to spark controversy.

Kenneth Wellesley, in the original introduction to his Penguin translation, made the following observation about the *Histories*: 'In all the records of Rome there can scarcely be another year that is so full of calamity, or that displays so clearly the strength and weakness of the Romans.' Without Tacitus, however, the rich potential of this historical material would never have been realized. Ever since the Elizabethan scholar Sir Henry Savile published the first English translation of Tacitus' *Histories* in 1591, this work has continued to fascinate translators and audiences. Indeed, Savile even went as far as to fill the gap between the beginning of the *Histories* and the end of the *Annals* by adding as a preface to his translation a supplement, *The Ende of Nero and the Beginning of Galba*, which was praised enthusiastically by Ben Jonson. It is inevitably a source of great frustration that neither of Tacitus' historical narratives has survived intact, but Savile's efforts to bridge the gap reflect the fact that reading what remains of the *Histories* is an utterly compelling experience. We are ultimately left wanting more, despite the grim subject matter. Tacitus' own expressive oxymoron, *misera laetitia*, 'melancholy delight' (*Histories* 2.45), describing the victors and vanquished as they contemplate the horrors of the self-destruction they have just lived through after the first battle of Bedriacum, is a memorable phrase. It could equally well be applied to the experience of reading Tacitus' extraordinary and moving historical narrative of the civil wars of 69.

Rhiannon Ash

Further Reading

The stimulating material presented by Tacitus in the *Histories* has naturally attracted analysis from many modern scholars, both historians and literary critics. This section is designed to offer some guidance to readers who wish to pursue their reading further. It is intended to be a selective and helpful overview, rather than a comprehensive bibliographical survey, and it is restricted to studies in English.

General studies of historiographical technique and Tacitus include R. Syme, *Tacitus* (Oxford 1958); R. Martin, *Tacitus* (London 1981; reprinted 1994); T. P. Wiseman, *Clio's Cosmetics* (Leicester 1979); I. S. Moxon, J. D. Smart and A. J. Woodman (eds.), *Past Perspectives: Studies in Greek and Roman Historical Writing* (Cambridge 1986); A. J. Woodman, *Rhetoric in Classical Historiography: Four Studies* (London and Sydney 1988), as well as his collection of essays, *Tacitus Reviewed* (Oxford 1998); T. J. Luce and A. J. Woodman (eds.), *Tacitus and the Tacitean Tradition* (Princeton 1993); R. Mellor, *Tacitus* (New York and London 1993); C. S. Kraus and A. J. Woodman, *Latin Historians, Greece & Rome New Surveys in the Classics* 27 (Oxford 1997); P. Sinclair, *Tacitus the Sententious Historian* (Pennsylvania 1995); J. Marincola, *Authority and Tradition in Ancient Historiography* (Cambridge 1997); and J. Marincola (ed.), *A Companion to Greek and Roman Historiography* (Oxford 2007). Any of these would offer a helpful starting point, although the studies by Martin and by Kraus and Woodman are probably the most accessible. There is also an excellent essay by D. S. Levene, 'Pity, Fear and the Historical Audience: Tacitus on the Fall of Vitellius', pp. 128–49, in S. Morton Braund and C. Gill (eds.), *The Passions in Roman Thought and Literature* (Cambridge 1997), which focuses on a particular section of Tacitean narrative, but raises broader historiographical issues.

For those specifically interested in the *Histories*, there is a range of studies to consult. K. Wellesley, *The Year of the Four Emperors* (3rd edition, London and New York 2000), offers a clear narrative of the year's events by one of the foremost authorities on the *Histories*; the new edition also has an introduction and a detailed bibliographical survey by B. Levick. For Tacitus' historiographical technique in the *Histories*, see R. Ash, *Ordering Anarchy: Armies and Leaders in Tacitus' Histories* (London 1999). Another study is by H. Haynes, *Tacitus on Imperial Rome: The History of Make-Believe* (Berkeley, Los Angeles, London 2003), who is concerned with the interaction of language and power in Tacitus and who uses the methodologies of psychoanalytic and Marxist scholars to underpin her analysis (although the book is probably not the most accessible starting point for relative beginners). D. Sailor, *Writing and Empire in Tacitus* (Cambridge, 2008), has a useful discussion of the *Histories*. Also useful for the general literary and ideological background are G. O. Hutchinson, *Latin Literature from Seneca to Juvenal* (Oxford 1993); S. Bartsch, *Actors in the Audience: Theatricality and Doublespeak from Nero to Hadrian* (Cambridge, Mass., and London 1994); and J. Henderson, *Fighting for Rome: Poets, Caesars and Civil War* (Cambridge 1998). P. Plass, *Wit and the Writing of History* (Madison, Wis., 1988), is an absorbing study of Tacitean language, while E. O'Gorman, *Irony and Misreading in the Annals of Tacitus* (Cambridge 2000), studies the relationship between language and power. On the reception of Julius Civilis, see K. Tilmans, 'Aeneas, Bato and Civilis, the Forefathers of the Dutch: the Origin of the Batavian Tradition in Dutch Humanistic Historiography', pp. 121–35, in J. R. Brink and W. F. Gentrup (eds.), *Renaissance Culture in Context: Theory and Practice* (Aldershot 1993); and W. Hessing, 'Foreign Oppressor versus Civiliser: the Batavian Myth as the Source for the Contrasting Associations of Rome in Dutch Historiography and

Archaeology', pp. 126–44, in R. Hingley (ed.), *Images of Rome: Perceptions of Ancient Rome in Europe and the United States in the Modern Age* (Portsmouth, Rhode Island 2001). On Tacitus and the Jews, see B. Wardy, 'Jewish Religion in Pagan Literature during the Late Republic and Early Empire', *Aufstieg und Niedergang der römischen Welt* II 19.1 (1979), pp. 592–644 (esp. pp. 613–31); and M. Goodman, 'Trajan and the Origins of Roman Hostility to the Jews', *Past and Present* 182 (2004), pp. 3–29.

Readers will gain valuable insights from the introductions of various commentaries on Tacitus, even if they do not have Latin. For the *Histories*, there is C. Damon, *Tacitus Histories Book I* (Cambridge 2003); R. Ash, *Tacitus Histories Book II* (Cambridge 2007); G. E. F. Chilver, *A Historical Commentary on Tacitus Histories I and II* (Oxford 1979); K. Wellesley, *Cornelius Tacitus The Histories Book III* (Sydney 1972); and G. E. F. Chilver, *A Historical Commentary on Tacitus' Histories IV and V* (Oxford 1985), completed and revised by G. B. Townend. For the *Annals*, there is F. R. D. Goodyear, *The Annals of Tacitus 1.1–54* (Cambridge 1972); F .R. D. Goodyear, *The Annals of Tacitus 1.55–81 and Annals 2* (Cambridge 1981); A. J. Woodman and R. Martin, *The Annals of Tacitus Book 3* (Cambridge 1996); R. Martin and A. J. Woodman, *Tacitus Annals Book IV* (Cambridge 1989); D. Shotter, *Tacitus Annals IV* (Warminster 1990); R. Martin, *Tacitus Annals V and VI* (Warminster 2001), which also offers a translation; E. C. Woodcock, *Tacitus Annals XIV* (London 1992); and N. Miller, *Tacitus Annals XV* (London 1994).

For those seeking translations of the parallel tradition, there is D. Little and C. Ehrhardt, *Lives of Galba and Otho: A Companion and Translation* (London 1998), for Plutarch's *Galba* and *Otho*; G. A. Williamson (trans. and revised by E. M. Smallwood), *Josephus The Jewish War* (Harmondsworth 2004); C. Edwards (trans.), *Suetonius Lives of the Caesars* (Oxford 2000); or M. Grant (trans.), *Suetonius The Twelve Caesars* (Harmondsworth 2003); or more specifically, D. Shotter, *Suetonius: The Lives of Galba, Otho and Vitellius* (Warminster 1993); and E. Cary (trans.), *Dio's Roman History*

Volume VIII Books LXI–LXX (Cambridge, Mass., 1925), with
C. L. Murison, *Rebellion and Reconstruction: An Historical
Commentary on Cassius Dio's Roman History Books 64–67
(AD 68–96)* (Atlanta 1999).

In Classical journals, there is a wealth of specialized studies
on individual sections of the *Histories*, including:

R. Ash, 'Waving the White Flag: Surrender Scenes at Livy 9.5–
6 and Tacitus *Histories* 3.31 and 4.62', *Greece & Rome* 45.1
(1998), pp. 27–44.

P. A. Brunt, 'The Revolt of Vindex and the Fall of Nero',
Latomus 18 (1959), pp. 531–59.

—, 'Tacitus on the Batavian Revolt', *Latomus* 19 (1960),
pp. 494–517.

T. Cole, '*Initium mihi operis Servius Galba*', *Yale Classical
Studies* 29 (1992), pp. 231–45.

A. Del Castillo, 'The Emperor Galba's Assumption of Power:
Some Chronological Considerations', *Historia* 51 (2002),
pp. 449–61.

A. Ferrill, 'Otho, Vitellius and the Propaganda of Vespasian',
Classical Journal 60 (1965), pp. 267–9.

P. A. Gallivan, 'The False Neros: A Re-examination', *Historia*
22 (1973), pp. 364–5.

B. Gibson, 'Rumours as Causes of Events in Tacitus', *Materiali
e Discussioni per l'Analisi dei Testi Classici* 40 (1998),
pp. 111–29.

J. B. Hainsworth, 'The Starting-Point of Tacitus' *Historiae*',
Greece & Rome 11 (1964), pp. 128–36.

E. Keitel, 'Otho's Exhortations in Tacitus' *Histories*', *Greece
& Rome* 34 (1987), pp. 73–82.

—, '*Foedum Spectaculum* and Related Motifs in Tacitus *Histories* II–III', *Rheinisches Museum* 135 (1992), pp. 342–51.

—, 'Principate and Civil War in the *Annals* of Tacitus', *American Journal of Philology* 105 (1984), pp. 306–25.

D. S. Levene, 'Tacitus' *Histories* and the Theory of Deliberative
Oratory', pp. 197–216, in C. S. Kraus (ed.), *The Limits of
Historiography: Genre and Narrative in Ancient Historical
Texts* (Leiden, Boston, Cologne 1999).

B. Levick, 'L. Verginius Rufus and the Year of the Four Emperors', *Rheinisches Museum* 128 (1985), pp. 318–46.

J. Marincola, 'Tacitus' Prefaces and the Decline of Imperial Historiography', *Latomus* 58 (1999), pp. 391–404.

—, 'Beyond Pity and Fear: the Emotions of History', *Ancient Society* 33 (2003), pp. 285–315.

N. P. Miller and P. V. Jones, 'Critical Appreciations III: Tacitus *Histories* 3.38–9', *Greece & Rome* 25 (1978), pp. 70–80.

M. G. Morgan, 'The Smell of Victory: Vitellius at Bedriacum (Tacitus *Histories* 2.70)', *Classical Philology* 87 (1992), pp. 14–29.

—, 'The Three Minor Pretenders in Tacitus *Histories* 2', *Latomus* 52 (1993), pp. 769–96.

—, 'Rogues' March: Caecina and Valens in *Histories* 1.61–70', *Museum Helveticum* 51 (1994), pp. 103–25.

—, 'Vespasian's Fear of Assassination', *Philologus* 138 (1994), pp. 118–28.

—, 'Galba, the Massacre of the Marines and the Formation of Legion I Adiutrix', *Athenaeum* 91 (2003), pp. 489–515.

C. L. Murison, 'The Historical Value of Tacitus' *Histories*', *Aufstieg und Niedergang der römischen Welt* II 33.3 (1991), pp. 1686–1713.

E. O'Gorman, 'Shifting Ground: Lucan, Tacitus and the Landscape of Civil War', *Hermathena* 159 (1995), pp. 117–31.

C. A. Perkins, 'Tacitus on Otho', *Latomus* 52 (1993), pp. 848–55.

J. Pigoń, 'Helvidius Priscus, Eprius Marcellus and *Iudicium Senatus*: Observations on Tacitus *Histories* 4.7–8', *Classical Quarterly* 42 (1992), pp. 235–46.

A. Pomeroy, 'Center and Periphery in Tacitus' *Histories*', *Arethusa* 36 (2003), pp. 361–74.

C. A. Powell, '*Deum ira, hominum rabies*', *Latomus* 31 (1972), pp. 833–48.

P. M. Rogers, 'Titus, Berenice and Mucianus', *Historia* 29 (1980), pp. 86–95.

M. Sage, 'Tacitus' Historical Works: A Survey and Appraisal', *Aufstieg und Niedergang der römischen Welt* II 33.2 (1990), pp. 851–1030.

Y. Shochat, 'Tacitus' Attitude to Otho', *Latomus* 40 (1981), pp. 365–77.

R. Syme, 'Partisans of Galba', *Historia* 31 (1982), pp. 460–83.

G. B. Townend, 'The Consuls of AD 69/70', *American Journal of Philology* 83 (1962), pp. 113–29.

—, 'The Restoration of the Capitol in AD 70', *Historia* 36 (1987), pp. 243–8.

C. J. Tuplin, 'The False Neros of the First Century AD', pp. 364–404, in C. Deroux (ed.), *Studies in Latin Literature and Roman History* V (Brussels 1989).

D. Wardle, 'Vespasian, Helvidius Priscus and the Restoration of the Capitol', *Historia* 45 (1996), pp. 208–22.

K. H. Waters, 'The Character of Domitian', *Phoenix* 18 (1964), pp. 49–77.

K. Wellesley, 'What Happened on the Capitol in December AD 69?', *American Journal of Ancient History* 6 (1981), pp. 166–90.

T. P. Wiseman, 'Flavians on the Capitol', *American Journal of Ancient History* 3 (1978), pp. 163–78.

The bibliographies of the studies of the *Histories* by R. Ash and H. Haynes offer further help, as does C. Damon's commentary on *Histories* 1 (Cambridge 2003) and R. Ash's commentary on *Histories* 2 (Cambridge 2007), and there is also a special volume of *Arethusa, Ingens Eloquentiae Materia: Rhetoric and Empire in Tacitus* 39 (2006), dedicated to Tacitus and co-edited by R. Ash and M. Malamud.

Historical studies of individual emperors relevant to the period are available by M. Griffin, *Nero: The End of a Dynasty* (London 1984), B. Levick, *Vespasian* (London 1999), B. Jones, *The Emperor Titus* (London and Sydney 1984), P. Southern, *Domitian: Tragic Tyrant* (London and New York 1997), and J. D. Grainger, *Nerva and the Roman Succession Crisis of AD 96–99* (London 2003).

On military questions, see J. B. Campbell, *The Emperor and the Roman Army 31 BC–AD 235* (Oxford 1984), and A. K. Goldsworthy, *The Roman Army at War 100 BC–AD 200* (Oxford 1996). On propaganda, see J. Nicols, *Vespasian and the Partes Flavianae, Historia Einzelschriften* 28 (Wiesbaden 1978). For general help with a range of topics, from technical terms to information about individual authors and broader Classical themes, see S. Hornblower and A. Spawforth (eds.), *The Oxford Classical Dictionary* (3rd edition, Oxford 1996). Also useful are A. K. Bowman, P. Garnsey and D. Rathbone (eds.), *The Cambridge Ancient History Volume XI: The High Empire AD 70–192* (Cambridge 2000), and A. K. Bowman, E. Champlin and A. Lintott (eds.), *The Cambridge Ancient History Volume X: The Augustan Empire 43 BC–AD 69* (Cambridge 1996).

Finally, there are also some engaging historical novels available, including L. Davis, *The Course of Honour* (London 1997), about the love story between Vespasian and the freedwoman Caenis, and A. Massie, *Nero's Heirs* (London 1999), where a fictional character Scaurus writes a series of letters to Tacitus about the civil wars.

A Note on the Translation and Text

This translation is a revised version of Kenneth Wellesley's lively original 1964 Penguin of Tacitus' *Histories*. I quote from his original introduction: 'No translator of Tacitus can view his labours without some feeling of guilt and remorse. He may prove to have butchered his victim. He has inevitably robbed the original of its peculiar virtue, the living word.' Much the same can be said about the feelings of anyone engaged in revising a well-loved translation, particularly one produced by an eminent scholar such as Wellesley, who knew his text of Tacitus uniquely well. I hope that in revising the text I have managed to stay true to the spirit of Wellesley's prose, while making the translation more accessible to modern readers. For example, some changes have been made to individual words for the sake of clarity (e.g. regretfully, the Scottish word 'dirk' has gone); at other points, sentences have been slimmed down to try to reflect more closely the pithiness of Tacitus' original Latin. Also, the notes have been substantially expanded to help a reader who is coming to the text for the first time.

Scholars have argued that Tacitus' narrative of the *Histories* originally ran to twelve books, but our manuscripts unfortunately break off at 5.26. Nevertheless, we can deduce the chronological scope of the missing books from Tacitus' outline of the work at 1.1–3, from letters written by Pliny the Younger to Tacitus offering him 'raw material' for his historical narrative (e.g. *Epistles* 6.16 and 20 about the eruption of Vesuvius in AD 79), and from some small 'fragments' of the missing books cited by later writers.

THE HISTORIES

BOOK 1

The Setting of the Story

1. I shall begin my work with the year in which Servius Galba and Titus Vinius were consuls, the former for the second time.[1] For many historians have related events of the preceding 820 years dating from the foundation of Rome. So long as republican history was their theme, they wrote with equal eloquence and independence. Yet after the battle of Actium had been fought and the interests of peace demanded that power should be concentrated in one man's hands, this great line of historians came to an end.[2] Truth, too, suffered in various ways, thanks first to an ignorance of politics, which now lay outside public control; later came a passion for flattery, or else a hatred of autocrats. Thus, among those who were hostile or subservient, neither extreme cared about posterity. However, although the reader can easily discount a historian's flattery, there is a ready audience for detraction and spite. Adulation bears the ugly taint of subservience, but malice gives the false impression of being independent. As for myself, Galba, Otho and Vitellius were known to me neither as benefactors nor as enemies. My official career owed its beginning to Vespasian, its progress to Titus and its further advancement to Domitian.[3] I have no wish to deny this; but writers who claim to be honest and reliable must not speak about anybody with either partiality or hatred. If I live, I propose to deal with the reign of the deified Nerva and the imperial career of Trajan. This is a more fruitful and less thorny field, and I have reserved it for my old age.[4] Modern times are indeed happy as few others have been, for we can think as we please, and speak as we think.

2. The story which I am approaching is rich with disasters,

grimly marked with battles, rent by treason and savage even in peacetime. Four emperors perished violently.[5] There were three civil wars,[6] still more foreign campaigns, and often conflicts which combined elements of both.[7] Success in the East was balanced by failure in the West. The Balkans were in turmoil, the Gallic provinces were wavering, and Britain was conquered but immediately abandoned.[8] The Sarmatian and Suebian peoples rose upon us, the Dacian distinguished himself in desperate battles won and lost, and thanks to the activities of a charlatan masquerading as Nero, even Parthia was on the brink of declaring war. Now too, Italy itself fell victim to new disasters or ones which had not occurred for many centuries. Towns were swallowed up or buried along the richest part of the Campanian coast.[9] Rome was devastated by fires, her most venerable temples were destroyed and the very Capitol was set alight by Roman hands.[10] Things holy were desecrated, there was adultery in high places. The sea swarmed with exiles and cliffs were stained with blood. Still fiercer savagery gripped Rome.[11] Rank, wealth and office, whether surrendered or retained, provided grounds for accusation, and the reward for virtue was inevitable death. The profits of the prosecutors were no less hated than their crimes. Some obtained priesthoods and consulships as the prize of victory, others acquired official posts and backstairs influence, creating a universal pandemonium of hatred and terror. Slaves were bribed to turn against their masters, freedmen against their patrons, while those who lacked an enemy were ruined by their friends.

3. Nonetheless, the period was not so barren of merit that it failed to teach some good lessons as well. Mothers accompanied their children in flight, wives followed their husbands into exile. There were resolute kinsmen, steadfast sons-in-law and slaves obstinately faithful even in the face of torture. Distinguished men driven to suicide faced the last agony with unflinching courage, and there were death scenes equal to those praised in the history of early Rome. In addition to multiple tragedies on the human plane, portents occurred in the sky and on earth, premonitory thunderbolts and tokens of things to come, auspicious or ominous, doubtful or obvious. Indeed, it has never

been verified by more terrible disasters for the Roman people or by fuller portents that the gods care not for our peace of mind, but only for vengeance. 4. However, before embarking on my theme, it seems desirable to go back a little and consider the state of affairs in Rome, the mood of the army, the attitude of the provinces and the elements of strength and weakness throughout the Roman world. In this way it may be possible to appreciate not only the actual course of events, whose outcome is often dictated by chance, but also their underlying logic and causes.

Although the death of Nero[12] had been welcomed initially by a surge of rejoicing, it had stirred conflicting emotions not only among the senate, the people and the urban garrison in Rome, but also in all the legions and their commanders overseas. A well-hidden secret of the principate had been revealed: it was possible, it seemed, for an emperor to be chosen outside Rome. Still, the senators were overjoyed, and promptly permitted themselves considerable freedom of speech in their negotiations with an emperor who was new to his task and absent from the capital. The leading members of the equestrian order were hardly less delighted than the senators. Hopes were raised among respectable Roman citizens who were connected to the great households, and among the dependants and freedmen of condemned men and exiles. The low-life types who had grown accustomed to the circus and theatres, the most villainous of the slave population and the squanderers who had been the recipients of Nero's degrading charity were gloomy and hungry for the latest rumours. 5. The city garrison, long steeped in a tradition of sworn allegiance to the Caesars, had been induced to desert Nero more by cunning and suggestion than from any inclination of its own. It now discovered that payment of the bounty promised in the name of Galba was not forthcoming, and that there was not to be the same scope for great services and rewards in peace as in war. These troops also realized that it was too late for them to ingratiate themselves with an emperor created by the legions. Already disaffected, they were stirred up further by the unscrupulous intrigues of their prefect, Nymphidius Sabinus, who was plotting to make himself emperor.[13]

It is true that Nymphidius was caught in the act, but although the head of the plot had been removed, many of the troops retained a guilty conscience.

There were rumours, too, about Galba's old age and miserliness. His strictness, once well spoken of and much talked about among the soldiers, now irritated men who rejected the discipline of the past and who, in the course of fourteen years under Nero, had come to like the vices of emperors no less than they had once feared their virtues. In addition to this, there was the famous remark by Galba – 'I select my troops, I don't buy them.'[14] Impeccable as a public statement, the epigram proved double-edged for Galba himself, for everything else fell short of this standard. 6. Old and feeble, Galba was dominated by Titus Vinius[15] and Cornelius Laco.[16] The former was the most vicious of men, the latter the most idle. Between them, they burdened the emperor with resentment caused by Vinius' crimes and ruined him with contempt for Laco's sluggishness.

Galba's march had been slow and blood-stained, thanks to the executions of Cingonius Varro, a consul-designate, and the ex-consul Petronius Turpilianus.[17] The grounds were that the former was an associate of Nymphidius and the latter a commander appointed by Nero. Allowed no proper trial or defence, these two had perished by what seemed a miscarriage of justice. The entry into Rome was marked by the massacre of thousands of unarmed troops, ill-omened and alarming even the perpetrators themselves. After the arrival of the Spanish legion[18] and the retention in Rome of the formation which Nero raised from the fleet, the capital was crowded with an unfamiliar army. In addition, there were numerous drafts from Germany, Britain and Illyricum. Nero had selected these men and sent them on ahead to the Caspian Gates for the campaign which he was mounting against the Albani, but had later recalled them to deal with the revolt of Vindex.[19] Here was fuel in plenty for a revolution, lacking indeed a clear-cut preference for any one leader, but nevertheless readily available to any daring opportunist.

7. It happened that news of the executions of Clodius Macer and Fonteius Capito arrived simultaneously. Macer, obviously

bent on causing trouble in Africa, had been put to death by the imperial agent Trebonius Garutianus on the orders of Galba.[20] Capito, who harboured similar designs in Germany, had been assassinated by the legionary commanders Cornelius Aquinus and Fabius Valens, who did not wait for instructions.[21] There were people who believed that despite Capito's unsavoury reputation for greed and lust, he nevertheless had no thought of rebelling. However, after his legionary commanders had urged him to declare war but failed to persuade him, they themselves had allegedly plotted to trap and accuse him, whereupon Galba's lack of firmness, or perhaps his anxiety not to probe too deeply, however suspicious the circumstances, had approved what could not be altered.

Whatever the truth of the matter, both executions were ill received, and once the emperor was hated, good deeds and bad brought him equal discredit. Everything had its price. The imperial freedmen wielded excessive influence and Galba's own slaves were eager to grab any unexpected windfall, for they knew time was short when dealing with an elderly emperor. The new court exhibited the same evils as the old – equally serious, but not equally tolerable. Even Galba's age provoked sneers and discontent among a populace accustomed to the young Nero, and comparing the two emperors, as the crowd will, for their looks and physical attractiveness.[22]

8. So much for public opinion at Rome, naturally complex in view of the large numbers of people involved. Of the provinces, Spain was governed by Cluvius Rufus, a man of eloquence and civility, but untried in wars.[23] The Gallic provinces were linked to the regime by their memory of Vindex, and, in addition, by the recent grant of Roman citizenship and the corresponding prospect of tax relief. However, the Gallic communities closest to the armies stationed in Germany had not been so well treated. Some had actually suffered loss of territory and were just as upset when considering the concessions accorded to others as from reckoning their own sufferings.

The armies of Germany presented a particular danger in view of their strength. Anxious and resentful, they plumed themselves on their recent success, yet feared the consequences of having backed the wrong side. They had been slow to abandon Nero, nor had Verginius declared for Galba immediately. Whether he really was unwilling to become emperor himself is doubtful, but it was common knowledge that the troops had offered him the position. Fonteius Capito's assassination still rankled, even with those who were in no position to complain. What was lacking was a leader, for Verginius had been removed, under the pretence of imperial friendship. The troops, observing that he had not been sent back to Germany and indeed faced prosecution, felt that they were incriminated themselves. 9. The army of Upper Germany despised its commander-in-chief, Hordeonius Flaccus.[24] Debilitated by old age and gout, Flaccus lacked personality and prestige. Even when the troops were quiet, he could not maintain discipline; and by the same token, if the men were raging, his feeble attempts to control them only inflamed them further. The legions of Lower Germany were left without a governor for some time. Finally Galba's nominee appeared – Aulus Vitellius, son of the Vitellius who had held the censorship and three consulships. This, it seemed, was sufficient qualification.

In the army of Britain there were no angry outbursts. Indeed, throughout all the disturbances of the civil wars, no other legions acted with greater propriety. The reason may lie in the fact that they were far away and cut off by the North Sea; or perhaps they had learnt from continual campaigning to reserve their hatred for the enemy. There was peace, too, in Illyricum, though the legions mobilized by Nero had sent deputations to court Verginius while they waited in Italy. But the troops were widely dispersed (always a very sound method of ensuring military loyalty) and they could not mingle their failings nor join forces.

10. The East remained as yet undisturbed. Syria, with four legions, was governed by Licinius Mucianus.[25] He was a man equally notorious in good times and bad. In his youth, he had courted friendship with great men with an eye to his own advancement. Then he ran through a fortune and his standing became precarious, for even Claudius was thought to be hostile to him. Removed to an isolated corner of Asia, he came as near

to being an exile as later to being emperor. He was a curious mix of self-indulgence and energy, courtesy and arrogance, good and evil. Excessively self-indulgent in his spare time, yet he showed remarkable qualities when actively employed on a task. In public you would praise him, but his private life was criticized. Yet by a supple gift for intrigue he exercised great influence on his subordinates, associates and colleagues, and he was the sort of man who found it more congenial to make an emperor than to be one.

The conduct of the Jewish war, with the command of three legions, lay in the hands of Nero's nominee, Flavius Vespasian.[26] He had neither the will nor the intent to oppose Galba. Indeed, he had actually sent his son Titus to do homage and pay his respects to the emperor, as I shall record in the appropriate context.[27] Perhaps mysterious prophecies were already circulating, and portents and oracles promising Vespasian and his sons the principate; but it was only after the rise of the Flavians that we believed in such stories.

11. Egypt, and the forces designed to keep it in order, has been governed ever since the deified Augustus' day by Romans of equestrian rank in place of the Pharaohs. It seemed sensible that a province of this sort – difficult to reach, fertile in corn, yet divided and unsettled by strange cults and irresponsible excesses, ignorant of law and lacking knowledge of civil government – should be kept under the control of the imperial house. It was ruled at that time by Tiberius Alexander, himself an Egyptian.[28]

As for Africa and its legion, following the execution of Clodius Macer, they were content with any kind of emperor after experiencing a lesser master. The two Mauretanias, together with Raetia, Noricum, Thrace and the other provinces governed by procurators, took their cue from nearby armies, and were driven to support or hostility through contact with more powerful influences. The ungarrisoned provinces – and above all Italy itself, the helpless victim of every overlord – were doomed to be the spoils of war.

This, then, was the state of the Roman Empire when Servius Galba entered upon his second consulship as the colleague of

Titus Vinius, at the start of a year which was deadly to them and nearly destroyed Rome.[29]

The Murder of Galba

12. A few days after 1 January, a letter came from Pompeius Propinquus,[30] the procurator of Belgica, announcing that the legions of Upper Germany had broken their oath of loyalty and were calling for a new emperor, although they were entrusting the final choice to the senate and people of Rome in order to mitigate the offence. This event accelerated a measure which Galba had for some time been debating in his own mind and with his friends – the adoption of an heir.[31] In recent months, the matter had undoubtedly been the main topic of discussion throughout the country, for in the first place, there was opportunity and craving for such talk, and in the second, Galba was old and failing. Few people showed sound judgement or any real desire for the public good. Indeed, many day-dreamers talked glibly of the chances of this candidate or that in order to curry favour with a friend or a patron, or else to vent their spite on Titus Vinius, whose unpopularity grew every day along with his power.

Galba's indulgence only sharpened the desires of his courtiers, who were greedy for more after their first taste of success. For under such a weak and credulous emperor, wrongdoing involved less fear of the consequences and greater rewards. 13. The power of the emperor was shared between Titus Vinius, the consul, and Cornelius Laco, the praetorian prefect. No less influential was Icelus, Galba's freedman, who had been given the status of knight and as such was commonly called 'Marcianus'.[32] These three were at loggerheads, and each pursued an individual policy in minor matters, but on the question of electing a successor they were divided into two factions. Vinius supported Marcus Otho, while Laco and Icelus agreed in rejecting him, though they had no single alternative candidate in mind. Galba himself was well aware of the friendship existing between Otho and Titus Vinius, while rumours spread by inveterate gossip-mongers speculated that, as Vinius had an unwedded daughter and Otho was single, the pair would soon be father-in-law and son-in-law.

I believe that Galba had begun to be anxious, too, about the welfare of his country, fruitlessly wrested from Nero if it were left in Otho's control. After all, the latter had spent a thoughtless childhood and riotous youth, winning Nero's favour because he mimicked his vices. This was why Nero, until such times as he could get rid of his wife, Octavia, had planted Poppaea Sabina, the imperial whore, on Otho, who knew all about his sexual antics. Later he suspected him of an involvement with this same Poppaea, and packed him off to the province of Lusitania in the guise of its governor.[33] Otho administered his province affably, and was the first to side with the revolt. So long as the campaign lasted he showed energy, and was the most eminent among those supporting Galba. He had hoped to be adopted from the start, and now each passing day saw his ambition intensified. Most of the soldiers supported him, and Nero's courtiers naturally fell for one who resembled him.

14. After being informed of the revolt in Germany, Galba was anxious about the extent of the outbreak, although so far there was no certain information about Vitellius. The emperor had no confidence in the city garrison either. He therefore resorted to what he believed to be the one and only cure for the disease – an imperial election. He summoned Marius Celsus,[34] the consul-designate, and Ducenius Geminus, the city prefect, as well as Vinius and Laco, and after a few prefatory remarks about his own old age, sent for Piso Licinianus.[35] It is not clear whether this was his own choice, or whether, as some have believed, Laco was pressurizing him, after making friends with Piso at the house of Rubellius Plautus.[36] However, in supporting him Laco astutely pretended that he was a stranger, and Piso's good reputation made the policy plausible enough. As the son of Marcus Crassus and Scribonia, Piso came of distinguished parentage on both sides. His severe expression and general appearance belonged to an earlier age, and upright observers spoke of his strict morality, although he was seen as bad-tempered by those who viewed him less favourably. Yet it was

precisely that aspect of his character which aroused suspicion
in the pessimists that pleased his adoptive father.

15. So it seems that Galba took Piso's hand and spoke to him
roughly as follows: 'If I were a private citizen adopting you
before the pontiffs by a curial statute in the traditional way,[37]
it would have been gratifying to me to have a descendant of
Gnaeus Pompey and Marcus Crassus entering my family, and
for you it would be an honour to enhance your own noble
ancestry with the distinctions of the Sulpician and Lutatian
families.[38] As things are, the unanimous will of heaven and
earth has called me to supreme power, and it is rather your
character and patriotism which have impelled me to offer you
the principate. For this power, our forefathers fought on the
battlefield, and I myself won it in war, but I now give it to
you in time of peace, following the precedent set by Emperor
Augustus. He it was who promoted to a position immediately
below his own his sister's son Marcellus, then his son-in-law
Agrippa, later his own grandsons, and finally Tiberius Nero,
his stepson. However, Augustus sought a successor within his
family: I have done so throughout the state. This is not because
I lack relatives or army colleagues, but I myself did not accept
power from selfish motives, and the proof of my reasoning
should be plain from the fact that, for your sake, I have passed
over the claims not only of my relatives but of yours. You have
a brother as nobly born as you, and older, who is worthy of
this elevation, but you are the better man.[39]

'You are old enough now to have escaped the waywardness
of youth, and you have nothing to apologize for in your past.
Until today, you had to tolerate only misfortune. Yet success
probes a man's character more keenly. Men put up with bad
times, but prosperity spoils us. Loyalty, independence and
friendship are the finest flowers of human character. These
qualities you will of course continue to display as sturdily
as ever, but others will seek to weaken them by sycophancy.
Flattery, honeyed words and the poison most fatal to sincerity
– individual self-interest – will beset you. Even if you and I are
conversing with perfect frankness today, others will prefer to
engage with our high status rather than with us as people.

Persuading a ruler to adopt the right course is a fatiguing business, but flattery of any emperor is accomplished without the need for real affection.

16. 'If it were possible for our gigantic empire to stand erect and keep its balance without a ruler, I should be the right sort of person to inaugurate a republican constitution. However, we have long ago reached a point where drastic measures are necessary. Hence, my declining years can make Rome no greater gift than a good successor, nor your youth any greater gift than a good emperor. Under Tiberius, Gaius and Claudius, our empire was the heirloom of a single family. A substitute for freedom will be that our emperors are starting to be selected. Now that the dynasty of the Julii and Claudii has come to an end, the process of adoption will find the best man for the job. To be born and bred of emperors is a matter of chance and is valued accordingly, but adoption involves unfettered judgement, and if one wants to choose well, public opinion points the way. Picture Nero, puffed up with pride on being the heir of a long line of Caesars. It was not Vindex with his undefended province, nor I with my one legion, who dislodged this incubus from the shoulders of Rome. It was his own monstrous excesses, his own life of pleasure that did so, although there was no precedent at that time for the condemnation of an emperor. We ourselves, elevated by armed force and by those who judged us worthy, are bound to attract envious glances, whatever our merits. However, you must not lose confidence if two legions have not yet settled down after the shock which the Roman world has suffered.[40] My accession too was far from tranquil. Besides, once men hear of your adoption, I will stop being seen as an old man – the only criticism people level at me now. Nero will always be missed by the morally bankrupt types. You and I must make sure that he is not missed by good men as well.

'This is not the moment for further words of advice, and indeed every precaution has been taken if I have done right in choosing you. The soundest and simplest criterion of good and bad policy is to reflect what actions you would yourself approve or disapprove of if another were emperor. Rome is not like countries ruled by kings, where one house dominates and the rest are slaves. You will be ruling men who can tolerate neither total slavery nor total liberty.'

Such was the tenor of Galba's remarks. They sounded as if he were still creating an emperor, but the rest addressed Piso as if the process were complete.

17. They say that Piso betrayed no emotion or exultation to his immediate audience or afterwards to the general public who riveted their gaze upon him. He addressed his father and emperor in suitably respectful language, and referred to himself modestly. His unaltered looks and manner seemed to imply that he had the ability rather than the desire to be emperor.

It was then debated whether the adoption should be announced from the rostra, in the senate or the praetorian barracks. It seemed best to proceed to the barracks. This, it was felt, would be a tribute to the army: although its favour ought not to be sought by bounties and cajolery, it should not be despised if won by honourable means.[41] Meanwhile, an expectant public impatient to hear the great secret surrounded the palace, and attempts to suppress rumours which had leaked out merely intensified them.

18. The tenth of January was an unpleasantly rainy day, abnormally disturbed by thunder, lightning and a threatening sky. From time immemorial this had been interpreted as an omen calling for the cancellation of political assemblies, but it did not deter Galba from making his way to the barracks. He despised such things as being chance events; or perhaps the future is predestined and inevitable whatever the warning signs. His proclamation, addressed to a crowded assembly of troops, was brief, as befitted a supreme commander. He said that in adopting Piso he was following the precedent of divine Augustus and the military practice whereby one man used to pick another.[42] Furthermore, so that an exaggerated version of the revolt would not gain credibility through concealment, he went out of his way to insist that the aberrations of the Fourth and Twenty-Second Legions, prompted by a few ringleaders, had not gone beyond mere words and talk, and they would soon return to their duty. Nor did he round off the speech by pandering to the troops or bribing them. Even so, the tribunes,

centurions and front-ranks responded with a gratifying cheer. The rest remained gloomy and silent, as if they felt that active service had lost them the bounty customarily exacted even in peacetime. There is general agreement that they could have been won over by a tiny act of generosity from the stingy old emperor.[43] His old-fashioned rigidity and excessive strictness spelt ruin, for we cannot rise to these standards nowadays.

19. After that, Galba addressed the senate just as simply and briefly as he had spoken to the soldiers. Piso made a courteous and formal speech, which went down well. Many senators felt genuine goodwill, his opponents spoke even more effusively and the uncommitted majority was quick to grovel. They were too busy calculating their private prospects to worry about the public interest. In the following four days, the time which intervened between his adoption and murder, Piso made no public utterance or move.

As reports of the German revolt increased day by day in a country prepared to hear and believe all the latest news provided it is bad, the senate had decided that legates should be sent to the army of Germany. The question of Piso's joining the embassy was discussed in secret. This would look more impressive: the others would carry the authority of the senate, Piso the prestige of a Caesar. They decided to include Laco, the praetorian prefect; but he promptly vetoed this plan. Besides, the selection of the other commissioners, which had been entrusted by the senate to Galba, was marked by scandalous indecision. Men were nominated, and then excused or substituted, as each man's fears or hopes induced him to pull strings to stay behind or be included in the mission.

20. The next matter of concern was finance. A comprehensive survey showed that the fairest thing would be to demand repayment from those who were responsible for the crisis: Nero had squandered 2,200 million sesterces[44] in largesse. Galba ordered the recipients to be sent individual demand notices, on the understanding that each was to retain one tenth of what he had received. However, the people concerned had barely this amount left, for they had spent other men's money as lavishly as their own. The really greedy and unprincipled beneficiaries

no longer disposed of any landed property or capital invest-
ments: only the minor trappings of depravity remained. The
collection of the money was to be supervised by an equestrian
committee of thirty, an unprecedented commission and burdensome because of the numbers involved and the personal interests in play. Auctioneers and dealers in confiscated property
were everywhere, and Rome was distracted by lawsuits. Yet
there was also intense delight at the thought that the recipients
of Nero's bounty would henceforth be as poor as those he had
robbed.

   In the course of these days some tribunes were discharged:
Antonius Taurus and Antonius Naso of the praetorian guard,
Aemilius Pacensis of the urban cohorts, and Julius Fronto of
the watch.[45] This did not prove salutary for the rest, but only
triggered fear that, if individuals were being cunningly removed
by a policy of terror, they were all under suspicion.

   21. Meanwhile, Otho had nothing to hope for from settled
conditions, and his whole policy required chaos. Many combined factors spurred him on: his extravagance which would
have burdened even an emperor, his lack of resources barely
tolerable for a private individual, his anger towards Galba and
jealousy of Piso. To stimulate his ambition, he invented dangers,
too. He told himself that Nero had found him too much of a
burden, and he could not expect a second Lusitania and the
compliment of another exile. Suspicion and hatred must always
be the reaction of rulers towards the man talked of as the next
in succession. It was this, he reflected, that had harmed him
before an elderly emperor, and it would do so even more with a
truculent youth soured by prolonged exile. His own assassination, Otho reflected, was always possible. So he must act with
daring, while Galba's authority was disintegrating and Piso's had
not yet established itself. There was scope for great enterprises
when power changed hands, and hesitation was misplaced where
inaction could do more harm than recklessness. Death came alike
to everyone as a condition of existence: the only demarcation
was in being forgotten or celebrated by posterity. If the same
end awaited the guilty and the innocent, a man of spirit should
at least embrace the death which he deserved.[46]

22. Otho's character was not as flabby as his physical condition. His confidential freedmen and slaves, who were given a freer hand than one expects in a private household, dangled enticements before his greedy gaze: a court and life of pleasure like Nero's, liaisons, marriages and all the gratifications of tyranny. These could be his if he had the courage. If he did nothing, they taunted, these prizes would go to someone else. The astrologers also spurred him on, declaring that their observation of the stars heralded great changes and a year of glory for Otho. Such men betray the powerful and deceive the ambitious: in our country they will always be banned, but retained.[47] The backstairs deliberations of Poppaea had involved many astrologers, the worst possible tool for an imperial spouse. One of these, Ptolemaeus, had gone with Otho to Spain. He had promised that Otho would survive Nero, and after that happened his reputation was secured. Now, proceeding by guesswork and the gossip of those who reckoned up Galba's age and Otho's youth, Ptolemaeus had managed to persuade the latter that he would be called to become emperor. However, Otho accepted the predictions as if they were based on knowledge and the voice of destiny, man's character being such that he will always prefer to believe in mysteries. Ptolemaeus pressed his advantage and proceeded to urge Otho to take the fatally easy step from evil ambition to evil deeds.

23. Yet whether the plot was the result of a sudden impulse is unclear. Otho had been angling for the support of the troops for some time, in the hope of succeeding to the principate or in preparation for a coup. On the move from Spain, during the march or at halting places, he habitually addressed the oldest soldiers by name, and called them 'comrades' – an allusion to their service together under Nero. He greeted some as old friends, asked after the occasional absentee and helped them with money or favours, often dropping complaints and double-edged remarks about Galba and using all the other tricks which tend to stir up simple people. The tiring marches, short rations and strict discipline were not well received by men who were used to travelling to the lake district of Campania and the cities of Achaia on board ship, but who now found themselves

plodding wearily over the Pyrenees and Alps and along inter-
minable roads under the weight of their arms and equipment.

24. The already smouldering discontent of the troops was
fanned to a blaze by one of Tigellinus' associates, Maevius
Pudens.[48] Getting hold of the men who were most easily led, or
who were short of money and therefore ready for any desperate
plunge, he worked upon them little by little and finally went so
far as to hand out a tip of 100 sesterces to each and every
member of the cohort on duty whenever Galba dined with
Otho, ostensibly for their meal. This semi-official bounty was
enhanced by more confidential rewards to individuals. His
methods of corruption were enterprising. A member of the
emperor's personal bodyguard called Cocceius Proculus happened to be in dispute with a neighbour over part of the latter's
land. Otho bought up the whole of this neighbour's farm with
his own money and presented it to Proculus as a free gift. He
was only able to do this by the inefficiency of the praetorian
prefect, who was blind to all scandals, whether notorious or
clandestine.

25. Anyway, Otho now entrusted the imminent plot to his
freedman Onomastus. The latter introduced two members of the
bodyguard, a corporal called Barbius Proculus and a warrant-
officer, one Veturius. In the course of a wide-ranging interview
Otho recognized them to be competent and unscrupulous, and
heaped bribes and promises on them. Money was given to them
for trying out the mood of further potential supporters. Thus,
two common soldiers undertook to hand over the empire of
the Roman people – and hand it over they did. Only a few
associates were let into the secret. They goaded the indecision
of the others by various techniques, dropping hints to senior
non-commissioned officers that they were under a cloud because Nymphidius had promoted them, and inducing in the
remainder, that is the common soldiers, a mood of anger and
despair at the repeatedly postponed bounty. If a few regretted
Nero and missed the slack discipline of the past, all without
exception were panic-stricken at the prospect of being posted
to less favoured units.

26. The rot spread to the legionaries and auxiliaries, already

stirred up after news had circulated that the loyalty of the army of Germany was crumbling. The troublemakers were ready for mutiny, and even the better sort were prepared to connive at it, so that on 14 January they were on the point of carrying Otho off to their barracks as he was returning home from a dinner. However, they were scared off by the uncertainties of night-time, the scattered location of the troops throughout Rome and the fact that it was difficult to coordinate drunken men. It was not their country which concerned them, for they were preparing in sober earnest to desecrate it with the blood of their emperor, but they feared that in the darkness any chance person who met the Pannonian or German units might be mistaken for Otho, who was not personally known to most people. There was substantial evidence of this incipient outbreak, but those in the know hushed it up. The few hints which reached Galba's ears were played down by the prefect Laco, who was clueless about what his men thought, hostile to any plan, however excellent, which he had not himself proposed, and stubbornly disregarded expert opinion.

27. On 15 January, Galba was offering sacrifice in front of the Temple of Apollo.[49] The soothsayer Umbricius, declaring the entrails of the victim to be ill-omened, predicted an imminent plot and an enemy close to home. As Otho was standing next to Galba, he overheard this and gleefully interpreted it in the contrary sense as a happy omen, favourable to his own designs. Shortly afterwards, his freedman Onomastus brought him a message: the architect and builders were waiting for him. This was the prearranged code indicating that the troops were already assembling and the plot ripe. As people asked Otho why he was leaving, he pretended that he was buying some dilapidated property which he first needed to survey. Supported by his freedman, he made his way through the palace of Tiberius into the Velabrum, and from there to the Golden Milestone near the Temple of Saturn. Here twenty-three members of the bodyguard hailed him as emperor. Otho was alarmed that they were so few in number, but they quickly placed him in a chair, drew their swords and hurried him off. Roughly the same number of soldiers joined them on the way – some knew about

the plot, many were curious, a proportion were shouting and flourishing their swords, others again were keeping quiet, intending to suit their reaction to the event.

28. The tribune on duty at the barracks was Julius Martialis.[50] Most people thought he was involved in the plot, either because of the magnitude of the unexpected crime, or because he feared that the rot ran deep among the men and that he might be killed if he resisted. The other tribunes and centurions also preferred the advantage of the moment to the uncertain risks of honour. This was their state of mind: a few individuals brazenly committed a shocking crime, more people wanted it to happen, but everyone passively allowed it to take place.

29. Meanwhile, Galba, utterly unaware and preoccupied with his sacrifice, continued to importune the gods of an empire no longer his. Suddenly, word came that some senator – it was not known who – was being hurried off to the praetorian barracks, and next, that Otho was the man. News came from every part of Rome at once, brought by whoever had met the procession. Some panicky informants gave an exaggerated account. A few used understatement, unable even at that point to forget their habitual flattery.[51] Therefore they put their heads together and decided to test the mood of the cohort on duty in the palace, although without resorting to Galba himself. The prestige of the emperor was to be kept intact for when more drastic remedies were required. So after the soldiers had been summoned, it was Piso who addressed them from the steps of the palace along the following lines:

'This is the fifth day, fellow-soldiers, since I was created a Caesar by adoption, not knowing what was to come, nor whether this name was to be desired or dreaded. What this implies for my family and for the state rests with you. Not that I fear a grimmer fate on my own account. I have experienced adversity already, and at this very moment I am learning that success itself is no less dangerous. However, on account of my father, the senate and the empire itself, I grieve if today it is necessary for us either to die or – something which is just as miserable for good men – to kill. We found comfort in the most recent crisis from the lack of bloodshed in Rome and from the undisputed transfer of power. In this case, the fact of my adoption appeared sufficient precaution against fighting, even after Galba's death.

30. 'I shall make no claims for myself in point of ancestry or strict morality. For there is no need to catalogue my virtues in comparison with Otho. His sole boast is a vicious life, which involved the ruin of the empire even when he was playing the part of the emperor's friend. Could he have earned the principate by his mincing airs? Or by his effeminate dress? Extravagance deceives some people, who wrongly take it for generosity. Otho will be skilled in squandering, but not in giving. At this moment seduction, revelry and couplings with women are engaging his imagination. These he deems the prizes of the principate – prizes whose lusts and pleasures are to be his, while the shame and degradation falls to everyone. No one has ever made good use of power evilly gained.

'The unanimous voice of mankind called Galba to be Caesar, and Galba awarded the title to me, with your approval. If "constitution", "senate" and "people" are merely empty phrases, it is up to you, fellow-soldiers, to see that the dregs of the army do not create an emperor. One has sometimes heard stories of legionaries rising in mutiny against their commanders, but your reliability and reputation have remained intact to this day. Even Nero himself deserted you; you did not desert him.[52] We are faced with fewer than thirty renegades and deserters – men in whom no one would tolerate choosing even a centurion or a tribune. Will they have the empire in their gift? Do you concede this precedent, and make yourselves accessories to the act by keeping quiet? These liberties will spread to the provinces and will spell death for us and warfare for you. Murdering your emperor brings no greater reward than keeping your hands clean, and from us you will get an equally generous bonus for loyalty as you would from others for treason.'[53]

31. The men of the bodyguard had slipped away, but the rest of the cohort took no exception to Piso's speech. As tends to happen during turbulent events, it was aimlessly and with no fixed plan that they seized their standards, more than, as was afterwards believed, to hide their complicity. Marius Celsus,

too, was sent off to negotiate with the select units from Illyricum quartered in the Vipsanian Colonnade,[54] and instructions were given to two senior centurions, Amullius Serenus and Domitius Sabinus, to summon from Freedom Hall[55] the troops of the German army. Little confidence was placed in the naval legion, which was hostile after the butchery of their comrades by Galba right on his first entry into Rome. In addition, the tribunes Cetrius Severus, Subrius Dexter and Pompeius Longinus proceeded to the praetorian barracks to see if the still incipient outbreak could be made to yield to saner counsels before it was too late. Of the tribunes, Subrius and Cetrius were assailed by threats from the troops, while Longinus was actually manhandled, arrested and disarmed. This was because his loyalty to his emperor depended not on military rank but friendship with Galba, and so he was particularly suspect to the rebels. The naval legion promptly went over to the praetorians, and the drafts from the army of Illyricum drove Celsus away at the point of their javelins. The detachments from Germany remained undecided for some time, being still physically unfit, as well as calmly disposed. They had formed the advance party sent on to Alexandria by Nero, and after they had fallen ill on the long return voyage, Galba was nursing them back into condition with lavish care.

32. The whole populace now was mobbing the palace together with some slaves. With discordant shouts they demanded Otho's head and the execution of the conspirators, as if the crowd were clamouring for some sort of entertainment in the circus or theatre. They showed no judgement or sincerity, for on the very same day they were to make diametrically opposed demands with equal alacrity, albeit in the traditional manner of those who acclaimed any emperor at all with extravagant applause and empty enthusiasm.

Meanwhile, Galba was hesitating between two proposals. Titus Vinius urged staying in the palace, using the household slaves for protection, barricading the doors, and avoiding contact while tempers ran high. Galba, he said, should give the offenders a chance to repent, and loyal subjects a breathing space for concerted action. After all, crimes profit from speed, good counsels from delay. Finally, the emperor would have the same opportunity to venture out at will later, if this seemed sensible, but if he were to do so and regret it, any return would lie at the mercy of others.

33. The other advisers favoured speedy action, before the conspiracy, so far a feeble business confined to a few plotters, could grow. Otho, too, was likely to be in a panic, they pointed out. He had left furtively and been carried off to a group of strangers, but thanks to the idle delays of the time-wasters, he was at this very moment learning the part of an emperor. They must not wait for him to establish his hold on the barracks, invade the Forum and enter the Capitol under Galba's nose, while the distinguished emperor and his heroic courtiers bolted the palace (to the extent of a door and doorframe), intending, of course, to endure a state of siege! And the slaves would be splendid help, once the unity of the great crowd and its initial outburst of indignation petered out! Such a plan was as dangerous as it was degrading. Even if they were fated to die, they should meet the danger face-to-face. This would win Otho the greater infamy, and themselves honour.

When Vinius opposed this plan, Laco set about him with threats, goaded on by Icelus, who obstinately persisted in a private vendetta to the ruin of his country. 34. Galba hesitated no longer, and went along with those who advised the better-looking plan. However, Piso was told to go on ahead to the barracks, as he was a young man of great name recently promoted, and he was hostile to Titus Vinius. Perhaps Piso really hated him, or the malicious types willed him to do so; but the story that Piso loathed Vinius is easier to believe.

Piso had scarcely left the palace when word came that Otho had been killed in the camp. At first the rumour was vague and uncertain. Then, as so often is the case with daring lies, certain individuals asserted that they had been present and had witnessed the deed. The story was lapped up by a jubilant and uncritical public. Many people thought that the rumour had been invented and exaggerated by Othonian agents who had already blended with the crowd and spread the bogus good news in order to lure Galba out.

35. This prompted a burst of applause and exaggerated enthusiasm, not only from the populace and the ignorant lower classes, but also from many of the knights and senators. Abandoning their fear, they threw caution to the winds. After forcing the doors of the palace, they poured inside, presented themselves to Galba and complained that they had been forestalled in their revenge. The greatest cowards among them – those who, as events proved, were to lose their nerve in the moment of danger – spoke extravagantly, making fierce protestations. Ignorance and assertion went hand in hand. Finally, the absence of reliable information and the united chorus of delusion overcame Galba. He buckled on his breastplate, and being too old and too infirm to resist the crowd's onslaught, was lifted up in a chair. While still in the palace area, he was met by one of his bodyguard, Julius Atticus, who flourished a blood-stained sword and cried out that he had killed Otho. Galba replied: 'Fellow-soldier, who ordered this?'[56] This remark shows his striking determination to check indiscipline. Indeed, he did not fear threats and was immune to flatterers.

36. By this time the minds of all the soldiers in the praetorian camp were made up. So great was their enthusiasm that they were not content with surrounding Otho with a throng of bodies. They put him, amid massed flags and standards, on a dais which had recently supported a gold statue of Galba. The tribunes and centurions were allowed no access to Otho, and the common soldiers warned him to be on his guard against the officers. The whole place re-echoed with shouting, tumult and mutual encouragement. It is not unusual for the civilian populace and the lower classes to voice their idle flattery in confused cries, but this was quite different. Whenever the troops caught sight of a fresh adherent coming over to them, they shook him by the hand, put their arms around his neck, placed him near Otho and administered the oath of allegiance, now praising the emperor to his troops, now praising the troops to their emperor. Nor did Otho fail to salute the crowd, stretching out his hands, throwing them kisses and in every way playing the slave to achieve domination. When the whole naval legion had taken the oath, he began to trust his strength. Believing that the men

whom he had provoked one by one should be fired up by a general appeal, he addressed the praetorians as follows from the rampart of the camp:

37. 'I find it hard to say in what capacity I stand before you, fellow-soldiers. I can scarcely call myself a subject after you have nominated me as emperor. Nor can I describe myself as emperor while another rules. Your own designation will be just as ambiguous so long as there is doubt whether the man you are harbouring in your barracks is the ruler of Rome or a traitor. Do you hear them? They are calling in the same breath for my punishment and your execution. This makes it quite obvious that we fall or stand together.

'Knowing Galba's clemency, no doubt he has already promised to carry out the sentence. After all, he slaughtered thousands of completely innocent troops although no one was clamouring for this.[57] I shudder whenever I think of his grisly entry into Rome – the only victory Galba ever won – when he ordered that men who had surrendered, thrown themselves on his mercy and been accepted as his loyal followers, should suffer decimation before the eyes of the city. After this auspicious entry, what prestige did he bring to the office of emperor except his executions of Obultronius Sabinus and Cornelius Marcellus in Spain, Cilo Betuus in Gaul, Fonteius Capito in Germany, Clodius Macer in Africa, Cingonius on the march, Turpilianus at Rome, Nymphidius in the barracks? What province, what camp is there anywhere, which is not stained and polluted with blood, or, to use Galba's language, "reformed and straightened up"? For what others call "crimes", he calls "remedies". By a misuse of terms, he describes "cruelty" as "severity", "greed" as "economy" and the "executions and insults" you have suffered are a "discipline".[58]

'Barely seven months have passed since the death of Nero, and already Icelus has stolen more money than was ever squandered by creatures like Polyclitus, Vatinius and Aegialus.[59] The exactions of Titus Vinius would have displayed less greed and lawlessness if he had been emperor himself. As it is, he has both kept us in subjection as if we belonged to him, and held us cheap as though we were the property of another. His mansion

alone is enough for that bounty which is never given to you,
yet serves as a source of reproaches on a daily basis.

38. 'What is more, to make sure that there is no hope from
his successor, Galba has restored from exile the one man who
in his opinion most closely resembled himself for surliness and
avarice. You have observed, fellow-soldiers, the remarkable
storm by which even the gods signified their disgust at this
ill-omened adoption. The same mood animates the senate. The
same mood animates the Roman people. All they are waiting
for is your courageous intervention, for you alone can make
good policies effective, and without you the best endeavours
are paralysed.

'I am not calling upon you to fight a war or risk your lives.
The armed forces without exception are on our side. As for the
one solitary toga-clad cohort manning the palace, its function
is not so much to protect Galba as to guard him. When this
unit catches sight of you, when it receives my signal, the only
struggle that will take place will be a competition to see who
can earn my deepest gratitude. There is no room for hesitation
in an enterprise that can only win praise if it is concluded
successfully.'

Otho then ordered the arsenal to be opened. Weapons were
hastily grabbed. Tradition and discipline went by the board.
The troops disregarded the distinctions of equipment between
praetorians and legionaries, and seized helmets and shields
meant for auxiliaries. All was confusion. No encouragement
came from tribunes or centurions. Each man followed his own
lead and prompting, and the chief stimulus for the worst
elements was the sorrow of the good. 39. By this time Piso was
seriously alarmed by the mounting tumult and cries of mutiny,
audible even in Rome itself. He joined Galba, who had in the
interval left the palace and was approaching the Forum. Celsus,
too, returned with gloomy news. Some suggested returning to
the Palatine. Others wanted to make for the Capitol. A number
of them were for securing the rostra. The majority, however,
just disagreed with the views of their companions, and as so
often happens when things go wrong, the best option seemed
to be what it was now too late to do. It is said that Laco,

without telling Galba, toyed with the idea of killing Titus
Vinius. Perhaps he thought his execution would mollify the
troops, or believed that he was collaborating with Otho, or
ultimately just hated him. The time and the place gave him
pause, because once killing starts, restraining it is difficult.
Besides, alarming news and the flight of his associates upset
Laco's plan. Indeed, all those keen supporters who had osten-
tatiously paraded their loyalty and courage at the start now lost
heart.

40. By this time, Galba was being carried this way and that
by the erratic pressure of the surging multitude. Everywhere
the public buildings and temples were crowded with spectators,
which made for a dismal view. Yet not a cry came from the
citizens or rabble. Their expressions were astonished, their ears
sensitive to every sound. There was neither uproar nor quiet
calm, but only the hush associated with great fear or great
anger.

Otho, however, was informed that the mob was being armed.
He ordered his men to move in at full speed and seize the danger
points. Thus the Roman troops set off, as if they were set on
deposing a Vologaeses or Pacorus from the ancestral throne of
the Arsacidae[60] – and not setting out to murder their emperor,
a defenceless old man. Scattering the people, trampling the
senate under foot, with weapons at the ready and horses spurred
to a gallop, they burst into the Forum. Neither the sight of the
Capitol, nor the sanctity of the temples that looked down upon
them, nor the thought of past and future emperors deterred
such men from committing a crime which the next ruler-but-one
inevitably avenges.

41. On seeing the column of armed men close at hand, the
standard-bearer of the cohort which formed Galba's escort –
Atilius Vercilio, according to the tradition – tore off the effigy
of Galba and dashed it to the ground.[61] That signal indicated
that all the troops enthusiastically supported Otho. It also triggered a mass exodus of the people from the Forum. Swords
were drawn to deal with the stragglers. Near the Pool of
Curtius,[62] Galba was flung sprawling from his chair by the
panic of his bearers. People give different versions of his last

words, depending on whether they hated or admired him. Some
say that he grovelled, and asked what he had done to deserve
his fate, begging a few days' grace to pay the bounty. Most
accounts say that he voluntarily bared his throat to the
assassins, telling them to come and strike him, if this seemed
best for the country. It hardly mattered to the murderers what
he said.

The identity of the killer is in doubt. Some name a veteran
called Terentius, others call him Laecanius. The more usual
version holds that a soldier of the Fifteenth Legion named
Camurius thrust his sword deep into Galba's throat. The rest
of them disgustingly hacked at his legs and arms (for his breast
was protected by armour). In their wildness and savagery, they
even inflicted further wounds on the already headless torso.

42. Then they attacked Titus Vinius. Here, too, accounts
differ. Was he rendered speechless by a paroxysm of fear? Or
did he call out that Otho had given no instructions that he
should be killed? Whether this remark was in fact invented due
to fear or a confession that he was in the plot, his life and
reputation incline me to think that he had prior knowledge of
a crime he certainly caused. In front of the Temple of the deified
Julius Caesar he was struck down by an initial blow on the
back of the knee, then a legionary, Julius Carus, pierced him
right through from one side to the other with a sword.

43. Our own era can look upon one heroic man from that
day, Sempronius Densus.[63] He was a centurion of the praetorian
cohorts and had been appointed by Galba to watch over Piso.
With dagger drawn, he faced up to armed men and denounced
their crime. Now by gestures, now by words, he turned the
assassins' attention upon himself. This gave Piso a chance to
escape, wounded though he was. He got away to the Temple
of Vesta, where he was taken in through the pity of a state slave
and hidden in his humble lodging. Thus, for a while, Piso
managed to postpone the fatal moment, not thanks to the
sanctity of the building or its daily ritual, but by lying low. At
that moment came two men sent by Otho, who was burning to
have Piso killed. One of these was Sulpicius Florus of the auxiliary cohorts serving in Britain, who had only recently been

given Roman citizenship by Galba. The other was the imperial bodyguard Statius Murcus. These two dragged out Piso and murdered him at the door of the temple.

44. Otho is said to have welcomed no other murder with greater joy and to have gazed on no other severed head with such greedy eyes. Perhaps this was because then for the first time his mind was relieved of all worry and he felt free to exult. Or perhaps the thought of his treason towards Galba and his friendship with Titus Vinius had cast a shadow over Otho's spirit, for all its ruthlessness, whereas the murder of an enemy and rival like Piso may have seemed a right and proper reason for rejoicing.

The heads were impaled on poles and carried about amongst the cohort standards and a legionary eagle. The mutineers vied with each other in displaying their bloody hands, whether they had actually done the killing or had merely been there, and whether their boasting of what they called a fine and memorable deed was true or false. More than 120 individuals presented petitions demanding a reward for some noteworthy service on this day. These documents were later discovered by Vitellius, who instructed that all the petitioners were to be rounded up and put to death. This was not a tribute to Galba, but the traditional method by which emperors secure self-defence for the present and warn of retribution in the future.

45. You would have thought that the senate and the people were different men. They all stampeded towards the barracks, each trying to beat his neighbour in the race and catch up with those who led the field. They cursed Galba, complimented the soldiers on their choice, and covered Otho's hand with kisses.[64] These demonstrations were multiplied in proportion to their insincerity. Otho welcomed even single individuals who came up to him, and restrained the greed and menaces of his men by word and look. Marius Celsus, the consul-designate, had been a loyal friend to Galba to the bitter end. For this the soldiers now demanded his head, for they resented his energy and high principle as if they were character flaws. It was all too clear that they were seeking an excuse for bloodshed and plundering and the annihilation of every decent man, but Otho so far had

no authority to prevent outrage – though he could already command it. So he pretended to be angry, and by ordering Celsus to be put in irons and declaring that he would soon face a heavier punishment, rescued him from immediate death.

46. After that, the troops got their way in everything. They chose their own praetorian prefects, including Plotius Firmus. Once one of the common soldiers, then given command of the watch, he joined Otho's faction while Galba's position was still secure. His colleague was Licinius Proculus, whose close association with Otho suggested that he had encouraged his designs. As city prefect, the troops chose Flavius Sabinus, following the lead of Nero, under whom Sabinus had held the same post. In making this choice many of them had their eye on his brother, Vespasian.[65]

There was a demand that the payments traditionally made to centurions to secure exemption from duty should be abolished. For the common soldiers paid this as a kind of annual tax. As much as a quarter of a company's strength could be scattered about on leave or loitering in the actual barracks, so long as they paid the centurion his fee. There was nobody who had any scruples about the extent of these burdensome exactions nor the methods employed to meet them. Highway robbery, theft or taking on jobs as slaves were means by which the soldiers paid for their time off. Besides this, any soldier who was wealthy was harassed by hard work and savage treatment until he agreed to purchase exemption. Finally, when he had been bled dry by his expenses and had also lost his vigour through laziness, he would return to his unit, a pauper instead of a rich man and sluggish instead of energetic. This process was repeated interminably; and the same destitution and indiscipline ruined man after man, driving them herd-like towards mutiny, dissension and, in the last resort, civil war. However, Otho had no wish to alienate his centurions by bribing their men. So he promised that he would pay for the annual leave from his imperial exchequer. This was certainly a beneficial reform, which in due course hardened into a permanent rule of the military service under the good emperors who succeeded.

The prefect Laco was given the impression that he was being

exiled to an island. In fact, he was struck down by a veteran whom Otho had already sent ahead to murder him. Marcianus Icelus was a freedman, and, as such, he was publicly executed.[66]

47. So the day was spent in crimes, but the crowning horror was the mood of jubilation. The senate was summoned by the urban praetor, the other magistrates competed in flattery and the senators tore off to the meeting. A decree was passed giving Otho tribunician power, the title 'Augustus' and all the imperial prerogatives. Everybody made a desperate effort to obliterate the taunts and insults which had been freely bandied about; no one was actually made to feel that they rankled in Otho's mind, and whether in fact he had renounced revenge or merely postponed it was uncertain, as his principate was too short.

The Forum was still blood-stained and littered with bodies when Otho was carried through it to the Capitol, and from there to the palace. He allowed the bodies to be handed over for burial and to be cremated. Piso was laid to rest by his wife Verania and his brother Scribonianus, Titus Vinius by his daughter Crispina. They had to search for the heads and pay a ransom for them, as the assassins had kept them to sell.

48. Upon his death, Piso was nearing his thirty-first birthday. His reputation had been better than his luck. Two of his brothers had been executed: Magnus by Claudius and Crassus by Nero. He himself was an exile for a long time, and for four days a Caesar. His hurried adoption gave him only one advantage over the elder brother to whom he was preferred: he was the first to be murdered.

As for Titus Vinius, during his fifty-seven[67] years he played many parts, both good and evil. His father came from a family which had produced praetors, and his maternal grandfather[68] was a victim of the proscriptions. His initial military service won him notoriety. The wife of his commanding officer Calvisius Sabinus had an unfortunate passion for inspecting the camp-site. One night, she entered it disguised as a soldier, and with no less effrontery tried her hand at guard duties and other military activities. Finally, she dared to commit adultery, in the headquarters building of all places. The man involved was proved to be Titus Vinius. So he was put in chains by order of

Gaius Caesar,[69] but when times changed soon afterwards, he was released, rising smoothly in the public service as praetor, and then as a legionary commander who proved his worth. His reputation was later sullied by a degrading scandal on the grounds that he had stolen a gold cup at a banquet given by Claudius. On the following day, Claudius gave orders that Vinius alone of all his guests was to be served on earthenware. Still, as proconsul he governed Narbonese Gaul austerely and honestly. After that his friendship with Galba drew him into the abyss. Unscrupulous, cunning and quick-witted, he could (depending on his mood) be either vicious or hard-working, with equal effectiveness. Titus Vinius' will was set aside because of his enormous wealth, but Piso's poverty guaranteed that his last wishes were respected.

49. Galba's corpse lay disregarded for many hours, and under cover of night suffered much insulting treatment. Finally his steward Argius, one of his former slaves, buried it in a humble grave in the grounds of Galba's private villa. The head fell into the hands of camp-followers and servants, who impaled it on a pole and mutilated it. It was only found on the following day in front of the tomb of Patrobius (Nero's freedman who had been sentenced by Galba). It was then laid with the ashes of the body, which had already been cremated.

Such was the fate of Servius Galba. Over seventy-three years he had lived through the principates of five emperors enjoying success, but he was luckier under others' regimes than under his own. In his family there was ancient nobility and great wealth, but his own personality was something of a compromise: he was lacking in vices rather than endowed with good qualities. As for his reputation, he was not indifferent about it, but did not exploit it. He did not covet other people's money and was thrifty with his own, but he was a positive miser with public funds. He was blamelessly tolerant towards friends and freedmen when they happened to be honest; but if they were not, his lack of perception was quite inexcusable. However, distinguished birth and the perils of the era disguised his apathy, which was described as wisdom. In the prime of life he attained military distinction in Germany; as proconsul, he administered

Africa with moderation, and his control of Nearer Spain in his latter years showed a similar sense of fair play. Indeed, so long as he was a subject, he seemed too great a man to be one, and everyone judged him capable of being an emperor – but then he took power.

50. Rome was in a state of fear. Men were alarmed at the atrocity of the crime, still fresh, and they also feared Otho's character, which they knew from the past. An additional source of panic was the fresh news about Vitellius. This had been hushed up before Galba's assassination, so that the mutiny was thought to be confined to the army of Upper Germany. Here then were the two most despicable men in the whole world by reason of their unclean, idle and pleasure-loving lives, apparently appointed by fate for the task of destroying the empire. Not only the senate and the knights, who had some stake and interest in the country, but the masses, too, expressed sorrow openly. Conversation no longer centred on recent precedents for the brutality of peace. Minds went back to the civil wars, and they spoke of the many times Rome had been captured by its own armies, of the devastation of Italy, of the sack of provinces, of Pharsalus, Philippi, Perusia and Mutina, famous names associated with national disasters.[70] The whole world, they reflected, had been practically turned upside down when the duel for power involved good men, but the empire had survived the victories of Julius Caesar and Augustus. The republic would have done the same under Pompey and Brutus. Yet were they now to visit the temples and pray for Otho? Or for Vitellius? To pray for either man would be impious, to offer vows for the victory of either equally blasphemous. In any war between the two, the only certainty was that the winner would turn out the worse. Some observers predicted the possibility of intervention by Vespasian and the forces of the East. Although Vespasian was better than either Otho or Vitellius, yet they dreaded fresh hostilities and fresh disasters. In any case, there were ambiguous stories about Vespasian – and he was the only emperor up to that point who changed for the better.[71]

The Vitellian Advance

51. I shall now explain the origin and causes of the uprising in favour of Vitellius. After the destruction of Julius Vindex and his entire force, the Roman army had acquired a taste for loot and glory. This was only natural, for without exertion or danger it had won a war that had been extremely profitable. The men now preferred campaigns and set battles, and the rewards of war rather than their normal pay. They had long endured hard and unrewarding service in an uncongenial area and climate, under strict discipline. Yet discipline, however inflexible in peacetime, is relaxed in civil conflicts, where agents are ready to encourage disloyalty on either side, and treachery goes unpunished.

Recruits, equipment and horses were in ample supply, whether for use or show. Besides, before the war with Vindex, the men had only known their own company or troop, as the two armies were kept apart by the provincial boundaries.[72] Now, however, having joined forces to deal with Vindex, the legions had been able to assess their own strength and that of the Gallic provinces. Hence they began to look around for fighting and new quarrels. No longer, as in the past, did they call the provincials 'allies', but 'the enemy' or 'beaten men'. The Gallic communities bordering the Rhine played their part too. These threw in their lot with the Roman garrisons, and now venomously incited them against 'the Galbians', for they gave their fellow-countrymen this tag out of contempt for Vindex. Thus the troops were hostile to the Sequani, Aedui and other communities (depending on how wealthy they were). Their imaginations greedily lapped up the sacking of cities, the plundering of fields and the looting of homes. On top of their natural greed and arrogance, which are typical vices of the stronger side, the Roman troops were also irritated by the insolence of Gauls who insulted the army by boasting that Galba had excused them a quarter of the tribute and made grants of territory to their states.[73]

Provocation was added by a rumour cunningly circulated and rashly credited. The legions, it was alleged, were being decimated and the most enterprising centurions discharged. From everywhere there came bad news and the reports from Rome were ominous. The city of Lyons was disaffected, and its persistent loyalty to Nero cultivated a rich crop of rumours there.[74] However, it was the military camps themselves that contained the most plentiful material for imagination and credulity, thanks to the soldiers' hatred, fear and conviction, once they realized their strength, that the risk was slight.

52. Shortly before 1 December in the previous year,[75] Aulus Vitellius had entered Lower Germany as its governor and carefully inspected the winter-quarters of the legions. A number of centurions were given back their rank, discharged men were reinstated and sentences reduced. Most of these interventions reflected a desire to curry favour, but some showed judgement, including an honest reform of the mean and greedy ways in which Fonteius Capito had promoted or demoted men. Whatever he did was interpreted not according to the standard of an ex-consular governor but as a hint of something greater. Although Vitellius demeaned himself in the eyes of strict disciplinarians, nevertheless his supporters described as 'affability' and 'good nature' the excessive and imprudent generosity with which he squandered both his own resources and those of other people. Besides, his men were so eager to get what they wanted that they took his very faults for virtues. Both armies contained many orderly, quiet soldiers, but there were also many disgruntled and active ones. However, for boundless ambition and a notable lack of scruple, two men stood out above the rest – the legionary commanders Alienus Caecina and Fabius Valens.

Valens for his part was hostile to Galba. He felt that after he had uncovered Verginius' hesitation and thwarted Capito's plans, the emperor had been ungrateful. So he proceeded to work upon Vitellius, pointing out how keen the troops were. Vitellius, he said, was well spoken of everywhere, and Hordeonius Flaccus could do little to hold things up. Britain would rally to them, and the German auxiliaries would follow. There was disaffection in the provinces. The elderly emperor held power on sufferance, and this power would soon pass to another. Vitellius should spread his sail and meet the good fortune that was coming towards him. It was understandable, he added, that Verginius should have had his hesitations. He came from an equestrian family, and his father was a nobody. Such a man might well think himself unequal to the task, if he had accepted the principate, whereas there was safety in refusal. Yet Vitellius had a father who had been consul on three occasions, as well as censor and the colleague of a Caesar.[76] This had long since imposed upon the son the dignity proper to an emperor and taken away from him the safety afforded by remaining a private citizen.

Vitellius' lazy temperament was shaken by the strong impact of these arguments. The result was an idle longing rather than real hope.

53. In Upper Germany, however, it was Caecina who had coaxed support from the troops. He was young, good-looking and had a huge stature and ambitious spirit, as well as being a clever speaker and having an upright bearing.[77] Galba put him in charge of a legion despite his youth after he had eagerly joined his cause when he was serving as quaestor in Baetica. However, Galba later learnt that he had misappropriated public funds, and ordered him to be prosecuted for embezzlement. Taking this badly, Caecina decided to cause general chaos and to camouflage his personal grievances with the ruin of his country. In the army, too, the seeds of disturbance were in plentiful supply. The whole force had been involved in the campaign against Vindex; it had not gone over to Galba until after Nero's death; and finally, when it did take the oath, its accession had been anticipated by the units in Lower Germany. So, too, the Treviri, Lingones and other Gallic communities, whom Galba had hit hard by means of severe edicts or loss of territory, mingled rather closely with the legions in their winter-quarters. As a result there was seditious talk, deterioration of the soldiers through contact with civilians, and the possibility that the support offered to Verginius would profit some other imperial challenger.

54. The civic authorities of the Lingones had sent the legions the traditional token of mutual hospitality – symbolic 'hands'.[78] The envoys who brought them carefully assumed the squalid

guise of mourning and went around the headquarters building and the barrack blocks complaining about their own sufferings and the privileges granted to their neighbours. When the story found a ready hearing among the troops, the Lingones went on to lament the dangers and humiliation of the army itself and fired up the soldiers' feelings. They were close to mutiny when Hordeonius Flaccus ordered the envoys to go, telling them to leave the camp at night in order that their departure should attract less attention.[79] This only led to a shocking rumour. It was widely held that the men had been murdered, and that, unless the troops took steps to defend themselves, their most vocal representatives, who had denounced the present state of affairs, would be put to death when it was dark and the rest knew nothing. The legions bound themselves by a secret under-standing to act together. This was extended to cover the aux-iliary units. At first they were distrusted, as their infantry cohorts and cavalry regiments had been posted around as though an attack on the legions was being planned. However, in due course the auxiliaries embraced the plan more keenly than their companions. Troublemakers find it easier to agree on war than on the means to achieve harmony in peacetime.

55. Yet the legions of Lower Germany were made to take the usual New Year oath of loyalty to Galba on 1 January, though they showed considerable reluctance. Here and there indi-viduals in the front ranks spoke up, but the rest were silent. Everybody was waiting for a bold move from his neighbour, for it is only human nature to follow promptly, however much we dislike taking the lead. Still, the legions themselves had varying feelings. The men of the First and Fifth were so rowdy that some of them stoned the portraits of Galba. The Fifteenth and Sixteenth Legions, on the other hand, confined themselves to muttering threats and looked around for others to start the outbreak.

However, in the army of Upper Germany, the Fourth and Twenty-Second Legions, who were billeted in the same winter camp, tore the portraits of Galba to pieces.[80] This actually happened on 1 January. At first the Fourth took the initiative, while the Twenty-Second was relatively backward, but they soon cooperated. Not wanting it to appear that they were abandoning all respect for authority, they introduced the now outworn formula of 'the Senate and People of Rome' into their oath of allegiance. None of the senior officers made any effort on Galba's behalf, and some of them, as often happens in such chaos, played a conspicuous part in causing the trouble. However, no one mounted the platform and addressed the troops collectively – after all, there was as yet no emperor with whom they could ingratiate themselves. 56. Looking on at this disgraceful scene stood the consular governor, Hordeonius Flaccus. He made no attempt to restrain the mutineers, rally the waverers or encourage the loyal soldiers. Too frightened to lift a finger, he avoided offence by doing nothing. Four centurions of the Twenty-Second Legion – Nonius Receptus, Donatius Valens, Romilius Marcellus and Calpurnius Repentinus – tried to protect the portraits of Galba, but the troops charged at them and hustled them off to a place of confinement. Nobody showed any loyalty or remembered his previous oath after that, but as tends to happen in mutinies, they all followed the lead of the majority.

On the night of 1 January, a standard-bearer from the Fourth Legion entered the city of Colonia Agrippinensium and announced to Vitellius, who was dining at the time,[81] that the Fourth and Twenty-Second Legions had thrown down the portraits of Galba and sworn allegiance to the senate and people of Rome. It was felt that this was an empty oath; they should strike while the iron was hot and offer the troops an emperor. Vitellius sent messengers to his legions and their commanders to announce that the army of Upper Germany had risen against Galba, and put it to them that they must either fight the rebels or else, if they preferred agreement and peace, they must nominate an emperor. He added that it was safer to take up an emperor promptly than to engage in a long search.

57. The camp of the First Legion was the closest to hand,[82] and Fabius Valens was the keenest of the legionary commanders. On the following day, entering the city of Colonia Agrippinensium with the cavalry component of his legion and of its auxiliaries, he saluted Vitellius as emperor. The other

legions of the province of Lower Germany followed his example with remarkable eagerness, while the army of Upper Germany dropped its lip-service to 'the Senate and People of Rome' and on 3 January went over to Vitellius. Whatever authority they had recognized during the preceding two days had obviously not been that of a republican government. The people of Colonia Agrippinensium, as well as the Treviri and Lingones, were just as enthusiastic as the armies. They offered to contribute reinforcements, horses, equipment and money in accordance with their strength, wealth and natural abilities. Offers came not only from the leaders in the cities and army camps, who had the means to give ready money and much to hope for from victory. Even whole companies and ordinary soldiers handed over their savings or, in lieu of cash, their sword-belts, medals and silver parade equipment, stimulated by the encouragement of others or their own initiative and greed.

58. So Vitellius, gratefully acknowledging the prompt response of his men, distributed amongst knights the court functions normally carried out by freedmen, paid the centurions from the imperial exchequer for their men's leave, confirmed on more than one occasion the savage demands of his soldiers for successive executions, and only now and again foiled them by pretending to impose a term of imprisonment. Pompeius Propinquus, the procurator of Belgica, was immediately put to death, but Vitellius craftily extricated Julius Burdo, the commander of the German fleet. The army was violently incensed with Burdo because they thought he had engineered a false accusation against Capito and backed it up by conspiracy. They had fond memories of Capito, and in their present savage mood executions could be carried out in public but acts of mercy only by stealth. So the accused was kept in confinement and only let out after victory when the resentment of the troops had subsided. Meanwhile, the centurion Crispinus was tossed to the men as an expiatory offering. He had actually sullied himself with Capito's blood, so he was a more obvious target for those clamouring for revenge and a cheaper sacrifice for the agent of retribution.

59. Julius Civilis was the next to be removed from danger.[83]

He was extremely powerful among the Batavians, and it seemed
desirable to avoid alienating a fierce nation by executing him.
Besides, there were eight cohorts of Batavians stationed in the
territory of the Lingones. These were an auxiliary force normally attached to the Fourteenth Legion, but in this troubled
period they had separated from their legion, and their friendship
or hostility would have a significant impact on the balance of
power, depending on their inclination. I have already referred
to the centurions Nonius, Donatius, Romilius and Calpurnius.[84]
Vitellius now ordered their execution after condemning them
of loyalty – a most serious charge in the eyes of rebels. Vitellius'
party found two new adherents in Valerius Asiaticus, governor
of the province of Belgica and later taken up by Vitellius as his
son-in-law, and in Junius Blaesus, governor of Lugdunese Gaul,
who brought over the Italian Legion and the Taurian cavalry
regiment, both stationed at Lyons. The garrison of Raetia was
also prompt in its adhesion.

Not even in Britain was there any sign of hesitation. 60. Its
governor was Trebellius Maximus, whose greed and miserliness
had earned him the contempt and hatred of his army.[85] His
unpopularity was enhanced by the attitude of the commander
of the Twentieth Legion, Roscius Coelius. The two men had
long been at odds, but the quarrel had erupted with more
intensity thanks to the convenient accident of civil war. Trebellius accused Coelius of sedition and undermining the chain of
command, while Coelius charged Trebellius with depriving the
legions of money and resources. Meanwhile, this degrading
feud between two senior officers ruined the discipline of the
army. The dispute became so bad that the auxiliaries also noisily
denounced Trebellius and drove him away, while the cohorts
and cavalry regiments flocked to Coelius' side. Trebellius, left
high and dry, had to take refuge with Vitellius. Despite the
removal of the consular governor, the province stayed quiet. It
was administered by the legionary commanders, theoretically
on an equal footing, though Coelius' lack of scruple made him
more powerful.

61. Thanks to the adhesion of the army from Britain, Vitellius
had vast resources and manpower at his command and now

decided on two commanders and a twofold advance. After winning over the Gallic provinces or crushing them if they refused, Fabius Valens was to invade Italy by way of the Cottian Alps. Caecina was told to take a shorter route over the Pennine pass and then descend into Italy. Valens received some units selected from the army of Lower Germany, together with the eagle of the Fifth Legion and a force of auxiliary cohorts and cavalry. This amounted to about 40,000 armed men in all. As for Caecina, he was given 30,000 troops from Upper Germany, with the Twenty-First Legion forming the main strength. Each commander was also allotted German auxiliary units, and Vitellius used the same source to supplement his own force. He was to follow with the full weight of the attack.[86]

62. There was a remarkable contrast between the army and its emperor. The troops applied pressure and demanded action while the Gallic provinces were still unnerved and the Spanish ones undecided. Winter was no impediment, nor would a cowardly respect for peace slow them down! It was vital, they said, to invade Italy and seize the capital. In civil war, speed was the only safe policy, and deeds were wanted, not deliberation.[87] Yet Vitellius dozed away his time and took for granted the privileges of an emperor, giving himself up to idle pleasures and sumptuous banquets. Even at midday he was drunk and stuffed with food,[88] but such was the passion and energy of his men that they actually carried out the general's duties themselves, just as though he were there to inspire the energetic or frighten the lazy ones. Ready and at the alert, they clamoured for the signal to start. Vitellius was given the title 'Germanicus' on the spot, although he would not allow himself to be addressed as 'Caesar' even after his final victory.[89]

Fabius Valens and the army he was leading to war were given a happy omen on the very day they set off, when an eagle floated effortlessly before the advancing column, as if guiding it on its way. For many miles the soldiers shouted joyfully, so calm and untroubled was the bird. This was interpreted as an omen clearly presaging a great and successful enterprise.[90]

63. Indeed, they approached the territory of the Treviri confidently, for they counted them as allies. Yet at Divodurum, the

capital of the Mediomatrici, although the troops were received with every civility, a sudden panic gripped them, and they hastily seized their weapons to slaughter the innocent civilians. They did this not from an appetite for plunder or a desire for spoils, but because they were gripped by frenzy and motives which defy analysis, which meant that the appropriate remedy was more difficult to find. Eventually placated by their commander's appeals, they held back from completely wiping out the town. Still, almost 4,000 people lost their lives and such terror descended on the Gallic provincials that when the marching column approached, whole cities would go out to meet it, attended by their magistrates and pleading for mercy. Women and children prostrated themselves along the roads, and every possible appeasement of an enemy's anger was made to secure peace, even though there was no formal war taking place.

64. News of Galba's murder and Otho's accession reached Fabius Valens when he was at the capital of the Leuci. His troops were neither pleased nor frightened. They were only contemplating war. The Gauls now cast aside their hesitation. They hated Otho and Vitellius to the same extent, but the latter inspired fear as well. The next community was the Lingones, who were faithful to the Vitellian cause. The army received a cordial welcome and responded by behaving well, but the happy mood was cut short by the insubordination of the Batavian cohorts which, as I have already described, Fabius Valens had added to his army after they had split from the Fourteenth Legion. First there were quarrels, then a brawl between the Batavians and the legionaries, which almost exploded into a battle as the enthusiastic soldiers flocked to one side or the other until Valens punished a few of the offenders and reminded the Batavians of what they had forgotten – that they were under his command.

An excuse for war against the Aedui was sought in vain. Although they were ordered to supply money and weapons, they also offered food supplies without payment. What the Aedui had done from fear, the people of Lyons did with pleasure. Nonetheless, the Italian Legion and the Taurian cavalry regiment were withdrawn from the city, though it was decided to leave the Eighteenth Cohort at Lyons, its normal winter-quarters. Manlius Valens, the commander of the Italian Legion, got no credit from Vitellius despite his services to the cause. This was because Fabius had made allegations against him behind his back. Manlius knew nothing of this, and was lulled into a false sense of security by being praised in public.

65. The recent fighting had caused the long-standing friction between Lyons and Vienne to blaze up. Each had dealt the other many blows, and incidents had occurred with more frequency and venom than appropriate merely to fighting a battle on behalf of Nero and Galba. Moreover, in a fit of pique, Galba had confiscated the revenues of Lyons to the imperial treasury, but he had heaped honours on Vienne. Hence sprang rivalry, envy and a hatred that locked together cities parted by a single river.[91] So the inhabitants of Lyons began to work upon individual soldiers and urge them to sack the rival city. They reminded them that Vienne had laid siege to Lyons, assisted the rebel Vindex, and in the recent past recruited legionaries to protect Galba. After they had suggested these pretexts for hatred, they revealed the immense possibilities of loot. By this time, private approaches had been reinforced by an official appeal: the avenging soldiers should rise up and destroy the stronghold of Gallic rebellion. Vienne, it was claimed, was utterly foreign and hostile to Rome, but Lyons was a Roman city closely connected with the army[92] and allied to them through thick and thin: the Vitellians must not leave it at the mercy of angry enemies if luck turned against them.

66. By these arguments, and more of the same kind, they had stirred the feelings of the troops to such an extent that even the senior officers and generals of Vitellius' party thought that it would be impossible to cool them down. Meanwhile, the people of Vienne were well aware of the peril they faced. Headed by white flags and tokens of surrender, they met the approaching troops and managed to soften the soldiers' hearts by grasping their weapons, knees and feet in a gesture of entreaty. Valens added the incentive of a bounty of 300 sesterces for each man.[93] Then – and only then – were they influenced by the fact that Vienne was a historic and imposing city, and Fabius' appeal

that there should be no loss of life or damage to property was given an unprejudiced hearing. Nonetheless, as a community Vienne was penalized by confiscation of its weapons, and the inhabitants gave the troops all sorts of unofficial gifts. Even so, the rumour persisted that Valens had himself been heavily bribed. For a long time he had been miserably poor, so he found it hard to conceal his sudden transformation from shabbiness to affluence. His greedy desires had been inflamed by protracted need. These were now given full scope, and the penniless youth became an extravagant old man.

The army was next led on a slow march through the lands of the Allobroges and Vocontii, with Valens actually auctioneering the length of the day's march and the moves from one camp to another, and striking discreditable deals with property owners and local officials. Menaces were employed, too. For instance, at Lucus, a town in the territory of the Vocontii, he threatened to set fire to the place until he got a financial sweetener. When money was not available, he could be persuaded by sexual favours and adultery. In such fashion they made their way as far as the Alps.

67. Caecina indulged more freely in looting and bloodshed. It was the Helvetii who managed to provoke his unruly temper. This Gallic tribe, once famous for its fighting qualities, has in more recent times lived on its reputation. These people knew nothing of Galba's murder and refused to recognize Vitellius as emperor. Hostilities were triggered by the greed and impatience of the Twenty-First Legion in stealing a sum of money sent as pay for the garrison of a fort which the Helvetii themselves maintained with native soldiers paid at their own expense. The Helvetii took this badly and intercepted some dispatches which were being delivered in the name of the German army to the legions in Pannonia, putting the centurion and his small escort under arrest.[94] Caecina was spoiling for a fight and eager to punish the first offender he could find before a change of heart took place. Suddenly moving camp, he devastated the countryside and plundered a spa which, over the long years of peace, had developed into a fair-sized town that bustled with visitors who came to take the waters in agreeable surroundings. Instruc-

tions were sent to the auxiliaries in Raetia to attack the Helvetii from the rear as they turned to face the legion.

68. Plucky before the crisis, the Helvetii proved cowards in the hour of danger. When the alarm was first sounded, although they had selected Claudius Severus as their general,[95] they showed a total lack of military skill, discipline and coordination. An encounter with veteran troops would be fatal, while their walls, now crumbling and decayed, were not up to withstanding a siege. They were caught: on one side was Caecina at the head of his powerful army, on the other the cavalry and infantry auxiliaries from Raetia, supported by the local Raetian levies, soldiers accustomed to fighting and well trained. Everywhere the scene was one of devastation and slaughter. Drifting helplessly between the two enemy forces, the Helvetii threw away their arms and, many of them wounded or stragglers, fled to Mount Vocetius. Thereupon a cohort of Thracians was promptly sent in and dislodged the fugitives, while the troops from Germany and Raetia pursued them throughout the forest and slaughtered them in their hiding places. Many thousands were killed and many sold into slavery.

After the mopping-up operations were complete, the soldiers marched to attack the capital, Aventicum.[96] Envoys were sent out to offer the surrender of the town, and this was accepted. Caecina executed one of their chieftains, Julius Alpinus, whom he regarded as responsible for the rebellion. The rest he left to Vitellius' mercy or vindictiveness. 69. It is hard to say which the Helvetian envoys found the more implacable: Vitellius or the army. The troops demanded the destruction of the town, and thrust their weapons and fists in the envoys' faces. Even Vitellius permitted himself to bluster and threaten until one of the envoys, Claudius Cossus, a well-known speaker, but good at concealing his skilful rhetoric behind an apt display of nervousness and therefore more persuasive, managed to calm the soldiers' feelings. A crowd is typically mercurial. Once excessively vindictive, the men were now just as prone to take pity. So, by shedding copious tears and persistently demanding better treatment, the envoys secured pardon and survival for Aventicum.

70. Caecina spent a few days in Helvetian territory waiting until he was informed of Vitellius' decision on this matter, and using the time in preparing to cross the Alps. It was now that he received from Italy the cheering news that a unit stationed in the Po valley had declared for Vitellius. This was the Silian cavalry regiment,[97] which had served in the province of Africa during Vitellius' period as governor. Later mobilized by Nero so that it could be sent ahead to Egypt, it had been recalled owing to the rebellion of Vindex, and at the moment was waiting in Italy. Its officers, who knew nothing about Otho, but were attached to Vitellius, repeatedly emphasized the strength of the approaching legions and the good reputation of the German army. At their instigation, the regiment went over to Vitellius and by way of a gift to their new emperor presented him with the strongest towns in the Transpadane Region – Mediolanum, Novaria, Eporedia and Vercellae.[98] Caecina was informed of this by the unit itself, but since such an extensive portion of Italy could not be defended by a single cavalry regiment, he sent ahead cohorts of Gauls, Lusitanians and Britons as well as some German mounted units and the Petrian cavalry regiment.[99] He himself hesitated for a time. Should he make a detour over the Raetian mountains into Noricum to confront its governor, Petronius Urbicus, who, after mustering his auxiliary forces and cutting the bridges over the rivers, was considered to be an adherent of Otho? Yet he feared that he might lose the infantry and cavalry already sent on ahead. He also reflected that there was more glory in consolidating his Italian gains.[100] In any case, wherever the clash took place, Noricum was sure to be among the other prizes of victory. So he decided on the Great St Bernard route, and led his main body and the heavy legionary force across the Alps although they were still in the grip of winter.

71. Meanwhile, to everybody's surprise, Otho did not sink into a lethargic state of hedonism. Pleasures were postponed, indulgence disguised and his entire conduct was adjusted to the high standards expected of a ruler. Yet this only intensified people's fears that the sham virtues were an inevitable prelude to further vices.

Marius Celsus, the consul-designate, had been saved from the venom of the troops by a pretended imprisonment. Otho now gave orders for him to be summoned to the Capitol, seeking a reputation for clemency in his treatment of a famous man who was a political opponent.[101] Celsus sturdily admitted the charge of keeping faith with Galba, and indeed claimed credit for setting a good example. It was not as if Otho were simply forgiving him, but, calling on the gods to witness their mutual reconciliation, he immediately treated Celsus as an intimate friend and later chose him as one of his generals. Celsus remained solidly but haplessly loyal to Otho as well – this seemed to be his predestined role. Welcomed happily by leading Romans and much discussed by the general public, Celsus' pardon was not unpopular even with the troops, who admired the very quality that irritated them.

72. Then came a similar gratification, though for different reasons, when Otho was persuaded to put Ofonius Tigellinus to death. Tigellinus, who was humbly born, disgraceful as a boy and dissolute in maturity, was appointed as commander of the watch and the praetorian guard. He also won other prizes normally associated with virtuous character, although he found it quicker to win them by vices. In due course, he took to more robust forms of transgression, first cruelty and then greed. While luring Nero to every form of wrongdoing, he daringly embarked on some crimes without the emperor's knowledge, and finally deserted and betrayed him. That was why people demanded his punishment more insistently than anyone else's – those who hated Nero and those who missed him came together, despite their polarized feelings. During Galba's principate, Tigellinus was sheltered by the influential Titus Vinius, whose excuse was that the man had saved his daughter's life. No doubt he had done so, although this was not prompted by mercy (given his numerous killings). He was seeking an escape route for the future, for every criminal, distrusting the present and fearing a change of fortune, stockpiles private gratitude as a protection against loathing from the public. Such men are not concerned with keeping their hands clean, but merely hope for a similar immunity in exchange. This only made the public

more bitter. To their old hatred for Tigellinus was added the recent unpopularity of Titus Vinius. People ran from the whole city to the palace and the squares, and overflowing into the circus and theatres, where the mob can demonstrate with the greater impunity, raised a seditious clamour. In the end, Tigellinus received the order to commit suicide at Sinuessa Spa where he was indulging in sexual romps with his prostitutes, exchanges of kisses and other degrading delays, but finally he slit his throat with a razor and crowned his notorious life with a belated and disreputable death.

73. Around this same time, there arose an emphatic public demand for the execution of Calvia Crispinilla, but she was saved from this fate by various contrivances (Otho's collusion evoked hostile comment). This woman had been Nero's tutor in vice before going over to the province of Africa to instigate Clodius Macer to revolt. Her plan was quite obvious – a corn blockade of Rome and her people.[102] Later she became a popular figure throughout the country as a whole, securing her position by marriage to a former consul, and the successive regimes of Galba, Otho and Vitellius brought her no harm. Eventually she enjoyed great influence as a wealthy woman who had no heirs – for, whether times are good or bad, such qualities retain their power.

74. Meanwhile, Otho wrote a stream of letters to Vitellius. His correspondence was disfigured by alluring and unmanly bribes – money, influence and whichever quiet spot he cared to choose for a life of indulgence. Similar baits were held out by Vitellius, with some degree of restraint at first, so long as the rivals still maintained a foolish and degrading hypocrisy. Then, like men quarrelling, they accused each other of debauchery and wickedness. Here at least both were in the right.

Otho recalled the envoys sent by Galba and dispatched a fresh deputation, chosen ostensibly from the senate, to approach both armies in Germany, the Italian Legion and the forces at Lyons. With an alacrity which belied any notion of compulsion, these envoys threw in their lot with Vitellius, but the praetorian escort provided by Otho as a guard of honour was hurriedly sent back to Rome before it could come into contact with the legionaries. Fabius backed up this move by sending a letter addressed in the name of the German army to the praetorian and urban cohorts, boasting of the strength of the Vitellian side and offering to come to an understanding. He actually went as far as to criticize them for making Otho emperor long after power had been handed to Vitellius.[103] 75. In this way the city garrison was being worked on by both promises and threats: too few to fight, they were not likely to lose anything by making peace. Despite this, the praetorians remained inflexibly loyal.[104]

However, secret agents were sent by Otho to Germany, and by Vitellius to the capital. Both parties failed to achieve anything, Vitellius' agents going undetected and unpunished because they were lost amid the vast population of Rome, all strangers to one another. On the other hand, the Othonians were fresh faces in a community where each man knew his comrades personally, and their identity was thus betrayed. Vitellius composed a letter to Otho's brother Titianus in which he threatened to put the latter and his son to death in the event of any harm befalling his own mother and children. In fact, both families survived. Under Otho the reason for this is unclear (perhaps he was afraid), but the victorious Vitellius was certainly credited with clemency.

76. The first event to boost Otho's confidence was the news from Illyricum that the legions of Dalmatia, Pannonia and Moesia had sworn allegiance to him as emperor. Identical reports came from Spain, and a proclamation was issued praising Cluvius Rufus. Yet in no time at all it was discovered that Spain had gone over to Vitellius. Even Aquitania soon shifted its ground, despite the oath of loyalty to Otho imposed by Julius Cordus. Nowhere could one rely on loyalty or affection: through fear or compulsion the provinces were changing sides this way and that. The same sort of panic impelled Narbonese Gaul to rally to Vitellius: it took the easy step of joining neighbours stronger than itself. The distant provinces and such forces as lay overseas remained true to Otho, not from enthusiasm for his cause but because of the considerable prestige exercised by the mere name of Rome and the imposing façade of senatorial

support. In any case, Otho had already established his position psychologically, for he had been heard of before Vitellius was. The army of Judaea had the oath of allegiance to Otho administered to it by Vespasian, the legions of Syria by Mucianus. At the same time, the authorities in Egypt and all the eastern provinces expressed nominal support. Africa showed the same allegiance. Here the initiative came from Carthage, which did not wait for a lead from the governor, Vipstanus Apronianus. One of Nero's freedmen, Crescens – for even these creatures play their part in affairs of state when times are bad – had offered the public a feast in celebration of the recent accession, and the reckless people rushed to express their support in various ways. The remaining African communities followed the example of Carthage.

77. This split in the armies and provinces meant that Vitellius had to fight for the position of emperor. Otho, however, went on with his imperial duties as if there were not a cloud in the sky. He sometimes displayed a proper sense of statesmanship, more often an unseemly haste based on immediate needs. With his brother Titianus he became consul until 1 March, making some attempt to soothe the army of Germany by allotting the succeeding months to Verginius, with Pompeius Vopiscus as his colleague, allegedly because he was an old friend, although many took this as a compliment to Vienne. The remaining consulships were allocated according to the selections of Nero or Galba. Thus Caelius Sabinus and Flavius Sabinus were to hold office until 1 July, and Arrius Antoninus and Marius Celsus until 1 September. Even Vitellius refrained from vetoing these arrangements after his victory. Otho also made appointments to the colleges of pontiffs and augurs as a crowning distinction for old men who had already had a distinguished career, or afforded young men of rank recently back from exile the solace and satisfaction of occupying priesthoods held by their fathers and grandfathers. Membership of the senate was restored to Cadius Rufus, Pedius Blaesus and Scaevinus Propinquus,[105] who had been condemned for extortion under Claudius and Nero. In pardoning them, the senators decided to find a new name for what had actually been 'greed', calling it

instead 'treason'. This charge was then so hated for its misuse that it made even beneficial laws dead in the water.

78. The same lavishness marked Otho's approaches to civic communities and provinces. At Hispalis and Emerita additional families of settlers were enrolled, the Lingones received a block grant of Roman citizenship, and the province of Baetica was awarded some Moorish communities. New constitutions devised for both Cappadocia and Africa looked good but would not survive. All these proposals can be excused by the needs of the moment and imminent worries, but Otho still remembered his love-life and restored Poppaea's statues by senatorial decree. It was believed that he even contemplated some ceremony in memory of Nero, in order to entice the mob. Indeed, some people did exhibit portraits of Nero, and on certain occasions the populace and the troops actually saluted the emperor as 'Nero Otho' as if this represented an additional ennoblement. Otho himself left the matter in the air, for he was afraid to forbid the title or else ashamed to acknowledge it.

79. While attention was diverted to the civil war, foreign affairs were being disregarded. As a result, the Rhoxolani, a Sarmatian tribe, had become more daring, and after slaughtering two auxiliary cohorts in the previous winter, they had embarked on a hugely optimistic invasion of Moesia with a force numbering some 9,000 wild and exulting horsemen, keener on booty than battle. So, while they were roaming about and off their guard, the Third Legion and its auxiliaries suddenly attacked. On the Roman side everything was ready for a battle. Not so the Sarmatians. Scattered about through desire for plunder or laden with heavy spoils, while their swift horses were being slowed down because the tracks were slippery, the men were being slaughtered like chained prisoners. It is indeed amazing to report how all the courage of the Sarmatians depends on such an extraneous factor. They show unique cowardice when fighting on foot, but when advancing on horseback, scarcely any battleline could withstand them. However, this particular day was wet, and a thaw had set in. Neither their lances nor their enormous two-handed swords were of any use, because the horses lost their footing and the dismounted men

were hampered by their heavy body-armour. Their chiefs and nobles wear this protective covering, which consists of iron-plating and extremely tough leather. Although it is impenetrable to blows, it is cumbersome for anyone trying to get up after being sent sprawling by an enemy charge. At the same time, the Sarmatians were being swallowed up in the deep, soft snow. The Roman soldiers moved easily in their breastplates and attacked by hurling their javelins or using their lances and, as occasion required, their lightweight swords. At close quarters they hacked at the unprotected Sarmatians (for it is not their custom to defend themselves with shields). Finally, a few men who had survived the battle took refuge in swampy country, where they succumbed to the severity of the weather or their wounds.

When this news reached Rome, Marcus Aponius, the governor of Moesia, was granted a triumphal statue,[106] and the legionary commanders Aurelius Fulvus, Tettius Julianus and Numisius Lupus received consular decorations.[107] Otho was delighted, and plumed himself on the victory as if he had been the successful general and had extended the empire by means of commanders and armies that were his.

80. Meanwhile a mutiny broke out which almost destroyed the capital, although it arose in a place where no danger was feared and out of a trivial incident.[108] Otho had ordered the Seventeenth Cohort to move to Rome from the city of Ostia and a praetorian tribune named Varius Crispinus was entrusted with the task of issuing arms to it. This man, aiming to carry out his orders with greater freedom from distraction while the praetorian barracks were quiet, had the armoury opened and the cohort's transport loaded up at nightfall.[109] The hour aroused suspicion, the motive was misconstrued, and the bid for peace and quiet developed into an uproar. Just seeing the weapons made some drunken praetorians want to seize them. The troops began to grumble and accused the tribunes and centurions of a treacherous plot to arm the senators' household slaves and murder Otho. Some were ignorant of the real circumstances and slow-witted from drink, every scoundrel saw the chance of loot, while the majority of the men were, as usual,

ready for any kind of excitement. Besides, the darkness had dissipated the better men's tolerance for orders. The mutinous soldiers cut down the tribune as he tried to restrain them, together with the strictest disciplinarians among the centurions. The men seized weapons, drew their swords, mounted their horses and rode off to Rome and the palace.

81. Otho was entertaining a packed dinner party of society men and women.[110] The guests were alarmed. Was this a meaningless outbreak on the part of the troops or a trick from the emperor? Would it be more dangerous to stay and be caught, or escape and scatter? At one moment, they put on a brave face, at the next, their fears betrayed them as they watched Otho's expression. As is the way with suspicious minds, although Otho felt fear, he also inspired it. However, he was just as scared for the senators as for himself and had promptly sent off the praetorian prefects to soothe their angry men. He also told all his guests to hurry away from the banqueting room. This was the signal for a general stampede. Magistrates threw away their badges of office, eluding the masses of retainers and slaves who were waiting upon them, while old gentlemen and their wives vanished down the darkened streets of the capital in every direction. One or two made for their mansions, but most of them fled to the homes of their friends and sought obscure hiding places with their humblest dependants.

82. Not even the doors of the palace could stop the troops surging irresistibly into the banqueting-hall and demanding that Otho should show himself to them. A tribune, Julius Martialis, and a legionary prefect, Vitellius Saturninus, were wounded in their attempt to stem the rush. The whole place was a hubbub of weapons and threats, hurled now against the centurions and tribunes, now against the whole senate. In their blind and panic-stricken frenzy, finding no single target for their anger, they clamoured for a free hand against everybody. Finally Otho threw imperial dignity to the winds, clambered up on a couch, and with some difficulty restrained the mutineers by means of prayers and tears. So they returned to barracks, but grudgingly and with guilty consciences. On the next day Rome resembled a captured city.[111] The great houses were shuttered, the streets

almost empty, the populace gloomy. The downcast glances of
the troops displayed sullenness rather than regret. Company by
company, they were addressed by Licinius Proculus and Plotius
Firmus, with the differing degrees of severity according to the
characters of the two prefects. They concluded their remarks
by announcing that each soldier was to be paid 5,000 sesterces.[112] Only then did Otho venture into the barracks. He was
immediately surrounded by the tribunes and centurions, who
stripped off their uniform and asked for a safe discharge. The
troops felt this reproach against themselves and resumed obedient conduct in an orderly way. They themselves actually
demanded the execution of the ringleaders in the mutiny.

83. Otho faced a dilemma, as the situation was turbulent and
the soldiers had divided opinions – the best sort were demanding a remedy for the present wave of indiscipline, while the
average man, that is, the majority of them, delighted by mutinies
and power based on solicitation, could be driven to civil war
with greater ease by means of rioting and looting. Nevertheless,
Otho also reflected that a principate won by criminal means
could not be retained by sudden doses of discipline and old-
fashioned strictness, but he was still worried at the insecurity
to which Rome was exposed and the threat to the senate. In the
end he made a speech to the troops along these lines:[113]

'My fellow-soldiers, I have not come to fire your hearts with
affection for me or to spur your spirit to heroism. For, in
commendable fashion, you already have more than enough of
both these qualities. Instead, I have come to ask you to keep
your valour under control and to restrain your friendly feelings
for me. Yesterday's riot was not triggered by the cupidity or
hatred that have prompted disorder in many armies, nor was it
started by a cowardly refusal to face danger. Your excessive
devotion provided a stimulus that was keen but misguided. For
deadly results often follow honourable intentions, unless one
applies sound judgement.

'You and I are going to war. Surely you don't think that the
need for carefully weighing up the situation and arriving at a
quick decision when the hour strikes allows scope for every
intelligence report to be read in public and every plan to be

studied before the whole army? Sometimes it is just as crucial for the ordinary soldiers to remain in the dark as to know things. The nature of a general's authority and the strict observance of discipline requires that even centurions and tribunes should often obey orders without question. If every single man is to have the right to ask why orders are being given, then the habit of obedience is sapped, and with it the whole principle of command. Are we still going to have men seizing weapons in the dead of night when we are on campaign? Shall a couple of drunken louts – for I feel sure that only a few lost their heads in last night's affair – stain their hands with the blood of a centurion and a tribune and force their way into their general's tent?

84. 'Of course you acted to protect me. However, commotion, darkness and general confusion can open the way for my assassination. If Vitellius and his minions could choose what mood and what state of mind to call down upon us, surely they would pray for mutiny and dissension, for the private to disobey his centurion and the centurion his tribune, for us to rush blindly to our destruction in a confused mass of infantry and cavalry? Successful fighting, fellow-soldiers, depends on obedience, not on questioning the generals' orders, and the bravest army in the hour of danger is the one that is best behaved before that hour strikes. Arms and courage should be your business: leave to me the job of planning policy and guiding your bravery.

'Just a few individuals only were to blame, but only two will be punished. As for the rest of you, wipe out the memory of that most terrible night! I only hope that no army anywhere hears the dreadful words you uttered against the senate. By Hercules, this is the supreme council of state, with members recruited from men of distinction in every province, and clamouring for its destruction is conduct which even the Germans whom Vitellius is mustering against us at this very moment would surely not permit themselves.[114] Can any sons of Italy, any true Roman warriors, cry out for the bloodthirsty butchery of an order by whose radiance and glory we eclipse the obscure and shabby following of Vitellius? Yes, he has got hold of a few native tribes and has raised some poor shadow of a proper army, but on our side is the senate. So the state takes its stand here: over there, against us, are the enemies of that state. Do you really imagine that this most beautiful city depends on mansions, buildings and piles of masonry? These are dumb, lifeless things, and one and all can fall or be rebuilt. The survival of our empire, peace between the nations and your life as well as mine find a firm support in the continued preservation of the senate. The senatorial order was solemnly instituted by the patriarch and founder of our city. From the regal period up to the principate it has survived in unbroken continuity. We received it from our fathers. Let us as surely transmit it to our sons. You are the source of new blood for the senate, and the senate in its turn supplies our emperors.'[115]

85. This speech, nicely calculated to reprimand the troops and calm their feelings, and also Otho's restrained show of severity – no more than two men were to be punished – were well received. For the moment he had calmed troops who could not be dealt with firmly. However, peace and quiet had not returned to Rome, which clattered with arms and bore the look of war. Although the soldiers were not causing any concerted disorder, they had dispersed themselves around all the great houses disguised as civilians, and kept a jealous eye upon all whose station, wealth or some other uncommon distinction exposed them to gossip. Many people believed that Vitellian soldiers too had entered Rome to explore the degree of support for their cause.[116] As a result, the whole atmosphere was heavy with suspicion and even the privacy of the home was hardly secure. However, in public places anxiety reached a climax, as people constantly altered their attitudes and facial expressions to the latest rumour so as not to seem too upset by bad tidings and insufficiently gratified by good. Yet above all, it was when the senate was called to the house that there was strenuous moderation in all matters: silence might seem rebellious, while free speech was regarded with suspicion. Otho had recently been an ordinary senator and had used the same language as his peers, so he knew all about flattery. Therefore, the senators varied their opinions and twisted their words this way and that

to suit the moment. They denounced Vitellius as an enemy and a traitor to his country, but the most wary politicians confined themselves to perfunctory abuse. Some hurled real insults, but only did so during moments of uproar when people were shouting over one another, or else blurted them out in an incoherent torrent of words which nobody could quite catch.

86. There were alarming prodigies too, reported by a number of independent sources.[117] At the entrance to the Capitol, it was said, the reins of the chariot in which Victory rides had slipped from her grasp; an apparition of superhuman size had suddenly emerged from the Chapel of Juno; on a sunny, windless day the statue of the divine Julius on the Tiber island had turned round so as to face east instead of west;[118] an ox had spoken in Etruria; there had been monstrous animal births and many other signs and wonders of the kind that in primitive centuries were noted even in peacetime, but are now only heard about in times of fear. Yet the most serious panic was caused by a disaster combining immediate destruction with the threat of trouble in the future. This was the sudden flooding of the Tiber, which demolished the Pile Bridge[119] thanks to the tremendous rise in its waters, and after being dammed by the ruins, overwhelmed not only the flat and low-lying parts of the capital, but also areas thought to be immune from disasters of this kind. A number of people were swept away in the streets, and even more were cut off without warning in their shops and beds. Famine gripped the poor, since they were unable to work and there was a shortage of food. The standing flood water weakened the foundations of large tenement blocks, which collapsed as the river retreated. No sooner had the public recovered from this shock than it was faced by another. As Otho was preparing his expeditionary force, it was found that the Campus Martius and the Flaminian Way[120] were blocked. This was the route to the front, and although the obstruction sprang from chance or natural causes, it was interpreted as a sign from heaven and an omen of imminent disaster.

87. Otho held a service of purification[121] throughout the city and weighed up his plans for war. As the Pennine and Cottian Alps and all the other landward approaches to the Gallic

provinces were being blocked by Vitellius' armies, he decided
to invade Narbonese Gaul with the help of his powerful navy.[122]
This was loyal to his cause because he had enrolled as a legion
the survivors of the Milvian Bridge massacre; they had been
kept in prison by the cruel Galba, while the rest of the navy
men were promised prestigious military promotion in due
course. Otho reinforced his fleet with urban cohorts and a large
group of praetorians. These were the strong backbone of his
army, who were to give the generals the benefit of their advice
and protection. The expedition was commanded by the senior
centurions Antonius Novellus and Suedius Clemens, as well as
by Aemilius Pacensis, to whom Otho had restored the tribune's
rank of which Galba had deprived him. The freedman Moschus
– kept on in order to spy upon the loyalty of his superiors –
maintained control of the fleet.

Suetonius Paulinus,[123] Marius Celsus and Annius Gallus were
chosen to lead the main force of infantry and cavalry, but Otho
put most faith in Licinius Proculus, the praetorian prefect. This
man had been energetic while serving in Rome, but had no
experience of real wars. However, by criticizing respectively
Paulinus' influence, Celsus' energy and Gallus' seasoned judgement, this wicked and cunning man easily outdid his restrained
and honest colleagues.

88. Over this same period Cornelius Dolabella was banished
to the city of Aquinum,[124] although without being subjected to
close or humiliating custody. No charge had been brought
against him, but critics pointed to his ancient lineage and close
connections with Galba.[125]

Otho now gave orders that many of the magistrates and most
of the former consuls should accompany him, ostensibly as his
suite, not as active participants or to assist in the war. Even
Lucius Vitellius was included in their number, for he was treated
no differently from the rest and not as the brother of an emperor
– or of a traitor.

All this caused a wave of anxiety in the capital, where none
of the upper classes was exempt from fear or danger. The
leading senators were incapacitated by age or enervated by a
long peace, the aristocracy was lazy and had forgotten about

warfare, the equestrians were ignorant of active service. The more these people strove to hide and conceal their fear, the more obvious it became. On the other hand there were fools who tried to cut a dash by purchasing showy armour, fine horses and even, in some cases, luxurious paraphernalia for feasts and items to titillate the appetites, as if these were weapons of war. Sensible men were worried about peace and the state of the country, the irresponsible and the improvident were puffed up with idle hopes, and many bankrupts, at their wits' end in peace, drew new vigour from confusion, and found their greatest safeguard in insecurity.

89. The common people and a population too vast to sense collective political responsibilities gradually began to feel the hardships of war. Owing to the channelling of all available money into the war effort, the cost of food rose. This problem had not worn down the people to the same extent during the revolt of Vindex, for at that time Rome had remained safe and the fighting had been restricted to the provinces, during what was virtually a foreign war between the legionaries and the Gauls. Indeed, ever since the divine Augustus had settled the constitution of the principate, the Roman people had fought their campaigns far away, with the result that the wars worried or adorned the emperor alone. Under Tiberius and Gaius, the only disasters that affected the state were associated with peace. The plot of Scribonianus[126] against Claudius was no sooner reported than crushed, and Nero was driven from power by messages and rumours rather than by force of arms. Yet now legions and fleets were taken into the front-line, along with the praetorian and urban troops (something which had rarely happened before). Behind them were arrayed the East and the West with all their respective forces. This had the makings of a lengthy war, had it been fought under different leaders.

There were some people who tried to delay Otho as he was setting out by pointing out that the ceremony of Laying up the Shields had not yet been completed,[127] but he scorned all hindrances, which had, after all, been deadly to Nero. The fact that Caecina had already crossed the Alps also spurred him on.

90. On 14 March, after formally handing over affairs of the

state to the senate, Otho granted to those recalled from exile whatever was left over from Nero's auctions of confiscated property which had not yet been paid into the treasury. This concession was perfectly fair, and it looked generous, though in fact it yielded little, as for some time the money had been processed at top speed.

Otho then summoned a public meeting, in which he stressed the prestige of Rome and the united support of senate and people as factors which favoured his cause. He talked about the Vitellian party in moderate terms, blaming the legions for ignorance rather than outrageous conduct and making no mention of Vitellius himself. Perhaps this reflects his own self-control, or possibly his speech-writer held back from insulting Vitellius out of fear for his own skin. For just as Otho relied upon Suetonius Paulinus and Marius Celsus for advice in military matters, so he was believed to consult Galerius Trachalus[128] about affairs at Rome. Indeed, there were some who thought they could recognize Trachalus' manner of speaking, which was ample, sonorous and perfectly judged to satisfy public tastes, as well as being well known from his frequent appearances in the courtroom.

The cheers and cries of the crowd were excessive and insincere, according to the usual pattern of flattery. As if people were seeing off Julius Caesar or Emperor Augustus, they vied with one another in their enthusiastic good wishes. They did this neither from fear nor real affection, but as a result of their passionate devotion to servility. They were just like household slaves, for each man was prompted by selfishness and the dignity of the state now meant nothing. On leaving Rome, Otho handed over the policing of the capital and the daily responsibilities of an emperor to his brother Salvius Titianus.

BOOK 2

Flavian Caution

1. In a very different part of the world fortune was already planning the origins and causes of a new dynasty, which was, with varying lot, happy for the state or terrible, and for the emperors themselves prosperous or deadly. Titus Vespasianus had been sent off from Judaea by his father while Galba was still alive, alleging that the reason for his journey was a desire to pay homage to the emperor and the fact that he was now of an age to stand for public offices.[1] However, the people, eager to fabricate stories, had spread the rumour that he had been summoned to Rome for adoption. The fuel for such gossip was Galba's advanced age and childlessness, and the extravagance of Rome in designating many candidates until one is selected. Titus' reputation was rated all the higher because of his personal qualities, as his intelligence fitted him for the most exalted station, while he had good looks, too, and a certain dignity of manner.[2] Moreover, Vespasian's affairs were going well, the prophecies were favourable, and there were also the coincidences which a credulous society took as omens. At the city of Corinth in Achaia, when he was reliably informed of Galba's death, and people were at hand who assured him that Vitellius was arming for war, troubled at heart he gathered round him a few friends and examined all the possibilities on either side. If he proceeded to Rome, he would earn no gratitude for a duty undertaken to honour another man, and would merely be a hostage for either Vitellius or Otho. If, on the other hand, he returned to Judaea, it would be a definite affront to the winner, but as it was the victorious side was still uncertain, and if his father went over to the successful party, the son would be

excused. If, however, Vespasian claimed the principate, men pondering war would have to forget about causing offence.[3]

2. These and similar arguments kept him hovering uneasily between hope and fear. Finally, hope triumphed. Some people believed that his passion for Queen Berenice[4] fired him to turn back. It is quite true that the young man was far from insensible to Berenice's charms, but his practical efficiency never suffered from this. (Titus led a life of pleasure in his youth, and proved more self-disciplined during his own reign than during his father's.) So he sailed along the shores of Achaia and Asia, skirting the coastal areas to the left and making for the islands of Rhodes and Cyprus, and then, crossing more boldly by the open sea, for Syria. Thereupon, he was seized by a desire to go and visit the Temple of Venus at Paphos,[5] which is famous among natives and visitors alike. It may perhaps be of some interest to discuss briefly the origin of this cult, the temple ritual and the form of the goddess, for she is not represented in this way anywhere else.

3. An ancient tradition declares that the temple was founded by King Aerias,[6] while some authorities say that this is the name of the goddess herself. A more recent version tells us that the temple was consecrated by Cinyras[7] and that it was here that the goddess landed after her birth from the sea. However, it seems that the knowledge and skill of divination was introduced from abroad (Tamiras the Cilician was the one who imported it), and an arrangement was made that the descendants of both families should preside over the rites. Later, to avoid a situation where the royal line failed to outrank the foreigners by any mark of esteem, the immigrants relinquished control of the very lore they had introduced, and now the only priest consulted is a descendant of Cinyras. The worshipper selects whatever sort of victim he has vowed to sacrifice, but the choice is restricted to male animals. The livers of kids are held to offer the surest prediction. Spilling blood upon the altar is forbidden; only prayers and pure fire are offered upon it. Although the altars are out in the open, they are never dampened by rain. The goddess is not portrayed in the likeness of a human, but resembles a conical turning-post, rising without interruption

from a rather broad base up to a top of slender circumference.[8] The reason for this is obscure.

4. Titus inspected the rich treasures, the gifts from kings and the other objects to which the Greeks, passionate about antiquities, attribute an origin lost in the mists of the past. Then he consulted the priest in the first place about his voyage. On being assured of a clear passage and calm sea, he enquired in veiled language of his own future, offering a number of victims. Sostratus – for so the priest was named – observed that in every case the entrails showed favourable indications and that the goddess was clearly giving her blessing to a great enterprise. So for the time being he made a short and conventional reply, but after asking for a private interview, he disclosed the future to Titus. Heartened by these assurances, he sailed on to rejoin his father. Amidst the mood of uncertainty prevailing throughout the provinces and armies, his arrival inspired a surge of confidence.

Vespasian had already given the decisive turn to the Jewish war, although the siege of Jerusalem still remained.[9] This was a difficult and uphill task, more because of the peculiar character of its mountain site and the bigotry of its inhabitants than because the besieged had enough strength left to endure a desperate struggle. I have already mentioned above that Vespasian himself had three legions, seasoned in war. Mucianus commanded four others[10] which had seen no active service, but rivalry and the distinction of the neighbouring army in Judaea had eliminated any laziness. Danger and hard work had toughened Vespasian's men just as much as the uninterrupted peace and passion for the war which they had not experienced had invigorated Mucianus' men. Each of these two armies had its auxiliary cohorts and cavalry regiments, its fleets and clientkings and a great name based upon differing reputations.

5. Vespasian was a born soldier. He marched at the head of his troops, chose the place to camp and struggled against the enemy night and day by his generalship and, if occasion required, by personal combat, eating whatever food happened to be available and dressed much the same as a private soldier. All in all, apart from his avarice, he was a match for the generals

of old. Mucianus was quite different. His lavish generosity, great wealth and the fact that all his activities exceeded the limits of a private citizen made him stand out. He was the better speaker and a talented and far-sighted administrator. This was an excellent blend of imperial qualities, if only the vices of the two men could be removed, leaving just their positive traits in the mix. However, as governors of Syria and Judaea respectively, Mucianus and Vespasian had been divided by the jealousy which usually develops between the administrations of neighbouring provinces. Finally, at Nero's death they put aside their hatred and collaborated for the common good, initially by means of friends, but then Titus served as the special assurance of a harmonious relationship. He managed to remove petty frictions by an appeal to their common interests and he was inclined by nature and by training to entice the sophisticated Mucianus, too. Tribunes, centurions and common soldiers were won over by playing upon their industry and licence, their virtues and vices, depending on each man's character.

6. Before Titus returned, both armies had taken the oath to Otho, since news travels quickly in such cases while the massive machinery of civil war is slow and cumbersome. In any case the long-peaceful and dormant East was now for the first time embarking upon such a war. For previously the most fierce civil conflicts had erupted in Italy or Gaul, relying upon the resources of the West. Pompey, Crassus, Brutus and Antony, who drew civil war in their wake across the sea, had met disastrous ends, and in Syria and Judaea the Caesars had been heard about more often than seen. The legions had avoided mutiny and only made threats against the Parthians,[11] with varying success. In the most recent civil war, turmoil elsewhere contrasted with unbroken peace here, followed by allegiance to Galba. Later, when it became generally known that Otho and Vitellius were setting out to seize the Roman state in a sacrilegious war, the troops began to grumble that others would earn the prizes of empire and themselves nothing but the compulsion of slavery. So they reckoned up their own strength. For a start, there were their seven legions, as well as Syria and Judaea with their considerable auxiliary forces. On one side they were bordered by Egypt

with its two legions, while on the other side lay Cappadocia and Pontus and all the camps located on the Armenian frontier. Asia and the remaining provinces were rich and populous; and as for all the islands, they were surrounded by sea, and during the interim period of mobilization the sea itself offered support and protection.

7. The generals could not fail to notice the ardour of the soldiers, but so long as the others were fighting they decided to play a waiting game, convinced that the winners and losers in a civil war never form a sincere and lasting union. It did not matter whether it was Vitellius or Otho who happened to survive. In success, even good generals become overbearing, but these men had to face dissension, laziness and self-indulgence: so, by their own vices, one would perish in war, one in victory.[12] Therefore, they postponed the war until the time was right. Vespasian and Mucianus were relatively recent conscripts to the campaign, but the others had long since decided to fight, albeit from a variety of motives. Men of the highest character acted from love of their country. Many were stimulated by the attractive prospect of booty, others by financial embarrassment. Thus though their reasons differed, good men and bad all desired war with equal enthusiasm.

8. At about this same time Achaia and Asia were upset by a false alarm, thanks to a rumour that Nero was at hand.[13] There had been conflicting stories about his death, and so quite a few people imagined – and believed – that he was alive. I shall describe the adventures and attempts of the other claimants in the course of my work.[14] On this occasion it was a slave from Pontus, or, according to other accounts, a freedman from Italy, who was skilled at playing the cithara and singing, but he also had a marked facial resemblance, and because of this, the impersonation was all the more plausible. He was joined by some army deserters who had been roaming about in destitution until he bribed them to follow him by lavish promises. With these men he set out to sea, but after a violent storm he was forced to land on the island of Cythnus,[15] where he recruited some troops returning from the East on leave, or had them murdered when they refused. He also robbed businessmen and

armed the sturdiest of their slaves. A centurion named Sisenna, representing the army of Syria, happened to be bringing some symbolic 'hands' to the praetorians as a token of friendship. He tried to influence this man by a variety of artful means, but Sisenna, taking fright, secretly slipped away from the island and fled in fear of his life. As a result, panic spread. Many men were attracted by Nero's famous name, eager for revolution and hating the current state of affairs.

Although the rumours were growing on a daily basis, they were abruptly dispelled by a coincidence. 9. Galba had appointed Calpurnius Asprenas[16] governor of the provinces of Galatia and Pamphylia. He had been given two triremes from the fleet at Misenum as his escort, and with these he docked at the island of Cythnus. Here agents were at hand to summon the captains of the triremes in the name of Nero. Assuming a pathetic air, the fellow appealed to 'the allegiance of his former soldiers' and asked them to land him in Syria or Egypt. Half convinced, or to trick him, the captains declared that they would have to talk to their crews and would return when they had got them all into the right frame of mind. However, they faithfully made a full report to Asprenas, at whose instance the ship was overwhelmed and the man of mystery put to death. His head, remarkable for its eyes, hair and savage expression, was taken to Asia and from there to Rome.[17]

10. In a capital riven by dissension and hovering between liberty and licence as one emperor followed on the heels of another, even trivial matters were being dealt with in a highly emotional atmosphere. Vibius Crispus,[18] whose wealth, influence and intelligence ranked him among the well-known rather than the good, attacked the knight Annius Faustus,[19] who had been a professional informer in Nero's day. He impeached him before the senate, since, in Galba's principate, the senators had recently resolved that the cases of informers should be brought to trial. This senatorial decree had been bandied about in different ways, varying from ineffectual to formidable depending on whether the defendant was powerful or helpless, but it still retained some power to intimidate. Besides, Crispus had done his utmost to ruin his brother's accuser, and had won over a

considerable proportion of the senate to demand that Faustus should be executed without defence or hearing. Yet in the eyes of other senators, nothing helped the defendant so much as his accuser's excessive power. They proposed that the proper time should be allocated, the charges should be published, and the man's case should be heard in the traditional way, however unpopular and guilty the accused might be. At first this view prevailed, and the case was postponed for a few days, but Faustus was soon condemned, albeit without the public approval which he had richly deserved in view of his evil character. For people remembered that Crispus himself had made his fortune by the same kind of prosecutions. It was not the penalty which rankled, but the instrument of retribution.

The First Battle of Bedriacum

11. Meanwhile, the war started auspiciously for Otho. At his command, the armies had set off from Dalmatia and Pannonia. They comprised four legions, from each of which 2,000 men were sent ahead. The main group was following at no great distance. These were the Seventh Legion, raised by Galba, and three veteran legions – the Eleventh, the Thirteenth, and above all the Fourteenth, whose men had won renown by quelling the rebellion in Britain.[20] Nero had enhanced their reputation by choosing them as his most special troops, so their devotion to him was enduring and their support for Otho was enthusiastic. However, the greater their strength and power, the more their over-confidence slowed them down. The auxiliary cavalry and infantry preceded the legions on the march, and from Rome itself came a sizeable contingent consisting of five praetorian cohorts and some detachments of cavalry, together with the First Legion. In addition, there were 2,000 gladiators – a shameful force to call upon, although during civil wars even strict commanders made use of such support. These troops were placed under the command of Annius Gallus, who was sent ahead with Vestricius Spurinna to secure the banks of the Po, since the original plan had fallen through after Caecina had successfully crossed the Alps, although the emperor had at first

hoped to contain him within the Gallic provinces. Otho himself
was attended by chosen detachments of his bodyguard together
with the remaining praetorian cohorts, by veterans from
the praetorians and by a large naval brigade. His march was
not slow or marred by luxurious comfort, but wearing a steel
cuirass he marched on foot before the standards, unshaven,
without finery and quite different from his reputation.

12. Fortune smiled upon these enterprises at first.[21] Through
command of the sea, Otho dominated the greater part of Italy
right up to the frontier with the Maritime Alps. To try to gain
possession of this province and to attack Narbonese Gaul, he
had selected Suedius Clemens, Antonius Novellus and Aemilius
Pacensis as generals. However, Pacensis was clapped in irons
by his unruly men and Antonius Novellus had no authority.
Suedius Clemens commanded only in a way designed to make
him popular, being as shamelessly neglectful of military discipline as he was eager for battle. Nobody would have guessed
that they were invading Italy or the towns and homes of their
fatherland. They proceeded to burn, plunder and ravage them
as if they were foreign shores and cities of the enemy. The
savagery was all the more terrible because no precautions had
been taken anywhere to meet the threat. The fields were packed
with workers, the farmhouses open and defenceless. As the
landowners ran out with their wives and children, they were
lured to their doom by the complacency brought about by peace
and by the evil of war.

The governor of the Maritime Alps at that time was Marius
Maturus. He roused the people, who were well supplied with
men of military age, and set about repelling the Othonians from
the frontiers of his province, but at the first charge the mountain
people were cut down or scattered. This was only to be expected
of hastily gathered recruits with no idea about military camps
or commanders, and who took no pride in victory and saw no
dishonour in defeat.

13. Goaded by that battle, Otho's men turned their anger
upon the town of Albintimilium.[22] For they had taken no booty
in the fighting, as the farmers were poor and their paraphernalia
worthless, while the fighting men who were swift-footed and

knew the area intimately could not be captured. Nevertheless, their greed was satisfied at the cost of disasters inflicted on innocent civilians. What intensified bitterness was the exemplary courage of a Ligurian woman, who hid her son and, when the soldiers, thinking that money was concealed with him, asked her under torture where she was concealing him, pointed to her womb and indicated in response that he was hiding there. From then on, not by means of any terrors, even fear of death, did she change her consistently heroic reply.[23]

14. Quaking messengers brought word to Fabius Valens that Otho's fleet was threatening the province of Narbonese Gaul, which was bound by an oath to Vitellius. Representatives from the colonies also arrived, begging for help. Fabius dispatched two Tungrian cohorts, four squadrons of cavalry and a whole regiment of Treviran horsemen, with Julius Classicus[24] as commander. Part of this force was kept back in the colony of Forum Julii, because if the whole force had marched inland and the coast were left unprotected, the Othonian fleet could advance quickly. Twelve squadrons of cavalry and men selected from the auxiliary cohorts set off to confront the enemy, supported by a cohort of Ligurians which had long formed the local garrison, and 500 Pannonians not yet regularly enrolled in the legion. Battle was not long delayed. The Othonian battleline was arranged as follows: a group of the marines, mixed together with some civilians, occupied the rising ground of the hills near the sea, while the praetorians filled the flat land between the hills and the shore, and on the sea itself the fleet maintained contact, ready for action and extending a menacing array of prows turned shorewards. The Vitellians, inferior in infantry but well provided with horsemen, placed their Alpine troops on the neighbouring hills, with their infantry cohorts in close order behind the cavalry.

The Treviran squadrons charged the enemy recklessly, given that veteran soldiers were facing them, and at the same time, on the flank, the band of civilians assailed them with rocks. This sort of thing even they could manage, and being interspersed among troops they showed the same daring in the moment of victory, whether they were energetic or cowards.

Additional terror gripped the shattered Vitellians when the fleet delivered an attack on their rear while they were still fighting. Thus encircled all around, the whole force would have been annihilated if the darkness of night had not hampered the victorious army and provided cover for the fugitives.

15. Although the Vitellians were beaten, they did not refrain from action. They brought up reinforcements and attacked the enemy while they were complacent and taking their ease after their successful encounter. The sentries were cut down, the camp was penetrated and there was panic amongst the ships, but gradually the alarm subsided, and after rallying on a nearby hill the Othonians defended themselves and then went on the attack. At this point there was appalling slaughter, and the commanders of the Tungrian cohorts, who made a prolonged effort to hold out, were finally overwhelmed by a rain of missiles. Even the Othonians did not score a bloodless victory. Some of them launched a blind pursuit, and the cavalry faced about and surrounded them. A kind of truce was then concluded, and to prevent any sudden alarming move by the fleet on the one side or the cavalry on the other, the Vitellians returned to Antipolis in Narbonese Gaul and the Othonians to Albingaunum, a town within Liguria.

16. Corsica, Sardinia and the other islands of the Tyrrhenian Sea were kept on Otho's side by the prestige of the victorious fleet. However, Corsica was nearly destroyed by the recklessness of the governor Picarius Decumus, which in such a colossal war was not at all useful for the struggle as a whole, but proved deadly to himself. Since he hated Otho, he determined to help Vitellius by mobilizing the resources of Corsica, which would have had no impact on the outcome, even if the help had been forthcoming. He summoned the leading men of the island and explained his plan. Those who dared to contradict him – Claudius Pyrrhicus, captain of the galleys stationed off Corsica, and Quintius Certus, a Roman knight – he ordered to be executed. Their deaths frightened those who were there, and, sharing the others' fear, a flock of people who did not know what was afoot promptly swore allegiance to Vitellius. However, when Picarius began to enlist troops and burden undisci-

plined men with military duties, they loathed this unaccustomed graft and pondered their powerlessness, telling themselves that it was an island they inhabited, while Germany and the might of the legions were far away. Even those who had cohorts and cavalry to protect them had been plundered and devastated by the fleet. Suddenly the mood changed, although without any openly violent outbreak. Instead, they chose the right time for a plot. When Picarius' entourage had left him and he was naked and helpless in the baths, he was cut down, and his staff shared his fate. The murderers themselves took their heads, like those of enemies, to Otho, but they received neither reward from Otho nor punishment from Vitellius, for in the worldwide upheaval of the times they were utterly lost in the confusion amongst more significant crimes.

17. As I have mentioned above,[25] the Silian cavalry regiment had already opened the way into Italy and brought the war across the Alps. Nobody favoured Otho, but this was not because they preferred Vitellius. In fact, a long period of peace had crushingly prepared the Italians for every kind of slavery: they were easy pickings for those who arrived first and they did not care which was the better side. As some cohorts sent ahead by Caecina had also arrived, the forces of Vitellius now controlled the most prosperous area of Italy, including all the farmland and cities between the Po and the Alps. A cohort of Pannonians was captured at Cremona. A hundred cavalrymen and 1,000 sailors were rounded up between Placentia and Ticinum. These successes meant that the Vitellian army no longer found its way barred by the river and its banks. Indeed, the mere presence of the Po was a challenge to the Batavians and the Germans from beyond the Rhine. They crossed it without warning, opposite Placentia, and by surprising a few scouts so demoralized the rest that they brought back a false and panic-stricken report that Caecina's whole army was at hand.[26]

18. Spurinna, who was holding Placentia, was convinced that Caecina had not yet arrived, and if the enemy did approach, he had resolved to keep his men behind the fortifications and avoid exposing to a seasoned army his own force – three praetorian cohorts, 1,000 infantry drafted from the legions and a small

cavalry contingent. However, the men were unruly and had seen no active service. Seizing the standards and flags, they burst out and aimed weapons at their general as he tried to restrain them, ignoring their centurions and tribunes. Indeed they kept howling that Otho was being betrayed and that Caecina had been invited into Italy. Spurinna went along with these other men's rash behaviour, at first under compulsion, but later he feigned acquiescence so that his advice would carry more weight if the mutiny should peter out.

19. When the Po was sighted and night was closing in, they decided to entrench camp. The physical labour (a novelty for troops normally stationed in the capital) broke their spirit. Then every longest-serving soldier began to deplore their own credulity and pointed out the critical danger, if Caecina and his army surrounded their slender force of cohorts in the open terrain. By this time the language of restraint ran throughout the camp, and when the centurions and tribunes went among the ranks, there was praise for the foresight of the general because he had chosen a powerful and wealthy colony as a strong base for the campaign. Finally, Spurinna himself addressed them, not so much blaming them as explaining the situation, and, leaving a reconnaissance party behind, he led the rest back to Placentia in a less disorderly mood, ready to listen to orders. The city-walls were reinforced, defences added, towers heightened, while not just weapons were provided and prepared, but military obedience and an acceptance of discipline – the only thing that was missing from the Othonian side, since one could not complain about their lack of courage.

20. As for Caecina, he seemed to have abandoned savagery and unruly behaviour north of the Alps, and marched through the Italian countryside in an orderly fashion. The inhabitants of the country towns and colonies took his manner of dress as a sign of arrogance, for he made speeches to toga-clad audiences while he himself was decked out in a multicoloured cloak and trousers (typically barbarian garb).[27] Moreover, they also grumbled about his wife Salonina and seemed wounded, although it was not intended to offend anyone, that she was conspicuously riding her purple-decked horse. It is only human

nature to scrutinize other people's new-found fortune with jealous eyes and to demand moderation in displaying success above all from the ones the critics have recently seen on a par with themselves.

Caecina, having crossed the Po, tried to lure the Othonians from their allegiance by negotiation and promises, and he himself was subjected to the same process. At first some pretentious language about 'peace' and 'concord' was bandied about to little purpose. Then he turned all his attention and plans to the siege of Placentia, inspiring great fear. He knew perfectly well that the outcome of the opening phase of the campaign would determine his reputation for the rest of the war.

21. However, the first day's action was carried out impulsively rather than in a manner that showed the skilled techniques of a veteran army. The enemy, unprotected and careless, approached the walls after a heavy session of eating and drinking. It was during this fighting that a most splendid amphitheatre, located outside the walls, went up in flames. Perhaps it was set on fire by the besiegers while they were hurling torches, slingshots and incendiary missiles at the besieged, or else it was set alight by the blockaded men because they were hurling fire in return. The ordinary townspeople, primed to suspect the worst, believed that inflammable material had been furtively brought in by certain people from neighbouring cities who were jealous and envied them because there was no other building so capacious throughout Italy. However it happened, it was regarded as trivial so long as worse disasters were feared, but once safety was restored they lamented it as if they could have suffered no heavier blow. In any case, Caecina was repulsed with serious casualties, and the night was spent preparing siege-equipment. The Vitellians got ready screens, bundles of brush and moveable defenses in order to undermine the walls and protect the assault parties, while the Othonians provided themselves with stakes and immense masses of stone, lead and bronze designed to crush and annihilate the enemy. Both armies felt a sense of honour and a desire for glory, but there were differing sorts of exhortation on each side. One side stressed the strength of the legions and the army of Germany, the other the prestige

of the urban garrison and the praetorian cohorts. The Vitellians mocked the enemy soldiers as flabby layabouts who had been ruined by the circus and the theatre, while the Othonians scorned their opponents as a bunch of foreigners and aliens. At the same time, while Otho and Vitellius were being celebrated or condemned, the men found richer stimulus in exchanging insults than in delivering praise.

22. The day had scarcely begun, but the walls were crammed with defenders and the plains glittered with arms and men. The legionaries in close formation and the auxiliary forces in extended order assailed the top of the walls with arrows or stones and closed in upon stretches which had been neglected or were crumbling with age. The Othonians hurled down their javelins from above with surer and more careful aim against the rashly advancing cohorts of Germans who, with wild battle-songs and bodies naked as is their custom, clashed their shields together with upraised arms. The legionary troops, protected by screens and wicker barriers, undermined the walls, built up a mound and assailed the gates. The praetorians facing them rolled down with almighty crashes the huge millstones which had been arranged at various points along the wall for this very purpose. Some of those below were crushed to pieces by the stones, while others were pierced by weapons and left senseless or maimed. Panic made the slaughter worse and those on the walls inflicted wounds with greater intensity. The Vitellians retreated and the party's reputation was shattered. Caecina, who was ashamed of his reckless and ill-considered attack,[28] and afraid of looking ridiculous and useless if he stayed put in the same camp, recrossed the Po and made for Cremona. As he was departing, he received the surrender of Turullius Cerialis with a number of naval personnel and of Julius Briganticus with a few cavalrymen. The latter officer was a cavalry prefect of Batavian birth, the former a senior centurion known to Caecina because he had commanded a company in Germany.

23. On learning of the enemy's route, Spurinna informed Annius Gallus by letter about recent events, including the defence of Placentia and Caecina's plans. Gallus was at that moment leading the First Legion to assist Placentia, as he lacked

confidence that such a small number of cohorts could face a prolonged siege and the powerful army of Germany. When he heard that the defeated Caecina was making for Cremona, it was only with difficulty that he held back his legion, since the troops were on the brink of mutiny in their burning eagerness to fight. He halted them at Bedriacum, a village between Verona and Cremona, which thanks to two Roman catastrophes is now infamous and ill-omened.[29]

In the course of these same days, Martius Macer fought a successful battle near Cremona. This enterprising general ferried his gladiators across the Po and staged a lightning raid on the opposite bank. Some Vitellian auxiliaries there were thrown into disorder, and when the rest of them were fleeing to Cremona, those who had stood firm were cut to pieces. However, the offensive was kept in check in case the enemy brought up reinforcements and turned the tables upon the victors. So the Othonian troops, who assessed everything their generals did in a negative way, became suspicious. Every cowardly bigmouth vied with one another in assailing Annius Gallus, as well as Suetonius Paulinus and Marius Celsus, who had also been given command by Otho. The accusations were varied, but the most violent incitement to mutiny and sedition came from the murderers of Galba, who were crazed by guilt and fear. These men caused chaos, both by provocative remarks openly made and by writing secret letters to Otho. The emperor was always ready to listen to the lowest of the low, and it was good advice he feared. He now fell into a panic, being a man who was indecisive in success and more competent in the thick of disaster. So he summoned his brother Titianus and put him in charge of the war.

24. Meanwhile, a brilliant action was fought under the command of Paulinus and Celsus.[30] Caecina had been tortured by the failure of all his moves and the fast-fading reputation of his army. Driven from Placentia, his auxiliaries recently cut to pieces, he had come off worse even in clashes between patrols, skirmishes which were more frequent than worthy of mention. Now that Fabius Valens was approaching, Caecina, anxious to prevent all the glory of war falling to his colleague, hurried to

retrieve his reputation with more greed than judgement. At a point called the 'Castores',[31] twelve miles from Cremona, he posted his most formidable auxiliaries hidden in some woods overlooking the road. The cavalry was ordered to go further forward, provoke a battle and, by deliberately turning tail, to entice the enemy into a hasty pursuit until the ambush struck. This plan was betrayed to the Othonian generals. Paulinus assumed responsibility for the infantry, while Celsus took charge of the cavalry. A detachment of the Thirteenth Legion, with four cohorts of auxiliaries and 500 cavalry, was posted on the left. Three praetorian cohorts held the high road on a narrow front. On the right, the First Legion moved forward with two auxiliary cohorts and 500 cavalry. In addition, 1,000 horsemen from the praetorians and the auxiliaries were introduced to provide the finishing touch to success or assistance if they were struggling. 25. Before the two sides made contact, as the Vitellians were turning about, Celsus, knowing this was a trick, held back his men. The Vitellians rashly surged up from their hiding place, and as Celsus slowly retreated, they followed him too far and themselves fell headlong into a trap. For they had the cohorts on their flanks, the legions opposite them, and by a sudden dividing movement the cavalry had surrounded them in the rear. Suetonius Paulinus did not immediately give the infantry the signal to engage. He was a natural dawdler and the sort of man who liked cautiously laid plans rather than accidental success. So he had the ditches filled, the flat ground opened up and the line extended, thinking that it would be soon enough to start winning when precautions had been taken against defeat. This delay gave the Vitellians time to take refuge amidst vines that had become entangled because of their criss-crossed side branches. There was a small wood close by, too. Venturing a counter-attack from here, they managed to kill the most eager of the praetorian troopers. Among the wounded was Prince Epiphanes,[32] who was eagerly leading his men into battle on Otho's side.

26. At that point the Othonian infantry charged and crushed the enemy battleline. Even the troops who were coming to help turned and fled. For Caecina had not summoned his cohorts

simultaneously, but one by one. This factor increased the confusion on the battlefield, for these men, arriving in scattered groups and nowhere pooling their strength, were swept up by the rout of the fugitives. Besides this, there was mutiny in the camp, triggered because the whole army had not been led out to battle together. They arrested the prefect of the camp, Julius Gratus, on the grounds that he was engaging in treachery in the interest of his brother, who was serving with Otho. Yet at the same time, the brother, a tribune named Julius Fronto, had been arrested by the Othonians on the very same charge. However, there was such consternation everywhere among the fugitives and those coming up against them, in the battleline and before the camp, that the rumour spread on both sides that Caecina might have been destroyed with all his forces if Suetonius Paulinus had not sounded the retreat. Paulinus for his part asserted that he had been wary of so much additional labour and marching, fearing that the Vitellian troops, fresh from camp, might have attacked the wearied Othonians, and if they were repulsed there would have been no reserves to back them up. A few men approved of the commander's reasoning, but it was generally not well received.

27. This defeat did not so much drive the Vitellians to despair as restore them to discipline. This happened not just in the army of Caecina, who blamed his men for being readier to mutiny than fight, but in addition the forces of Fabius Valens, who had by this time reached Ticinum, abandoned their contempt for the enemy and obeyed his orders with greater respect and consistency in their eagerness to retrieve their reputation.

As a matter of fact, a serious mutiny had blazed up, which I will retrace from its start earlier on in the narrative – it would have been wrong to interrupt the sequence of Caecina's operations.[33] I have already described how the Batavian cohorts, having separated themselves from the Fourteenth Legion during the fighting which took place in Nero's principate, were on their way to Britain when they heard of Vitellius' uprising and joined Fabius Valens in the territory of the Lingones. These Batavians now started to behave arrogantly, and whenever they approached the tents of a legion they boasted that they had put

the Fourteenth in its place, robbed Nero of Italy and now held
the whole outcome of the war in their hands. This was an insult
to the legions and rankled bitterly with the general. Discipline
deteriorated amidst disputes and brawls. In the end, Valens
suspected that their insubordination was a prelude to treachery.
28. So when news came that the Treviran cavalry regiment
and the Tungrians had been routed by Otho's fleet and that
Narbonese Gaul was being surrounded, Valens, concerned both
to protect allied communities and by a clever stratagem to split
up unruly cohorts that could be dangerously strong if united,
ordered some Batavians to go to the rescue. When this leaked
out and became common knowledge, the auxiliaries became
gloomy and the legions grumbled. They complained that they
were being deprived of the help of the bravest troops. Now that
the enemy was within sight, the seasoned heroes who had won
so many battles were to be practically withdrawn from the
front-line! If a mere province were more important than the
capital and the safety of the empire, then they should all follow
the Batavians to Gaul. If, however, victory depended on Italy
being safe, the strongest limbs, so to speak, should not be
amputated from the body of the army.[34]

29. As they were fiercely hurling out these words, Valens sent
in the lictors and set about trying to control the mutiny, but
the men attacked him personally, bombarded him with stones
and chased him as he ran for it, yelling out that he was hiding
the Gallic loot and the gold of Vienne, which were the rewards
for their labours. They tore the general's baggage to shreds,
ransacked his tent and poked about in the very ground with
spears and lances. They were able to do this because Valens
meanwhile was hiding in a cavalry officer's quarters, disguised
as a slave. Then, as the mutiny was gradually cooling down,
Alfenus Varus, the prefect of the camp, accelerated the process
by a sensible decision. He told the centurions not to make their
usual inspection of the sentries, and omitted the trumpet-calls
which summon the troops to their duties. They all seemed
paralysed and numb as a result, looking round at each other in
bewilderment and unnerved by the very fact that there was no
one in charge. By their silence, their submissiveness, and finally

their appeals and tears, they begged for pardon. When Valens came out of hiding in his degrading garb, weeping and unexpectedly unharmed, there was joy, sympathy and goodwill. Just as a crowd always veers between one emotional extreme and the other, they were transformed into a state of happiness. Heaping praise and congratulations on him, they exultantly gathered the eagles and standards about him and bore him to the platform in the square. Valens was practical in his moderation and did not demand that anyone should be executed, but in order to avoid arousing further mistrust by pretending to ignore the mutiny, he denounced a few men as trouble-makers. He knew perfectly well that in a civil war the troops can take more liberties than their commanders.

30. His men were entrenching camp at Ticinum when news came of Caecina's defeat. The mutiny almost repeated itself,[35] for they believed that they had been kept away from battle by Valens' underhand methods and repeated time wasting. The troops did not want to rest, nor did they wait for the general to act, but they marched ahead of the standards, telling the bearers to get a move on. A rapid march brought them up with Caecina.

Valens had a bad reputation with Caecina's troops. They complained that despite being inferior in number they had been exposed to the full force of the enemy, and at the same time they made a bid to excuse themselves, magnifying by flattery the strength of the reinforcements so as to avoid being looked down upon as men who were beaten and cowardly. Besides, although Valens had a more powerful force and almost twice the number of legions and auxiliary units, yet the troops liked Caecina better. He was thought to be readier to show kindliness, and he was also a tall and well-built man in the prime of life, and possessed a sort of superficial charm. This was why the generals were jealous of each other. Caecina mocked his colleague as dirty and depraved, while Valens responded by deriding the other as pompous and vain. Yet they concealed their hostility for now and pursued a common goal, writing a stream of insulting letters to Otho without any consideration for the possibility of future pardon. The leaders of the Othonian faction abstained from abusing Vitellius, despite the fact that the field for invective was exceedingly rich. 31. Admittedly, until their respective deaths, in which Otho won glory and Vitellius complete infamy, the idle pleasures of Vitellius seemed less frightening than Otho's burning lusts. In addition, the murder of Galba had intensified the terror and hatred felt towards Otho, whereas no one held Vitellius responsible for beginning the fighting. Vitellius' gluttonous appetite was a disgrace to himself, but the hedonistic, cruel and unscrupulous Otho seemed a deadlier threat to the state.[36]

After the armies of Caecina and Valens had come together, the Vitellians had no further reason to delay committing their combined forces. Otho held a council-of-war to decide whether to wage a long campaign or try his luck immediately.[37] 32. At this meeting Suetonius Paulinus thought he owed it to his military reputation – he was considered the cleverest general at that time – to review the whole strategic position. He made a speech explaining that haste would help the enemy, whereas a waiting game would increase their own chances. Vitellius' army had now arrived in full, but was weakly supported in the rear since the Gallic provinces were bursting with unrest and it would be inadvisable to abandon the Rhine frontier when such hostile tribes would surely surge across. The troops of Britain were kept at bay by their enemies and the sea. The Spanish provinces were not exactly overflowing with soldiers. Narbonese Gaul, invaded by the fleet and defeated in battle, had received a severe shock. Italy north of the Po was enclosed by the Alps and could not be reinforced by sea, while the mere passage of an army through it had wrought havoc. There was no corn available to the enemy army anywhere, and without supplies an army could not be kept together. Even the Germans, the most aggressive troops on the other side, would not stand up to the change of latitude and climate and their strength would wilt if the war was extended into the summer. Many campaigns which were forceful at the first onset had dwindled to nothing through tedious delays. On their own side, all was different. There were rich and devoted resources everywhere. They had at their disposal Pannonia, Moesia, Dalmatia and the East, with armies fresh and unimpaired; Italy and the city which was the capital of the world; the Roman senate and people – whose reputation always shone out, even if at times they were overshadowed. They had public and private resources, and boundless riches, which are stronger in civil dissensions than the sword; soldiers whose constitutions were accustomed to Italy or to other hot climates. They had the River Po as a barrier, and cities securely defended by men and walls. That none of these would go over to the enemy was abundantly clear from the defence of Placentia. Otho should therefore draw out the war. In a few days, the Fourteenth Legion would arrive – itself very famous and now supplemented by forces from Moesia. Then the emperor could consider the situation afresh, and if he decided on battle they would fight with augmented strength.

33. Marius Celsus added his approval to Paulinus' assessment of the situation. Annius Gallus, who had been injured a few days before after falling from his horse, was consulted by messengers sent to ask what he thought and they had brought back word that he, too, agreed. Otho was determined to fight the decisive battle. His brother Titianus and the praetorian prefect Proculus, impetuous through inexperience, claimed that fortune, the gods and Otho's guardian spirit smiled upon their plans and would smile upon their performance: they had fallen back on flattery to prevent any attempt at opposition.

Once they had decided to fight, they considered whether it was better for the emperor to participate in the battle or keep aloof. Paulinus and Celsus, reluctant to appear to expose him to danger, raised no further objections, and the same group of mistaken advisers prevailed upon Otho to retire to Brixellum and to reserve himself for the most crucial decisions relating to the empire, safely removed from the hazards of battle. That day was the first blow to the chances of Otho's party.[38] Not only did a strong force of praetorians, bodyguards and cavalry go with the emperor as he departed, but the spirit of those who remained behind was shattered. This was because the soldiers, suspicious of their generals, were loyal to Otho alone, who likewise trusted only his men, and so he had left the authority of the officers on an uncertain footing.

34. The Vitellians knew all about this, thanks to the stream

of desertions which always happen during civil war. Besides, the Othonian scouts were so eager to learn about the enemy's plans that they failed to conceal their own. Quietly concentrating on when the enemy would rashly burst out, Caecina and Valens did something that is a substitute for shrewd action – they waited for other people to make stupid mistakes. Meanwhile, pretending that they were going to cross the River Po, they began to build a bridge so as to confront a band of gladiators on the other bank and so that their own troops should not while away time in idleness.[39] A line of boats was arranged facing against the current, equally spaced and secured by heavy timbers at the prow and stern, with anchors cast off besides to strengthen the bridge, but with sufficient slack on the anchor cables to allow the boats to ride the mounting waters without losing formation. A tower was put on board to enclose the further end of the bridge, and was moved out successively to whichever was the last boat. From it they could drive off the enemy with catapults and artillery.

The Othonians, meanwhile, had erected a tower on the bank and were hurling stones and flaming missiles. 35. There was also an island in midstream. The gladiators were struggling towards it in boats, while the Germans were gliding forwards by swimming. By chance the latter had got across in some strength, and Macer then manned some galleys and attacked them, using the keenest of his gladiators. However, gladiators do not exhibit the same steady courage as soldiers, and they found it harder to shoot effectively from the bobbing decks of the boats than did their enemies, who had a firm footing on the bank. Thanks to the erratic lurching of the quivering boats, the rowers and fighters fell over each other in confusion. The Germans took the initiative, plunged into the shallow water, latched onto the sterns, climbed up the gangways or drowned their opponents in hand-to-hand tussles. The whole scene was played out under the eyes of the two armies. The greater the delight of the Vitellians, the more bitterly the Othonians cursed the cause and architect of their defeat. 36. The battle was broken off by flight, after the surviving ships had been hauled away. The army clamoured for Macer's execution. After wounding him with a lance thrown from some distance, they closed in with swords drawn, but the tribunes and centurions intervened and rescued him. Not long afterwards Vestricius Spurinna arrived with his cohorts, in accordance with Otho's orders, having left a small garrison to hold Placentia. Then Otho sent the consul-designate, Flavius Sabinus, to take over the force previously commanded by Macer.[40] The troops were delighted at the change of generals, while the generals were reluctant to take on such an intimidating command owing to the continual mutinies.

37. I find it stated by certain writers[41] that in their dread of war or contempt for both emperors – whose wickedness and degradation was becoming notorious through increasingly candid daily reports – the two armies wondered whether they should not cease fighting and either come to a consensus themselves or leave the choice of an emperor to the senate. According to these authorities, this was why the Othonian leaders suggested waiting for a while: Paulinus, it is alleged, was particularly keen on this because he was the senior officer of consular rank and a distinguished general who had earned a brilliant name for himself in the British campaigns. For myself, although I am prepared to admit that in their heart of hearts a few men may have prayed for peace instead of strife and for a good and honest ruler instead of two worthless and infamous scoundrels, nevertheless I do not think that in such a degenerate era the prudent Paulinus had any hope that the mass of ordinary soldiers would exercise such self-control as to lay aside war from an attachment to peace after disturbing the peace from love of war. Nor do I think that armies so different in language and habits were capable of coming together into a union of this kind, or that officers and generals who were nearly all guiltily aware of progressing from hedonism, to poverty, to crimes would have tolerated any emperor who was not disreputable and obliged to them for the services they had rendered.[42]

38. From time immemorial, humans have had an innate passion for power, but with the growth of the empire it has ripened and run wild.[43] For, as long as resources were limited, equal standing was easily maintained, but after the world was

subjugated and rival cities or kings were cut down to size, we
were free to covet wealth in safety and the first struggles
between the senate and people blazed up. Unruly tribunes alternated with excessively powerful consuls, and there were trial
runs for civil wars in the city and in the Forum. Then Gaius
Marius, who rose from the lowest ranks of the people, and
Lucius Sulla, the most savage of the nobles, destroyed the republican constitution by force of arms and replaced it with despot-
ism.[44] After them came Gnaeus Pompey. He was more guarded,
but no better, and from then on the one goal was autocracy.
The legions of citizens did not shrink from civil war at Pharsalus
or Philippi,[45] so it is hardly likely that the armies of Otho and
Vitellius would have laid aside war voluntarily. The same divine
anger, the same human madness, the same criminal incentives
drove them into conflict. The fact that each war was decided as
it were by a single knock-out blow is only down to the feeble-
ness of the emperors. However, my reflections on ancient and
modern ways have made me stray too far, so now I return to
the proper sequence of events.

39. After Otho departed for Brixellum, the prestige of the
command lay with his brother Titianus, but the prefect Proculus
had real power and control. Celsus and Paulinus, whose prudent advice was universally ignored, were generals in name
only, but they served as a screen for the faults of others. The
tribunes and centurions were unreliable, since the best of them
were passed over and power lay with the worst. The ordinary
soldiers were enthusiastic, but they still preferred to interpret
the generals' orders to suit their own purposes rather than obey
them.

It was decided to advance and set up camp four miles from
Bedriacum, but this was done so unskilfully that they suffered
from a lack of water, even though it was springtime and there
were numerous rivers all around. At this point, there was hesitation about how to handle the battle, as Otho's dispatches were
pressing for speed, while the troops were demanding that the
emperor should be present at the combat, and many were
requesting that the troops operating across the Po should be
summoned. It is difficult to judge what would have been best

to do, but certainly what was done was the worst possible choice. 40. They set out as if embarking on a long campaign, not a decisive battle. Their objective was the confluence of the Po and a tributary, sixteen miles away.[46] Celsus and Paulinus were against exposing a footsore and heavily laden army to an enemy who would not pass up the chance of attacking them while they were out of order in their marching column or else scattered and constructing the rampart – and the Vitellians were lightly armed and would have barely four miles to advance. Titianus and Proculus were beaten in the deliberations, but they resorted to their rights as supreme commanders. It is true that a Numidian was at hand after a swift gallop, bearing aggressive instructions from Otho, who reprimanded the generals for dragging their feet and ordered that the matter should be brought to a head. He was sick of delay and could no longer bear the tension.

41. On the same day,[47] the tribunes of two praetorian cohorts approached Caecina while he was busy with the construction of the bridge, and asked for an interview. He was preparing to listen to their proposals and give them answers, when his scouts rushed up with news that the enemy was at hand. The tribunes' remarks were cut short, so it was difficult to say for sure whether they were initiating a trick or treachery or even some honourable scheme. Dismissing the tribunes, Caecina rode back to camp and found that Fabius Valens had issued the signal for battle and that the troops were under arms. While the legions were drawing lots to determine the order of march, the cavalry charged out of the camp.[48] Remarkably, they would have been forced back against the rampart by a smaller number of Othonians, but this was prevented by the courage of the Italian Legion, whose men drew their swords and forced the retreating cavalry to return and resume the fight. The battleline of the Vitellian legions was arranged without any fuss, for although the enemy was near, it was impossible to see any sign of an armed force because of the thick plantations. However, among the Othonians, there were nervous generals, common soldiers hostile to their superiors, a confusion of vehicles and camp-followers, and a road with steep ditches on either side, which

would have been narrow even for a column advancing calmly. Some Othonians were massed round their respective standards, others were looking for them. Everywhere there was the confused noise of men running about and calling. Depending on each man's audacity or fearfulness, individuals would surge forward or drift back, making for front or rear.

42. While their minds were numb in the face of this sudden threat, their initiative was further sapped by unwarranted delight after the discovery of some men who mendaciously claimed that Vitellius had been abandoned by his army. It has not been fully established whether the Vitellian scouts spread this rumour or if it actually arose on Otho's side, either by design or chance.[49] The Othonians lost all heart for fighting and spontaneously greeted their opponents. They were met with antagonistic muttering, and, as many troops on their own side had no idea what had prompted their greeting, the Othonians feared treachery. At this point, the enemy advanced, with unbroken ranks and superior in strength and numbers. As for the Othonians, although they were scattered, outnumbered and weary, they still undertook to fight fiercely. Indeed, as the battle was fought over a wide area obstructed by trees and vines, it had many different aspects. They clashed at close quarters and from a distance, sometimes in clusters, sometimes in wedge formation. On the high road, there was a hand-to-hand struggle, as the men threw the weight of their bodies and shield-bosses against each other. They abandoned the usual volley of javelins and hacked through helmets and armour with swords and axes. Knowing each other, watched by their comrades, they were contesting the outcome of the whole campaign.

43. By chance, two legions made contact in open country between the Po and the road. These were the Vitellian Twenty-First, commonly known as 'Hurricane' and long renowned, and on the Othonian side the First (Adiutrix) Legion, which had never fought before, but was in high spirits and eager for fresh distinction. The men of the First overran the front ranks of the Twenty-First, and carried off their eagle. Fired up by that humiliation, the legion responded by charging at the ranks of the First, killing their commanding officer, Orfidius Benignus,

and seizing a great number of standards and flags from the enemy. In another part of the battlefield, the Fifth pushed back the Thirteenth Legion, while the men of the Fourteenth were attacked and surrounded by superior numbers. Long after the Othonian commanders had fled, Caecina and Valens were still bolstering their men with reinforcements, and as a fresh reserve, there was also Alfenus Varus with his Batavians. These cohorts had confronted and routed the band of gladiators, who had been carried across in boats, and killed them in the river itself. Having won the day there, the Batavians delivered their onslaught on the Othonian flank.

44. After the centre of the battleline had collapsed, the Othonians fled in all directions in a bid to reach Bedriacum. The distance was enormous, the roads choked with heaps of corpses, which only increased the slaughter. After all, in civil war prisoners cannot be converted into profit.[50] Suetonius Paulinus and Licinius Proculus took different routes and avoided the camp. Vedius Aquila, the commander of the Thirteenth Legion, suddenly panicked and brought himself right into the hands of the angry troops. It was still broad daylight when he entered the rampart and was immediately surrounded by a shouting mob of mutinous fugitives. They did not hold back from either insults or violence and reproached him as a deserter and traitor, not because they had any particular charge against him, but like a typical crowd the men accused others of their own guilty conduct. Night brought assistance to Titianus and Celsus. By this time, sentries had been posted and the soldiers got under control by Annius Gallus, who used advice, appeals and his own authority to persuade them not to aggravate the disaster of defeat by butchering each other. Whatever happened, he remarked – whether the end of the war had arrived or whether they chose to take up arms again – the only solace for conquered men was to act together.

Although the spirit of the other troops had been broken, the praetorians angrily protested that they had been beaten by treachery, not by the enemy's courage. Even the Vitellians, they added, had not obtained their victory without bloodshed, as their cavalry had been routed and a legionary eagle captured.

The Othonians still had Otho himself and the troops stationed
with him across the Po. The legions from Moesia were coming
and a large part of the army had stayed behind at Bedriacum.
These men had certainly not yet been beaten and, if need be,
would find a more honourable death on the battlefield. Amidst
such thoughts, the praetorians became defiant or anxious, but
in their utter desperation they were more often goaded to anger
than fear.

45. However, the Vitellian army bivouacked five miles from
Bedriacum, as the generals were wary of storming the camp on
the same day and also hoped that the enemy would surrender
voluntarily. The lightly armed Vitellians had marched out only
to fight a battle, but arms and victory were their safeguard. On
the next day, the intention of the Othonian army was clear,
and the wilder elements had come to their senses. So a deputation was sent to the Vitellians. The generals had no hesitation
in granting peace, but the envoys were held up for a time, which
caused some disquiet since the Othonians did not know whether
their request had been granted or not. Once the deputation
returned, the camp was opened up. At this point victors and
vanquished alike burst into tears, finding a melancholy delight
in cursing the evil fate of civil war. In the same tents, they
nursed their wounded brothers or other relatives. Their hopes
for reward were in doubt, but funeral rites and bereavement
seemed guaranteed. Everybody was involved in the tragedy and
had someone's death to mourn. A search was made for the
body of the legionary commander Orfidius, and it was cremated
with the customary honours. A few were buried by their relatives, but the vast majority of the dead were left lying on the
ground.[51]

Otho's Suicide

46. Otho, waiting for news about the battle, was utterly calm
and resolved about his plan.[52] First came a gloomy rumour,
then fugitives from the battlefield revealed that his cause was
utterly lost. Otho's men were so eager that they did not wait for
him to make any statement. They urged him to keep cheerful,

pointing out that his new forces were still intact and that they themselves were ready to suffer or to dare the utmost. And this was not mere flattery. In some kind of furious enthusiasm, they were burning to join the fight and restore the fallen fortunes of their side. Those at a distance stretched out their hands to Otho and the nearest bystanders grasped his knees in supplication. First and foremost among them was Plotius Firmus. As praetorian prefect, he appealed to the emperor again and again not to abandon a most faithful army, not to abandon soldiers who served him so excellently. It showed greater spirit, he said, if troubles were tolerated rather than evaded. Brave and active men clung to hope even when fortune was against them, while only cowards and weaklings hurried headlong to despair through fear. During this speech, whenever Otho relaxed or hardened his expression, they cheered or groaned. It was not just the praetorians – Otho's personal troops – who urged him on, but units sent ahead from Moesia who informed him that the advancing army was just as determined, and that some legions had entered Aquileia. No one therefore doubts that the war could have been resumed – one which was cruel, mournful and full of uncertainties for vanquished and victors alike.

47. Otho, turning his back on plans for war, said:[53] 'To expose this spirit, this courage of yours, to further danger would, I think, be too high a price to pay for my life. You hold out great hopes, in the event of my deciding to live on, but this will merely make death all the more splendid. We have put each other to the test, fortune and I. Nor must you count up the length of my principate. It is more difficult to exercise moderation in good fortune when you do not think you will possess it for long. Civil war began with Vitellius, and he is responsible for the fact that we struggled over the principate in an armed conflict.[54] Yet it will be in my power to set an example by making sure that we do not fight more than once. Let this be the act by which posterity judges Otho.[55] Vitellius shall enjoy the company of his brother, wife and children: I have no need either for vengeance or consolation. Although other men may have held the principate for longer, nobody can ever have relinquished it so bravely. Am I to allow all these young

Romans, all these fine armies, to be trampled underfoot a
second time, to be torn from their country's hands? Let this
thought accompany me, that you would have died on my behalf
– but you must live on after me. I should no longer impede your
chances of survival, nor you my resolution. To waste further
words on death smacks of cowardice. Take this as your best
proof that my decision is final, that I complain about no one.
For blaming gods or men is the mark of someone who wishes
to live.'

48. After this speech, he addressed his entourage kindly
according to each man's age and rank. He urged them to hurry
away with all speed and to avoid provoking the victor's anger
by remaining, using his personal authority to stir the young
men and appeals to move his elders. His look was calm, his
words intrepid, and when his followers wept he restrained
their untimely tears. He allocated ships and vehicles for their
departure. Any petitions or letters that showed outspoken support of himself or insults to Vitellius he destroyed. He distributed money sparingly, quite unlike a man facing death. Then
he dealt with a young lad called Salvius Cocceianus, his
brother's son, who was scared and sorrowful. Otho went out
of his way to comfort him, praising his family devotion but
reprimanding his fear. Did he really think that Vitellius would
be so cold-hearted as to refuse to make even this tiny repayment
for the immunity granted to his whole family? He, Otho, was
earning the victor's clemency by committing suicide quickly.
For it was not in a moment of final desperation, but while the
troops were demanding battle that he had spared his country
from the ultimate catastrophe. He had won enough of a name
for himself, enough distinction for his descendants. After all
the Julians, Claudians and Servians, he had been the first to
bring the principate into a new family.[56] So the young lad must
face life in a confident mood. He should never forget that Otho
had been his uncle – nor remember it too well.[57]

49. After this, he dismissed everyone from his presence and
rested for a while. While he was turning over in his mind some
worries that were already his last, he was distracted by a sudden
commotion and the news that the troops were mutinous and

beyond control. They kept threatening to murder those who were leaving, but showed particularly aggressive force against Verginius, whom they were keeping under siege within his house. Otho reprimanded the ringleaders, and returning to his quarters made time for conversations with those who were leaving, until such time as they had all got away unhurt. As twilight was drawing in, he quenched his thirst with a drink of iced water. Then after two daggers were brought to him and he had tested both, he tucked one beneath his pillow. After it had been established that his friends had already set off, he passed a quiet night and (so sources report) he actually slept.[58] At first light, he fell upon his dagger. Hearing the dying man's groan, his freedmen and slaves came in, together with the praetorian prefect Plotius Firmus, and found a single wound, in the chest.

There was a swift funeral. He had sought that with insistent prayers, for he feared that his head might be cut off and subjected to mockery.[59] The praetorian cohorts carried his body along amidst tributes and tears, showering kisses on his wound and hands. Some of the troops committed suicide beside the funeral pyre, not because they felt guilty or afraid but because they loved their emperor and wished to share his glory. Afterwards, at Bedriacum, Placentia and other camps in all quarters, this kind of death became common. They built for Otho a modest tomb which was more likely to survive. Such then was the end of his life in his thirty-seventh year.

50. He came from the town of Ferentium. His father had achieved the consulship, his grandfather had been praetor. On his mother's side his birth was less distinguished, but not lowly. His childhood and youth were such as I have described. By two actions, one utterly appalling, one heroic, he has earned just as much renown as disgrace in the eyes of posterity.

Although I believe that ferreting out fabulous stories and amusing my readers' minds with fictional tales is quite inappropriate in a serious work of this type, all the same I should not go so far as to discredit accounts which have been widely talked about and passed down. The locals report that on the day when the battle was fought at Bedriacum, a species of bird that had never been seen before[60] perched in a much-frequented grove at Regium Lepidum. Thereafter, neither the crowds of people nor the flocks of birds that circled around succeeded in scaring it or driving it away, until the very moment when Otho killed himself. Then it vanished from sight, so the story goes, and for those calculating the times, the beginning and end of the marvel coincided with the final stages of Otho's life.

51. At his funeral, the grieving and sorrowful troops renewed their mutinous behaviour, and this time there was no one to restrain it. Turning to Verginius, they demanded menacingly now that he should assume the principate, now that he should become their ambassador before Caecina and Valens. Verginius sneaked out by the back door of his house and foiled the soldiers just as they broke in at the front.

Rubrius Gallus[61] carried a petition from the cohorts stationed at Brixellum, and a pardon was immediately granted, while Flavius Sabinus handed over to the victor the forces under his command. 52. The fighting had now ceased everywhere, but the majority of senators faced an extremely dangerous situation since they had set off from Rome with Otho and had then been left behind at Mutina. It was here that news of the defeat reached them, but the soldiers rejected the report as a misleading rumour, and because they believed that the senators were hostile to Otho, they kept watch on their conversations and put the worst interpretation on their expressions and demeanour. Finally, by means of insults and abuse, they sought an initial pretext for massacre, just when another peril too loomed over the senators. Now that the Vitellian side was all-powerful, observers might think that they had dragged their feet in welcoming the victory. Therefore, fearful and anxious on two counts, they came together, although nobody formulated a plan individually and each man felt safer sharing the blame among many. The town council of Mutina heaped further worries on the terrified senators by offering them weapons and money and by addressing them formally as 'Conscript Fathers'[62] in an ill-timed compliment.

53. There was one notorious brawl in which Licinius Caecina attacked Eprius Marcellus[63] for making an ambiguous speech. Not that the rest were speaking candidly; but Marcellus was

loathed because people remembered his activities as an informer, which left him open to feelings of envy, and his very name spurred on Caecina, who, as a newly fledged senator of unknown family, wanted to make his mark by attacking someone important. The two antagonists were parted by the good sense of the moderate senators.

Indeed, the whole group now moved back to Bononia, intending to discuss the situation further, while in the meantime hoping for further news. At Bononia, men were sent separately along different roads to question every newcomer. One of Otho's freedmen, upon being asked the reason for his journey, replied that he was bringing his master's last wishes. When he left Otho, it seemed, the emperor was still alive, but his only concern was with posterity after abandoning the pleasures of life. At this there was admiration and a reluctance to probe further, and their feelings unanimously turned to Vitellius.

54. Vitellius' brother Lucius was present at their deliberations and was making himself available to the senators, who were already fawning. That was when Nero's freedman Coenus suddenly appeared and caused general consternation by telling an atrocious lie. He asserted that with the arrival of the Fourteenth Legion, which had joined forces with the soldiers from Brixellum, the victorious Vitellians had been slaughtered and the fortune of Otho's party had been turned around. His reason for telling this lie was to enable the travel warrants[64] approved by Otho, which were now being disregarded, to regain their validity thanks to this happier news. True enough, Coenus succeeded in getting to Rome at full speed – only to pay the penalty a few days later on Lucius Vitellius' instructions.[65] Yet the threat to the senators was increased, since the Othonian troops thought the news was true. What intensified their alarm was the thought that the departure from Mutina and abandonment of Otho's cause looked like official acts. After that, they held no more meetings, and each senator looked after his own interests until a dispatch from Fabius Valens dispelled their fears. Indeed, the nobility of Otho's death helped to spread the news of it like wildfire.

55. At Rome, however, there was no panic. The festival of

Ceres was being celebrated in the usual way.[66] When reliable informants brought word to the theatre that Otho had died and that the city prefect, Flavius Sabinus, had made such soldiers as were in the city take the oath to Vitellius, the audience applauded Vitellius. Adorned with laurel and flowers, the people carried busts of Galba around the temples, and heaped their garlands into a kind of funeral mound near the Pool of Curtius, which was the place that the dying Galba had stained with his blood. In the senate all the powers accumulated over the long principates of previous emperors were immediately decreed. Congratulations and thanks to the armies of Germany were paid in addition, and a deputation was sent off to convey their joy formally. A letter was read out in the senate written by Fabius Valens to the consuls in very restrained terms. Yet Caecina's self-control was more pleasing to the senators, for he had not written at all.[67]

56. However, Italy was being plagued more severely and dreadfully than it had been during the war. Scattered throughout the towns and settlements, the Vitellians pillaged, plundered and perpetrated violent and vicious rapes. Driven by natural greed or mercenary instincts, they were ready for anything, right or wrong, and they did not hold back from attacking any target, regardless of whether or not it was sacred. There were also civilians who disguised themselves as soldiers in order to kill their own personal enemies, while the soldiers themselves, knowing the local area, picked out prosperous farms and rich landowners as targets for plunder, or, if they resisted, death. The generals were at their mercy and lacked the guts to intervene. Caecina was the less greedy of the pair, but more given to popularity seeking. Valens, notorious because of his ill-gotten gains and profits, was therefore prepared to turn a blind eye to the transgressions of others as well. Italy's resources had long since been worn down, which meant that such vast numbers of infantry and cavalry, the financial losses and the acts of injustice were only barely tolerated.

Vitellius in Northern Italy

57. Meanwhile Vitellius, unaware that he had won, began to gather the remaining strength of the German army as if the war had yet to be won. A few veterans were left in the winter-quarters, and recruiting was stepped up in the Gallic provinces in order that the enlistments of the remaining legions could be raised to full strength. Responsibility for the Rhine frontier was entrusted to Hordeonius Flaccus. Vitellius supplemented his own army with 8,000 men drawn from the army of Britain. He had only completed a few days' march when he heard about the victory at Bedriacum and that armed resistance had collapsed on the death of Otho. So he called a meeting and heaped fulsome praise on the valour of the troops. While the army was demanding that he reward his freedman Asiaticus with equestrian status, he put a stop to this degrading flattery. Then with characteristic inconsistency, he granted at a private banquet the very privilege which he had refused to grant in public, and he honoured Asiaticus with the rings of a knight, despite the fact that he was a disgusting slave who was aiming for the top by his evil ways.[68]

58. Over these same days, the news arrived that both provinces of Mauretania had gone over to Vitellius as a sequel to the murder of their governor Albinus.[69] Lucceius Albinus had been put in charge of Mauretania Caesariensis by Nero, with Galba entrusting to him the control of Mauretania Tingitana as well. The forces at the governor's disposal were considerable – nineteen cohorts, five cavalry regiments and a large force of Moors, a band ready for war thanks to their brigandage and robbery. On Galba's death, Albinus was inclined to back Otho, and, not content with Africa, threatened to invade Spain which was separated from it only by a narrow strait. At this, Cluvius Rufus was alarmed, so he moved the Tenth Legion down to the shore as if in preparation for a crossing. Centurions were sent ahead to win over the Moors to Vitellius – not a difficult task, given that the army of Germany enjoyed a great reputation in every province. A rumour was also being spread that Albinus, scorning the title 'governor', had assumed the distinction of a

king and the name 'Juba'.[70] 59. So there was a change of feeling.
The cavalry commander Asinius Pollio, one of Albinus' most
loyal supporters, and Festus and Scipio, two cohort commanders, were assassinated. Albinus himself, who was on his
way from Tingitana to Mauretania Caesariensis, was murdered
when he put in to land. When his wife faced up to the assassins,
she met the same fate, although Vitellius did not investigate any
of these events.[71] With a cursory hearing he used to pass over
reports, however important they were, since he was unequal to
the more serious responsibilities of his position.

He ordered his army to proceed by road, while he himself
travelled by boat down the River Arar. He had no imperial
trappings, but was conspicuous only for his long-standing poverty until the governor of Lugdunese Gaul, Junius Blaesus, a
man of high birth, who was as generous spirited as he was
wealthy, surrounded the emperor with attendants and accompanied him in sumptuous style. For precisely that reason Blaesus
proved disagreeable, although Vitellius concealed his resentment beneath cringing compliments.[72] At Lyons, the leaders of
the victorious and vanquished sides were at hand. Valens and
Caecina received a glowing tribute from Vitellius at a military
parade, and were stationed close to his official chair. Then he
ordered the whole army to march out to meet his infant son,
who was solemnly conducted to the spot and enveloped in a
general's cloak. Holding the child in his arms, Vitellius gave
him the name 'Germanicus' and surrounded him with all the
emblems of imperial rank. This lavish honour conferred in
prosperity proved fatal in adversity.[73]

60. Then the leading Othonian centurions were executed,
which above all caused the armies of Illyricum to become
estranged from Vitellius. At the same time, the other legions
began to contemplate war since their association with the German armies had bred hatred for them. As for Suetonius Paulinus
and Licinius Proculus, Vitellius kept them waiting miserably,
dressed filthily in defendants' clothing until he finally granted
them an audience and they resorted to defence pleas which
were more mandatory than honourable. They actually claimed
credit for treachery and attributed to their own duplicity the

long march before the battle, the exhaustion of the Othonians, the jumbled column of marching men and vehicles, and several other factors which were purely accidental. In fact, Vitellius believed their claims of treachery and acquitted them of loyalty. Otho's brother Salvius Titianus was not in danger, for he was excused by his indolence and his family obligations. Marius Celsus retained his consulship, but it was commonly believed and afterwards alleged in the senate that Caecilius Simplex had been willing to buy the distinguished office and to secure Celsus' destruction as well. Vitellius rejected the charge and later awarded Simplex a consulship which cost him neither murder nor money. Galeria, the wife of Vitellius, protected Trachalus from his accusers.

61. While great men went in peril of their lives, shameful to report, a certain Mariccus, a humble member of the Boian tribe, had the nerve to push himself to prominence and to challenge the armed might of Rome by pretending to have divine power. This liberator of Gaul and god (for he had bestowed those titles upon himself) had raised a force of 8,000 men and was already coercing the neighbouring Aeduan cantons when that most responsible state, using chosen men of military age together with some additional cohorts contributed by Vitellius, scattered the fanatical mob. In the battle, Mariccus was captured. Later, he was thrown to the beasts, but because they refused to tear him to pieces the common people stupidly believed that he was indestructible – until he was executed as Vitellius watched.

62. No further severe measures were taken against the rebels or anyone's property. The wills of those who had fallen in battle fighting for Otho were ratified, or else the law of intestacy was applied. Indeed, you should not have feared Vitellius' avarice, if he were in control of his love of luxury, but he displayed a revolting and insatiable appetite for banquets. Stimulants for his gullet were being brought from Rome and Italy, while the routes from the Tuscan and Adriatic seas were bustling noisily. Leading members of the various cities had their pockets drained by providing feasts, and the very cities were being devastated. The Vitellian troops became flabby and work-shy as they became accustomed to pleasures and despised their leader.

Vitellius forwarded to Rome a decree postponing his acceptance of the title 'Augustus' and refusing that of 'Caesar',
although he did not reduce his real power at all. Astrologers
were expelled from Italy,[74] and strict orders issued that Roman
knights should not disgrace themselves by performing in the
games and the arena. Previous emperors had driven them to
take part by offering money or, more often, by using force, and a
number of the provincial towns vied with one another in
attracting with enticements the most decadent of the young men.

63. With the arrival of his brother and the crawling intrusion
of tutors in tyranny, Vitellius became more overbearing and
brutal and ordered the execution of Dolabella, whose banishment to the city of Aquinum by Otho I have already recorded.[75]
Dolabella had heard about Otho's death and entered the capital. The ex-praetor Plancius Varus, once one of Dolabella's
closest friends, had laid this charge against him before Flavius
Sabinus, the city prefect. The allegation was that he had broken
out of custody and offered himself as general to the beaten side.
The accuser added that an attempt had been made to seduce
the cohort stationed at Ostia. In the complete absence of any
proofs for such serious charges, Varus in due course repented
of his action and begged for forgiveness, but it was too late and
the damage had been done. As Flavius Sabinus hesitated over
such a grave matter, Lucius Vitellius' wife, Triaria, aggressive
to a degree scarcely credible in a woman, terrified him through
hints that he was seeking to win a reputation for clemency by
endangering the emperor. Sabinus, lenient when left to his own
devices, easily changed his tune whenever fear pressed down
upon him. Alarmed for himself although the danger threatened
another man, he shoved someone who was already falling, lest
he should appear to have helped him to his feet. 64. Therefore
Vitellius, who feared and hated Dolabella because he had later
married his divorced wife Petronia, summoned him by letter,
and gave orders that he should turn off from the busy Flaminian
Way to Interamna,[76] where he was to be put to death. The
assassin thought this far too elaborate. On the journey, he
threw his victim to the ground in a wayside inn and cut his
throat, bringing enormous resentment upon the new regime,

since this was taken as the first sign of its character. Moreover, the outrageous conduct of Triaria was made more burdensome by the exemplary moderation of someone close at hand, the emperor's wife, Galeria, who was not mixed up in these grim events. No less virtuous was the mother of the two Vitellii, Sextilia, a woman of old-fashioned morals. The story went that in response to the first letter from her son as emperor, she said that she had not borne a 'Germanicus', but a 'Vitellius'. She was not moved to exultation subsequently by any allurements of rank or flattery from the public, but felt only the calamities of her house.

65. Once Vitellius had departed from Lyons, Cluvius Rufus caught up with him after relinquishing his responsibilities in Spain. He showed an expression of delight and congratulation on his face, but at heart he was worried and aware that charges had been levelled against him. An imperial freedman named Hilarus had denounced him because on hearing about the imperial claims of Vitellius and Otho, Rufus had allegedly planned to make a bid for power himself with the Spanish provinces as his base, and for this reason he had not endorsed his travel warrants with the name of any emperor. The accuser also construed some passages from his speeches as insults towards Vitellius and rabble rousing in favour of himself. Yet Cluvius' personal clout was strong enough that Vitellius actually gave orders for his own freedman to be punished. Cluvius was given a place in the emperor's entourage without losing Spain, which he governed by proxy according to the precedent set by Lucius Arruntius.[77] However, Tiberius Caesar kept Arruntius at court because he feared him, whereas Vitellius was not the least bit frightened of Cluvius. The same honour was not paid to Trebellius Maximus, who fled from Britain because of his troops' angry temperaments. Vettius Bolanus, one of those on the spot, was sent to replace him.

66. The spirit of the conquered legions, which was far from broken, was making Vitellius worried. Scattered throughout Italy and mingled in with the victors, they were engaging in hostile talk, with particular defiance shown by the Fourteenth Legion, whose men would not concede that they had been

beaten. For at the battle of Bedriacum, they asserted, only some advance detachments had been routed, but the backbone of the legion had not been present.[78] It was decided that they should be returned to Britain, from where Nero had summoned them. Meanwhile, they were to share camp with the Batavian cohorts, on the grounds that these auxiliaries had a long-standing dispute with the men of the Fourteenth. Amidst such hostile feelings between armed men, peace and quiet was inevitably short-lived. At Turin, while a Batavian auxiliary was attacking a certain workman for cheating him and a legionary was defending the man as his host, each man was joined by his respective comrades and insults turned into bloodshed. Indeed, a fierce battle would have blazed up but for the fact that two praetorian cohorts took up the cause of the Fourteenth, bolstering the legionaries and intimidating the Batavians. Vitellius ordered that the Batavians should be attached to his marching column on the grounds that they were loyal soldiers, while the legion should cross the Graian Alps by a roundabout route avoiding Vienne (for its citizens were also a source of fear). On the night of the legion's departure, fires were carelessly left alight everywhere and part of the city of Turin was burnt down. This loss, like many catastrophes of war, has been effaced by more substantial disasters which struck other cities. After the men of the Fourteenth had descended from the Alps, the most unruly elements were all for marching to Vienne, but they were stopped by the united efforts of the better soldiers and the legion crossed over into Britain.

67. The next source of anxiety for Vitellius came from the praetorian cohorts. The men were first split up, and then offered the appeasement of an honourable discharge, so they began to hand in their weapons to their tribunes until the news spread that Vespasian's bid for power had gathered momentum. Then they rejoined the army and became the main strength of the Flavian party.

The First Legion of marines was sent to Spain to cool down in an atmosphere of peace and quiet. The Eleventh and Seventh were returned to their winter camps, while the Thirteenth was ordered to build amphitheatres, as Caecina and Valens were preparing to put on gladiatorial shows (at Cremona and Bononia respectively) and Vitellius was never so preoccupied by the cares of office as to forget his pleasures.

68. Indeed, Vitellius had managed to split up the defeated using restrained measures, but a mutiny arose amongst the victors: it started off as fun, but the number of men slaughtered enhanced the feelings of resentment against Vitellius. At Ticinum, Vitellius was at dinner and Verginius had been invited to the feast. Legates and tribunes tend to emulate the behaviour of their supreme commanders, either copying their strictness or indulging in prolonged dinners, and accordingly the ordinary soldier either does his duty conscientiously or gets out of hand. In Vitellius' circle, everything was chaotic and drunken, an atmosphere more in tune with all-night orgies than the discipline of the camp. So it happened that two soldiers – one belonging to the Fifth Legion, the other a Gallic auxiliary – were fired up by high spirits to engage in a bout of wrestling. After the legionary had taken a tumble and the Gaul was jeering at him, and after those who had gathered to watch had taken opposite sides, the legionaries launched themselves against the auxiliaries and two cohorts were annihilated.[79] One alarming outbreak was only cured by another. In the distance could be seen a cloud of dust and the glint of arms. The sudden cry went up that the Fourteenth Legion had turned on its tracks and was coming to the attack. However, the troops were in fact the rearguard of their own column. Once they were recognized, this set their minds at rest.

Meanwhile a slave of Verginius happened to appear on the scene and was accused of being Vitellius' assassin, whereupon the troops stormed the dinner-party and clamoured for Verginius' head. Nobody doubted his innocence, not even Vitellius, although he quaked in his boots at the slightest hint of a plot. These men, who were pressing for the execution of an ex-consul and their own former commander, were only restrained with difficulty. Indeed, nobody more than Verginius was the target of every mutinous act. Admiration and esteem for the man remained, but they hated him because he had scorned them.

69. On the next day after Vitellius had given a hearing to a

senatorial embassy which had been told to wait at Ticinum, he went over to the camp and actually heaped praise on the troops for their devotion, although the auxiliaries noisily protested that the legionaries had been allowed to get away with such arrogant behaviour without being punished. To prevent the Batavian cohorts daring some even more truculent act, they were sent back to Germany – this was the beginning of a war that was both civil and foreign, for which destiny was preparing the way.[80] The Gallic auxiliaries were returned to their various communities. They formed a numerous contingent whose help had been accepted at the very beginning of the Vitellian uprising as a form of military window-dressing. However, to enable the already depleted resources of the empire to meet the drain of lavish bounties, Vitellius ordered the strength of legionary and auxiliary units to be reduced by a veto on recruiting, and men were being offered discharges without distinction. This policy was fatal to the country and unpopular with the troops, who found that the same number of duties was divided between a small number of men, so that danger and toil came round with greater frequency. Moreover, their strength was being sapped by pleasures, in a way totally at variance with old-fashioned discipline and the traditions of our ancestors, in whose hands the Roman state found a firmer footing in character than in money.

70. From Ticinum Vitellius turned off to Cremona, and after watching Caecina's gladiatorial show conceived a desire to set foot on the plain of Bedriacum and to cast his eyes over the traces of his recent victory.[81] It was a dreadful and revolting sight. Less than forty days had elapsed since the engagement, and mutilated corpses, severed limbs and the decaying carcasses of men and horses lay everywhere. The ground was tainted with gore, the trees and crops had been trampled down – the devastation was appalling. No less callous was the part of the road which the people of Cremona had strewn with laurel and roses, after building altars and sacrificing victims in the manner appropriate for a king. These signs of present happiness soon proved devastating to them. Valens and Caecina were there, pointing out the significant locations for the battle: from here

the battleline of the legions had burst forth; from that point the cavalry had attacked; from there the auxiliaries had over-whelmed the enemy.[82] Now each of the tribunes and prefects magnified his own contribution, blending lies with the truth (or an exaggeration of the truth). The ordinary soldiers, too, turned off the high road with shouts of glee, retracing the extent of the fighting and gazing admiringly at the heaps of weapons and piles of corpses. There were indeed some who were moved to tears and pity by the mutability of human life, but not Vitellius. He did not avert his gaze or feel horror at so many thousands of Roman citizens lying there unburied.[83] He was actually happy, and, utterly ignorant about how close his fateful day was, he offered a sacrifice to the gods of the place.

71. Next, a gladiatorial show was put on by Fabius Valens at Bononia after the equipment was brought from Rome. Indeed, the closer the emperor got to the capital, the more riotous his journey became since he was joined by actors, gangs of eunuchs and everything else that was typical of Nero's court. For Vitellius had always been an admirer of Nero, habitually attending the emperor's song recitals, not – like the better sort – under compulsion,[84] but because he was enslaved and bound to luxury and gluttony.

To open up a few spare months of office for Valens and Caecina, Vitellius cut short the consulships of other men, pass-ing over the tenure of Martius Macer because he had been a leader of Otho's party, and postponing the consulship to which Valerius Marinus had been nominated by Galba. Valerius had done nothing to annoy Vitellius, but he was a mild man likely to accept the snub without resentment. The name of Pedanius Costa was omitted from the list because the emperor resented his activities against Nero and support of Verginius, although he put forward other reasons in public. In addition they all thanked Vitellius, a sign of the habitual servility of the time.

72. A masquerade now took place which lasted for no more than a few days, although it caused great excitement at the start. A man had turned up passing himself off as Scribonianus Camerinus[85] and claiming that during the Neronian reign of terror, he had gone into hiding in Histria. This was because in

this area there were still some retainers and estates belonging to the ancient family of the Crassi and respect for their name endured. Therefore after every scoundrel was assigned a role in the plot of the impostor's play, the gullible lower classes, together with some of the troops, eagerly flocked to join him, whether genuinely misled or just bent on causing trouble. That was when the man was brought before Vitellius and asked who on earth he was. After nobody believed his story and he was recognized by his master as a runaway slave called Geta, he was executed in the manner appropriate to slaves.[86]

73. It is scarcely believable to relate how much Vitellius' arrogance and indolence increased when couriers from Syria and Judaea brought word that the East had sworn allegiance to him. For there was nevertheless widespread talk about Vespasian, however vague and unreliable the sources, and Vitellius was generally agitated at any mention of his name. At that point, however, he and his army, as though without a rival, erupted into patterns of behaviour more usually associated with foreigners and marked by savagery, debauchery and plundering.

Vespasian's Imperial Challenge

74. By contrast, Vespasian was pondering war, weapons and the forces available to him far and near.[87] The troops were devoted to him, so much so that when he dictated the oath of allegiance to them and prayed that everything would be favourable for Vitellius, they listened to him in silence. Mucianus, while not unfriendly to Vespasian, was still more attached to Titus. The prefect of Egypt, Tiberius Alexander, had already come to an understanding with him.[88] The Third Legion was counted by Vespasian as his own, since it had crossed into Moesia from Syria.[89] It was hoped that the other legions from Illyricum would follow any lead it gave, as the whole army was incensed by the arrogance of the soldiers coming from Vitellius, who (despite being savage in appearance and talking raucously) derided everyone else as their inferiors. However, men generally hesitate when confronted by the

prospect of such a huge war; and Vespasian was no exception. Excited and optimistic at one moment, at other times he reflected on the dangers. What would that day mean – the day on which he committed his sixty years and two young sons to the hazards of war? In private deliberations a steady advance was possible, and just as people wished, they could advance more boldly or cautiously, depending on how they fared. However, for those pursuing the principate there was no halfway point between the summit and the abyss. 75. There danced before his eyes the strength of the German army, which was of course well known to a military man. He reflected that his own legions had no experience of civil war, while Vitellius' soldiers had been victorious in it; and the beaten side was better supplied with complaints than with military strength. Amidst civil strife, the loyalty of troops was precarious and danger could come from individual men. What was the use of cohorts and cavalry regiments if by a well-timed crime one or two traitors should seek the reward offered from the other side? That was how Scribonianus had been killed during Claudius' principate; that was how his assassin Volaginius was promoted from a common soldier to the highest rank. It was easier to set whole armies in motion than to avoid lone killers!

76. As Vespasian was faltering because of these anxieties, he was being heartened by his legates and friends, including Mucianus. After many confidential discussions, Mucianus now also made an appeal to Vespasian in public along the following lines:[90]

'Everyone who plans some great exploit must reckon whether his initiative is helpful to the state, likely to bring glory to himself, and easy to achieve – or at least not unduly difficult. At the same time the man who gives the advice must be scrutinized carefully to see whether he backs his advice by involving himself in danger, and to establish who is likely to gain the highest distinction if fortune lends her support to the undertaking.

'I call you, Vespasian, to the principate, to take up an office as beneficial to the state as it will be honourable to yourself. By the will of the gods, it has been placed in your hands. Do not

fear what might seem to be mere flattery: it is perhaps closer to
an insult than a compliment to be chosen to succeed Vitellius.
We are not rising in revolt against the very sharp intellect of
the divine Augustus, nor against the supremely wary old age of
Tiberius, nor even against Gaius or Claudius or Nero, a dynasty
put on a firm basis through long rule. You even yielded to
Galba's aristocratic lineage, but any further passivity while our
country is left to suffer inevitable defilement and decay would
seem slothful and cowardly, even if such slavery were as safe
for you as it would be dishonourable. Now the time has gone
and is long past when you could have appeared to covet power.
At the moment the principate is your only refuge. Has Corbulo's
murder slipped your mind?[91] He came from a more distinguished family than either of us, I grant you, but Nero, too,
was more highly born than Vitellius.[92] A fearful ruler regards as
sufficiently illustrious any humble man who makes him afraid.
Besides, Vitellius' own case proves to him that an army can
create an emperor. He was a man with no record of army
service, no military reputation, elevated only by Galba's unpopularity. Not even Otho was beaten by skilful generalship or
a mighty army, but by his own premature despair. Vitellius has
now made his predecessor seem a great and desirable emperor,
given that in the meantime he scatters his legions, disarms his
cohorts and sows fresh seeds of conflict every day. Whatever
keenness and dash his troops had in the past is being steadily
dissipated in eating-houses and revels while they imitate their
emperor. You, Vespasian, can draw on Judaea, Syria and Egypt
for nine fresh legions not sapped by any battle, not infected by
mutiny, with soldiers in good training and victorious in a
foreign war; and you also have strong fleets, cavalry regiments
and cohorts, devoted native kings, and your own experience,
in which you excel all others.

77. 'For myself I shall claim nothing beyond not being
counted below Valens and Caecina. However, you must not
despise Mucianus as an ally because you have not experienced
him as a rival. I rank myself before Vitellius and after you. Your
family can boast the distinction of a triumph and two young
sons, one of whom is already capable of holding power and in

his first years of military career became renowned amongst the German armies. It would be illogical not to yield power to a man whose son I should adopt if I were emperor myself.[93] However, our relative positions will not be the same in success as in failure. For if we win, I will have whatever status you grant me, but before then we will endure the risks and dangers on an equal footing. Actually, no: better still, you should exercise supreme command over your armies, and leave the fighting and uncertainties of battle to me.

'At this moment the defeated are better disciplined than the victors, for their resentment, hatred and thirst for revenge fire them to be courageous, while boredom and insubordination continue to blunt the efficiency of the Vitellians. The war itself will open up and expose the hidden festering wounds of the victorious side. I am relying less on your vigilance, restraint and wisdom than on Vitellius' sloth, ignorance and malice. However, we have better prospects if we declare war than if we kept the peace, for those who plan rebellion are already rebels.'

78. After Mucianus' speech, the rest clustered around Vespasian more confidently, encouraging him and citing the prophecies of soothsayers and the conjunctions of the stars. Vespasian was considerably influenced by such superstitious beliefs, for after he gained supreme power he was the sort of man to retain openly at court a certain Seleucus, an astrologer, as his guide and seer. His thoughts now went back to omens from the past.[94] For instance, a remarkably tall cypress tree on his estate had suddenly toppled over, but on the following day it had sprung up again on the same spot, and in due course it grew just as tall with even broader foliage. The seers were unanimous that this was a notable sign of future prosperity and that Vespasian, still a very young man, was destined for the highest distinction. At first his triumphal awards, the consulship and the renown of his Jewish victory seemed to have provided confirmation of the omen, but once he obtained these honours he began to believe that it was his destiny to hold imperial power.

Between Judaea and Syria lies Carmel.[95] This is what people call the mountain and its god. Yet this god has neither an image

nor a temple (that is the ancient tradition), only an altar and
the reverence of his worshippers. While Vespasian was offering
sacrifice in this place and was turning over in his mind his secret
ambitions, the priest Basilides repeatedly examined the entrails
of the victims and finally said to him: 'Whatever you are planning, Vespasian – be it building a house, enlarging your estate
or engaging more slaves – you will be granted a mighty house,
far-flung boundaries and a host of people.' Rumour had
immediately pounced on this ambiguous statement and was
now starting to reveal its meaning. Indeed, ordinary people
talked of little else. There were more frequent discussions in
Vespasian's company to the extent that optimism always
prompts more grandiose talk. With their resolve strong, they departed, Mucianus going to Antioch and Vespasian to Caesarea.
These are the capitals of Syria and Judaea respectively.

79. The first move to confer imperial power on Vespasian
took place at Alexandria, as Tiberius Alexander speedily got
his legions to swear the new imperial oath on 1 July. This
date was subsequently celebrated as the day of his accession,
although it was on 3 July that the army of Judaea had sworn
the oath before Vespasian with such passion that they would
not even wait for his son Titus, who was returning from Syria,
where he had acted as an intermediary between Mucianus and
his father in their negotiations.

It all happened because of a spontaneous move from the
troops, although no assembly had been prepared and the legions
had not been marshalled. 80. While the party was still looking
for a suitable time and place, and – the most difficult thing in
such a situation – the man to speak first, and while hope and
trepidation, reason and chance passed through their minds, one
day Vespasian came out of his bedroom when a few soldiers
were standing on duty in the usual way to greet him as imperial
governor. However, they saluted him as emperor. Then the rest
rushed up and heaped on him all the imperial titles, including
'Caesar' and 'Augustus'. They all banished fear from their
minds and turned their thoughts to imperial power. Vespasian
himself showed no sign of pride, arrogance or transformed
personality in the face of his transformed situation. As soon as

the dizziness that had blurred his vision after such a great elevation had cleared, he addressed his men in the manner of a soldier and received a whole torrent of congratulations. For in addition, Mucianus, who had been waiting for just this moment, made his eager troops swear loyalty to Vespasian. Then he entered the theatre at Antioch, which those people customarily use for their political meetings, and addressed the crowd which had flocked to the spot with flattering effusiveness. Mucianus was quite a graceful speaker, even in Greek, and was a skilful showman in displaying to advantage whatever he said and did. There was nothing that kindled the province and army more than the fact that Mucianus asserted that Vitellius had decided to transfer the legions of Germany to a lucrative and quiet posting in Syria, while those in Syria were to be moved to the bases in Germany, where the climate was severe and conditions hard.[96] The fact is that even the provincials liked dealing with familiar troops, and many had formed ties of intimacy and kinship with them, while the troops took pleasure in the camp where they had served so long and which felt like home.

81. By 15 July the whole of Syria had sworn allegiance to Vespasian. In addition support came from Sohaemus and his kingdom, whose resources were not to be despised, and Antiochus, who was mighty in ancestral wealth and the richest of the kings offering their services.[97] Then Agrippa was called from Rome by secret messengers from his people and while Vitellius was still in the dark, he had sailed double quick to Vespasian.[98] No less enthusiasm to support the cause was shown by Queen Berenice, who was at the age where her beauty was in full bloom, while even the old man Vespasian was pleased by her generous gifts. Every province located on the seaboard up to and including Asia and Achaia, and the whole Roman territory extending inland towards Pontus and Armenia, swore to support Vespasian, but governors who had no troops at their disposal controlled these lands, since at this date legions had not yet been posted to Cappadocia. A council was held at Berytus to decide the most important issues. To this meeting came Mucianus with his legates and tribunes, as well as his

most distinguished centurions and soldiers and the pick of
the crop from the army of Judaea. The simultaneous array
of infantry and cavalry, and the spectacle of client-kings out-
bidding each other in splendour, immediately created the
impression of imperial grandeur.

82. The first priority of the campaign was to levy troops and
to recall the veterans. Some powerful cities were selected for
the manufacture of armaments, while at Antioch gold and silver
coins were struck. All these measures were rapidly put in hand,
each in the proper place, by appropriate officials. Vespasian
himself made inspections, encouraging efficient men by praise
and spurring on the idle by example rather than correcting
them, more ready to see his friends' merits than their faults. He
honoured many men by making them prefects and procurators,
while he adorned a number with senatorial status. These were
men of exceptional calibre, who would soon obtain the highest
offices, but in some cases luck took the place of merit. As for a
bounty to the troops, Mucianus had only conjured up the
prospect of a modest sum at the initial parade, and even
Vespasian offered no more under conditions of civil war than
other emperors had in peacetime. He was impressively resistant
to bribing the troops and therefore he had a better army.
Ambassadors were sent to Parthia and Armenia, and precautions were taken to protect their backs while the legions
were preoccupied with civil war. It was decided that Titus
should maintain pressure on Judaea while Vespasian should
take hold of Egypt,[99] which was the key to power. Against
Vitellius it seemed adequate to deploy only a part of their forces
with Mucianus as general, given the magic of Vespasian's name
and the irresistible trend of destiny. Letters were written to all
the armies and legates with instructions to entice the praetorians
who hated Vitellius with the prize of readmission to the service.

83. Mucianus set off with his troops in battle-order, behaving
as the emperor's colleague rather than as his subordinate.[100]
Not advancing so slowly as to look as though he was dawdling,
but still not hurrying, he allowed his army's reputation to grow
by mere distance. He realized only too well that his force was
small, but that people form inflated ideas of what they cannot

see for themselves. However, the Sixth Legion and a force of 13,000 men in special detachments were following along behind in a mighty marching column. He had ordered the fleet to sail from the Black Sea to Byzantium, since he was in two minds about the strategy, pondering whether he should bypass Moesia, take Dyrrachium with his infantry and cavalry, and shut off the Adriatic with his warships. This would secure Achaia and Asia behind him, and, as unarmed provinces, they would otherwise be at Vitellius' mercy unless they were reinforced especially. What is more, Vitellius would not know which part of Italy to protect if enemy ships were threatening Brundisium, Tarentum and the coasts of Calabria and Lucania.

84. So the eastern provinces now hummed with the preparation of ships, soldiers and weapons, but nothing exhausted them as much as the financial levy. Mucianus kept on saying that money formed the sinews of civil war, and in judicial inquiries he had no regard for the principles of law or truth, but only the lavishness of a man's resources. Informers were everywhere, and all the richest men were seized as plunder. These burdens were grievous and intolerable, but measures which could be excused by the needs of war continued to be imposed even in peacetime, since, while Vespasian himself over the early stages of his principate was not exactly determined to maintain unjust practices, he learned the knack from indulgent fortune and wicked advisers, and became daring. Mucianus also helped the war effort with his own fortune, but his lavish expenditure of private means only meant that he could help himself to public money even more liberally. Others followed his lead in contributing their wealth, but very few had the same opportunities to recoup themselves.

85. Meanwhile, Vespasian's initial plans were accelerated by the eagerness with which the army of Illyricum joined his party.[101] The Third Legion set an example to the other forces in Moesia, namely the Eighth Augustan and the Seventh Claudian Legions, who were deeply devoted to Otho, although they had not been on hand for the battle of Bedriacum. After advancing as far as Aquileia, they attacked the messengers who brought news of Otho's defeat and tore up the colours which displayed

the name of Vitellius, finally seizing the camp funds and dividing them among themselves. They had behaved in a thoroughly hostile manner. As a result they became afraid, but fear generated a plan that credit could be claimed with Vespasian for conduct which would require an apology before Vitellius. So the three legions in Moesia wrote letters inviting the Pannonian army to join their cause, but they also prepared to use force in the event of a refusal. In this fluid situation, Aponius Saturninus, the governor of Moesia, dared to commit an appalling crime. He sent a centurion to assassinate the legate of the Seventh Legion, Tettius Julianus. The motive was a private dispute, camouflaged as a bid to help the Flavian cause. Julianus discovered he was in danger, and, seeking help from locals who knew the area intimately, made his escape through the trackless wilds of Moesia and travelled beyond Mount Haemus. From then on he took no part in the civil war, spinning out his journey to Vespasian by various means, and either loitering or hurrying forward according to the latest news.

86. In Pannonia, however, the Thirteenth and Seventh Galbian Legions, maintaining their resentful fury about the battle of Bedriacum, promptly declared for Vespasian, being influenced in particular by Antonius Primus.[102] This man had been found guilty before the laws and in Nero's principate was convicted of fraud. It was one of the unfortunate results of civil war that he had managed to recover his senatorial rank. After being put in charge of the Seventh Legion by Galba, he was believed to have written more than once to Otho, offering himself as a general for the party, but he was ignored and played no practical part in the Othonian campaign. As Vitellius' power crumbled, he switched his allegiance to Vespasian and added tremendous force to the campaign. Physically energetic and a ready talker, he made an art of cultivating hatred against other men and was a powerful force with regard to riots and mutinies; a grasping crook who gave out bribes, he was a scoundrel in peacetime, but a force to be reckoned with in war.

After that the united front of the armies of Moesia and Pannonia drew in the troops from Dalmatia, although their consular legates were by no means actively rebellious. Pannonia and Dalmatia were governed respectively by Tampius Flavianus and Pompeius Silvanus, who were rich and elderly, but there was also the imperial agent Cornelius Fuscus, who was in the prime of life and came from a good family.[103] In early youth Fuscus had resigned from the senatorial order through his desire to pass up an official career. All the same, he was the leading force in getting his colony to support Galba, and for his services he won the office of procurator. Once he had rallied to the Flavian side, he applied the strongest torch to the war. Exulting less in the rewards generated by danger than in danger for its own sake, he preferred a novel and hazardous gamble over what was certain and long established. So the Flavians proceeded to stir and shake elements anywhere that were tottering. Letters were written to the Fourteenth Legion in Britain and the First in Spain, because both had supported Otho and opposed Vitellius. Messages were sprinkled throughout the Gaulish provinces, and in an instant a mighty war was ablaze, as the legions of Illyricum were in open revolt and the rest were likely to follow their lead if they proved successful.

Vitellius in Rome

87. While this was what Vespasian and his generals were doing in the provinces, Vitellius was becoming more despicable and lazy every day, stopping to enjoy all the delightful towns and country houses as he headed towards Rome with a ponderous marching-column. In his wake followed 60,000 armed men, ruined by loose discipline. The number of soldiers' attendants was even larger, together with the camp-followers, who were particularly undisciplined even by the standard of slaves. The vast escort of officers and friends was not cut out for obedience, even if it had been controlled by the strictest discipline. The unwieldy mob was further encumbered by the senators and knights who came out from the city to meet it. Some came because they were afraid, many wanted to engage in flattery, while the rest, and in due course all of them, joined in because they did not want to be left behind. Men from the low-born populace also flocked to join the column: these jokers, actors

and charioteers were known to Vitellius through their degrading services and he took remarkable pleasure in these ignoble
friendships. It was not only the colonies and the towns that
were being devastated to furnish supplies: the very farmers and
the fields now ready for harvest were being stripped bare, as if
this were enemy soil.

88. There were many vicious fights among the troops, for the
legionaries and auxiliaries still did not see eye to eye after the
original outburst at Ticinum,[104] although when they had to
fight civilians they agreed well enough. Yet the worst slaughter
took place at a point seven miles from Rome. Vitellius was
distributing cooked food among the individual soldiers there as
if he were fattening up a lot of gladiators, and the common
people had poured out from the capital and were milling
about everywhere in the camp. In what passed with the likes of
them for wit, some people disarmed the oblivious soldiers by
cutting off their belts surreptitiously and kept on asking the
soldiers whether they were wearing their swords. The soldiers
were not used to being made fun of and took the joke badly,
attacking the unarmed populace with their swords. Among
other casualties, the father of one of the soldiers was killed
while accompanying his son. Then he was recognized, and as
news of his murder spread they held back from attacking innocent people.

However, there was panic in Rome, as the first soldiers to
arrive were dashing about everywhere. They made chiefly for
the Forum, in their desire to see the spot where Galba had
fallen. No less grim was the spectacle they themselves presented,
as they bristled with shaggy animal hides and huge weapons.
Not being used to crowds, they made little effort to avoid
collisions, and sometimes fell over because the street was slippery or someone had got in their way, whereupon they became
abusive and soon used their fists and swords. Furthermore,
their tribunes and prefects were flitting about everywhere with
terrifying squadrons of armed men.

89. Vitellius himself, after crossing the Milvian Bridge[105]
mounted on a fine horse, wearing a general's cloak and kitted
out with a sword, drove the senate and people before him.

However, his entourage deterred him from entering Rome as if it were a conquered city; so he exchanged his uniform for a bordered toga and marched on foot before a carefully arranged column. Four legionary eagles surrounded by four banners representing the other legions formed the front. After that came twelve cavalry standards and the serried ranks of the infantry, followed by the cavalry. Then followed thirty-four auxiliary cohorts arranged according to their nationality or type of equipment. In front of the eagles went the camp prefects, the tribunes and senior centurions wearing white, while the other centurions were marching with their respective companies and shone with weapons and decorations. The troops, too, were resplendent in their medals and honorific collars. It was a noble sight, and an army worthy of an emperor – though not when that emperor was Vitellius. In this way he entered the Capitol and there embraced his mother and honoured her with the title 'Augusta'.

90. On the following day he delivered a boastful speech about himself as if he were addressing the senate and people of a foreign state, extolling his own energy and restraint, despite the fact that those present were well aware of his scandalous behaviour, as was all of Italy through which he had made his shameful way in sloth and luxury. However, the carefree people, unable to distinguish between what was false and true, and thoroughly versed in the customary flatteries, shouted and yelled their approval, and although Vitellius rejected the title 'Augustus', they compelled him to assume it. The acceptance was as pointless as the refusal.

91. In a city which puts an interpretation on everything, it was regarded as a deadly omen that Vitellius took up the office of Pontifex Maximus on 18 July and issued a decree concerning public worship. This date has long been considered unlucky because it is the anniversary of the disasters on the Cremera and the Allia.[106] He was that ignorant about all civil and religious precedent, but his friends and freedmen were just as complacent, and he used to transact business as if surrounded by drunkards. However, at the consular elections he canvassed with his candidates like a common citizen, and courted constant talk from the dregs of the people by appearing at the theatre as

a member of the audience and at the racecourse as a punter. This behaviour would indeed have been graceful and democratic had it been prompted by virtuous impulses, but the memory of his past life deprived it of honour and value.

He habitually attended the senate even when the agenda was about trivial matters. Once it happened that the praetor-designate, Helvidius Priscus, made a proposal which conflicted with the emperor's own wishes.[107] Vitellius was put out at first, but he did nothing more than summon the tribunes of the people to come to the aid of his scorned authority. In due course when his friends, who feared his deeper resentment, were trying to soothe him, Vitellius remarked that there was nothing unusual in a difference of opinion between two senators on a matter of politics and that he himself had often opposed even Thrasea.[108] Most people laughed at the impertinence of this comparison, but others found it pleasing that he had chosen Thrasea and not one of the powerful political giants as the pattern of true glory.

92. To command the praetorians he had selected Publilius Sabinus, who had been prefect of an auxiliary cohort,[109] and Julius Priscus, at the moment a centurion. Priscus flourished through Valens' support, while Sabinus prospered with Caecina's help. In this conflict between rivals, Vitellius was a mere pawn: Caecina and Valens in fact carried out the functions of government. They had long been wary of one another, but the dishonesty of friends and a city prolific in generating quarrels had sharpened their mutual hatred, which had barely been concealed in the camp during the war. They competed and courted comparison by their ostentatious retinues and the huge columns attending their morning receptions, while Vitellius leaned now towards one, now the other. For power is never completely trustworthy, even when it is excessive. As Vitellius alternated between suddenly taking offence and untimely flat-teries, they felt contempt, but feared him at the same time. Yet they had not for that reason been any slower to seize mansions, parks and the riches of the empire, although the tearful and destitute crowd of nobles who had been allowed by Galba to return home from exile with their children got no pity or assist-

ance from the emperor. One measure welcome to the leading men of the state, and also endorsed by the people, was that Vitellius had allowed returned exiles to resume rights over their freedmen, although these wily creatures tried in every way to get around the edict by concealing their money in the pockets of obscure or ambitious men.[110] Some of them passed into the imperial household and became more powerful than their former masters.

93. As for the soldiers, the barracks were packed, so an overflowing crowd of men camped in colonnades or temples and roamed around the whole city. There was no question of parades, proper sentry duty or a training programme. Amid the lures of the capital and pursuits too shocking to be described, they were ruining their physique by idleness and their morale by debauchery. Finally, careless of life itself, a great number camped in the unhealthy Vatican district, as a result of which death frequently descended on the throngs of soldiers. Since the Tiber was flowing near at hand, the Germans and Gauls, who are in any case susceptible to illness, damaged their health in their eagerness for the river because they were unable to bear the heat. What is more, the organization of military service was thrown into confusion by misguided policy or corruption. Sixteen praetorian and four urban cohorts were being formed, each to consist of a thousand men.[111] Valens was more audacious in levying these troops because he felt that it was he who had saved Caecina from danger. It is true that Valens' arrival had bolstered the Vitellians, and the bad name he had won by marching so slowly had been effaced by victory. In any case, all the troops from Lower Germany were enthusiastic devotees of Valens, as a result of which it is believed that Caecina's loyalty first began to deteriorate.

94. However, Vitellius' indulgence towards his generals was nothing compared with the licence he allowed his soldiers. Each man chose his division of service for himself. Anyone, however undeserving, was enrolled in the urban garrison if that was his preference. On the other hand, really good soldiers were permitted to stay with the legions or cavalry if they so desired. There was no dearth of such volunteers among those who were

worn out with sickness and blamed the extremes of the Italian climate. Nevertheless, the legions and cavalry lost their strongest elements, and the prestige of the urban units was shattered, after 20,000 men were randomly recruited from the whole army rather than carefully chosen for service.

While Vitellius was making a speech to the soldiers, a demand was raised for the execution of the Gallic leaders Asiaticus, Flavus and Rufinus on the grounds that they had fought for Vindex. Vitellius made no effort to curb outcries of this sort. Quite apart from his natural indolence, he was aware that the gratuity for the soldiers was almost upon him and that he had no money, so he lavished every other sort of concession on the troops. The freedmen of leading citizens were ordered to pay a kind of extraordinary tax which was proportionate to the number of their slaves. Vitellius himself was concerned only with wasting money. He constructed stables for his charioteers, filled the circus with gladiatorial and wild beast shows, and frittered away his money as if it were a boom time.

95. Moreover, Caecina and Valens celebrated Vitellius' birthday by giving gladiatorial shows throughout the city, in every district, on a lavish scale unknown before that day.[112] It delighted the rabble, but earned the contempt of good men that the emperor had set up altars in the Campus Martius and made ritual funeral offerings to Nero, after sacrificial victims were slaughtered and burnt at public expense. The torch was applied to the pyre by the Augustales, a college of priests which Tiberius Caesar had instituted for the worship of the Julian clan, in imitation of Romulus' foundation in honour of King Tatius.[113]

Four months had not yet elapsed since the victory, yet Vitellius' freedman Asiaticus had already rivalled the efforts of Polyclitus, Patrobius and the hated names of the past. Nobody in that court sought distinction by honesty or hard work. The one route to power was to try to gratify the insatiable appetites of Vitellius with lavish banquets, expenditure and gluttonous meals. The emperor himself was more than happy if he enjoyed the present without considering the longer term. It is believed that he squandered 900 million sesterces within a very few months. Mighty and wretched, Rome had endured an Otho and a Vitellius in the same year and suffered every variety of humiliations at the hands of men like Vinius, Fabius, Icelus and Asiaticus, until finally Mucianus and Marcellus succeeded them – fresh faces rather than a new outlook.

96. The defection of the Third Legion was the first to be announced to Vitellius, after Aponius Saturninus sent a letter with the news before he, too, joined Vespasian's side. However, Aponius had not described everything that had happened, since he was wavering at this sudden development, and Vitellius' flattering friends played down the news. Only one legion was mutinous, they assured him, but the other armies were unshakably loyal. Vitellius gave a speech to the soldiers along just the same lines, blaming the recently discharged praetorians who were spreading false rumours and emphatically asserting that there was no reason to fear civil war. Any reference to Vespasian was censored, and troops patrolled the city to stop people gossiping. This offered ample fuel to encourage rumours.

97. However, Vitellius summoned reinforcements from Germany, Britain and the Spanish provinces, but he did so sluggishly and pretending that there was no need for urgency. The governors and provinces were just as slow to act. Hordeonius Flaccus suspected the Batavians by now and was alarmed at a possible war of his own, while under Vettius Bolanus, Britain was never peaceful enough; and each man's loyalty was in doubt.[114] Nor did the Spanish provinces make any haste, as there was no consular governor there at the time. The three legionary commanders held equal authority, and while they would have bent over backwards to please Vitellius if he had looked like winning, they all kept their distance from his misfortunes. In Africa, the legion there, together with the auxiliary cohorts recruited by Clodius Macer and later disbanded by Galba, were marshalled again at Vitellius' command, and at the same time the remaining men of military age signed on promptly. This was because Vitellius had been an upright and popular proconsul there, but Vespasian had been notorious and hated.[115] So the provincials speculated that they would display the same qualities as emperors, but experience proved them wrong. 98. Indeed, at first the legate Valerius Festus

faithfully backed up the enthusiastic provincials, but he soon
began to waver. In official correspondence and proclamations
he supported Vitellius, but was in secret contact with Vespasian,
intending to use in his defence one set of exchanges or the other,
depending on which strengthened his position. In various parts
of Raetia and the Gallic provinces, some soldiers and centurions
were arrested in possession of letters and proclamations of
Vespasian. They were sent to Vitellius and put to death. Most
escaped capture after being hidden by loyal friends or their
own cunning ruses. In this way, Vitellius' preparations became
known, but Vespasian's plans for the most part remained un-
disclosed. This was partly due to Vitellius' slackness, but also
to the fact that the garrisons occupying the Pannonian Alps
detained all messengers. Also, thanks to the Etesian winds, the
sea favoured those sailing eastwards, but hampered the voyage
in the opposite direction.[116]

99. Vitellius finally ordered Caecina and Valens to mobilize
for war when he became terrified at the prospect of an enemy
invasion amidst alarming news on all sides. Caecina was sent
on ahead, but Valens was just getting back on his feet after a
severe illness and was being slowed down by his convales-
cence.[117] The appearance of the German army as it left Rome
was vastly different from before. There was no physical vigour,
no passion in their hearts; the column was slow and straggling,
their weapons were being carried any old how, their horses
were sluggish. The soldiers could not endure sun, dust or hot
weather, and as their ability to put up with hard work was
blunted, so their readiness for making trouble grew. In addition
to these problems, there was Caecina. He had always courted
popularity, but was now gripped by something new – apathy.
Excessive indulgence in the spoils of power had turned him
into a flabby hedonist, or, perhaps for someone contemplating
treachery, sapping the army's morale was just another trick.
Many believed that Caecina's loyalty was undermined by the
strategy of Flavius Sabinus, with Rubrius Gallus acting as the
go-between in their negotiations and promising that any conditions agreed for changing sides would be validated by
Vespasian. At the same time, Caecina was also reminded of the

dislike and jealousy he felt for Fabius Valens. If his rival stood higher with Vitellius, Caecina could always win influence and power by courting a new emperor.

100. After an embrace from Vitellius and much courteous treatment, Caecina set off and sent on part of his cavalry in advance to occupy Cremona. Next came units from the First, Fourth, Fifteenth and Sixteenth Legions, then the Fifth and Twenty-Second. The rearguard was formed of the Twenty-First Hurricane and First Italian Legions, accompanied by detachments from the three British legions and selected auxiliaries. Once Caecina had gone, Fabius Valens wrote to the army which he himself had commanded to wait for him on the march. This, he said, was what he had agreed on with Caecina. However, Caecina was on the spot and had more influence, so he pretended that this plan had been changed in order that they could confront the impending war with their full strength. Thus the legions made haste, some with orders to head for Cremona, others for Hostilia. Caecina himself made a diversion to Ravenna, ostensibly to address the fleet. Later, it became clear that he had sought a secret interview for concocting treachery. For Lucilius Bassus, after commanding a cavalry regiment, had been appointed by Vitellius as admiral of both the Ravenna and Misenum fleets, but because he had not at once been made praetorian prefect, he quite unjustifiably took umbrage and was now planning this scandalous betrayal as his revenge.[118] It is impossible to be sure whether Bassus induced Caecina to desert, or whether (since it often happens that bad men resemble each other) the same wicked impulse drove them both on. 101. The historians of the time who wrote accounts of this war during the Flavian dynasty have referred to 'concern for peace' and 'patriotism', twisting their explanations for the sake of flattery.[119] My own view is that in addition to the pair's innate fickleness and the low regard in which their loyalty was held after betraying Galba, they were apparently also prompted by their rivalry and jealousy to ruin Vitellius himself, in case other men outpaced them in his affections.

After catching up with the legions, Caecina used various devices to undermine the obstinate devotion to Vitellius of the centurions and troops. Bassus had less difficulty in engineering a similar plot, since the fleet was ready at the least impulse to change its allegiance because it remembered its recent service on behalf of Otho.

BOOK 3

The Second Battle of Bedriacum

1. Under a luckier star and with more loyal supporters, the leaders of the Flavian party were shaping the plans for their campaign. They had met at Poetovio, the winter-quarters of the Thirteenth Legion. There they debated whether to resolve to close the Pannonian Alps and wait until all their forces were massed behind them, or whether it would show more spirit to grapple with the enemy and struggle to win Italy. Those who thought they should wait for reinforcements and drag out the war stressed the power and reputation of the German legions and the fact that the backbone of the British army had arrived more recently with Vitellius. They, on the other hand, did not have the same number of legions and had recently been defeated. For all their bluster, beaten troops were inevitably inferior in morale. However, if in the meantime they held the Alps, Mucianus would arrive with the forces of the East. Moreover, Vespasian controlled the sea and the fleets, as well as enjoying the support of the provinces. Thanks to these, he could set in motion the massive machinery for what would virtually be a second war. So, a salutary delay would mean the presence of new forces, without losing any of their current ones.

2. In reply to these arguments, Antonius Primus, who was the keenest advocate of war, urged that speed would help their own cause but be deadly for Vitellius. Victory had made Vitellius' forces lazier, not more confident, for they were not kept in a state of readiness in their barracks. In all the towns of Italy, they sat around in idleness, men to be feared only by their hosts, and the more ferociously they had acted before, the more greedily did they wolf down unaccustomed pleasures. In

addition they had been softened up by the circus, the theatres and the charms of the capital, and they were exhausted by illnesses.[1] Given a breathing space, however, even they would recover their toughness under training for war. Germany, the source of their strength, was not far away. Britain was only separated by a narrow body of water. The Gallic and Spanish provinces were close at hand, and from both came men, horses and money. Then there was Italy itself and the wealth of Rome. Finally, if the Vitellians wanted to take the offensive, they could rely on two fleets and a free run of the Adriatic. What good would the barricade of the Alps be then? Why should they drag out the fighting into the next summer? Where, meanwhile, were the Flavians to get money and supplies? Surely it would be better to profit from the very fact that the Pannonian legions had been cheated of victory rather than beaten in fair fight and were eager to get their own back, while the powerful armies of Moesia would come fresh to the attack?[2] If one counted men rather than legions, their own side was the stronger and unsullied by indulging in pleasures. Besides, their very humiliation had helped discipline. The cavalry, furthermore, had not been beaten even at Bedriacum. Despite a difficult situation it had scattered Vitellius' front-line.[3] 'On that occasion,' Antonius exclaimed, 'two Pannonian and Moesian cavalry regiments cut their way through the enemy: now sixteen will mass their colours and by their impact and din, by the very clouds of dust they raise, will bury and overwhelm riders and horses that have forgotten battle. Unless someone holds me back, at one and the same time I will both give the advice and carry out the plan. You, gentlemen, who are keeping your options open, hold back the legions! Lightly armed auxiliary cohorts will be sufficient for my purposes. Soon you shall hear that the gates of Italy have been unlocked and Vitellius' fortunes shattered. You will be glad enough to follow, and tread in the footsteps of the victor.'

3. These and similar remarks Antonius poured out with flashing eyes and strident voice, so as to be audible over a wider area (for the centurions and some of the soldiers had joined the meeting). The result was that he swept even cautious and

wary officers off their feet, while the ordinary soldiers and the others hailed Antonius as the one real man and leader, spurning the sluggishness of the other generals. This indeed was the reputation he had already won at the initial meeting when Vespasian's letter was read out. He had not, like the majority of the speakers, confined his remarks to ambiguities which he could later construe to suit events, but he was felt to have committed himself openly, and to that extent he carried greater weight with the troops as their partner in crime – or glory.

4. After Antonius, the most influential officer was the procurator Cornelius Fuscus.[4] He, too, made a habit of criticizing Vitellius bitterly and had left no escape route for himself if things went wrong. Then there was Tampius Flavianus. By nature dilatory in his old age, he was distrusted by the troops, who suspected that he had not forgotten that he was a relative of Vitellius. Moreover, by fleeing when the legions first became turbulent and then returning of his own free will, he was believed to have sought an excuse for treachery. For, after resigning command of Pannonia, Flavianus took himself off to the safety of Italy, but then his desire for revolution had induced him to resume the title of governor and join in the civil war. Cornelius Fuscus was the man persuading him to act – not that Fuscus needed such dynamism as Flavianus could offer, but he felt that the renown of an ex-consul should lend the incipient Flavian movement an air of respectability.

5. However, in order to transfer operations to Italy safely and efficiently, written instructions were sent to Aponius Saturninus to move up quickly with the army of Moesia, and in case the now-defenceless provinces should be left open to threats from the barbarian tribes, the rulers of the Sarmatian Iazyges,[5] who hold absolute power in their community, were enrolled in the Flavian army. They also offered to raise a mass levy and to supply a force of cavalry, their one effective arm, but the contribution was rejected for fear that during the dissensions they might engineer a foreign war or abandon their obligation and honour if offered greater rewards by the other side. The Flavians secured the support of the Suebian kings, Sido and Italicus,[6] who had shown long-standing compliance to Rome

and whose people were more ready to keep faith than to break it. Auxiliary forces were posted on the army's flank facing Raetia, which was hostile and whose governor Porcius Septiminus was a staunch adherent of Vitellius. This was why Sextilius Felix, together with the Aurian cavalry regiment and some auxiliary detachments from Noricum, was sent to hold the bank of the River Aenus, which forms the boundary between Raetia and Noricum. Neither side tried its hand at battle here and the success of the Flavians was decided elsewhere.

6. Antonius began his lightning invasion of Italy with some detachments from the cohorts and a part of the cavalry. He was accompanied by Arrius Varus, a vigorous military man whose reputation had been enhanced by service under Corbulo and successes in Armenia.[7] Yet he was also said to have denounced Corbulo's integrity in the course of private conversations with Nero. As a result of this discreditable action, he ingratiated himself with the emperor and earned himself the post of senior centurion, but although these dubious prizes made him happy for the present, they later came to ruin him.

However, Primus and Varus occupied Aquileia, and in the neighbouring towns, and at Opitergium and Altinum, they were warmly welcomed. A garrison was left at Altinum against a possible threat from the Ravenna fleet, whose defection had not yet been heard about.[8] After that, Patavium and Ateste joined the cause. At the latter place it was learnt that three Vitellian cohorts and a regiment of cavalry (the Sebosian) had encamped at Forum Alieni[9] after building a bridge there. This seemed a good chance to strike at an unwary foe, for that too was in the report. At first light the Flavians fell upon the enemy while they were still mostly unarmed. Instructions had been given that only a few should be killed and the rest frightened into changing sides; and in fact some surrendered immediately, although the majority managed to halt the enemy's advance by cutting the bridge.

7. When this victory became public knowledge and the first engagement in the war was seen to have been decided in favour of the Flavians, the Seventh (Galbian) and Thirteenth (Twin) Legions, with the latter's commander Vedius Aquila, moved

briskly to Patavium. There a few days were spent resting, and Minicius Justus, the camp prefect of the Seventh Legion, a disciplinarian who kept the troops on too tight a rein for civil war, was rescued from the anger of his troops and sent to Vespasian. A long-desired step was then taken, and indeed the positive comment it aroused lent it an exaggerated prestige. Antonius gave orders that the portraits of Galba, which had been overthrown due to the civil wars, should be restored to honour in all the towns. He believed that it would enhance their cause if people believed that the Flavians approved of Galba's principate and that his followers were regaining influence.

8. The next question was the selection of a base. Verona seemed preferable because the open territory around it lent itself to cavalry combat, in which the Flavians excelled. Moreover, to deprive Vitellius of a rich city seemed a practical step and good propaganda. Vicetia was occupied as the troops passed through. This was a small incident given the modest resources of the town, but significant in the eyes of observers who reflected that Caecina was born there and that the enemy commander had thus lost control of his native place. Verona was a real prize. Its people helped the Flavian cause by their example and material support: and the army, by inserting itself between Raetia and the Julian Alps, had established a blockade so that there was no way through for the German forces by that route.

These steps were taken either without Vespasian's knowledge or else against his instructions. For his orders were to halt the advance at Aquileia and to wait for Mucianus, and he re-inforced his command by an explanation of his strategy. Now that he had at his disposal both Egypt, which held the key to the corn supply, and the revenues of the richest provinces, Vitellius' army could be forced to its knees by lack of pay and supplies.[10] Mucianus gave the same advice in repeated letters. He put up a good smoke-screen by advocating a bloodless victory without casualties and so on, but in fact he was hungry for glory and keen to monopolize all the prestige of the war. Yet, because of the great distances involved, official instructions tended to arrive after events had already happened.

9. . . . .[11] so by a sudden assault Antonius overran the enemy

outposts, and after a small skirmish which put the fighting spirit of the combatants to the test, both sides disengaged on an even basis. After this, Caecina set up a fortified camp between Hostilia (a village in the territory of Verona) and the marshes of the River Tartaro, choosing a safe spot protected in the rear by a river[12] and on the flanks by a barrier of marshland. Had he been a loyal general, he could have used his concentrated Vitellian forces to crush the two enemy legions not yet reinforced by the army of Moesia; or else he could have driven back the Flavians and inflicted on them an ignominious retreat and the evacuation of Italy. However, Caecina contrived various delays and allowed the enemy to gain the initiative in the opening phases of the campaign. All the while he denounced in official dispatches an army which it was quite feasible to rout by force of arms until such a time as he could secure his treacherous deal with the enemy by means of his emissaries. During this lull, Aponius Saturninus arrived on the scene with the Seventh (Claudian) Legion, which was commanded by Vipstanus Messalla, a distinguished man from a famous family, and the only one to contribute an element of integrity to this campaign.[13] This then was the force – far inferior to the Vitellians and still only numbering three legions – to which Caecina sent his letters criticizing the folly of fighting for lost causes. At the same time, he lavishly praised the valour of the German army, seldom mentioning Vitellius and only in a perfunctory way, while refraining from all abuse of Vespasian. There was absolutely nothing here either to entice or to frighten the enemy. In their reply, the Flavian commanders made no attempt to justify their earlier defeat, but spoke up valiantly for Vespasian and boldly for their cause, expressing confidence in their army and displaying undisguised hostility towards Vitellius, although his tribunes and centurions were offered the hope of retaining any favours he had granted, and Caecina himself was openly encouraged to desert. Reading out this correspondence publicly in the parade-ground raised Flavian morale, since Caecina's tone was meek, as if he were afraid to offend Vespasian, whereas their own officers had written expressing their scorn and appeared to be insulting Vitellius.

10. When in due course two more Flavian legions appeared – the Third, led by Dillius Aponianus, and the Eighth, led by Numisius Lupus – they decided to make a show of strength and provide Verona with an outer rampart. The task of building this rampart on the side facing the enemy happened to fall to the Galbian Legion, and when some allied cavalry were spotted in the distance and taken to be enemies, this caused a false alarm. Fearing treachery, the legionaries grabbed weapons and turned the full weight of their anger on Tampius Flavianus. There was no proof for their accusation, but he had long been unpopular, and in a barrage of shouting they demanded his death. They screamed that here was a relative of Vitellius, a traitor against Otho, and the crook who had taken their bounty! He had no chance to defend himself, although he stretched out his hands in supplication, almost prostrate on the ground, his clothes torn, his chest heaving and his lips quivering with inarticulate sobs. This in itself spurred on the hostile men, for they took his excessive panic to be the sign of a guilty con-science. When Aponius tried to speak to them, his words were engulfed amidst the yelling men. They rebuffed other officers with jeers and shouts. To Antonius alone the soldiers' ears were open, for he was not only eloquent and had the knack of soothing a mob, but he also inspired respect as a leader. When the mutiny began to get out of hand and the troops passed from abuse and insult to arms and action, he ordered Flavianus to be put in chains. The soldiers saw through the farce, and scat-tering the guards around the officers' platform, they prepared for a lynching. Antonius put himself in their way with drawn sword and swore that he would die either at his troops' hands or his own. Whenever he saw a soldier known to him personally and wearing some decoration for valour, he appealed to him by name for help. Then, turning to the standards and the gods of war,[14] he prayed that they might inflict such fury and discord upon the armies of the enemy instead. Gradually the mutiny began to peter out, and with the gathering dusk the men slipped off to their separate tents. Flavianus left the same night, and after encountering a messenger bearing a letter from Vespasian, his danger came to an end.[15]

11. The rot was infectious, for the legionaries now attacked Aponius Saturninus, who commanded the forces from Moesia, and they did so all the more violently because their tempers had flared up at midday – not, as previously, in the evening, when they were exhausted by the physical labour of digging. The cause was the circulation of some correspondence which Saturninus was believed to have written to Vitellius. Although Roman soldiers had once competed in courage and discipline, now their rivalry was in insolence and insubordination – they wanted to be sure that they bayed for Aponius' blood no less violently than for Flavianus' life. The Moesian legionaries remembered that they had assisted the men of Pannonia to settle scores, while the Pannonian troops felt that the mutiny of others excused their own and so were happy to commit a second offence. They made for the mansion in which Saturninus was staying.[16] Primus, Aponianus and Messalla did their best, but it was not so much their efforts that saved Saturninus as the dark hiding place in which he was skulking – he had concealed himself in the furnace-house of some baths which happened to be empty. Afterwards, he got rid of his lictors and escaped to Patavium. Thanks to the departure of the two consular governors, Antonius alone now had effective control of both armies, for his colleagues yielded to him and the troops backed him with enthusiasm. There were some people who believed that Antonius had incited both these mutinies in order to enjoy sole command over the campaign.

12. On the Vitellian side, too, the mood was unsettled. Here the turmoil was even more fatal, since it sprang less from the suspicions of the men than from the treachery of their leaders. Lucilius Bassus commanded the Ravenna fleet, whose men were wavering, since many came from Dalmatia and Pannonia, and these provinces were now held by Vespasian. So the admiral had brought them over to the Flavian cause. Night-time was chosen for the act of treachery, so that the conspirators could meet in the headquarters building by themselves without the knowledge of the others. Bassus himself, whether he was ashamed or afraid of how the plot would turn out, was waiting for the end result in his house. During a chaotic outbreak, the

naval captains attacked the portraits of Vitellius, and when the few who offered resistance had been cut down, the rest of the men, who were keen on a change, came over to Vespasian. That was when Lucilius Bassus appeared and publicly put himself at the head of the movement. However, the marines chose Cornelius Fuscus, who had speedily hurried to the base, as their commander. As for Bassus, he was put under open arrest and taken in a fast flotilla as far as Atria. Here he was imprisoned by Memmius Rufinus,[17] who commanded a regiment of cavalry in the town, but his chains were promptly struck off by the intervention of the imperial freedman Hormus: he, too, was regarded as one of the generals.

13. To return to Caecina: when the defection of the fleet became known, he summoned to headquarters the senior centurions and a few of the soldiers, seizing upon a time when the camp was empty and the rest of the troops were scattered on their various duties. There he spoke highly of Vespasian's valour and the strength of his followers, whereas on their side, he pointed out, the fleet had changed allegiance, supplies were short, the Gallic and Spanish provinces hostile and Rome was thoroughly unreliable. He put a pessimistic spin on every aspect of Vitellius' position. Then, as those who were in the plot took the lead in swearing allegiance to Vespasian, Caecina made the others do the same while they were still shocked by the sudden turn of events. At the same time, Vitellius' portraits were torn down and the news sent to Antonius. However, the treasonable act became the talk of the entire camp, and as the men rushed back to the headquarters building they saw that Vespasian's name had been written up and Vitellius' portraits thrown down. At first, there was a great menacing hush, then one great explosion of protest. Had the dignity of the German army sunk so low, they cried, that without a battle, without a single blow, they were tamely to put their hands into chains and surrender their weapons to the captors? After all, what sort of legions could the other side muster? Surely these were beaten men? Besides, the only strong formations in Otho's army, the First and Fourteenth, were not there, although even these they had routed and cut to pieces on those very plains. Were many

thousands of armed men to be handed over as a gift to the outlaw Antonius, like a gang of slaves bought and sold in the market? It seemed that eight legions were to be the appendage of one miserable fleet! That was what Bassus wanted, that was what Caecina wanted – after stealing palaces, villas and fortunes from Vitellius, they were now determined to rob the troops of their emperor, and the emperor of his troops! Unscathed and unscarred, cheap even in the eyes of the Flavians, what would they say to those who legitimately demanded to see the balance sheet of victory or defeat?[18]

14. Such were the cries of indignation that sprang from one and all. Following the lead given by the Fifth Legion, they restored the portraits of Vitellius, put Caecina in chains, elected as their leaders Fabius Fabullus, commanding officer of the Fifth, and Cassius Longus, the prefect of the camp, and massacred the crews of three galleys who chanced to cross their path, ignorant and innocent of what had happened. Then, after abandoning their camp and cutting the bridge,[19] they marched back to Hostilia and from there to Cremona to join the First Italian and Twenty-First Hurricane Legions, which Caecina had sent ahead with part of the cavalry to hold Cremona.

15. When news of this reached Antonius, he decided to attack the enemy forces while they were still emotionally unbalanced and their resources were separated. He could not wait until their leaders recovered their hold and the troops their discipline, or until a rendezvous restored confidence. He reckoned that Fabius Valens had left Rome and would increase his pace on learning of Caecina's betrayal; and Fabius was faithful to Vitellius, as well as being a talented general. At the same time, the possible advance of large masses of Germans through Raetia was a frightening thought. As a matter of fact, Vitellius had indeed called for reinforcements from Britain, Gaul and Spain, presaging a war of boundless havoc, but Antonius, fearing this very possibility,[20] snatched a timely victory by forcing an engagement. After two days' march from Verona, he arrived at Bedriacum with his whole army. On the next day,[21] keeping his legions back to entrench camp, he sent his auxiliary cohorts into the territory of Cremona, ostensibly to forage, but actually

to acquire a taste for plundering Roman civilians. He himself, with 4,000 cavalry, advanced to a point eight miles from Bedriacum so that they could indulge in devastation with more freedom. The scouts, as usual, rushed on ahead.

16. It was about eleven in the morning when a rider galloped up with the news that the enemy was approaching, headed by a small advance party, and movement and tumult could be heard over a wide area. While Antonius was still debating a plan of action, Arrius Varus, who was impatient for results, dashed out with the keenest members of the cavalry and drove back the Vitellians, inflicting only slight losses. For as greater numbers hastened to the scene, the tables were turned, and the most eager of the pursuers now found themselves at the rear of the retreat. Such haste had not been Antonius' wish, and he had all along been expecting what had in fact happened. Telling his men to engage the enemy with brave hearts, he moved his troops of horse to the flanks and left a free passage in the middle for Varus and his cavalry. The legions were ordered to take up arms. A trumpet-call was sounded throughout the area to indicate that the foragers should abandon their hunt for spoil and make for the fighting at the nearest point. Meanwhile, the frightened Varus linked up with the main body of cavalry, infecting it with his own panic. The fresh forces were driven back together with the wounded men, colliding with one another because of their own panic and the narrowness of the roads. 17. In this chaos Antonius did whatever a resolute general or brave soldier could do, confronting the panic-stricken and holding back the fugitives.[22] Where most effort was required, or where there was any glimmer of hope, by his strategy, his fighting and his shouting he made himself a marked man in the eyes of the enemy and a beacon to his own men. Finally, he got so fired up that he thrust a spear through a retreating standard-bearer, then caught up the flag and turned it to face the enemy. Ashamed by this, some troopers, numbering no more than a hundred, stood their ground. The place helped them, since the road narrowed at that point and a bridge had been destroyed – and the stream which flowed between the two armies made escape difficult because of its slippery bed and

steep banks. This circumstance, whether we call it necessity or luck, gave fresh heart to a side which was apparently already beaten. They formed up in close ranks and met the rash and scattered charges of the Vitellians. It was now the enemy's turn to suffer disaster. Antonius assailed his devastated opponents and laid low those who confronted him, while his troops, according to their individual character, plundered the fallen, took prisoners or carried off weapons and horses. Indeed, their exulting cries alerted those who had just now been scattering over the countryside in flight, and they too got involved in the victorious action.

18. Four miles from Cremona, the glint of standards marked the approach of the Hurricane and Italian Legions, which had marched out as far as this during the initial success of their cavalry. However, when luck turned against them, they did not open out their ranks, they did not receive their disorganized comrades and they did not advance, nor take the initiative in attacking an enemy exhausted by marching and fighting over such a great distance. If they had, perhaps they would have won.[23] When things were going well, they had not seriously felt their lack of a commander, but now, at the crisis point, they realized it to the full. As the front ranks wavered, the victorious cavalry charged into them, closely followed by the tribune Vipstanus Messalla leading the auxiliaries from Moesia, who had been brought up by a forced march which many of the legionaries had matched despite its lightning pace. Thus a mixed force of infantry and cavalry broke through the column of Vitellian legions, to whom the nearby walls of Cremona offered greater hope of escape and correspondingly less will to resist. However, Antonius did not press home his advantage, being mindful of the exhaustion and wounds inflicted on the cavalry and their horses during a fight in which the chances had gone both ways, despite their final success.

19. As evening was falling, the Flavian army arrived in full strength. After marching over the heaps of dead and the fresh traces of slaughter, they felt as if the fighting was over and clamoured to proceed to Cremona where they could receive, or enforce, the surrender of the beaten enemy. This at any rate was

their fine-sounding talk in public, but each man was thinking to himself something rather different: a city situated on a plain could be stormed, and if they burst in during the hours of darkness, they would be just as brave, but they would enjoy greater licence to plunder. If, however, they waited until light, there would be peace terms and appeals for mercy, and in return for all their exertion and wounds, the only recompense would be the useless glory of having granted clemency, while the riches of Cremona would be pocketed by the auxiliary and legionary commanders. When a city was stormed, its booty fell to the troops; if it surrendered, the profit went to the commanders. So they ignored their centurions and tribunes, and drowned out any protests by clashing their weapons to indicate that they would mutiny if they were not led onwards.

20. Then Antonius pushed his way into the thick of the companies. When his appearance and prestige had secured silence, he assured them that he had no intention of robbing such deserving troops of credit or reward, but added that commanders and men had different functions to perform.[24] A fighting spirit was excellent in soldiers, but commanders more often rendered service by deliberation and caution than by recklessness. In the past he had done his bit to secure victory by fighting with sword in hand, but in the future he would serve them by calculation and planning, which were the proper attributes of a general. There was no question about the dangers confronting them – darkness, the layout of an unfamiliar city and, within it, an enemy enjoying every chance for a surprise attack. Even if the gates were wide open, they must not enter except after a reconnaissance, and by day. Or did they propose to begin the attack blindfold, without knowing the favourable approaches or the height of the walls, or whether the assault upon the city called for catapults and missiles or siege-works and moveable defences? Antonius then turned to individuals, asking one man after another whether he had brought with him axes and picks and all the other equipment necessary for storming cities. When they shook their heads, he retorted: 'Can brute strength breach and undermine walls with swords and javelins? Suppose it proves necessary to build a mound, suppose we must shelter

behind screens and hurdles: are we going to stand about helplessly like an unsuspecting crowd, admiring the height of the
towers and our opponents' defences? Why not wait just for
one night, bring up the catapults and engines and then sweep
forward carrying victory with us by force?' Without further
ado, Antonius sent the camp-followers and servants back to
Bedriacum with the freshest members of the cavalry to bring
up supplies and anything else that was likely to be useful.

21. This indeed was almost too much for the men, who were
on the verge of mutiny when the cavalry, riding right up to the
walls of Cremona, captured some drifters from the town who
told them that six Vitellian legions – that is the whole army
which had previously been stationed at Hostilia – had covered
thirty miles that very day, and on hearing of the defeat of their
comrades were now arming for battle and would turn up at
any moment. It was this frightening report that opened the deaf
ears of the troops so that they listened to their commander's
advice. He ordered the Thirteenth Legion to take up a position
on the actual embankment of the Postumian Way. In contact
on its left stood the Seventh Galbian Legion on open ground,
then the Seventh Claudian, its front protected by one of the
drainage ditches (such was the character of the area). On the
right were the Eighth, deployed along a side road without cover,
and after that the Third, interspersed among a dense plantation
of trees. This at least was the order in which the eagles and
standards were placed; the troops themselves were mixed up
haphazardly in the darkness. The contingent of praetorians lay
next to the Third, with the auxiliary cohorts on the flanks of
the line and the cavalry protecting the wings and rear. The
Suebians, Sido and Italicus, patrolled the front line with a
picked force of their countrymen.

22. As for the Vitellian army, reason dictated that it should
rest at Cremona. After some food and sleep to recover its
strength, it could have attacked and annihilated the shivering
and hungry enemy on the next morning. Yet it had no leader
and no plan of action. Shortly before nine at night, the Vitellians
hurled themselves violently at the enemy, who were prepared
and already in position. I should hesitate to give conclusive

evidence about the Vitellian order of battle, which was chaotic because of the fury and darkness, although others have recorded that their right front was held by the Fourth Macedonian Legion, their centre by the Fifth and Fifteenth supported by detachments of the Ninth, Second and Twentieth Legions from Britain, and their left front by the men of the Sixteenth, Twenty-Second and First Legions. Elements of the Hurricane and Italian Legions had attached themselves to all the companies, while the cavalry and auxiliaries chose their own posts.

Throughout the night, the fighting was varied, indecisive and bitter, inflicting destruction first on one side and then on the other. Clear heads and strong arms did not help at all, and even their eyes could not penetrate the darkness. On both sides weapons and uniform were identical,[25] frequent challenges and replies disclosed the watchword and flags were inextricably confused as they were captured by this group or that and carried hither and thither. The formation under heaviest pressure was the Seventh Legion recently raised by Galba. Six centurions of the leading companies were killed and a few standards lost. Even the eagle was only saved by the senior centurion Atilius Varus, who slaughtered many of the enemy, but then finally was killed himself.

23. Antonius stiffened the wavering line by bringing up the praetorians. After taking up the fighting, they drove back the enemy, only to be driven back themselves. The reason for this was that the Vitellians had concentrated their artillery upon the high road so as to command an unobstructed field of fire over the open ground. Their shooting had at first been sporadic, and the shots had struck the trees without hurting the enemy. The Sixteenth Legion[26] had an enormous catapult which hurled massive stones and was now mowing down the enemy battle-line. It would have inflicted extensive havoc but for a conspicuous act of daring on the part of two soldiers. They concealed their identity by seizing shields from the dead enemies, and severed the torsion springs by which the catapult was operated. They were cut down immediately and so their names have perished, but there is no doubt that the deed was done.

Fortune had not favoured either side, until in the middle

of the night the moon rose, displaying – and deceiving – the combatants.[27] However, as the moonlight shone from behind the Flavians, it favoured them; on their side the shadows of horses and men were exaggerated, and the enemy weapons fell short because they mistakenly thought that they were on target to hit actual bodies. The Vitellians, on the other hand, were brilliantly illuminated by the light shining full in their faces, and so, without realizing it, they provided an easy mark for an enemy aiming from what were virtually concealed positions.

24. Therefore, since Antonius and his men could now recognize each other, he spurred on some by shameful taunts, many by praise and encouragement, all by hope and promises. Why, he asked the Pannonian legions, had they taken up arms again? These were the very battlefields where they could wash away the stain of past humiliating defeat and restore their glorious reputation. Then, turning to the troops from Moesia, he called on them as the leaders and architects of the campaign: they had challenged the Vitellians by threats and words, but this meant nothing if they could not bear their looks and attacks. This is what he said as he reached the successive contingents; but he spoke at greater length to the men of the Third Legion, reminding them of their early and recent history, how under Mark Antony they had beaten the Parthians, under Corbulo the Armenians, and in the immediate past the Sarmatians. Then he provoked the praetorians. 'As for you,' he said, 'you soldiers are mere civilians unless you beat the enemy. What other emperor and what other camp will you have to protect you? There on the battlefield are the standards and equipment which are really yours. Death is waiting if you are defeated, for you have already drunk your full measure of disgrace.'

Everywhere there were cheers of enthusiasm, and as the sun rose, the men of the Third saluted it in accordance with the Syrian custom.[28] 25. This generated a rumour from an uncertain source (or perhaps it was intentionally spread by the Flavian commander) that Mucianus had arrived and that the two armies had been greeting one another in turn. The men moved forward thinking that they had been reinforced by fresh troops, while the Vitellian line was now thinner than before, as one might expect of a force which in the absence of all leadership bunched and spread according to individual impulse or panic. When Antonius sensed that the enemy was under pressure, he threw them into confusion by using massed columns of troops. The disintegrating ranks broke and could not be closed again because vehicles and catapults were getting in the way. Down the long straight road the victors charged, drawing away from each other in the fervour of pursuit.

That massacre was particularly notable because of an incident where a son killed his own father.[29] I shall give details of the event and the names of the protagonists on the authority of Vipstanus Messalla. Julius Mansuetus from Spain had joined the Hurricane Legion, leaving a young son at home. Soon after, the boy came of age, and having been conscripted by Galba for service in the Seventh, happened to encounter his father in this battle and laid him low with a wound. As he was looking over the half-dead man, the pair recognized one another. Embracing his father's corpse, the son prayed in words choked by sobs that his father's spirit would be appeased and not turn against him as a parricide. This crime was down to the state, he cried, and one soldier was only a tiny fraction of the forces engaged in civil war. With these words, he took up the body, dug a grave and performed his final duty to his father. The nearest soldiers noticed this, then more and more; and so throughout the ranks spread astonishment, complaints and cursing of this cruellest of all wars. However, this did not mean that they killed and robbed relatives, kinsmen and brothers any more slowly: they denounced the crime that had been committed, but still carried out the same crime themselves.

26. When the Flavians reached Cremona, a new and formidable task confronted them. During the war with Otho, the troops from Germany had built a camp near the walls of Cremona and a rampart round the camp; and since then, they had strengthened these defences still further. This sight gave the victors pause and the officers were uncertain what orders to issue. To begin the assault with an army exhausted by a long day and night seemed difficult, and, if no reserves were standing by, dangerous. If, on the other hand, they were to return to

Bedriacum, the impact of such a long and exhausting march would be intolerable and meant throwing away their victory. Even entrenching camp was a fearful prospect with the enemy so close, for there was the threat that scattered parties of men engaged in digging would be thrown into disorder by a sudden sortie. Yet the factor that terrified the generals above all was their own troops, who would rather endure danger than delay. For the men felt that playing safe was dull, but taking a chance offered possibilities. Whatever the cost in death and wounds and bloodshed, it counted for nothing compared with their greed for plunder.

27. Antonius was inclined to agree, and ordered a ring of troops to surround the rampart. At first they fought at a distance by unleashing arrows and stones at one another, which caused greater damage to the Flavians, against whom weapons plunged down from above. Then Antonius assigned the different legions to separate sections of the rampart and gates so that a division of labour might sort out the brave from the cowardly and fire up the men by a competition for honour. The area nearest to the road to Bedriacum was allotted to the men of the Third and Seventh Legions, and the wall further to the right to the Eighth and Seventh Claudian Legions, while the detachments of the Thirteenth advanced impetuously as far as the Brixian gate. There was a slight delay after that, while some of the legionaries collected mattocks and axes from the adjacent fields, and others hooks and ladders. Then, lifting their shields above their heads, they moved up in a tight testudo arrangement.[30] Both sides used Roman fighting techniques. The Vitellians rolled down heavy stones, and then, when the testudo was split and wavering, probed it with lances and poles until the compact structure of shields fell apart and they could flatten their bleeding or maimed opponents with deadly slaughter. The Flavian attack began to slacken, but their generals, finding the men worn out and deaf to exhortations which seemed pointless, pointed suggestively to Cremona.[31] 28. (I find it difficult to decide whether this ingenious suggestion came from Hormus, as Messalla tells us, or whether in his accusation of Antonius, Gaius Plinius is the more authoritative source.[32] The only clear thing is that neither

Antonius nor Hormus went against the grain of his reputation and way of life in committing this appalling crime.) Henceforward, bloodshed and wounds could not check the Flavians' determination to undermine the rampart and shatter the gates. Climbing on one another's shoulders and mounting on top of the re-formed testudo, they grasped at the enemy's weapons and limbs. The unwounded and wounded, the maimed and the dying were all piled together in a shifting kaleidoscope of death and destruction of every variety.

29. The keenest competition was between the Third and Seventh Legions, so the general Antonius at the head of a picked auxiliary force pressed the attack in this sector. Their grim rivalry in the offensive was too much for the Vitellians, while the missiles hurled down on the testudo glanced harmlessly off, so finally the defenders tipped over the catapult itself upon the enemy beneath. For the moment this made a gap, as it crushed the men on whom it fell, but it also took with it in its fall the battlements and the upper part of the wall, and at the same time an adjacent tower succumbed to a hail of stones. Here, while the men of the Seventh pressed the attack in close formation, the soldiers of the Third managed to break through the gate with their axes and swords. There is agreement between all our authorities that the first to penetrate the camp was Gaius Volusius, a soldier of the Third Legion. He climbed up to the rampart, threw down any men still attempting resistance and, waving and yelling to attract attention, cried out that the camp was captured. The others, now that the Vitellians were on the run and hurling themselves headlong from the rampart, surged through to join him. Whatever space there was between the camp and the walls of Cremona was filled with slaughter.

30. Once again now an unfamiliar setting for their labours confronted the Flavians: lofty city-walls, towers made of stone, iron barriers to the gates, a garrison brandishing its weapons and Cremona's teeming populace devoted to the Vitellian cause, as well as a crowd of visitors from the whole of Italy who had flocked to the fair regularly held at that time of year – their numbers proved helpful to the defence and their wealth an allurement to the assailants. Antonius ordered torches to be

brought quickly and applied to the most attractive buildings outside the city to see if the people of Cremona might be persuaded to change sides by the loss of their property. Those buildings that stood close to the walls and overlooked them he filled with his best troops, who dislodged the defenders with joists, tiles and blazing torches.

31. Some of the legionaries were already forming up into a testudo formation and others were discharging missiles and stones, when the morale of the Vitellians gradually began to fade. The higher the rank, the less the will to resist the inevitable. They feared that if Cremona, too, were taken by storm, there would be no further possibility of pardon and the conqueror's anger would fall entirely on the tribunes and centurions (where killing was profitable) rather than on the lower ranks who had nothing to lose. The common soldiers stood firm, not caring about the future and thinking themselves relatively safe because they were unknown. Roaming through the streets or hidden in houses, these men refused to ask for peace even when they had laid aside war. The camp prefects took down the name and portraits of Vitellius. They removed the chains from Caecina, who was still imprisoned even at that point, and begged him to plead for the Vitellians' cause. When he arrogantly refused, they wore down his resistance with tearful requests, which was the utmost iniquity – all those supremely brave men begging for help from a traitor. Soon after, they displayed from the walls olive branches and priestly headbands to indicate their surrender.[33] Once Antonius had given the order to stop fighting, the Vitellians brought out their standards and eagles. These were followed by a dejected column of disarmed men with downcast eyes. The victors had crowded around them, initially jeering and aiming blows at them, but after a while, when the defeated men faced up to the insults and impassively endured everything, the Flavians remembered that this was the army which, not long previously, had shown restraint after its victory at Bedriacum. However, when Caecina stepped forward in his capacity as consul, distinguished by his bordered toga and lictors, who thrust aside the crowd, the victors flew into a rage. They taunted him as arrogant and cruel, and

on top of that, as a traitor (so hated is that crime). Antonius intervened, and sent him off to Vespasian with an escort.

32. Meanwhile the people of Cremona were being roughed up by the armed troops, and it was only when a massacre was imminent that the appeals of the generals managed to calm the men. Moreover, Antonius summoned the soldiers to a parade, addressing the victors proudly and the vanquished with clemency, but he did not give any clear indication about the fate of Cremona. Quite apart from the army's natural taste for plunder, the soldiers were bent on wiping out the Cremonese, thanks to an old score. It was believed that the town had also aided the Vitellians during the war against Otho; and later the men of the Thirteenth, left there to build an amphitheatre, had been the target of their mockery and insults (this sort of conduct was typical of impudent city mobs).[34] The Flavians' resentment was sharpened by a gladiatorial show Caecina had given at Cremona, its renewed employment as a base and the way in which they offered the Vitellians food in the fighting line. This had involved the death of certain women who in their enthusiasm for the cause had gone out onto the battlefield. In addition to this, it was the season of the fair, so a city which was in any case opulent was stuffed with an even greater display of wealth. The other generals were shadowy figures, but Antonius' success and reputation had placed him completely in the public gaze. He hurried off to the baths to wash away the bloodstains from the battle, and there, as he grumbled about the temperature of the water, he was overheard to say: 'Luke-warm! Things will heat up soon enough, though.' This cheap joke was a magnet for everyone's hatred, for people thought that he had given the signal to set fire to Cremona, which was in fact already burning.

33. Forty thousand armed men burst into the city, accompanied by servants and camp-followers in greater numbers who were even more viciously addicted to lust and violence.[35] Neither rank nor age saved the victims: rape alternated sickeningly with murder and murder with rape. Elderly men and frail old women, who had no value as loot, were dragged off to raise a laugh. Any marriageable girl or good-looking lad who crossed their path was torn this way and that between the violent hands

of would-be captors, until finally the plunderers themselves destroyed one another. Anyone hauling off money or temple offerings laden with gold was often cut to pieces by other looters who were stronger. Some, turning up their noses at the obvious finds, hunted out hidden valuables and dug for buried treasures after flogging and torturing the property owners. In their hands they held flaming torches, and once they had carried out their booty they wantonly flung these into the empty houses and the temples which had been stripped bare. Since the army was a mixture of citizens, allies and foreigners with different languages and habits, the men manifested a correspondingly diverse array of wild desires and had wide-ranging conceptions of what was right, even if there was no kind of wrongdoing that they ruled out. Cremona lasted them four days. While all its buildings, sacred and secular, collapsed in flames, only the Temple of Mefitis outside the walls remained standing, defended by its position or the power of the divinity.[36]

34. Such, then, was the fate of Cremona, 286 years after its first beginnings. It had been founded in the consulship of Tiberius Sempronius and Publius Cornelius,[37] at the time when Hannibal was menacing Italy, to serve as a fortification against the Gauls living north of the Po or any other violent invasion by way of the Alps. As it turned out, the abundance of settlers, the convenient presence of rivers and the fertility of its territory, as well as kinship and intermarriage with the local tribes, made it grow and flourish, but a city which had been unscathed by foreign invasion proved unlucky in civil wars.

Antonius, ashamed of this criminal act and worried by the mounting resentment, issued a proclamation that no one should keep prisoner a citizen of Cremona. Indeed, the troops had already found their booty useless to them owing to a concerted refusal throughout Italy to buy slaves of this sort, so they began to murder them. When this became known, the prisoners were stealthily ransomed by their relatives by blood or marriage. In due course, the surviving inhabitants returned to Cremona. The squares and temples were restored thanks to the generosity of other Italian towns; and Vespasian gave them his encouragement.[38]

35. However, since the ground was tainted with putrid matter, it was impossible to encamp for long by the ruins of the dead city. The Flavians moved out three miles, and formed up the frightened and straggling Vitellians in their respective units. The defeated legions were dispersed throughout Illyricum, in case they engaged in suspicious activities while the civil war was still being mopped up. Next, messengers were sent with the news to Britain and the Spanish provinces. Julius Calenus, a tribune, was dispatched to Gaul, and Alpinius Montanus, a cohort commander, to Germany. Since Montanus was a Treviran and Calenus an Aeduan, while both were former supporters of Vitellius, the intention was to make a decisive show of Vespasian's victory. At the same time, the Alpine passes were garrisoned out of concern that Germany might stir herself to come to the aid of Vitellius.

Vitellius and the Crisis

36. Once Vitellius had induced Fabius Valens to leave for the front a few days after Caecina's departure,[39] he camouflaged his worries in luxurious living. He made no preparations for war and failed to toughen his troops by addressing or training them. He did not spend time in the public eye, but hid himself away in the shady retreat of his gardens, and just like those miserable animals that are content to lie and doze so long as food is put in front of them, he let everything slide and was equally oblivious to past, present and future. As he sat there idly and apathetically among the groves of Aricia, the news of Bassus' betrayal and the defection of the Ravenna fleet proved utterly shocking. Not long afterwards, reports about Caecina's desertion and then his arrest by the army filled him with a combination of gloom and joy. In such a feeble character, happiness outweighed concern. Exultantly he rode back to Rome, and before a crowded assembly he heaped praises on the devotion of his troops. He gave orders that Publilius Sabinus, the praetorian prefect, should be arrested because of his friendship with Caecina, and Alfenus Varus was appointed as his replacement.

37. Vitellius then addressed the senate in a speech carefully designed to impress, and the senators commended him with studied flattery. Lucius Vitellius set in motion a move for a severe ruling against Caecina. The others soon joined in and expressed studied outrage against the consul who had betrayed the state, against the general who had betrayed his emperor and against the man piled high with so much wealth and honour who had betrayed his friend and benefactor. They were pretending to protest on behalf of Vitellius, but they were really expressing their own annoyance.[40] Not a single speaker reproached the Flavian generals, but blaming the armies for their misguided lack of judgement, they anxiously used roundabout language and avoided mentioning Vespasian's name. There was even a senator who wheedled himself into a consulship lasting one day (for that was what still remained from Caecina's tenure), which earned both donor and recipient huge ridicule. On 31 October, Rosius Regulus entered – and resigned – office. Constitutional experts noted that never before had a suffect magistrate been appointed without the formal cancellation of the magistracy by legislation before the people.[41] That was the novelty, for there had been a one-day consul before, namely Caninius Rebilus under Julius Caesar's dictatorship, at a time when rewards for services in the civil war were being hurriedly distributed.

38. Around this time, the fact that Junius Blaesus had died became known and generated much talk.[42] This is what I have heard about it. Vitellius was lying seriously ill at his house in the Servilian Park when he noticed that a lofty neighbouring dwelling was ablaze with umpteen lights which shone through the night. On enquiring the reason, he was told that Caecina Tuscus was holding a large dinner-party, and that the guest of honour was Junius Blaesus. His informants gave an exaggerated account of lavish display and a relaxed and convivial atmosphere. Critics readily came forward to denounce Tuscus himself and others, but particularly venomous charges were laid against Blaesus for spending his days in merriment while the emperor was ill. There are always people who keep a sharp lookout for signs of an emperor's displeasure. When it became clear enough

to them that Vitellius had been provoked and that Blaesus could be ruined, they assigned the role of informer to Lucius Vitellius. He was Blaesus' enemy, bitterly jealous of a man whose excellent reputation towered above his own life, sordidly marked by every type of scandal. Lucius suddenly flung open the door of the emperor's bedroom and knelt down before him, clasping Vitellius' young son in his arms. When Vitellius asked him what the trouble was, he said that it was not because of his own personal fears and private anxieties that he had brought his tearful appeals, but from concern for his brother and his brother's children. There was no point in fearing Vespasian: all those German legions, all those brave and loyal provinces, a huge and immeasurable sweep of land and sea served as a defence against him. It was in Rome and in his own intimate circle where the emperor must guard against an enemy who boasted the Junii and Antonii as his ancestors, and who sought to show himself off to the soldiers as an affable and generous member of a ruling family. He was the centre of all public attention, while Vitellius, paying no attention to who were his friends and who were his enemies, was nurturing a rival who contemplated the emperor's sufferings from a banqueting table. This man should pay the price for such untimely festivity by a night of misery and death, in which he would learn to his cost that Vitellius was still alive and still emperor, with a son to succeed him in the event of his death.[43]

39. Vitellius was hesitating between murder and his fear that if he postponed Blaesus' execution his own ruin might soon follow; but to order it openly would cause a terrible scandal, so he decided it was best to use poison. What made people believe him guilty was the conspicuous pleasure he took in visiting Blaesus. Indeed, Vitellius was heard to make a most vicious remark, boasting that 'he had feasted his eyes on the spectacle of his enemy's death'. I quote his actual words.[44]

Blaesus not only came from an illustrious family and possessed gracious ways, but he was also stubbornly loyal. Even while Vitellius' position was still sound, he was approached by Caecina and other prominent members of the party who were already turning against the emperor, but he persisted in refusing to join any plot. Despite being a model of goodness and a calm man who turned his back on any sudden promotion, let alone the principate, he had not been able to avoid being thought worthy of it.

40. Meanwhile, Fabius Valens, together with a long and luxurious train of prostitutes and eunuchs, was advancing at a pace too sluggish for a campaign when couriers arrived with the urgent news that the Ravenna fleet had been betrayed by Lucilius Bassus. If Valens, who had just started on his journey, had hurried, he could have caught up with Caecina in time to confront his wavering loyalty, or overtaken the legions before the decisive battle. Some of his colleagues did in fact advise him to take his trustiest men by secret tracks to Hostilia or Cremona, avoiding Ravenna. Others thought it best to summon the praetorians from Rome and break through the blockade in strength. Valens himself frittered away in deliberation days that called for action and merely waited, which was useless. Then, rejecting both proposals, he compromised, which is always the worst possible solution in a crisis, and failed to act with sufficient daring or caution. 41. He wrote to Vitellius to ask for reinforcements, and received three cohorts together with a cavalry regiment from Britain. This was a contingent too large to escape detection and too small to cut its way through.

Even at such a critical moment, ugly stories still circulated about Valens. People were convinced that he was grabbing forbidden pleasures and dishonouring the homes of his hosts by seducing their wives and sleeping with their offspring.[45] He certainly had power and money on his side, and the urgent passion of a doomed man to have a final fling.

At last the arrival of the infantry and cavalry revealed how misguided his plan was, since he could not move straight through enemy territory with such a small force, even if it had been completely trustworthy, but these newcomers were of questionable loyalty. However, a sense of shame and the respect inspired by the presence of their commander restrained them for the time being – although these were ephemeral ties for men who feared danger and were unconcerned by dishonour. Scared by the situation, Valens sent the cohorts ahead to Ariminum and ordered the cavalry to protect the rear, while he himself accompanied by only a few companions who were steadfast amid disaster left the main road and made for Umbria and then Etruria. In Etruria he heard about the outcome of the battle of Cremona, and hatched a plan which actually showed some spirit and would have had dire consequences if it had worked. The idea was to seize some ships, land somewhere or other in the province of Narbonese Gaul and incite the Gallic provinces, the armies and the German tribes to renew the war.

42. Since Valens' forces garrisoned at Ariminum were demoralized by his departure, Cornelius Fuscus moved up his troops, dispatched a fast naval force along the adjacent coast and surrounded the town by land and sea. The victors now occupied the Umbrian plain and the Adriatic seaboard of Picenum, so that the Apennines divided the whole of Italy between Vespasian and Vitellius. Fabius Valens set sail from the Portus Pisanus, but was compelled by sluggish seas or contrary wind to put in at the harbour of Hercules Monoecus. Not far from here was the base of Marius Maturus, the governor of the Maritime Alps and a staunch Vitellian who had not yet forgotten his oath of allegiance despite the hostility of the whole area around him.[46] He welcomed Valens courteously, but warned his guest not to take the rash step of entering Narbonese Gaul. This frightened Valens, but at the same time the loyalty of his followers was now undermined by fear. 43. For Valerius Paulinus, the procurator, was an energetic soldier and he made the neighbouring communities swear allegiance to Vespasian, who had been his friend before his elevation to power. After recruiting all those who had been discharged from the praetorians by Vitellius, and who were only too ready to join the fight, Paulinus was now holding with his garrison the town of Forum Julii, the gateway which controlled the sea. His lead had all the more impact because this was his native town, and he was held in esteem by the praetorians whose commander he had once been. The civilians, too, favoured a fellow-townsman, and hoped that he would be in a position to pull strings for them in the future, so they supported the cause with enthusiasm. While these robust preparations were magnified by rumours

which gained momentum among the wavering Vitellians, Fabius Valens, accompanied by four bodyguards, three friends and the same number of centurions, returned to the ships. Maturus and the rest were content to stay behind and take the oath to Vespasian. As for Valens, the sea seemed less dangerous than the coast and its towns, but his future plans were undecided, and he was more confident about what to avoid than whom to trust. In the event, bad weather forced him to land in the Stoechades, islands which belonged to Marseilles, and there a flotilla of fast galleys sent by Paulinus took him into custody.

44. With the capture of Valens the whole Roman world rallied to the winning side. The movement began in Spain with the First Adiutrix Legion, which remembered Otho and hated Vitellius: its lead was followed by the Tenth and Sixth. Nor were the Gallic provinces reluctant. Support also came from Britain, which was naturally inclined to support Vespasian, since he had been appointed by Claudius to command the Second Legion and had fought there with distinction.[47] Even so, the other legions in Britain were restless, for they contained a number of centurions and soldiers who owed their promotion to Vitellius and were worried about accepting a new emperor in exchange for one they knew.

45. Thanks to these disagreements and the spate of rumours about civil war, the Britons plucked up courage, prompted by a man called Venutius, who, quite apart from his natural ferocity and a hatred of all things Roman, was being fired up by a personal feud with Queen Cartimandua. She was queen of the Brigantes, a powerful woman of noble descent whose influence had increased after her treacherous capture of King Caratacus had apparently paved the way for Claudius' triumph.[48] That meant wealth and the self-indulgence of prosperity. She tired of Venutius (he was her husband) and gave her hand and kingdom to his armour-bearer, Vellocatus. The royal house was instantly rocked by this scandal. The enthusiastic support of the people was at the disposal of the discarded husband, while the lover was backed by the cruel and lustful queen. So Venutius summoned help, and a simultaneous revolt on the part of the Brigantes themselves brought Cartimandua

face to face with extreme danger. That was when she appealed
for Roman assistance. In the event, our auxiliary cohorts of
infantry and cavalry rescued the queen from a tight corner by
fighting a number of battles with varying success. Venutius got
the throne, and we were left with the fighting.

46. It was at this same time that trouble broke out in
Germany, where the slackness of our commanders, the mutinous nature of our legions, foreign invasion and allied treachery
nearly caused the downfall of Rome. This war, with its various
causes and incidents – for it was a protracted struggle – I shall
deal with in due course.[49] There was also a disturbance among
the Dacians. Never a trustworthy people, at that time they
feared nothing as the Roman army had been withdrawn from
Moesia.[50] They looked on quietly at the initial phases of the
civil war, but when they heard that Italy was ablaze with war
and that everything was alternating in cycles of violence, they
stormed the winter-quarters of the cohorts and cavalry, and
began to occupy both banks of the Danube. They were just
about to destroy the legionary camp as well, when Mucianus
sent the Sixth Legion against them. He knew about the victory
at Cremona, but was anxious in case a double foreign invasion
threatened if the Dacians and the Germans had broken in from
opposite directions. As so often at other times, Rome's good
fortune saved the day, having brought Mucianus on the scene
with the forces of the East, and because meanwhile we settled
matters at Cremona. Fonteius Agrippa, who had governed Asia
as a proconsul for the normal period of one year, was appointed
to administer Moesia, and was given additional forces from
the army of Vitellius.[51] To distribute this army among the
provinces and to tie it down in a foreign war was an act at once
of statesmanship and peace.

47. Nor did the other peoples of the empire keep quiet. In
Pontus there had been a sudden uprising led by a foreign slave
and one-time commander of the royal fleet called Anicetus. He
was a freedman of Polemo,[52] and having once been supremely
powerful could not stomach the change which turned the kingdom into a Roman province. So, in the name of Vitellius, he
called to arms the tribes which border on Pontus, luring on all

the most destitute men to hope for plunder. At the head of a considerable force, he suddenly attacked Trapezus, an ancient and famous city founded by the Greeks at the farthest point of the Pontic coast. Here they slaughtered a cohort which had once formed part of the royal army but had later been given Roman citizenship as well as Roman standards and equipment, while retaining the idle and licentious habits of the Greeks. A rebel fleet added fresh fuel to the blaze, sailing where it pleased over the unpoliced sea, because Mucianus had withdrawn the best of the galleys and all the crews to Byzantium. Even the natives were insolently roving the seas in hastily constructed boats. These they call 'arks': they are narrow above the water-line, but broad in the beam, and constructed using neither bronze nor iron rivets. When the sea is choppy, as the waves get higher, they increase the height of these boats' sides by adding planks successively, until they are wholly enclosed by a sort of roof. In this way, they ride the waves. The boats have identical prows fore and aft so they can be rowed in both directions since it makes no difference whether they are beached stern or bow first: either way is equally safe.[53]

48. This state of affairs alerted Vespasian. So he selected a special force drawn from his legions and placed it under the command of an experienced soldier called Virdius Geminus. As the enemy was chaotically scouring the countryside in an eager search for loot, Virdius surprised them and forced them to take to their ships. Then, hurriedly building galleys, he caught up with Anicetus at the mouth of the River Chobus, where he had been protected and helped by the king of the Sedochezi, who had been driven into an alliance by a money bribe and other gifts. Certainly at first the king used threats and armed force to protect his guest, but after it came to a choice between being paid for his treachery or waging full-scale war, his loyalty evaporated in typical barbarian fashion. He struck a bargain for the death of Anicetus, and surrendered the other fugitives. That put an end to this slavish war.

That victory made Vespasian happy, but just when every-thing seemed to be going more smoothly than he could possibly have hoped, news reached him in Egypt about the battle of

Cremona. He hurried to Alexandria all the more quickly, with the intention of using starvation to put pressure on the shattered armies of Vitellius and the inhabitants of Rome, which depended on imports. To this end he was already preparing a naval and land invasion of the province of Africa, which is located on that same coast. By withholding the grain supplies, he was intending to impose famine and dissension on the enemy.[54]

The Flavian March on Rome

49. So in a convulsion felt around the world, imperial power changed hands. Meanwhile, the behaviour of Antonius Primus degenerated sharply after Cremona. He thought that he had done enough to settle the war and that the rest would be easy – or perhaps, in a character like his, it needed success to reveal his greed, pride and other hidden vices. He pranced through Italy as if it were a conquered country, ingratiated himself with the legions as if they were his own, and in everything he did and said prepared his route to power. To give the troops a taste for licence, he allowed the legions to appoint replacement centurions for those who had been killed. Their votes selected all the most unruly types. The soldiers were no longer under the control of their generals: it was the generals who were swept along by the violent whims of the soldiers. These were seditious methods which were bound to ruin good discipline, and Antonius soon exploited them to enrich himself. Mucianus was approaching, but Antonius was not at all afraid, despite the fact that this was a more deadly mistake than if he had scorned Vespasian himself.[55]

50. However, as winter approached and the Po valley became waterlogged, his column marched along without heavy baggage. At Verona they left the main parties of the victorious legions, the wounded soldiers or those too old for action and a number of fit soldiers as well. It was thought that the auxiliary cohorts, cavalry and some specially chosen legionaries would be sufficient, as the war was by this time practically won. The Eleventh Legion had now joined the advance. It had hesitated

at first, and then, when things turned out well, became uneasy because of its failure to cooperate. It was accompanied by a recent levy of 6,000 Dalmatian recruits. This whole force was led by the consular governor, Pompeius Silvanus, although real power lay with Annius Bassus, the legionary commander. Silvanus, too lazy for war, frittered away the time for action in talk, but Bassus knew how to manage him by a show of deference, and whenever there was work to be done he was always on the spot and ready to act with quiet efficiency. These units were reinforced by the pick of the naval personnel at Ravenna, who were eagerly demanding service in the legions.[56] Dalmatians made up the numbers in the fleet.

The army and its leaders halted at Fanum Fortunae, hesitating about their strategy, for they had heard that the praetorian cohorts had moved out from Rome, and concluded that the passes of the Apennines were by this time held by garrisons. What also alarmed the leaders was the lack of supplies in a region devastated by war, and the mutinous demands of the troops for a bounty called 'nail-money'.[57] The commanders had not made provision either for pay or for food. They were being hindered by the impetuous greed of their soldiers who stole what they could have had as a gift. 51. In some very widely read historians[58] I find endorsement of the following story. The victors displayed such disregard for right and wrong that a common cavalry soldier claimed to have killed his brother in the recent battle and demanded a reward from his leaders.[59] Common morality did not allow them to reward the murder, but the very nature of civil war prevented them from punishing it. So they decided to put the man off by claiming that the reward he deserved was too great to be paid on the spot. And there the story ends. However, an equally ghastly crime had occurred in a previous civil war, for in the battle against Cinna on the Janiculum,[60] a soldier of Pompeius Strabo killed his brother, and then, when he realized what he had done, committed suicide. So Sisenna relates.[61] So earlier generations were more sharply attuned than we are both to the glory created by good deeds and to the remorse caused by wicked actions. At any rate, it will be appropriate for me to cite these and similar anecdotes from ancient history when the context calls for examples of good conduct or consolation for evil.

52. Antonius and the other Flavian leaders decided that the cavalry should be sent forward to conduct a general reconnaissance of Umbria to see if they could approach the summit of the Apennines by a less forbidding route. A summons was also to be sent to the main body of the legions and whatever other troops were at Verona, and the Po and the Adriatic were to take a full complement of supply ships.

There were some generals who tried to drag their feet, feeling that Antonius was now too powerful, and that it would be safer to pin their hopes on Mucianus. For Mucianus, concerned that victory had come so quickly, was convinced that he would be excluded from the campaign and its distinctions unless he were personally present at the entry into Rome. So he wrote noncommittal dispatches to Primus and Varus, sometimes pointing up the need to exploit any opening, sometimes stressing the practical advantages of delay. His language was carefully chosen so that according to the outcome he could either distance himself from failure or take credit for success. Mucianus gave more candid advice to his other trusted supporters, including Plotius Grypus, who had recently been made a senator by Vespasian and put in charge of a legion, than to his other reliable adherents. All of these men wrote back in critical terms about the excessive haste of Primus and Varus, which was just what Mucianus wanted. By forwarding these accounts to Vespasian, Mucianus soon made sure that Antonius' intentions and achievements were not valued as highly as he had hoped.

53. Antonius resented this and blamed Mucianus, whose accusations, he said, had devalued his own desperate endeavours. He did not hold back in general conversation either, since he was an outspoken man who was not accustomed to obey orders. The letter he wrote to Vespasian was too boastful for an imperial addressee and contained veiled attacks on Mucianus. He pointed out that it was he, Antonius, who had got the legions of Pannonia to fight, who had spurred the Moesian commanders to action, and by steady persistence broke through the Alps, seized Italy, and cut off the enemy

reinforcements coming from Germany and Raetia. He had routed Vitellius' disunited and scattered legions, first by a whirl-wind cavalry charge, and then by a day and a night of hard infantry fighting. This was no mean achievement, and it was down to him. The sack of Cremona must be chalked up to the hazards of war. Previous civil conflicts had cost the country more dearly in that not one city but several had been destroyed. He served his emperor not by sending messages and writing dispatches, but by action and fighting, and he had not compro-mised the glory of those who, in the meantime, had established order in Dacia. The concern of these generals had been to impose peace in Moesia, his own had been to rescue and pre-serve Italy. By his own encouragement, the provinces of Gaul and Spain, one of the most powerful regions in the world, had gone over to Vespasian. However, all this hard work would have been for nothing, if the rewards for facing danger were to go only to those who had not faced it.

None of this escaped the notice of Mucianus, as a result of which there was a serious rift between the two. Antonius expressed his grievances more directly, whereas Mucianus nur-tured the dispute with a cunning that was much more relentless.

54. However, after the total collapse at Cremona, Vitellius foolishly tried to hush up news of defeat, which only postponed the remedy for the disease rather than the disease itself. The fact is that if he had admitted that he was in trouble and sought advice, there were still hopeful possibilities and resources avail-able. Yet by his diametrically opposite pretence that all was well, he just lied and made the problem more acute. Before the emperor there was a remarkable wall of silence about the war, while in Rome all rumours were quashed, which only made them multiply. People who would have told the truth, if this had been permitted, immediately spread more outrageous stories to spite the censorship. The Flavian generals also did their bit to intensify the gossip by taking captured Vitellian scouts on conducted tours of the victorious army to give them an insight into its strength, and then sending them back to Rome. Vitellius interrogated all these men in secret and then had them killed.

With remarkable persistence a centurion called Julius

Agrestis had many fruitless conversations with Vitellius in which he tried to spur the emperor to act heroically. Finally, Agrestis prevailed upon him so that he was sent in person to reconnoitre the enemy strength and see what had happened at Cremona. The centurion made no attempt to hide his mission from Antonius, but revealed the emperor's instructions and his own purpose, and asked permission to have a look at everything. Men were appointed to show him the site of the battle, the ruins of Cremona and the legions who had capitulated. Agrestis then returned to Vitellius, but when the emperor refused to admit that his report was accurate and actually alleged that he had been bribed, the centurion replied: 'Well, since you need conclusive proof and you have no further use for me whether living or dead, I will give you some evidence you can trust.' So he left the emperor and backed up his words by committing suicide.[62] Some sources say that he was killed by order of Vitellius, but they are unanimous about his fidelity and persistence.

55. Vitellius was like a man shaken from sleep. He ordered Julius Priscus and Alfenus Varus to hold the Apennines with fourteen praetorian cohorts and all the available cavalry units. The legion recruited from the marines followed hot on their heels. This force of so many thousands, including specially chosen men and horses, was quite strong enough to launch an offensive, if only the general had been a different man. The remaining cohorts were allocated to the emperor's brother Lucius to protect Rome. Vitellius himself abandoned none of his usual luxurious indulgences, but he acted hastily because he lacked confidence. He held hurried elections, appointing consuls in advance for a number of years. He lavished treaty status on the provincials and Latin rights on foreigners.[63] Some were excused payment of tribute, others were assisted by various exemptions. In short, with total disregard for the future, he hacked the empire to pieces. However, the common people gaped open-mouthed at such lavish bounty. Fools purchased his favours with money, but concessions which could neither be offered nor accepted without ruining the country were regarded as worthless by wise men. Finally, he yielded to the demands of the army, which was now at Mevania, and after

assembling a great retinue of senators, many of whom wanted
to curry favour, while still more were induced by fear, he
travelled with them to the camp, where his indecision put him
at the mercy of unreliable advisers.

56. As he was addressing the troops, an event which was
spoken of as a prodigy took place: a flock of ill-omened birds
flew overhead in such numbers that they blocked out the daylight in a black cloud.[64] There was an additional dreadful omen
when an ox which escaped from the altar and scattered the
implements of sacrifice was cut down some distance away in a
manner contrary to the proper ritual for killing victims. Yet the
chief portent was Vitellius himself, who was clueless about
military service and had no plan for the future. He was perpetu-
ally asking others about the proper march-order, the arrangement for reconnaissance and how far a military decision should
be pushed forward or postponed. Whenever a dispatch arrived,
he showed panic in his very looks and movements; and then he
turned to drink. Finally, bored with camp life, and hearing
about the defection of the fleet at Misenum, he returned to
Rome, frightened by each new blow he suffered but blind to
the supreme danger. Although it was open to him to cross the
Apennines with his army intact and attack an enemy exhausted
by the winter and lack of supplies, he scattered his resources
and consigned to slaughter and captivity a devoted army that
was ready to face any odds. His most experienced centurions
disagreed with him, and would have told the truth if consulted,
but Vitellius' closest friends kept them at bay. He himself was
predisposed to listen to sound advice in a sour mood and to
lend a ready ear only to what was agreeable – and fatal.

57. In civil wars, the daring escapades even of single individuals can have great influence. Claudius Faventinus, a centurion who had been ignominiously dismissed by Galba, induced
the fleet at Misenum to rebel after he had dangled before the
sailors a forged letter from Vespasian offering rewards for
treachery. The fleet was commanded by Claudius Apollinaris,
an officer who was neither robustly loyal nor enterprising as a
rebel. An ex-praetor, too, Apinius Tiro, happened to be at
Minturnae at the time, and put himself at the head of the rebels.

Incited by these two, the towns and the colonies in the area added their local rivalries to the confusion of civil war – Puteoli was particularly attached to Vespasian, while Capua was faithful to Vitellius.[65] To soothe the sailors' ruffled feelings, Vitellius now chose Claudius Julianus, who had recently commanded the fleet at Misenum without much insistence on discipline, and for this purpose gave him one urban cohort and some gladiators already under his command. When the two forces encamped within striking distance of each other, Julianus lost little time in going over to Vespasian. The rebels then occupied Tarracina, which was protected more efficiently by its walls and position than by the temper of its new garrison.

58. On hearing of this, Vitellius left part of his forces at Narnia with the praetorian prefects, and sent off his brother Lucius with six cohorts and 500 cavalry to confront the offensive which was being mounted throughout Campania. The emperor himself was depressed, but found some encouragement in the enthusiasm of his troops and the clamour of the people calling for war. For he gave the specious names of 'army' and 'legions' to a cowardly mob unlikely to translate its boasts into action. On the advice of his freedmen – for at Vitellius' court loyalty stood in inverse proportion to rank – he ordered the people to be mustered by tribes, and had volunteers sworn in. Since a huge crowd was pouring in, he allocated responsibility for the levy to the consuls. He imposed upon the senators specific contributions of slaves and money. The equestrian order offered its services and wealth, and freedmen, too, actually asked to shoulder the same burden. Thus a fake devotion created by fear had turned into real attachment. Most people took pity not so much on Vitellius as on the disastrous position of the principate. Besides, Vitellius did his best to stir sympathy by looks, words and tears, for he was lavish with his promises and displayed the emotional extravagances of panic. Indeed, he even consented to be addressed as 'Caesar', a title which he had previously refused.[66] Now the magic of the name appealed to his superstition, and in moments of fear the advice of wise men and the gossip of the mob are listened to with equal alacrity. However, mere emotional impulses, however strong originally,

always grow weaker over time. So senators and knights gradually melted away, at first reluctantly and in his absence, later
without respect or distinction. In the end, Vitellius grew
ashamed of his fruitless efforts and ceased to demand what no
one offered.

59. Although Italy had been frightened by the occupation of
Mevania and by the impression that the war was starting all
over again, the panic-stricken departure of Vitellius added a
decisive impetus to the popularity of the Flavian cause. The
Samnites, Paeligni and Marsi were in an excited state, jealous
that Campania had pre-empted them, and they were naturally
eager to emphasize their new-found loyalty by performing
every kind of military service. However, thanks to the severe
winter, the army had faced a difficult crossing of the Apennines,
and the difficulty it experienced in forcing a way through the
snow, even when unmolested, made it clear how much danger
it would have had to face if Vitellius had not happened to turn
back. So good fortune helped the Flavian leaders no less often
than strategy.[67] In the mountains they met Petilius Cerialis,
who had eluded the Vitellian guards by disguising himself as a
peasant and exploiting his personal knowledge of the area.[68]
Cerialis was closely related to Vespasian, and a distinguished
soldier in his own right, so he was taken up as one of the
generals. According to many accounts, Flavius Sabinus and
Domitian had a chance to escape too, and messengers from
Antonius repeatedly got through bringing details about a
rendezvous and an escort. Sabinus excused himself on the
grounds that his health was not up to such an exhausting and
daring escapade. Domitian had the spirit to act, but Vitellius
had put him in custody and, although his guards promised to
join him in the escape, he feared that this might be a trap. As it
was, Vitellius himself avoided any ill-treatment of Domitian
out of consideration for the safety of his own relatives.

60. When the Flavian generals reached Carsulae, they took a
few days' rest, and waited until the main body of the legions
caught up. The site of the camp appealed to them, too, for it
commanded a wide and distant prospect, and since there were
some very prosperous towns behind them, there was a good

flow of supplies. Furthermore, there was a chance of negotiations with the Vitellians who were only ten miles away and might hopefully be persuaded to surrender. This hardly pleased the common soldiers, who preferred to win a victory rather than negotiate a peace. They were not prepared to wait even for their own legions, in case they shared the prizes rather than the perils. Antonius summoned his men to a parade and pointed out that Vitellius still had considerable forces, which might well waver if they were given time to reflect, but they could become aggressive, if hope were denied them. The opening moves of a civil war, he claimed, must be left to chance, but final victory came with planning and calculation. The fleet at Misenum and the finest part of the coast of Campania had already abandoned Vitellius, who had nothing left of a worldwide empire but the strip of territory between Tarracina and Narnia. They had won sufficient glory by the battle of Cremona, but too much dishonour by Cremona's destruction. Their dearest wish should be to save Rome, not to capture it. He urged that greater rewards and supreme glory would be theirs if they sought the preservation of the senate and people of Rome without bloodshed. These and similar arguments succeeded in mollifying their feelings.

61. Not long afterwards, the legions arrived. Then, as the alarming news of their increased strength spread, the Vitellian cohorts began to waver. No one was encouraging them to fight, but many urged them to go over to the Flavians and competed with one another in surrendering their companies and squadrons to the victor as a free gift that would earn them his gratitude in the future. Thanks to them, it was learnt that Interamna, in the plains nearby, was garrisoned by a force of 400 cavalry. Varus was instantly sent off with a lightly armed force and killed the few who resisted, but most of them threw down their arms and asked for a pardon. A few fled back to the Vitellian camp, spreading demoralization everywhere and telling exaggerated tales of the fighting spirit and numbers of the enemy in order to diminish the scandal of losing the fort. In any case, on the Vitellian side there was no punishment for unsoldierly conduct, and the rewards earned by defection killed loyalty so

that all that remained was a competition in perfidy. There were constant desertions on the part of tribunes and centurions. The common soldiers, on the other hand, stubbornly adhered to Vitellius until Priscus and Alfenus, by leaving the camp and going back to him, freed everyone from the need to be ashamed of giving up.

62. It was during this period that Fabius Valens was put to death at Urvinum, where he had been imprisoned.[69] His head was displayed to the Vitellian cohorts to deter them from indulging in any further hopes, for they imagined that Valens had got through to the German provinces and was mobilizing existing and newly recruited armies there. At this gory sight, they were thrown into despair, whereas the Flavian army was vastly buoyed up and greeted the death of Valens as marking the end of the war.

Valens had been born at Anagnia and came from an equestrian family. Undisciplined in character but not without talent, he had tried to pass himself off as a witty man by behaving frivolously. During Nero's principate, he had appeared in a farce at the emperor's Youth Games, ostensibly under duress, but then voluntarily. He acted with some skill, but showed little sense of decorum. As the commander of a legion, he both supported Verginius and blackened his name. He killed Fonteius Capito after corrupting him – or perhaps it was because his allurements had failed. Although he betrayed Galba, he was loyal to Vitellius and his fidelity shone out positively in contrast with other men's treachery.[70]

63. Their hopes everywhere were shattered so the Vitellian troops decided to go over to the enemy. Even this act was not to be performed without a certain dignity. They marched down to the plains beneath Narnia with banners flying and standards borne aloft. The Flavian army, ready and armed as if for battle, had formed up in closed ranks on either side of the main road. The Vitellians marched forward until they were enveloped by them, and Antonius Primus then addressed them in a conciliatory tone. Some were ordered to stay at Narnia, others at Interamna. One or two of the victorious legions were also left behind with them, not so many as to be oppressive if the

ex-enemy troops behaved, but strong enough to quell any insubordination.

During this period, Primus and Varus sent Vitellius a stream of messages offering him his life, a pension and retirement in Campania if he would lay down his arms and entrust himself and his children to Vespasian's mercy. Mucianus wrote letters to him along the same lines. On the whole, Vitellius took the offer seriously, and talked about the appropriate number of slaves and the best seaside resort to choose. Indeed, his whole attitude was so lethargic that, if his courtiers had not remembered that he was an emperor, he would have forgotten it himself.

64. The leading men of the state, however, were engaged in secret conversations with the city prefect, Flavius Sabinus,[71] urging him to take his share of the glorious victory. They pointed out that he had his own military force in the urban cohorts, and could rely upon the cohorts of the city watch, their own slaves, the luck of the Flavians and the fact that nothing succeeds like success. He should not allow himself to be elbowed out of the limelight by Antonius and Varus. Vitellius' cohorts were few in number and alarmed by gloomy news from every quarter. The populace was easily swayed, and, given a leader, would be quick to transfer its flattery to Vespasian. As for Vitellius, he had not even been able to cope with success, and was now inevitably crippled by disaster. Credit for bringing the war to an end would go to the one who was the first to gain control of Rome. It was fitting for Sabinus to stake a claim to the imperial power on behalf of his brother, and for Vespasian to regard all others in second place to Sabinus.

65. Flavius Sabinus responded to these remarks with no eagerness, for age had enfeebled him, but some people furtively prompted suspicions that it was envy and jealousy that made him delay his brother's rise. It is true that, when both men were private citizens, the elder brother Sabinus overshadowed Vespasian in influence and wealth. People also believed that when Vespasian's credit was impaired, Sabinus had been stingy in providing assistance and had demanded a mortgage on his brother's house and land in return; hence, although they were

outwardly friendly, it was feared that there were hostilities between the pair in private. A more charitable interpretation was that this gentle man hated bloodshed and killing, and that this was why he took part in repeated interviews with Vitellius to discuss peace and an armistice upon agreed terms. They often met in private, and finally made a solemn settlement, it was said, in the Temple of Apollo. Only two men, Cluvius Rufus and Silius Italicus,[72] witnessed the actual terms of the agreement and the words exchanged between them, but observers at a distance marked their looks – Vitellius downcast and contemptible, Sabinus with an expression suggesting sympathy rather than a desire to humiliate.

66. If Vitellius had found it as easy to convert his followers as to give way himself, the army of Vespasian would have entered the capital without bloodshed. As it was, the greater their loyalty to Vitellius, the more passionately they opposed the notion of peace terms, pointing out the danger and discredit of a pact whose faithful observance depended on the conqueror's whim. However conceited Vespasian was, they said, he would not tolerate Vitellius as a subject, and even the beaten side would not accept such a situation. The victor's mercy only meant danger. To be sure, Vitellius himself was no longer young, and had had his fill of success and failure, but what name and status would his son Germanicus inherit? For the moment, there was an offer of money, household slaves and the delightful bays of Campania. However, when Vespasian had consolidated his power, neither he nor his court, nor indeed his armies, would feel safe unless the rival emperor were destroyed. After being taken prisoner and kept for a few days, Fabius Valens had proved too great a burden for them. It was clear therefore that Primus, Fuscus and that typical Flavian, Mucianus, would have no alternative but to kill Vitellius. Caesar had not spared Pompey, nor had Augustus given Antony his life.[73] What hope was there then that Vespasian would be above such things when he had been the dependant of a Vitellius when that Vitellius was a colleague of Claudius?[74] Indeed, even if he had no thought for his father's position as censor and his three consulships, or for the many other high offices filled by

his distinguished family, despair at least should arm him for a desperate bid. The troops stood firm, the people were still enthusiastic. In any case, nothing more dreadful could happen than the fate to which they were hurrying of their own accord. Defeated men must die, men who surrendered must die. The only important thing was whether they were to breathe their last amid mockery and insult, or on the field of honour.

67. Vitellius would not listen to those advising a brave response. He was overwhelmed by pity for his family and concerned that if he fought to the bitter end, he would make the victor less inclined to offer mercy to his widow and children.[75] He also had an elderly mother in poor health, but happily she died a few days before the ruin of her family. The only thing she got from her son's principate was sorrow and a good reputation.

On 18 December, after hearing news that the legion and cohorts at Narnia had deserted him and surrendered to the enemy, Vitellius, dressed in mourning garb, left the palace, surrounded by his sorrowful household. His little son was being carried in a small litter, as if to a funeral procession. The people's utterances were flattering and untimely; the soldiers remained threateningly silent. 68. Nobody was so mindless of human affairs as to be unmoved by that spectacle. A Roman emperor, shortly beforehand master of the human race, after leaving the seat of his authority, was now passing through the city and through the people, abandoning his power. They had neither seen nor heard about anything like it. Suddenly unleashed violence had done for the dictator Caesar, and a secret plot had removed Gaius, while night and the obscure countryside had hidden Nero's flight. Piso and Galba had practically fallen on the field of battle. Yet Vitellius, before an assembly of his own people and in front of his own soldiers, with even women looking on, made a few remarks suitable to his current sorrowful position: he said that he was yielding for the sake of peace and the state, but he begged them only to keep his memory in their hearts and take pity on his brother, his wife and his innocent young children. At the same time he held out his son and made his appeals, now to individuals, now to everyone, to look after him. Finally, as tears stopped him speaking, he turned to the consul (Caecilius Simplex was the man), who was standing close by, and unstrapped his dagger from his side and began to hand it over, the object which symbolized his power over the life and death of his subjects. While the consul was refusing it and the people standing by in the assembly were loudly contradicting him, Vitellius departed, intending to deposit the imperial regalia in the Temple of Concord and to head for his brother's house.[76] Hereupon there was a louder uproar, as they refused to let him enter a private house and called him to the palace. Every other way was blocked, and the only route available was the road leading to the Sacred Way.[77] Not knowing what else to do, Vitellius returned to the palace.

69. A rumour that Vitellius intended to abdicate had already leaked out, and Flavius Sabinus had written to the tribunes of the cohorts ordering them to confine their men to barracks. Assuming, therefore, that there had been a complete transfer of power to Vespasian, the leading senators, a number of knights, all the urban troops and the city guardsmen came in crowds to the house of Flavius Sabinus.[78] While they were there, news came of the people's enthusiasm for Vitellius and the threatening attitude of the cohorts from Germany. By this time Sabinus had gone too far to turn back, and although he was hesitant, they urged him to fight: each man was afraid for himself in case the Vitellians might hunt them down while they were scattered and therefore weaker. As tends to happen in situations of this sort, everybody offered advice, but only a few were prepared to face up to the danger.

Near the Pool of Fundanus,[79] as the armed escort of Sabinus came down the hill, the most active of Vitellius' supporters confronted it. The fracas was unexpected, but the Vitellians gained the upper hand in the skirmish there. In the chaos, Sabinus took the safest course currently open to him: he occupied the Capitoline Hill with a mixed force of soldiers and a few senators and knights. (It is not easy to establish their names, because after Vespasian's victory many people pretended to have served his cause in this way.) There were even some women among the besieged, most notably Verulana Gratilla, who followed the call to action and not the claims of her children and relatives.[80]

The Vitellian soldiers kept only a desultory watch after encircling the besieged, and that is why, late at night, Sabinus was able to get his children and his nephew Domitian to join him on the Capitol. He also managed to send a messenger through a carelessly guarded sector in the enemy lines to tell the Flavian generals that they were under siege and that the situation would get desperate unless help were forthcoming. The night was so quiet that Sabinus could have got away without any harm, for Vitellius' men, although full of dash in a tight corner, were pretty slack when it came to hard work and guard duty, and a sudden wintry rainstorm made seeing and hearing difficult.

70. At first light, before either side could begin hostilities, Sabinus sent one of the senior centurions, Cornelius Martialis, to Vitellius with instructions to complain that the agreement had been broken. The abdication, he protested, had apparently been no more than a pretence and an empty show, designed to deceive all those high-ranking men. For why, otherwise, after leaving the rostra, had Vitellius sought his brother's house, which overlooked the Forum and stimulated people's eyes, rather than the Aventine and his wife's home?[81] This would have been suitable for a private citizen and one trying to avoid all the show of imperial authority. Far from doing this, Vitellius had returned to the very stronghold of empire, the palace. From there an armed column had been sent out, a crowded area of the city had been strewn with the bodies of innocent victims, and not even the Capitol was to be spared. After all, he, Sabinus, was merely a civilian, an ordinary senator. While the issue between Vespasian and Vitellius was being settled by legionary battles, the capture of cities and the surrender of cohorts, and even when the Spanish and German provinces and Britain were already in revolt, he, Vespasian's brother, had remained loyal until Vitellius took the initiative and invited him to negotiate. Agreeing peace terms was crucial for the defeated, but was no more than an adornment for the winners. If Vitellius regretted

the pact, he had no business to launch an armed attack on Sabinus, whom he had perfidiously tricked, or on the son of Vespasian, who was little more than a child. What was to be gained by murdering one old man and one youth? Vitellius should go and face the legions and fight it out there. The result of such a battle would determine everything else.

Alarmed by these reproaches, Vitellius made a short speech in an effort to clear his name, throwing the blame on the troops: his own moderate character, he said, could not deal with their excessive passion. He also warned Martialis to slip away by a secret section of the palace to avoid being murdered by the soldiers as the intermediary of a pact that they detested. Vitellius himself was in no position either to command or to forbid. He was emperor no longer, only the cause of the fighting.

71. Martialis had scarcely returned to the Capitol when the raging soldiers arrived. They had no general, each man wrote his own script. Passing in a swift column the Forum and the temples overlooking the Forum, they charged up the hill opposite until they reached the lowest gates of the Capitoline citadel. There was a series of colonnades built long ago at the side of the slope on the right as you go up. Coming out onto the roof of these, the besieged showered the Vitellians with rocks and roof-tiles. These attackers were armed only with swords, and it seemed tedious to summon catapults and missiles. So they hurled torches into a projecting colonnade and followed the path of the fire. They would have broken through the burnt gates of the Capitol, had not Sabinus torn down statues everywhere (the adornment of our ancestors) and built a sort of barrier on the very threshold. They then attacked the Capitol by two different routes, one near the Grove of Refuge and the other by the hundred steps which lead up to the Tarpeian Rock.[82] Both assaults came as a surprise, but the closer and more vigorous was the one by the Refuge. The Vitellians could not be stopped as they climbed up by the adjoining buildings, which had been raised high (typical in prolonged peace) and were at the same level as the floor of the Capitol. It is uncertain whether the besiegers set fire to the houses, or whether it was the besieged (although this was the more common version) who were trying to dislodge

their enemies as they struggled and advanced.[83] From there the fire spread to the colonnades adjoining the temple.[84] Soon the gables supporting the roof, made from old wood, caught up and nourished the flames. So the Capitol, with its doors closed, undefended and unplundered, was burnt down.

72. This was the most lamentable and appalling disaster to befall the state of the Roman people since the foundation of the city. Although no foreign enemy threatened, although the gods favoured us as far as our failings permitted, the sanctuary of Jupiter Best and Greatest, solemnly founded by our fathers as a symbol of our imperial destiny – a temple which neither Porsenna on the surrender of the city nor the Gauls on its capture had been able to desecrate[85] – was now, thanks to the madness of our leaders, suffering utter destruction. It had already been burnt down in a previous civil war, but by an individual and mysterious act of arson.[86] Now, in broad daylight, it had been besieged, in broad daylight set on fire. For what military purposes had this happened? What prize would come from this enormous disaster?

The temple stood firm so long as we fought to defend our country. Tarquinius Priscus had vowed to build it during the Sabine war, and laid its foundations on a scale prompted rather by a hope of coming greatness than by the then modest resources of Rome. Later, Servius Tullius advanced the building with the support of our allies, as did Tarquinius Superbus with spoils taken from the enemy at the capture of Suessa Pometia.[87] However, the distinction of completing the structure was reserved for the free republic. After the kings were expelled, Horatius Pulvillus dedicated the temple in his second consulship.[88] Such was its magnificence that the enormous increase in Rome's wealth in later days served rather to adorn than to enlarge it. In the consulship of Lucius Scipio and Gaius Norbanus, 425 years later, it was burnt down and rebuilt on the same foundations.[89] The victorious Sulla undertook the responsibility, but he did not live to perform the dedication. This was the only case where his proverbial good luck deserted him. Despite all the great works of the Caesars, the inscription recording the name of Lutatius Catulus survived right up until the principate of Vitellius.[90] Such, then, was the temple which was now being reduced to ashes.

73. However, the fire caused more terror among the besieged than the besiegers. The fact was that in this crisis the Vitellian soldiers showed both cunning and determination, whereas on the opposing side were panic-stricken troops and a leader who was slow to act and seemed mentally paralysed and incapable of speaking or listening. He was neither guided by other people's advice, nor came up with his own plans. Turning now this way, now that in answer to each enemy shout, he countermanded what he had ordered, and ordered what he had countermanded. Soon the typical signs of collapse appeared: everybody gave instructions and no one carried them out. Finally, throwing down their arms, they started looking around them for an escape route and methods of concealment. The Vitellians forced their way in, creating a confused turmoil of blood, iron and flames. A few of the professional soldiers – the most notable being Cornelius Martialis, Aemilius Pacensis, Casperius Niger and Didius Scaeva – ventured to resist, and were struck down. Flavius Sabinus was unarmed and made no attempt to run. He was surrounded, together with the consul Quintius Atticus, who had attracted notice because of his empty distinction and his own pretentiousness in showering edicts upon the people, which glorified Vespasian and insulted Vitellius. The rest got away by various hazardous means, some dressed as slaves, others hidden by loyal dependants and concealed amid the baggage. A few overheard the Vitellian watchword and by actually challenging the enemy or giving the correct answer found concealment in daring.

74. As soon as the enemy broke in, Domitian had hidden himself in the house of the caretaker of the temple. Then, prompted by an ingenious freedman, he put on a linen mantle and escaped recognition by mingling with a crowd of worshippers and secreting himself with one of his father's dependants, Cornelius Primus, who lived near the Velabrum.[91] This is why, during Vespasian's reign, he demolished the caretaker's dwelling and put up a small chapel to Jupiter the Preserver and a marble altar with carvings of his own adventures. Later, on

becoming emperor in his turn, he built a large temple dedicated to Jupiter the Guardian, with an effigy of himself under the protecting arm of the god.[92]

Sabinus and Atticus were heavily chained and taken to Vitellius, who received them with words and looks that showed little hostility, although others clamoured noisily for the right to execute them and demanded a reward for services rendered. The cries, which were first raised among the bystanders, were taken up by the dregs of the city mob, who howled for Sabinus' execution with a combination of threats and flattery. Vitellius was standing at the top of the palace steps preparing to appeal to their better feelings, but they forced him to give up the attempt. Then Sabinus was stabbed and hacked to death, and after cutting off his head they dragged his decapitated body to the Gemonian Steps.[93]

75. Such was the end of a man of undeniable importance. He had served his country for thirty-five years, winning distinction in the civilian and military spheres. You could not question his honesty and fair-mindedness, but he did talk too much. This is the one charge that wagging tongues could level against him during the seven years in which he governed Moesia and his twelve-year tenure as prefect of the city.[94] At the end of his life, some regarded him as unenterprising, but many people believed that he was a moderate man who sought to prevent the bloodshed of his fellow-citizens. What everyone would agree is that before Vespasian's principate, Sabinus was the most distinguished member of his household. We have heard that his murder filled Mucianus with delight. Many observers maintained that it served the interests of peace by putting an end to the rivalry between the two men, of whom one might well have reflected that he was the emperor's brother, and the other that he was his colleague.

Vitellius, however, took a stand against the people's demand for the execution of the consul. Atticus had succeeded in mollifying the emperor, who felt that he owed him something in return, because when asked who had set fire to the Capitol, Atticus had taken responsibility. By this admission (unless it was a lie devised to suit the occasion) he had, so it seemed,

shouldered the resentment and guilt himself, thus exonerating
Vitellius and his followers.[95]

76. Over this same period, Lucius Vitellius had encamped at
Feronia[96] and was threatening to destroy Tarracina after pinning down there the gladiators and sailors, who did not dare
to leave the shelter of the walls or expose themselves to danger
in the open. As I have already mentioned,[97] the gladiators were
commanded by Julianus and the seamen by Apollinaris, but the
decadence and the idleness of the two men made them resemble
gladiators more than generals. They did not keep watch, nor
reinforce the weak places along the walls. Night and day, they
lolled about and made the pleasant beaches ring with sounds
of revelry. The soldiers were scattered everywhere on errands
of pleasure, and they spoke about the war only at their dinner-
parties. A few days earlier, Apinius Tiro had gone off and by
his merciless exaction of gifts and money throughout the towns
of the area he had earned more resentment than support.

77. Meanwhile, a slave belonging to Vergilius Capito[98]
deserted to Lucius Vitellius and promised that, if he were given
men, he would hand over the undefended citadel of Tarracina.
Late at night he led some lightly armed cohorts along the top
of the hills and positioned them overlooking the enemy. From
this point they swooped down to inflict massacre more than to
fight a battle. They cut down their opponents while they were
unarmed or scrabbling for their weapons. Some had just been
roused from sleep and were dazed by the darkness, panic,
trumpet-calls and shouts of the enemy. A few of the gladiators
put up a fight and inflicted some losses before they were killed,
but the rest made a rush for the ships, where the whole place
was caught up in the same panic – civilians were mixed up
with troops and the Vitellians were killing them all without distinction. Six galleys got away at the first alarm, with
Apollinaris the admiral of the fleet on board. The remaining
ships were captured on the shore or were overloaded with too
many fugitives and sank. Julianus was taken before Lucius
Vitellius, and suffered a degrading flogging before having his
throat cut under the victor's eyes.[99] Some criticized Lucius' wife,
Triaria, for putting on a soldier's sword and behaving with

arrogance and cruelty amid the misery and suffering of captured Tarracina.[100] Lucius himself sent a laurelled dispatch to his brother announcing his victory and asking whether he wanted him to return immediately or to press on with subjugating Campania. This delay was not only salutary for Vespasian's followers, but also for the whole state. For if the Vitellian troops – fresh from their victory and, on top of their natural determination, now made feisty by success – had hurried to Rome immediately after the battle, there would have been a desperate struggle which would certainly have culminated in the destruction of the capital. For Lucius Vitellius, despite his shady reputation, did get things done, and as good men derive their power from their virtues, the basis of his strength was his vices, as is the case with the most flawed individuals.

78. While this is what was happening on Vitellius' side, Vespasian's army, which had left Narnia, was celebrating the festival of the Saturnalia in idleness at Ocriculum.[101] The reason for this crass delay was so that they could wait for Mucianus. Some have suspected Antonius of treacherously wasting time after receiving a secret communication from Vitellius, and there was in fact a letter offering him a consulship, Vitellius' marriageable daughter and a rich dowry as a reward for changing sides. Others believe that this account was invented to please Mucianus. Certain writers have said that it was the strategy of all the Flavian generals to threaten Rome with war rather than to attack the city, since the most powerful cohorts had deserted from Vitellius, and in fact now that he was deprived of all his forces, it seemed inevitable that Vitellius would abdicate. However, according to this view, Sabinus spoiled everything first by his haste, then by his cowardice, after rashly resorting to arms and then proving unable to defend the Capitoline Hill against only three cohorts, although it should have been impregnable even to large armies. It is difficult to blame any one leader when they were all responsible. For Mucianus persistently delayed the victors by his ambiguously worded letters, while Antonius by ill-timed obedience earned himself condemnation just when he was trying to avert criticism. As for the other generals, they believed that the war was over, which made

its final stages all the more notorious. Petilius Cerialis had been
sent ahead with 1,000 cavalry to march cross-country through
Sabine territory and enter the city by the Salarian Way, but
even he had failed to make sufficient haste, and, at last, the
news that the Capitol was under siege shocked all the Flavian
commanders alike into action.

79. The night was almost over before Antonius marched
down the Flaminian Way and reached the Saxa Ruba,[102] but
his help came too late. There he heard that Sabinus had been
killed, the Capitol had been burnt down, the city was in a panic,
and that everything looked bleak. He also began to get news
that the common people and slaves were taking up arms for
Vitellius. Furthermore, Petilius Cerialis' cavalry engagement
had ended in defeat. For as he hurled himself recklessly against
an enemy he believed beaten, a mixed Vitellian force of infantry
and cavalry had caught him off his guard. The battle took
place near the city amidst buildings, gardens and winding lanes
familiar to the Vitellians but formidable to the enemy, who
were strangers to the area. Besides, the Flavian cavalry were
not cooperating as a group, since they had been joined by some
troops who had just surrendered at Narnia and were watching
to see which side was the lucky one. The commander of a
cavalry regiment, Julius Flavianus, was captured. The rest were
driven off in a degrading rout, although the victors did not keep
up the pursuit beyond Fidenae.

80. This success made the people more enthusiastic than ever.
The city mob armed. Only a few had proper military shields,
so most of them grabbed whatever weapons they could find
and demanded the signal for battle. Vitellius thanked them and
gave orders for them to go forth and defend the city. Then after
the senate had been summoned, a delegation was chosen to
meet the Flavian armies and urge a peace settlement, ostensibly
in the interests of the country.

The envoys had a mixed reception. Those who had approached
Petilius Cerialis faced an extremely dangerous situation, for the
troops flatly refused their terms. The praetor Arulenus Rusticus
was wounded.[103] What made this particularly scandalous was
his high personal reputation, quite apart from the violation of

his status as an ambassador and praetor. His colleagues were roughly handled, and his senior lictor was killed when he dared to clear a way through the crowd. Indeed, if the escort provided by the general had not come to their defence, the diplomatic immunity enjoyed by ambassadors even among foreign nations would have been violated by murder outside the very walls of Rome, thanks to the madness of civil war. The ambassadors sent to Antonius were received more calmly, not because the troops were more restrained but because their general had more hold over them. 81. Among these envoys was Musonius Rufus, a knight and a keen student of philosophy and the principles of stoicism.[104] Mixing with the troops in their companies, he now proceeded to lecture armed men about the benefits of peace and the dangers of war. Many of them laughed in his face, more still found him boring, and a few were even ready to knock him over and trample on him, but luckily the warnings of the most obedient men and the threats of the rest made him abandon his untimely moralizing. The Flavians also received a deputation of Vestal Virgins carrying a letter from Vitellius addressed to Antonius. In this, he asked for a delay of one day before the final conflict, and urged that if they would only interpose this deferral, it would be easier for them to agree a general settlement. The Vestals were sent away with due courtesy, and Vitellius was informed in the reply that with the murder of Sabinus and the burning of the Capitol all the deals normal in war were at an end.

82. However, Antonius did call the legions to a meeting and try to calm them, urging them to camp for the night by the Milvian Bridge and enter Rome on the following day.[105] His reason for waiting was his fear that the troops, once stirred up after a battle, would have no regard for the people and senators or even for the temples and shrines of the gods. However, the men suspected any postponement as being detrimental to their victory. Besides, the glint of banners displayed along the hills gave the impression of a hostile professional army, although in fact only untrained civilians were massed behind them.

The Flavians advanced in three columns. One went down the Flaminian Way where the soldiers had been assembled, a second advanced along the bank of the Tiber and a third approached the Colline Gate by the Salarian Way. The civilians were routed by a cavalry charge, but the Vitellian soldiers moved up to face the attack, also in three battle groups. There were many clashes outside the city with varying results, but the Flavians more often came off better since they were helped by better leadership. However, some of the attackers turned off along narrow and slippery tracks towards the eastern areas of the city and the Sallustian Park, where they were the only ones to meet with stiff resistance. The Vitellians, standing on the garden walls and using stones and javelins, withstood the attackers below them until the evening. Finally, the cavalry forced its way through the Colline Gate and enveloped the defenders. There was fierce fighting in the Campus Martius, too. Here good luck and numerous past victories helped the Flavians. It was only despair which made the Vitellians rush wildly onwards, and despite being routed they re-formed repeatedly inside the city.

83. The people of Rome stayed and watched the fighting as if they were spectators at a gladiatorial show, cheering and clapping now one side then the other in turn. Whenever one side gave way and soldiers would hide in shops or take refuge in some house, the people clamoured for them to be dragged out and killed. This meant that the people gained most of the loot, for the soldiers were bent on bloodshed and slaughter, so the spoils fell to the crowd.[106]

The whole city presented a brutal caricature of its normal self – fighting and casualties at one point, baths and restaurants at another, bloody heaps of corpses right next to prostitutes and their like. All the perverse passions associated with a life of luxury went hand-in-hand with whatever criminal acts you would expect during the most pitiless sacking of a city, so much so that you would have thought that the city was in the grip of a simultaneous orgy of violence and pleasure. Armies had clashed in the city before this, twice when Lucius Sulla gained control, and once under Cinna.[107] There was no less cruelty back then, but what was so inhuman now was the indifference of people who did not interrupt their pleasures even for a moment. As if this were one more entertainment for the holiday, they gloated over horrors and profited by them, careless which side won and glorying in the calamities of the state.

84. The storming of the praetorian camp[108] involved the heaviest fighting, since it was held by the most determined Vitellians who saw it as their last hope. This spurred on the victors all the more, particularly the ex-praetorians, and they simultaneously deployed all the resources ever designed to storm the most powerful cities – the testudo, artillery, earthworks and firebrands – and shouted out again and again that this operation was the climax of all the toil and danger they had endured in so many battles. Rome, they cried, had been handed back to senate and people, their temples to the gods, but the soldier's special pride lay in his camp: that was his country, that was his home! If they could not recover it at once, the night would have to be spent under arms. On the opposing side, the Vitellians, despite being outnumbered and doomed, embraced the final consolation granted to the defeated by marring the victory, delaying peace and desecrating homes and altars with blood. Many of them lost consciousness and died on the towers and ramparts, and after the gates were torn down a compact group of survivors charged at the victors. They all fell with their wounds in front, facing the enemy. Such was their concern to die honourably even as they were facing their final moment.

After the city was captured, Vitellius was taken in a chair through the back of the palace to his wife's house on the Aventine, with the intention of escaping to his cohorts and his brother at Tarracina, if he could lie low during the remaining hours of daylight. Then he returned to the palace, typically mercurial and true to the psychology of panic when someone who fears everything finds the present course of action the least palatable of all. The building was empty and deserted, for even the humblest of his slaves had slipped away or was making efforts to avoid him. The solitude and silence of the place frightened him. He tried locked doors and shuddered at the emptiness. Exhausted by his pitiful wanderings and concealed in some degrading hiding place,[109] he was hauled out by Julius Placidus, a tribune of the guards. His hands were tied behind his back. With his clothes torn to shreds he was led forth, a revolting spectacle, as the onlookers cursed him and not a single person shed a tear, for the squalour of his end had robbed it of pity. On the way, a soldier from the army of Germany angrily aimed a blow at Vitellius, or else perhaps he just wanted to spare him further humiliation or was trying to attack the tribune. In any event, he cut off the tribune's ear, and was immediately cut down.

85. Prodded by the swords of his enemies, Vitellius was forced now to look up and face their insults, now to watch the statues of himself as they came toppling down and above all to behold the rostra and the spot where Galba was murdered.[110] Finally, they drove him to the Gemonian Steps where the body of Flavius Sabinus had lain.[111] One remark of his was overheard which indicated that his spirit was not wholly degenerate. As a tribune was mocking him, he retorted that he had nevertheless been the man's emperor. Thereupon, he collapsed beneath a barrage of blows; and the mob ridiculed their dead emperor just as maliciously as they had flattered him while he was alive.

86. His father, as I have already recorded, was Lucius Vitellius the censor and three times consul.[112] His home town was Luceria. He was fifty-seven years old when he died, having won the consulship, various priesthoods and a name and place among the leading figures of Rome, all thanks to his father's eminence and without the slightest effort on his own part. The principate was offered to Vitellius by men who did not know him personally. Few commanders have made themselves so popular with the army by good actions as he did by doing nothing. However, he displayed frankness and generosity, although these qualities can prove disastrous if unchecked. Thinking that maintaining friendships depended on the lavishness of gifts, not on the steadiness of one's character, he deserved friends but did not have any. It was undoubtedly in the public interest that Vitellius was defeated, but those who betrayed him to Vespasian cannot claim credit for their act when they had treacherously abandoned Galba for Vitellius in the first place.

The day was turning into evening. It was impossible to call a meeting of the senate since the panic-stricken magistrates and senators had slipped out of the city or were hiding themselves in the houses of their clients. When there was nothing more to fear from the enemy, Domitian presented himself to the Flavian generals and was hailed as 'Caesar'. The troops crowded round and just as they were, still armed, escorted him to his father's home.[113]

BOOK 4

Trouble in the Senate

1. Murdering Vitellius had stopped the war without initiating peace. The armed victors were hunting down the defeated throughout the city with relentless hate: streets were choked with bodies, squares and temples ran with blood after men had been killed indiscriminately wherever they happened to be found. Soon the chaos escalated as they searched everywhere and dragged their victims from their hiding places. Whenever they caught sight of anyone who was tall and youthful, they cut down such men without making any distinction between soldiers and civilians. While their feelings of hatred still ran high, they satisfied their brutal instincts with bloodshed, but then it was transformed into greed. They left no corner untouched, no door unopened, as they pretended to be looking for Vitellius' supporters in hiding. That was when they started to break into private houses or, if they met resistance, they used this as a pretext for murder. There were plenty of destitute Romans or vicious slaves ready to betray rich masters.[1] Others again were denounced by their friends. Everywhere there was wailing and lamentation as Rome suffered the plight of a captured city, so much so that people longed for the unruly soldiers of Otho and Vitellius, although they had been hated at the time. The Flavian generals had been keen to set the civil war ablaze, but in victory they were incapable of exercising control. The truth is that in times of trouble and discord it is the utter rogues who have the most forceful impact, whereas peace and quiet call for the skills of good men.

2. Domitian had taken up the title of Caesar and the imperial residence, but although he was not yet prepared to focus on

his official responsibilities, he was already playing the part of an emperor's son by his rapes and adulteries. Arrius Varus was given the post of praetorian prefect, but supreme control rested with Antonius Primus, who helped himself to money and slaves from the emperor's palace as if they were the spoil from Cremona. Thanks to moderation or humble birth, just as the other generals had been marginalized in the war, they were now kept at arm's length from its profits.

The Roman populace, frightened and resigned to its servitude, urged that Lucius Vitellius should be intercepted on his way back from Tarracina with the cohorts and that the final dying flames of the war should be put out. Some cavalry were sent ahead to Aricia, while a column of legionaries marched out and stopped just before Bovillae. Vitellius speedily entrusted himself and his cohorts to the victor's discretion, and his men threw down their luckless arms as much in disgust as fear. A long line of prisoners hedged in by armed guards marched through the city. Nobody looked like he was angling for mercy, but grim-faced and truculent, they confronted the clapping and insults of the jeering mob with frozen expressions. A few tried to break away but were surrounded and dealt with. The rest were put into custody. Not a single man said anything discreditable, and despite being surrounded by troubles their reputation for valour remained intact. Lucius Vitellius was then executed. He was as unprincipled as his brother, but he showed more vigilance during Vitellius' principate, and although he was not the emperor's partner amidst success, he was still swept away by his fall.

3. Over this same period, Lucilius Bassus was sent off with a force of lightly armed cavalry to settle Campania, which was being disturbed by the mutually hostile feelings of the towns, rather than by any stubborn resistance against the new emperor. The sight of the troops had a calming effect, and the smaller towns were not penalized, but at Capua the Third Legion was left to spend the winter, which meant that the leading families suffered severely. The people of Tarracina, despite what one might expect, received no assistance,[2] which shows that men are more inclined to repay injury than kindness: the truth is

that gratitude is a burden, but vengeance can be turned to profit. It was some comfort that Vergilius Capito's slave, who, as I have mentioned,[3] had betrayed Tarracina to the enemy, was crucified, still wearing the very rings which Vitellius had given him to wear.

At Rome, however, the senate awarded Vespasian all the usual imperial titles. It felt pleased and confident: the civil war, begun in the Gallic and Spanish provinces, spreading to Upper and Lower Germany and then Illyricum, finally extending to Egypt, Judaea, Syria and every province and garrison, now seemed to have purged the whole world of evil and run its course. The senate was further encouraged by a letter from Vespasian, written under the impression that the war was still continuing. That, at any rate, was how it looked at the first glance, but he spoke like a proper emperor, making modest remarks about himself and demonstrating respect for the state. The senate in its turn showed due deference, decreeing a consulship for Vespasian and his son Titus, and a praetorship with the powers of a consul for Domitian.[4]

4. Mucianus, too, had sent a letter to the senate, which gave rise to comment. If he were a private citizen, why, it was asked, did he speak with the voice of authority? He could have given the same report verbally in a few days' time when called upon to speak in the senate from his proper place. Besides, even his criticism of Vitellius came too late to prove his independence. What showed true contempt for the state and really insulted the emperor was his boast that the principate had been in his hands and had been given to Vespasian as a gift. However, they kept their resentment hidden and displayed flattery. With many fine words, Mucianus was granted triumphal honours for a war waged against fellow-Romans, although his campaign against the Sarmatians was made the excuse.[5] Antonius Primus, too, received the insignia of consul, and Cornelius Fuscus and Arrius Varus those of praetor. After that it was the gods' turn: they decided to restore the Capitol.[6]

All these proposals were made by the consul-designate, Valerius Asiaticus.[7] The rest of the senators indicated their assent by a mere glance and gesture, but a few especially distinguished figures or those who had talent for flattery supported the resolutions with elaborate and insincere speeches. When the turn of the praetor-designate Helvidius Priscus came, he expressed himself in language which paid due respect to the new emperor, but showed no traces of insincerity, and the senate gave him a tremendous reception. For Helvidius this day above all saw him begin to offend powerful figures – but it also initiated his great distinction.

5. Since this is the second time that I have had occasion to refer to a man whom I will often have to mention, it seems appropriate to outline here his career and interests, and his fortune in life.[8] Helvidius Priscus came from the town of Cluviae,[9] and his father had been the senior centurion of a legion. From early youth he devoted his brilliant intellect to academic studies, not (as so often happens) in order to disguise ease and idleness under a pretentious name, but to arm himself more stoutly against the unpredictable chances of a public career. He followed the school of philosophy which counts moral virtue as the only good and vice as the only evil, while power, rank and factors extraneous to a man's character are counted as neither good nor evil.[10] When he was still only a quaestor, he was chosen by Thrasea Paetus to marry his daughter, and from his father-in-law's character he learnt, above all, how to be independent. As citizen, senator, husband, son-in-law and friend, he met the varied obligations of life in a consistent way, showing his contempt for wealth, stubborn adherence to the right course of action and courage in the face of danger.

6. There were some who thought that he was too eager to make a name for himself, for even philosophers find that the last frailty to be shed is a longing for glory. He was driven into exile by the fall of his father-in-law, but he returned on the accession of Galba and proceeded to impeach Thrasea's prosecutor, Eprius Marcellus.[11] This act of vengeance, perhaps excessive, perhaps justified, deeply divided the senate at the time. For if Marcellus were to be convicted, it meant the downfall of a whole army of potential defendants. The case opened with a menacing encounter, as the brilliant speeches of the two opponents show, but as time went on, Galba's ambiguous attitude

and the protests of many senators caused Priscus to drop the charge. Reactions varied, like men's characters. Some praised his restraint, others found him lacking in determination.

However, at the meeting of the senate that recognized Vespasian's imperial power, it had been decided that a delegation should be sent to the emperor. This led to a bitter quarrel between Helvidius and Eprius. Priscus demanded that the members of the deputation should be chosen individually by the magistrates under oath, while Marcellus called for the use of lot in accordance with the motion of the consul-designate. 7. Yet Marcellus' eagerness was really prompted by his own embarrassment, in case people believed that he was held in less esteem if others were chosen instead of him.

From brief exchanges, they gradually passed on to prolonged and bitter speeches, as Helvidius asked why Marcellus was so frightened of the verdict of the magistrates. After all, he had sufficient money and eloquence to give him a lead over many others, except that he was being hampered by men's memory of his crimes. If lots were drawn, no distinction was made between men's characters, but a senatorial vote and expression of opinion, on the other hand, was designed to probe the life and reputation of each and every candidate. It was crucial that, in the interest of the state and as a mark of respect for Vespasian, he should be met by the most irreproachable members of the senate – men who could accustom the emperor's ear to the language of honour. Vespasian had been friendly with Thrasea, Soranus and Sentius.[12] However inadvisable it might be that their prosecutors should be punished, they should not be paraded before him. By this senatorial verdict, they could give hints to the emperor about the men to favour and the men to fear. There was no instrument of good government more important than good advisers. Marcellus should be satisfied with having driven Nero to execute so many innocent victims. Let him enjoy his ill-gotten gains and his immunity from punishment, and leave Vespasian in the hands of better men.

8. Marcellus retorted that the proposal under attack was not his own, but it was the consul-designate who had made the recommendation in accordance with long-standing precedents

which had laid down that delegations should be chosen by
lot, in order to leave no room for self-promotion or personal
vendettas. Nothing had happened to make these ancient practices obsolete, or to transform a tribute to the emperor into an
insult to anybody else. They were all qualified to do homage.
What was more pressing was to make sure that they did not
allow the stubbornness of certain individuals to irritate the
emperor at the start of his principate, when his mood was
edgy and he was likely to be keeping an eye on everybody's
expressions and remarks. He said that he remembered the era
in which he was born and the constitution devised by their
fathers and grandfathers. Although he admired those earlier
times, he upheld the way things were done now, and while
praying for good emperors, he put up with them as they came
along. Thrasea had been brought low just as much by the
verdict of the senate as by his own speech. Sham trials of that
sort had delighted Nero's savage disposition, and Marcellus'
friendship with such an emperor had been just as agonizing an
experience for himself as exile had been for others. In short,
Helvidius was welcome to boast of his resolution and intrep-
idity, and class himself with the Catos and Brutuses of this
world.[13] He, Marcellus, was merely a single member of a senate
that had been slaves together. He had one further piece of
advice for Priscus. Let him not seek to climb above his emperor,
or try to play the schoolmaster to a man like Vespasian who,
no longer young, had held the honours of a triumph and was
the father of grown-up sons. Evil emperors wanted limitless
power, but even the best of them welcomed some threshold to
their subjects' independence.

These conflicting views were debated with great vigour on
both sides, and met with varying reactions. The contingent
which wanted the delegation to be chosen by lot won the day,
with even the moderates supporting tradition. All the most
prestigious senators also came down on this side because they
were afraid of their colleagues' jealousy if elected themselves.

9. Another dispute followed. The praetors, who at that time
administered the treasury, had complained about the impover-
ished public finances and demanded a limit on expenditure.

The consul-designate suggested that this problem should be left for the emperor, since the responsibility was so huge and the remedy so problematic, but Helvidius proposed senatorial action. When the consuls started to gauge the opinions of the senators in order of seniority, a tribune of the plebs called Vulcacius Tertullinus used his veto[14] to prevent any decision being taken on this important issue in the absence of the emperor. Helvidius had already proposed that the Capitol should be restored at public expense, with financial assistance from Vespasian. The moderates all passed over this proposal in silence and it was then forgotten, but there were some who remembered it all too well.

10. Then Musonius Rufus attacked Publius Celer, alleging that he had only managed to get Barea Soranus convicted by false testimony.[15] It seemed that this inquiry would revive the hatred that had been stirred by the professional accusers, but in this case the defendant was despicable and guilty, and there was no question of shielding him. For people remembered Soranus with reverence, while Celer, who claimed to be a philosopher, but still testified against Barea, was a traitor who had broken the very bonds of friendship which he professed to teach. The hearing was fixed for the next meeting of the senate, but now that vengeful feelings had been aroused, it was not so much Musonius or Publius they were waiting for as Priscus, Marcellus and the rest of them.

11. That was the state of affairs – disagreements between the senators, angry feelings amongst the defeated, no capacity amongst the victors to command respect, Rome uncontrolled by either laws or emperor – when Mucianus entered the capital and concentrated all power in his own hands. Antonius Primus and Arrius Varus now lost their influence, since Mucianus' resentment towards them was obvious, although he tried to conceal it in his expression. Rome, shrewd enough to detect a strained relationship, turned her back on them and transferred her allegiance to the new master: Mucianus was the only one to be courted and flattered. He played his part too by constantly moving from one palace or park to another, closely surrounded by an armed escort. This taste for ostentation, processions

and military guards shows how eagerly he embraced imperial power, while waiving the title of emperor.

The greatest alarm was caused by the execution of Calpurnius Galerianus, the son of Gaius Piso.[16] He had kept out of political adventures, but his distinguished name and the good looks of youth made him the subject of popular gossip, and in a city which was still unsettled and always relished the latest rumours, some people indulged in empty talk about him as a possible emperor. On the orders of Mucianus, he was put under military arrest, and to avoid a conspicuous execution in the city itself, it was at a point forty miles from Rome along the Appian Way that his veins were opened and he bled to death.[17] Julius Priscus, the praetorian prefect under Vitellius, committed suicide less from compulsion than a sense of shame, but Alfenus Varus managed to survive his own disgraceful cowardice. Asiaticus, being a freedman, paid for his evil influence at court by being executed in the manner appropriate for a slave.[18]

The Revolt of Civilis

12. Over this period rumours of disaster in Germany began to multiply, but Rome received them without concern. The annihilation of armies, the capture of permanent legionary camps and the defection of the Gallic provinces were indeed discussed – but not as if they were calamities. In order to explain the reasons why this war arose and blazed up to form such a widespread rebellion of foreign and allied peoples, I shall go back and explain its origins.[19]

The Batavians, so long as they lived beyond the Rhine, were a tribe of the Chatti.[20] Driven out by domestic dissensions, they occupied the uninhabited coastal fringes of Gaul, together with the neighbouring 'Island',[21] which is washed by the North Sea on the west and on the other three sides by the Rhine. They were not exploited financially by the Romans (which is rare when an alliance is made with a stronger power), but contributed only men and arms to the empire. After a long training in the German campaigns, the Batavian cohorts were moved across the Channel to Britain[22] where they added to their glorious

reputation, still commanded according to long-standing practice by their own nobles. They also had in their home country
a picked cavalry force specially trained for amphibious operations. These men could swim across the Rhine in perfect formation while keeping hold of their arms and horses. 13. By far
the most prominent of the Batavians were Julius Civilis and
Claudius Paulus,[23] who were of royal descent. Fonteius Capito
executed Paulus on a trumped-up charge of rebellion, while
Civilis was sent in chains to Nero. Although acquitted by Galba,
he found himself once more in danger under Vitellius, whose
army clamoured for his execution. This was why he hated Rome
and hoped for great things from our difficulties. However,
Civilis was unusually intelligent for a native, and passed himself
off as a second Sertorius or Hannibal, whose facial disfigurement he shared.[24] To avoid being targeted as an enemy if he
rebelled against Rome openly, he posed as a friend and supporter of Vespasian. It is true that Antonius Primus sent him a
letter with instructions to divert the reinforcements called up
by Vitellius and to delay the legions by the pretence of a German
revolt. Hordeonius Flaccus had given him the same advice in a
personal interview, since he was sympathetic to Vespasian and
concerned for his country, which faced disaster if fighting were
resumed and thousands of armed men poured into Italy.

14. So Civilis resolved to rebel, but for the time being he
concealed his real purpose, intending to shape the rest of his
actions in the light of future events. He initiated his uprising in
the following way. On Vitellius' orders, the young Batavians
were being conscripted, which was a heavy enough burden on
its own, but it was exacerbated by the greed and depravity of
the recruiting officers, who called up the old and unfit in order
to exact a bribe for their release, while young, good-looking
lads – for children are normally quite tall among the Batavians[25]
– were dragged off and raped. This caused bitter resentment,
so the ringleaders of revolt assembled and got their countrymen
to refuse service. Civilis invited the nobles and the most enterprising commoners to a sacred grove, ostensibly for a banquet.
When he saw that darkness and revelry had inflamed their
hearts, he spoke to them. He opened with patriotic remarks

about the glory and renown of their tribe, and then he went on to catalogue the injustices, the exactions and all the other evils of slavery. Once they had been regarded as allies, but now they were treated like slaves. When was the Roman governor coming? At least he exercised real control, despite his oppressive and arrogant entourage, but the Batavians were at the mercy of prefects and centurions. After these men had glutted themselves with spoil and blood, they were only replaced by others looking for fresh pockets to pick and new descriptions for plunder. They were faced with a levy which parted children from parents and brothers from brothers, apparently for ever. The Roman state had never been in such low water. The permanent legionary camps contained nothing but loot and old men. Let them just lift up their eyes and have no fear of legions which existed in name only. The Batavians, on the other hand, could rely on the strength of their infantry and cavalry, their kinsmen the Germans, and aspirations which united them with the Gallic provinces. Even the Romans would welcome such a war. If it ended in failure, they could still claim credit with Vespasian, but if they won, they would not have to give an account to anyone.[26]

15. The Batavians listened to the speech with wholehearted approval, so Civilis got them all to swear an oath of loyalty marked by barbarous ritual and traditional curses for perjury. Envoys were sent to the Canninefates to agree a joint plan of action. This tribe occupies part of the Island and closely resembles the Batavians in origin, language and fighting spirit, but they are less numerous. Then by secret communications he won over the auxiliaries from Britain, that is, the Batavian cohorts, which, as I have already mentioned, had been sent to Germany[27] and were now stationed at Mogontiacum.

Among the Canninefates there was a foolishly reckless man called Brinno, who came from a very distinguished family. His father had embarked on many daring escapades against the enemy, and he had also poured scorn on Gaius' ridiculous expeditions without being punished.[28] Thanks to the aura of celebrity surrounding this rebellious family, he was popular, and after being placed on a shield in the tribal fashion and carried on the swaying shoulders of his bearers, he was chosen as leader. Immediately calling upon the Frisii, a tribe beyond the Rhine, he attacked two Roman cohorts in their camp near the North Sea. The garrison had not expected the attack, nor indeed would it have been strong enough to hold out if it had, so the camp was captured and sacked. Then they fell upon the Roman camp-followers and traders who were scattered over the countryside and wandering about with no thought of war. The marauders were also on the point of destroying the frontier forts, but these were set on fire by the cohort-prefects because they could not be defended. The remaining troops with their standards and colours rallied to the upper part of the Island under a senior centurion called Aquilius, but this was an army in name only and it lacked real strength. That was because Vitellius had withdrawn the bulk of the cohorts' effective soldiers and saddled with arms a bunch of loafers from the nearest Nervian and German districts.

16. Civilis thought that he should try a ruse and took the initiative by blaming the prefects for abandoning their forts. He told them that with the cohort under his command, he would suppress the outbreak of the Canninefates, while the Roman commanders could go back to their respective winter-quarters. However, it was clear that treachery lay behind his advice, that scattered cohorts were more liable to be wiped out, and that the ringleader was not Brinno, but Civilis. Hints of this gradually leaked out and the Germans, a nation which delights in war, did not keep the secret for long. When the plot came to nothing, Civilis resorted to force and enrolled the Canninefates, Frisii and Batavians in three separate columns. The Roman battleline faced them, not far from the River Rhine, and their ships, which had landed here after burning the forts, were arrayed to face the enemy. The fighting had only just started when a Tungrian cohort went over to Civilis, and the Roman troops, dismayed by this unforeseen treachery, were slaughtered by a joint force of their allies and enemies. The naval force was equally disloyal. Some of the Batavian rowers feigned incompetence and got in the way of the sailors and marines as they performed their duties. Then they openly

resisted them and steered the ships towards the enemy-held bank, finally murdering the helmsmen and centurions who refused to join them. In the end the whole fleet of twenty-four ships either deserted or was captured.

17. This victory immediately made Civilis and his supporters famous, as well as proving useful subsequently. They had obtained the arms and ships they needed, and were acclaimed as liberators as the news spread like wild-fire throughout the German and Gallic provinces. Envoys were sent at once from the German provinces offering help, and Civilis used cunning and bribery to achieve an alliance with the provinces of Gaul. He returned the captured auxiliary commanders to their own communities and gave the men the choice between discharge and staying with him. Those who remained were offered service on honourable terms, while those who went received spoil taken from the Romans. At the same time, in confidential conversations, he reminded them of the ill-treatment which they had endured for so many years and which they wrongly called 'peace' although it was actually miserable slavery. The Batavians, he said, despite exemption from tribute, had taken up arms against the tyranny they all endured. The Romans had been routed and vanquished in the very first encounter. What if the Gallic provinces shook off the yoke? What reserves were left in Italy? It was at the cost of provincial blood that the provinces were crushed. They should not worry about the battle fought by Vindex. In this, the Aedui and the Arverni had been trampled underfoot by Batavian cavalry. Among the auxiliaries of Verginius had figured the Belgae, and sober reflection showed that Gaul had succumbed to her own Gallic armies. Now they were all on the same side, with the added advantage of such military discipline as had flourished in the Roman army in the past. They were supported by veteran cohorts, fresh from the defeat of Otho's legions. Slavery was good enough for Syria and Asia and the Orient with its tradition of kingship,[29] but in Gaul there were many men still living who had been born before the Roman tribute was imposed.[30] Not all that long ago the annihilation of Quinctilius Varus had certainly banished slavery from Germany, and in that case the emperor challenged was

not Vitellius, but Caesar Augustus.[31] Nature had given even the dumb beasts their freedom, but courage to act was the distinctive attribute of human beings. The gods helped the braver side. So, while they were unencumbered and fresh, they should attack the enemy who was bogged down and exhausted. While one lot was supporting Vitellius and another lot supporting Vespasian, there was scope to attack both.

So Civilis concentrated his efforts on Gaul and Germany. He was aspiring, had his plan succeeded, to become king of the strongest and richest nations in the world.

18. As for Hordeonius Flaccus, he actually helped Civilis' initial moves by pretending that there was nothing wrong, but when panic-stricken messengers arrived with news that a camp had been stormed, cohorts wiped out and everything Roman had been expelled from the Island of the Batavians, he instructed the legate Munius Lupercus to march out against the enemy. Lupercus, who commanded a camp containing two legions,[32] assembled a force consisting of legionaries from the garrison, Ubii from adjacent units and Treviran cavalry stationed at no great distance. These units he rapidly sent across the river, together with a Batavian cavalry regiment which, though long disaffected, pretended to be loyal in order to betray the Romans on the battlefield and derive greater profit from its flight. Civilis surrounded himself with the captured Roman standards so that his men would have before their eyes the newly won trophies, while their enemies would be terrified by reminders of their defeat. He also gave orders for his mother and sisters, accompanied by the wives and young children of all his men, to stand at their rear as a spur to victory or to shame them if they were beaten.[33] When his battleline rang out with the chant of his men and the shrill wailing of the women, it evoked only a feeble cheer from the legions and cohorts in response. The Roman left front was soon exposed by the defection of the Batavian cavalry regiment, which immediately turned about to face us. However, despite this frightening situation, the legionaries kept their arms and ranks intact. The Ubian and Treviran auxiliaries disgraced themselves by stampeding all over the countryside in wild flight. Against them the Germans directed the brunt of their attack,

which gave the legions a breathing space in which to get back to the camp called Vetera. The prefect of the Batavian cavalry regiment, Claudius Labeo, was involved in some petty local rivalry with Civilis. As murdering him might stir resentment amongst the Batavians, but his continued presence could encourage dissension, Civilis had him taken away to the Frisii.

19. At about the same time, the messenger sent by Civilis caught up with the cohorts of Batavians and Canninefates as they were setting off for Rome on Vitellius' orders. They immediately took on an air of ferocious arrogance, and as their price for making the journey they demanded a bounty, double pay and an increase in the cavalry contingent of their units.[34] No doubt Vitellius had promised these privileges, but the men were less concerned to obtain them than to secure a pretext for mutiny. Moreover, by his many concessions Hordeonius Flaccus had only encouraged them to clamour more noisily for what they knew he would refuse. Paying no attention to him, they made for Lower Germany to join Civilis. Flaccus called his tribunes and centurions together and consulted them about whether to bring the insubordinate troops to heel by force. Yet he was naturally sluggish and his anxious staff were worried by the unreliable mood of the auxiliaries and the fact that the legions had been diluted by hasty conscription, so he decided to keep his soldiers within the camp. Afterwards he changed his mind, and as his advisers themselves went back on the views they had expressed, he gave the impression that he intended pursuit, and wrote to Herennius Gallus, stationed at Bonna in command of the First Legion,[35] telling him to bar the passage of the Batavians and promising to follow closely on their heels with his army. The rebels could in fact have been crushed if Flaccus and Gallus had moved up from opposite directions and caught them in the middle. However, Flaccus abandoned his plan, and in a fresh dispatch to Gallus warned him not to trouble the departing cohorts. This caused suspicion that the commanders wanted to stir up the war, and that everything that had already happened, or was feared in the future, sprang not from the slackness of the army or the enemy's violence but from the treachery of the generals.

20. On approaching the camp at Bonna, the Batavian cohorts sent a representative ahead to lay their views before Herennius Gallus. They did not want to wage war against the Romans, for whom they had fought so many times, they said, but they were tired by long and fruitless service, and longed for their homeland and retirement. If no resistance were offered, they would march on without doing damage, but if faced with armed force, they would cut a way through with their weapons. This attitude made the legate hesitate, but his troops induced him to risk a fight. He had 3,000 legionaries and some untrained cohorts of Belgae, together with a number of civilians and camp-followers who were cowardly, although they were boastful enough before the crisis. This force burst from all the gates of the camp so as to surround the Batavians, who were numerically inferior. Yet these Batavians were experienced veterans and they formed up into squares, compact masses of men presenting an impregnable defence everywhere, front, rear and sides. In this formation they broke the thin Roman line. As the Belgae gave way, the legion was driven back and the panic-stricken fugitives made for the rampart and gates of the camp. This was where the heaviest losses occurred. The ditches were piled high with bodies, and the Romans suffered death and wounds not only at the hands of the enemy but as a result of falling and, in many instances, by their own weapons. The victors gave Colonia Agrippinensium a wide berth and did not try their hand at any further hostile act for the rest of the march. They made their excuses for the battle at Bonna, saying that they had asked for peace, but, when this was refused, they had been forced to act in self-defence.

21. The arrival of the veteran cohorts meant that Civilis now commanded a proper army, but he still hesitated about his plan and pondered that Rome was strong. So he made all the men he had swear allegiance to Vespasian, and sent envoys to the two legions which had been beaten in the previous battle and had retired to the camp at Vetera, asking them to accept the same oath. Back came the reply. They were not in the habit of taking advice from a traitor or from the enemy. They already had an emperor, Vitellius, and in his defence they would main-

tain their loyalty and arms to their dying breath. So a Batavian deserter should not sit in judgement on Roman affairs, but instead he should await the punishment he had earned by his crime.[36] When this reply reached Civilis, he flew into a rage, and quickly drove the whole Batavian nation into arms. They were joined by the Bructeri and Tencteri, and as the news spread, Germany awoke to the call of spoil and glory.

22. In the face of this threatening concentration of war, the legionary legates Munius Lupercus and Numisius Rufus proceeded to reinforce the rampart and walls. A settlement just outside the camp which had grown during the long peace to the size of a small town was now demolished to deny its use to the enemy. However, they had forgotten to arrange for the food supplies to be brought into the camp, and allowed them to be looted. Thus stocks which would have covered their needs for a long time were recklessly used up in a few days.[37] Civilis, leading the central expeditionary force consisting of the strongest Batavian troops, filled both banks of the Rhine with disorderly bands of Germans in order to look more ferocious, while the cavalry careered over the plains nearby. At the same time the ships were moving upstream. The besieged were dumbfounded at the sight. In one direction they saw the standards of veteran cohorts, in another direction the images of wild beasts which the various tribes had brought from the forests and sacred groves, for that is how they normally enter battle.[38] The whole appearance was an amalgam of civil and foreign war.

The attacking force was encouraged by the length of the rampart, for scarcely 5,000 armed men were defending a camp which had been designed for two legions. However, a crowd of camp-followers had flocked to Vetera owing to the disturbances and were on hand to help the war effort. 23. Part of the camp occupied a gentle slope, while the other was on level ground and approachable. Augustus had believed that this camp was sufficient to keep the German provinces under supervision and control, never imagining a situation so desperate that the enemy would actually dare to march on Vetera and attack our legions. As a result, no labour had been invested in either the site or the defences. The strength of the garrison had always seemed enough.

The Batavians and the Germans from across the Rhine formed up in separate tribal contingents to show off their individual fighting skills, and challenged us with long-distance volleys. After they found that most of their missiles sank harmlessly into the towers and crenellations of the walls, while they themselves were suffering wounds from the stones being fired from above, they attacked the rampart in a noisy charge. Most of them put ladders against it, while others clambered over a testudo formed by their comrades. A few had already climbed up some way when they were sent tumbling down under a rain of blows from swords and other weapons, to be overwhelmed by the enemy's stakes and javelins. These warriors are always excessively fierce at the outset and uncontrollable when the battle goes their way, but on that occasion their greed for booty made them put up with problems as well.[39] They even risked using siege-engines, although these were a complete novelty for them. Not that they had any technical knowledge themselves. Deserters and prisoners taught them how to build a timber structure rather like a bridge, then after fitting it with wheels how to move it forward. Thus, some of the attackers stood on top of it and so fought as though from a mound, while others hidden inside set about undermining the walls. However, a bombardment of stones from the catapults soon flattened this irregular contraption. As they were preparing bundles of brush and defensive huts, the catapults shot burning spears at the besiegers, who themselves became the target of flames. In the end, despairing of storming Vetera, they resolved on a waiting game, since they were well aware that the camp held only a few days' provisions and a huge crowd of non-combatants.[40] At the same time they hoped that famine might encourage treason, undermine the loyalty of the slaves and bring the chance elements of war into play.

24. Hordeonius Flaccus, meanwhile, hearing that Vetera was under siege, had sent officers to scour the Gallic provinces for reinforcements. He then handed over men specially chosen from the legions to the commander of the Twenty-Second Legion,

Dillius Vocula. The plan was that Vocula should march along the bank of the Rhine at top speed, while Flaccus himself travelled on board a naval squadron, being physically unfit and unpopular with his men. Indeed, the soldiers were quite blunt, grumbling that he had let the Batavian cohorts leave Mogontiacum, hushed up Civilis' designs and was now making an alliance with the Germans. Not even Antonius Primus or Mucianus had done more to promote Vespasian's rise. Obvious hostility and armed attack could be repelled in the open, but treachery and deceit worked in darkness and were therefore impossible to avoid. There, opposite them, stood Civilis, organizing his battleline, but Flaccus confined himself to a couch in his bedroom from where he gave whatever order best suited the enemy. All these armed units of the bravest fighters were being controlled by one sick old man. They were better off killing the traitor and disentangling their luck and bravery from this doomed creature! By such remarks they goaded each other on, but what made them blaze up further was a letter from Vespasian. Flaccus could not hide it, so he read it out to the assembled troops, and sent its bearers to Vitellius in chains.

25. This ploy settled the troops, and they marched to Bonna, the headquarters of the First Legion, but there the men were even more resentful, and blamed Hordeonius Flaccus for their defeat. It was by his orders, they reckoned, that they had been deployed against the Batavians under the impression that the legions from Mogontiacum were in pursuit, and it was thanks to his treachery, too, that they had been cut down when no reinforcements came to help; and, what is more, the other armies had no idea about these events, which were not being communicated to their emperor, although this treachery could have been nipped in the bud by swiftly bringing in reinforcements from the numerous provinces within reach.

Hordeonius Flaccus read out to the army copies of all the letters he had sent asking Britain and the provinces of Gaul and Spain for help, and introduced the disastrous practice of handing over dispatches to the standard-bearers of the legions, who read them to the troops before the officers had seen them. Then he had one of the mutineers arrested, more to assert his right of command than because a single man was to blame. The army now moved from Bonna to Colonia Agrippinensium, where Gallic auxiliaries started to stream in, for at first the Gauls energetically helped the Roman cause, although later, as German strength increased, numerous states took up arms against us, hoping for freedom and desiring to acquire an empire of their own once they had cast off their slavery. Among the legions there was growing resentment, and they had not been intimidated by the imprisonment of one solitary soldier. Indeed, this man actually tried to incriminate the general, alleging that he himself had carried messages between Civilis and Flaccus, but because he was a witness to the truth, he was being stifled on a trumped-up charge. Showing remarkable determination, Vocula got up on a platform and ordered the man to be seized and taken away, still yelling, to execution. This gave the troublemakers a shock, and the better sort obeyed orders. Then, as they unanimously called for Vocula to be their general, Flaccus handed over the command to him.

26. However, many factors exasperated the troubled soldiers. Pay and provisions were short; the Gallic provinces refused to provide either men or tribute; the Rhine was scarcely navigable because of a drought, unusual in this region, and this restricted the movement of supplies.[41] Moreover, units had been posted all along the river bank to prevent the Germans from crossing it, and this factor meant that there were more people to consume less food. Ignorant minds found the shortage of water in itself ominous, since it felt as if even the rivers, those ancient defences of the empire, were abandoning us. Something which in peacetime would have been regarded as a fluke or a natural event was now dubbed 'fate' and 'the anger of heaven'.[42]

On entering Novaesium, they were joined by the Sixteenth Legion. Its commanding officer, Herennius Gallus, was brought in to share the burden of command with Vocula. Not venturing to continue their advance against the enemy . . .[43] they encamped at a place called Gelduba. Here the generals strengthened the soldiers by manoeuvres, by building fortifications and ramparts and by various other military preparations. Wishing to raise morale by the prospect of plunder, Vocula led the army against the lands of the nearby Cugerni, who had accepted Civilis' offer of alliance. Part of the force remained behind with Herennius Gallus.

27. It happened that not far from the camp a heavily laden corn-ship had run aground, and the Germans proceeded to tow it to their side of the river. Gallus was not prepared to put up with this, and sent a cohort to the rescue. The Germans, too, brought up reserves, and as newcomers steadily joined in on either side, a regular battle was fought. After inflicting heavy losses on us, the Germans extricated the ship. The defeated troops adopted the now habitual tactic of blaming their general for treachery rather than themselves for cowardice. They dragged him out of his tent, tore his uniform and gave him a flogging, telling him to reveal what he had got for betraying the army, and who his accomplices were. They then rounded on Hordeonius Flaccus, calling him the mastermind whereas Gallus was just his dogsbody. In the end, terrified by repeated threats of murder, Gallus himself accused Flaccus of treachery. He was then put in chains, and only freed on the arrival of Vocula, who on the following day had the ringleaders of the mutiny executed. This army had the capacity for such diametrically opposed extremes of licentious conduct and submission. The common soldiers were without doubt loyal to Vitellius, while the senior officers favoured Vespasian.[44] This is why there were cycles of crime and punishment and why discipline alternated with insubordination with the result that it was possible to punish men without controlling them.

28. The whole of Germany was now supporting Civilis with vast reinforcements after a firm alliance had been sealed by exchanging hostages of the highest rank. He gave orders for the Ubii and Treviri to be plundered by their immediate neighbours, and another force was sent across the River Mosa to strike a blow at the Menapii and Morini in the north of Gaul. In both areas booty was gathered, but they were especially vindictive in plundering the Ubii because this tribe of German origin had renounced its nationality and preferred to be called by the Roman name of 'Agrippinenses'.[45] Some of their cohorts were cut to pieces in the village of Marcodurum, after they

had become complacent because they were so far from the Rhine. The Ubii in their turn did not hold back from plundering Germany, initially doing so without reprisal, but later they were rounded up, and indeed throughout this war they were less lucky than loyal.

After the crushing of the Ubii, Civilis became more dangerous. Success made him more feisty and now he pressed on with the siege of the legionary camp,[46] keeping tighter watch to prevent any messenger with news of the relieving army from slipping through his lines unobserved. He allotted the artillery and siege-works to the Batavians. He ordered the Germans from across the Rhine, who were clamouring for action, to advance and try to cut the rampart; if they were repulsed they were to renew the struggle, since there was a huge crowd of them and casualties mattered little. 29. Nightfall did not bring an end to their exertions. After heaping up piles of logs all around and setting fire to them, while they were feasting they would surge forward into battle with pointless recklessness as the wine went to each man's head, for their own shots went astray in the darkness, but the Romans could easily see the barbarian troops and aimed at anyone who was conspicuous because of his enterprise or glittering decorations.[47] Civilis, realizing what was happening, gave orders to put out the fires and to turn the whole area into a bewildering blend of darkness and battle. Now, indeed, there was a cacophony of howls and blind onslaughts in which it was impossible to see far enough to strike or to parry blows. Whenever there happened to be shouting, they would wheel in that direction and flail around. Courage was useless, chance ruled the chaos and often the bravest men were felled by the weapons of cowards. The German fighting was marked by incoherent fury, but the Roman soldiers, who knew all about dangerous situations, hurled their iron-tipped stakes and heavy stones to good effect. Whenever the sound of climbing or ladders being placed against the wall delivered the enemy into their hands, they would push back the assailants with their shield-bosses and follow this up with thrusts from their javelins. Many made it up onto the walls, but were stabbed by Roman swords.

This is how they passed the night, but dawn revealed a new form of assault. 30. The Batavians had built a high tower with two storeys which they brought up to the main gate, where the ground was flattest. The defenders responded by using sturdy poles and ramming it with beams until it fell to pieces, causing heavy losses to the men standing on it. The attackers were in a mess and a sudden sortie against them got results. At the same time the legionaries used their extraordinary experience and skill to contrive various engines of war. The one which caused most panic was a grab balanced in a raised position. This would suddenly be let down, whipping one or more enemy soldiers into the air before the eyes of their comrades and then dropped inside the camp by the rotation of the counterweight. Civilis gave up hope of storming the camp and resumed his leisurely blockade, trying in the meantime to wear down the loyalty of the legions by messages and promises.

31. Such was the course of events in Germany up to the battle of Cremona,[48] whose outcome was reported in a letter from Antonius Primus, which also included an edict from Caecina. As well as this, a prefect of one of the defeated auxiliary cohorts, Alpinius Montanus, gave evidence in person of the Flavian victory. Reaction to this news was varied. The auxiliaries from Gaul, who felt neither passion nor hatred for the contending sides and whose service implied no personal attachment, immediately abandoned Vitellius at the prompting of their commanders. The seasoned troops dragged their feet, but when Hordeonius Flaccus administered the oath of allegiance, they too accepted it under pressure from the tribunes, although with little conviction in their looks or hearts, and, while firmly reciting the other formulae of the solemn declaration, they hesitated at Vespasian's name or mumbled it; and most of them passed over it in silence.

32. A letter from Antonius to Civilis was then read to the assembled troops. It stirred their suspicions because it was written as if the recipient were an ally of the Flavians, while the army of Germany was alluded to as an enemy. When in due course the news reached the camp at Gelduba, it provoked the same sort of comments and reactions, and Montanus was sent

on to Civilis with instructions for him to abandon his fighting
and not to conceal a war against Rome under false colours. If
he had set out to help Vespasian, he was told, his mission had
already been fulfilled. Civilis replied artfully at first, but when
he saw that Montanus had an extremely violent character and
was ready for rebellion, he began to complain about the dangers
he had endured for twenty-five years in Roman camps. 'A fine
payment I got for my efforts,' he said, 'the murder of my
brother, my own imprisonment and the vicious clamour of this
army for my execution. For this I seek satisfaction according to
the law of nations. As for you Treviri and the others who are
born slaves, do you expect any reward for the blood you have
shed so often except thankless military service, endless taxation,
rods, axes and the whims of tyranny? Look at me. I command
a single cohort, but with the Canninefates and Batavians, only a
tiny fragment of the Gallic provinces, we have utterly destroyed
those enormous but useless bases or else we are now overwhelming them on all sides with war and hunger. One final
argument: we shall either make a daring attempt and achieve
freedom or lose nothing by defeat.' With these inflammatory
words, but with instructions to take back a milder reply, he
dismissed Montanus, who returned and pretended that his mission had failed.[49] He concealed the other developments, but the
explosion soon came.

33. Civilis held back a section of his forces, and sent the
veteran cohorts and the keenest of his German troops against
Vocula and his army, under the command of Julius Maximus
and Claudius Victor, his sister's son. They sacked the headquarters of a cavalry regiment at Asciburgium as they passed
by, and swooped upon the legionary camp so unexpectedly that
Vocula was unable to address his men or deploy them in battle
formation. All he could do in the chaos was to urge them to
form a central core of legionaries, around which the auxiliaries
clustered in a ragged array. The cavalry charged, but came face
to face with the disciplined ranks of the enemy and turned
about only to collide with their own men. What followed was
a massacre, not a battle. The Nervian cohorts, too, whether
through fear or treachery, left the Roman flanks bare, so the

attack penetrated to the legions. They lost their standards and were already suffering heavy losses within the rampart when fresh help suddenly altered the luck of battle. Some auxiliary cohorts of Vascones recruited by Galba had then been summoned to the Rhineland. As they neared the camp, they heard the shouts of men fighting and charged the enemy from the rear while they were distracted, causing a widespread panic out of all proportion to their numbers. It was thought that the whole army had arrived, either from Novaesium or from Mogontiacum. This misconception gave the Romans new heart: confident in the strength of others, they regained their own. All the bravest Batavian fighters (at least from the infantry) were killed; the cavalry got away with the standards and prisoners taken in the first phase of the battle. On that day a greater number of men were slain on our side, but they were the poorer fighters, whereas the Germans lost their very best. 34. The generals on both sides were equally culpable: they deserved defeat and failed to exploit success. For if Civilis had drawn up his battleline in greater strength, he could not possibly have been surrounded by this small number of cohorts, but would have broken into the camp and destroyed it. Vocula, on the other hand, failed to inform himself of the enemy's approach and was therefore beaten as soon as he came out; then, distrusting his success, he wasted several days before moving against the enemy. If he had quickly taken advantage of his success and kept the enemy on the run, he could have broken the siege of the legions[50] in the same momentous attack.

Meanwhile, Civilis had been making trial of the besieged garrison's morale by pretending that the Romans were finished and that his own force had won a victory. The captured standards and flags were paraded round the camp, and even the prisoners were put on show. One of these pulled off a superb act of daring by shouting out what had really happened for all to hear. He was cut down on the spot by the Germans, but that just confirmed his story. At the same time, the sack and smoke of burning farmhouses told them that the victorious army was coming. When Vocula was within sight of the camp, he ordered a halt, and had his position surrounded by ditch and rampart.

His instructions were for the baggage and heavy kit to be
dumped so that the army could fight unimpeded. This evoked
a storm of criticism against the general as the troops clamoured
for immediate action. They were used to making threats. Without even giving themselves time to form up properly, the dis-
arrayed and exhausted troops went into battle. Civilis was
ready for them, relying as much on the enemy's blunders as
upon the courage of his own troops. The Romans fought with
mixed success. The troublemakers turned out to be cowards,
but some men remembered their recent victory. Standing firm
and striking the enemy hard, they heartened themselves and
their neighbours, and when the line was restored they signalled
to the besieged to seize their chance. From the walls the garrison
could see everything, and they burst out from every gate of the
camp. Moreover, it happened that Civilis' horse fell and threw
his rider. Both armies believed the rumour that he was injured
or killed, and this had a tremendous impact in dismaying his
own men and encouraging their enemies, but Vocula let the
retreating Germans go, and strengthened the rampart and
towers of the camp, as if the siege were soon to be renewed.
After so many failures to exploit victory, there were good
grounds for the suspicion that he preferred fighting.

35. Nothing exhausted our troops so much as the lack of
supplies. The legionary baggage was sent to Novaesium with a
crowd of non-combatants so that they could bring up grain
from there by road, as the river was controlled by the enemy.
The first convoy got through safely, for Civilis was still reeling.
Then he got wind that the supply-train had again been sent to
Novaesium under the protection of auxiliary cohorts and was
proceeding on its way as if all were peaceful and that only a
few men remained at the command posts, with their weapons
stowed away in the wagons and everybody straying about wherever they liked. Civilis attacked in good order after sending
ahead men to hold the bridges where the roads narrowed.
Fighting developed along the straggling marching column, but it
was indecisive, and finally night stopped the battle. The cohorts
rushed on to Gelduba, which still had its camp as before,
guarded by the garrison left there. It was quite clear how much

danger the return trip would involve for the heavily laden and demoralized convoy. Vocula therefore reinforced his troops with 1,000 men taken from the Fifth and Fifteenth Legions which had been besieged at Vetera. These soldiers were insubordinate and hated their officers. More of them set off than had been ordered, openly grumbling on the march that they would no longer put up with short rations and the treachery of their generals. Those who had stayed behind, however, complained that withdrawing a portion of the legions had left them high and dry. So there was a double mutiny, with one group calling Vocula back and the others refusing to return to camp.

36. Meanwhile, Civilis besieged Vetera, while Vocula retreated to Gelduba and from there to Novaesium, near where he soon won a cavalry engagement. However, whether in success or defeat, the troops were just as eager to destroy their leaders. Once the legions were reinforced by the arrival of detachments from the Fifth and Fifteenth, they demanded a bounty, after discovering that Vitellius had sent the money for this. Flaccus quickly handed it over in the name of Vespasian, and it was this more than anything else which nurtured mutiny. In a wild riot of pleasure, feasting and seditious gatherings at night, their old hatred for Hordeonius Flaccus revived, and since none of the legates and tribunes dared to resist – the night had eliminated the last vestige of restraint – the troops dragged him out of bed and murdered him. The same fate was in store for Vocula, but he disguised himself as a slave and managed to get away through the darkness. 37. After the frenzy subsided, fear returned and they sent some centurions bearing letters to ask the Gallic communities for reinforcements and pay. A leaderless mob tends to be impetuous, panic-stricken and slack, and they were no different. As Civilis was approaching they hastily prepared to resist, then promptly dropped their weapons and fled. This failure generated dissension, for the contingents from the army of Upper Germany dissociated themselves from the others. However, the portraits of Vitellius were replaced in the camps and throughout the nearest communities in Belgica, although Vitellius was already dead.[51] Then the men of the First, Fourth and Twenty-Second repentantly followed Vocula

and in his presence once more swore allegiance to Vespasian. They were led off to relieve Mogontiacum, but by this time the besiegers, a mixed force of Chatti, Usipi and Mattiaci, had left the scene with their fill of spoil, but they paid for this with their blood when some of our troops had attacked them on their march, while they were scattered and off their guard. In addition, the Treviri built a battlement and rampart across their own territory, and fought the Germans with heavy losses on both sides. Their subsequent defection tarnished a fine record of service to Rome.

The New Year AD 70

38. While this was happening, Vespasian and Titus entered office as consuls, the former for the second time, although both men were absent. Rome was gloomy and tense thanks to a variety of fears. Quite apart from the calamities which were in fact impending, it was struck by a groundless panic because of a rumour that the province of Africa had revolted at the insti-gation of its governor, Lucius Piso.[52] He was the last man to make trouble, but shipping was being held up by severe winter storms, and the city populace, accustomed to buying its food on a daily basis and only concerned with politics if it involved the corn supply,[53] feared that the coast of Africa was being blockaded and the supplies were being kept back. Fear bred conviction, while the story was exaggerated by the Vitellians, as strongly partisan as ever, and not even the winners them-selves were displeased by the rumour – even foreign campaigns could not satisfy their greed, and no victory in civil war ever did so.

39. On 1 January, at a meeting of the senate called by the city praetor, Julius Frontinus,[54] decrees were passed praising and thanking commanding officers, armies and client-kings. Tettius Julianus[55] was deprived of his praetorship, ostensibly for abandoning his legion when it switched its allegiance to Vespasian, but in reality so that the vacant post could be trans-ferred to Plotius Grypus.[56] Hormus received the rank of knight.

Before long, Frontinus resigned and Caesar Domitian

assumed the praetorship. It was his name that stood at the
head of official letters and edicts, but real power rested with
Mucianus, although Domitian ventured a number of measures
at his friends' instigation or on his own whim. However,
Mucianus' main source of fear lay with Antonius Primus and
Arrius Varus. The fame of their achievements was still current
and bright, which meant that they had the enthusiastic support
of the soldiers, while the people also backed them because, once
the fighting was over, they had avoided any act of violence.
There was also a story that Antonius had encouraged Crassus
Scribonianus[57] to take power. This man derived his prominence
from his distinguished forebears and his brother's memory, and
there was a ready band of conspirators to hand, but Scribonianus refused. He was not an easy man to tempt, even if
success had been guaranteed, but he was all the more afraid of
a complete gamble. So Mucianus, not being able to suppress
Antonius openly, heaped lavish praise on him in the senate and
overwhelmed him with secret offers, pointing to Nearer Spain,
which was then vacant owing to Cluvius Rufus' departure. He
also distributed the posts of tribune and prefect generously
among Antonius' friends. Then, after Mucianus had filled Antonius' mind with empty hope and ambition, he crippled him by
removing to its winter camp the formation most devoted to
Antonius – the Seventh Legion.[58] The Third, too, long associated with Arrius Varus, was returned to Syria. Part of the
army was already on its way to the German provinces. All
troublesome elements were thus removed, and Rome regained
its normal aspect under the rule of law and the operation of
civil authority.

40. On the day when Domitian first formally entered the
senate, he made a short and restrained speech about his father's
and brother's absence and his own youthfulness. He was good
looking and those who did not yet know his character took his
repeated blushes as proof of his modesty.[59] When he proposed
a motion that all Galba's honours should be restored, Curtius
Montanus moved that Piso's memory should be honoured as
well. The senate approved both proposals, but the one about
Piso was never put into effect. Then a committee was chosen

by lot to supervise the restoration of property stolen during the fighting, and others were selected to survey and re-affix the bronze tablets containing the text of laws which had fallen down with the passage of time, to tidy up the official calendars which had become tainted by the current vogue for flattery,[60] and to impose restrictions on state expenditure. Tettius Julianus had his praetorship restored to him when it was discovered that he had fled to Vespasian, while Grypus retained his office. It was then decided to resume the hearing of the case between Musonius Rufus and Publius Celer.[61] Publius was convicted and satisfaction done to the spirit of the dead Soranus. A day that was remarkable for a commendably strict verdict in public matters also reflected positively on private individuals. By bringing the action it was felt that Musonius had done his proper duty, although opinions were divided about the Cynic philosopher Demetrius:[62] his defence of an obviously guilty man seemed to indicate self-promotion rather than a concern with morality. As for Publius himself, both his courage and his eloquence faltered in his hour of danger.

    This trial was the signal to take revenge on the prosecutors. Junius Mauricus[63] asked Domitian to put the imperial diaries at the disposal of the senate so that it could discover from them who had requested permission to impeach which victim. He replied that, in matters of this sort, the emperor must be consulted. 41. The senate, following the prompt given by its leading representatives, formulated a solemn oath which all the magistrates vied with one another to take, followed by the other senators in the order of their seniority. In this they called the gods to witness that they had never aided and abetted any action likely to compromise anyone's safety and had not received either reward or distinction from the downfall of fellow-Romans. Senators with guilty consciences were panic-stricken, and adopted various tricks to change the phrasing of the oath. The members showed approval to those who swore honestly, and stigmatized perjurors. This kind of informal public degradation fell especially harshly on Sariolenus Vocula, Nonius Attianus and Cestius Severus,[64] men notorious for their regular prosecutions during Nero's principate. Sariolenus also had to face the charge that he had recently engaged in the same activity under Vitellius, and the senators continued to shake their fists at Vocula until he left the chamber. They then turned their attention to Paccius Africanus, and hounded him out as well for prompting Nero to destroy the Scribonii, two brothers who had been famous for their wealth and their mutual devotion.[65] Africanus did not dare to confess his part in this, nor could he deny it, but he rounded on Vibius Crispus, who had been tormenting him with questions.[66] Implicating him in charges to which he had no defence, he parried odium by producing an accomplice.

42. On that day Vipstanus Messalla won a great name for loyalty and eloquence. Although under senatorial age,[67] he ventured to plead for his brother Aquilius Regulus, who had attained a detestable eminence after bringing to ruin the families of the Crassi and of Orfitus.[68] It seemed that as a very young man Regulus had volunteered to take upon himself their prosecution, not in order to save his own skin, but in the hope of becoming more influential. Crassus' wife, Sulpicia Praetextata, and their four children were poised for vengeance, if the senate was prepared to try the case. Therefore Messalla had avoided answering the charge or defending the accused, but simply by shielding his brother from dangers he had won over some senators. Curtius Montanus confronted him with a fierce speech and even went so far as to allege that after Galba's assassination Regulus had rewarded Piso's murderer, and had taken a bite at Piso's head. 'That, at least,' he said, 'Nero did not force you to do, and you did not procure either promotion or safety for yourself by such a savage action. No doubt we must tolerate the excuses of those who preferred ruining others to putting themselves in danger, but in your case, the exile of your father and the division of his fortune among his creditors left you free from worry. You were not yet old enough to stand for office, and Nero had no reason to desire anything from you, or to fear you. It was bloodthirstiness and insatiable greed that made you dabble your talents, still unexplored and untried in the defence of an accused, in the carnage of noble men. You stole the spoils of consuls from this fatally wounded state; and although gorged

on 7 million sesterces and decked out with a priesthood, you mowed down innocent children, distinguished old men and high-ranking women in a career of indiscriminate destruction, blaming Nero as a slacker because he drained his energy and that of his informers by only attacking families one by one. The whole senate, you cried, could be overturned by a single verdict! Gentlemen, you must protect and preserve such a quick-witted counsellor so that each future generation can receive instruction. Just as our seniors imitate Marcellus and Crispus, so let our young men model themselves on Regulus. Even when iniquity fails, it finds followers. What if it should flourish and grow strong? If we dare not offend someone who is still just a quaestor, will we be any bolder after he has become praetor and consul? Do you imagine that Nero will be the last of the tyrants? Those who survived Tiberius and Gaius thought so, although a more frightful and pitiless master was to follow. We are not afraid of Vespasian. Our present emperor is a man of maturity and moderation. However, forceful precedents outlast good emperors. We have lost our energy, gentlemen, and we are no longer the senate which on Nero's death demanded that his informers and attendants should be punished in the traditional way. After an evil emperor has gone, it is the first day which is the sweetest.'

43. The senate heard Montanus' speech and agreed with it so enthusiastically that Helvidius began to hope that even Marcellus might be toppled. So he started his speech by praising Cluvius Rufus, who, he said, although just as rich and outstanding in eloquence as Marcellus, had never impeached a single individual under Nero. Then he went on to attack Marcellus, both by pressing the charge against him and by citing the positive example of Rufus, while the senators grew increasingly excited. Marcellus sensed their reaction, and made as if to leave the house, saying, 'I am leaving, Priscus, and I leave in your hands your obedient senate. Carry on playing the tyrant in the presence of the emperor's son.' Vibius Crispus began to follow him. Both of them were furious, although their expressions were quite different: Marcellus flashed menacing looks, while Crispus was all smiles. Their friends, however, ran forward and

pulled them back. The conflict of opinion grew more and more extreme, and as the opposing parties – honest majority versus powerful minority – fought it out with bitter determination, the day was spent in dispute.

44. At the next meeting of the senate, Domitian opened the debate by stressing the need to drop their angry grievances and forget the measures forced on men by the previous regime, while Mucianus defended the professional prosecutors at length and also warned those who wanted to revive legal processes which had been set in motion and then dropped. His language was mild, and sounded like an appeal. As for the senate, it quickly abandoned its newly won freedom of speech as soon as it met with opposition. Mucianus, so as not to appear to be flouting the senate's views and condoning every crime committed under Nero, compelled Octavius Sagitta and Antistius Sosianus,[69] both former senators who had escaped from exile, to return to their islands of banishment. Octavius had seduced Pontia Postumina, who had refused to marry him, whereupon the frustrated lover had murdered her. Sosianus was an evil character who had ruined many victims. Both of these had been condemned to exile by a severe decree of the senate, and their sentences were now confirmed, although other offenders were allowed to come back home. This, however, did nothing to soothe the hatred inspired by Mucianus. After all, Sosianus and Sagitta counted for nothing, even if they were returned to exile. The real source of fear lay in the clever prosecutors, who were wealthy and experts at wielding their power with malicious skill.

45. An investigation conducted in the traditional way briefly restored the unity of the senate. A senator called Manlius Patruitus complained that he had been beaten up by a rowdy mob in the town of Sena, and indeed on the orders of the local officials. Nor, it seemed, had that been the end of the outrage. The people had made him the centrepiece of a mock funeral, complete with a dirge and lamentations right under his nose,[70] and they had also hurled insults and abuse at the whole senate. The accused were summoned to appear, and after a hearing, convicted and punished. In addition, a senatorial decree was

passed warning the common people of Sena to behave. Over this same period, Antonius Flamma, who had been prosecuted by the inhabitants of Cyrene, was condemned under the extortion law and exiled for cruelty.

46. While this was happening, a mutiny nearly flared up among the troops. The praetorians who had flocked to Vespasian after being dismissed by Vitellius were asking to be re-enlisted,[71] and the legionaries chosen for the same promotion were demanding the pay which they had been promised. Even the Vitellian soldiers alone could not have been dispersed without serious bloodshed, but such large numbers of men could only be kept on at vast cost. Mucianus entered the praetorian camp in order to consider more accurately each soldier's service record, making the victorious Flavians line up with their proper decorations and arms, and separating one man from the next with a little space. Then the Vitellians who had surrendered at Bovillae, as I have mentioned,[72] and the others who had been rounded up throughout the capital and its suburbs were marched out in rags. Mucianus ordered these men to be divided up in separate groups depending on whether they came from Germany, Britain or any of the other armies. Their first glimpse of the sight that greeted them had immediately caused consternation. Facing them they saw what looked like an enemy battleline, bristling with arms and equipment, whereas they themselves were encircled, naked and bedraggled. Once the process of sorting them out began, fear gripped them all, but the troops from Germany were particularly terrified as they thought this categorization was a prelude to execution.[73] They embraced their comrades tightly, threw their arms round their necks, and kissed them farewell for ever, protesting that they should not be left abandoned and alone, nor in a common cause suffer a different fate. They appealed in turn to Mucianus, to the absent emperor and finally to heaven and the gods. In the end, Mucianus addressed them all as soldiers of the same allegiance and the same emperor, and thus confronted their misguided fears. Indeed, the victorious army added its shouts to their tears. This concluded events on that day. When they heard a speech from Domitian a few days later, they had already

recovered their nerve. They now refused the offer of land, and pleaded for continued service and pay. This was a request – but one which could not be refused. They were therefore taken up as praetorians. Later, those who had reached the age limit and served their time were honourably discharged, while others were dismissed for misconduct, but they were demobilized selectively and one by one. This is the safest remedy when trying to diminish the strength of a mass movement.

47. However, whether because of a real financial crisis or to give the appearance of one, the senate resolved that a state loan of 60 million sesterces should be raised from private citizens. This responsibility was entrusted to Pompeius Silvanus, but not long afterwards the need disappeared or the pretence was abandoned. Then, a law was passed on the motion of Domitian rescinding the consulships granted by Vitellius,[74] and Flavius Sabinus was given a state funeral – striking proofs of the mercurial nature of fortune and her habit of distributing prosperity and disaster in equal measure.

48. At about the same time the senatorial governor, Lucius Piso, was killed. The best way to do justice to this murderous story is if I go back briefly and give some details which are not irrelevant to the origin and causes of crimes such as this.

During the principates of the divine Augustus and of Tiberius, the senatorial governor controlled the legion stationed in Africa and the auxiliary troops intended to defend the imperial frontiers. Then Gaius Caesar, who had a restless character and feared Marcus Silanus,[75] the official then in control of Africa, removed the legion from the governor's control and entrusted it to a legate sent out for the purpose. This deliberately fostered tensions, as the dispersal of patronage was shared equally between the two men, who had overlapping responsibilities, and the situation was exacerbated by an ugly spirit of competition. The power of the legates grew because of their long tenure of office, or else because inferior men are always more concerned to outdo their rivals. The senatorial governors on the other hand, being extremely eminent men, were more concerned with self-preservation than acquiring personal power.[76]

49. However, at that time, the legion in Africa was controlled

by Valerius Festus, a decadent young man with big ambitions, who was worried because he was related to Vitellius.[77] During their numerous conversations it is impossible to say whether Festus tempted Piso to rebel or whether he himself resisted Piso's temptations. No third person was present at their secret negotiation, and after Piso's murder most people were keen to butter up the murderer. What is beyond dispute is that the province and its garrison felt alienated from Vespasian; and some Vitellian fugitives from Rome were revealing incentives to Piso – the Gallic provinces were wavering, Germany was ready for a change, Piso himself was in peril, and war was safer for a man who was suspected during peacetime. While this was happening, Claudius Sagitta, the commander of the Petrian[78] cavalry regiment, crossed the sea quickly and got to Africa before Mucianus' envoy, the centurion Papirius, who had been instructed to murder Piso, or so Sagitta asserted. He added that the governor's cousin and son-in-law, Galerianus, had already been murdered.[79] The only hope of survival, he suggested, lay in a daring act, but there were two such courses open to him: he might prefer an immediate military revolt, or he could sail for Gaul and offer himself to the Vitellian armies as their leader. Piso did not react to this at all. As for the centurion sent by Mucianus, when he landed at Carthage, his voice constantly rang out with good wishes for Piso as though he were already emperor and he encouraged the people he met, who were amazed at this sudden development, to echo his acclamations. The mob was gullible enough. They made a rush for the Forum, and demanded Piso's presence. Their noisy and jubilant demonstrations created pandemonium, for they cared nothing for the truth and were passionate in their flattery. Thanks to Sagitta's information or his own natural reserve, Piso did not appear in public or give himself up to the enthusiastic crowd. He interrogated the centurion, and after establishing that the plan was to incriminate him and secure his death, he had him executed. In doing this he was motivated less by the hope of saving his own life than by his anger towards the assassin. The man had been one of the killers of Clodius Macer and he had returned to murder the proconsular governor while his hands still dripped with the blood of the legate. Then he reproached the people of Carthage in an agitated edict, and avoided even routine engagements, locking himself in his house to remove any excuse for fresh trouble, even if it arose quite by chance.

50. However, when the rioting of the mob, the centurion's execution, and an exaggerated cocktail of truth and lies so typical of rumours was revealed to Festus, he sent horsemen to kill Piso. They rode at speed, and in the half-light of dawn they were already breaking into the governor's palace with drawn swords. Many of them did not know Piso personally, for Festus had selected Punic and Moorish auxiliaries to carry out this murder. Near the governor's bedroom they happened to come across one of his slaves. They asked him who he was and where Piso was. When the slave responded with a gallant lie by saying that he was Piso, he was butchered on the spot. Not long afterwards Piso was killed, for there was somebody there who knew him, Baebius Massa, one of the imperial agents in Africa. Already at that point the deadly enemy of all the best men, this character is destined to figure again in the story as one of the causes of the troubles which we were later to endure.[80] Festus left Hadrumetum, where he had stopped to survey the situation, and, hurriedly rejoining the legion, he ordered Caetronius Pisanus, the prefect of the legionary camp, to be imprisoned. The real reason for this was a personal feud, but he denounced him as Piso's accomplice. He punished some of the soldiers and centurions and rewarded others – not to reflect what they deserved, but to foster belief that he had crushed an armed rebellion.

Later on Festus settled a dispute between Oea and Lepcis. It had started for trivial reasons, after the country people had stolen crops and herds, but now it involved full-scale hostilities and set battles. For the people of Oea, being outnumbered, had summoned the Garamantes, a wild tribe much given to plundering its neighbours.[81] So the people of Lepcis were in real trouble. Their lands had been extensively ravaged and they were now cowering behind the walls of their city. However, when the cavalry and infantry forces of the Roman auxiliaries intervened, the Garamantes were routed and all the loot was recovered, apart from what they had sold to the people of the interior as they travelled around the inaccessible settlements.

51. After the victory at Cremona and the arrival of good news from all sides, Vespasian now heard that Vitellius had died. He was told this by many people of every class who had gambled successfully on risking a crossing of the Mediterranean during winter. Representatives of King Vologaeses were also there, offering him 40,000 Parthian cavalry.[82] It was a glorious and happy situation to have such a considerable force of allies at one's disposal and yet be able to do without them. Vologaeses was thanked, and told to send envoys to the senate and conclude a formal peace treaty. Vespasian, with his mind set on Italy and events in the capital, now heard ugly stories about Domitian, who was said to be exceeding both the limits appropriate to his years and the privileges of a son. He therefore handed over the main part of his army to Titus to conclude the campaign in Judaea.[83]

52. There is a story that before Titus set off, he begged his father at some length not to be too readily incensed by these incriminating allegations against Domitian, but to remain unprejudiced and to adopt a conciliatory attitude towards his son. Neither legions nor fleets, he said, were such a sure defence of imperial power as a contingent of children. Time, chance and, sometimes, ambition or misjudgement could diminish, disaffect or terminate friendships, but a man's own flesh and blood was inseparable, particularly in the case of emperors. For while other men enjoyed their successes, their misfortunes only touched those nearest and dearest to them.[84] Not even brothers were likely to see eye to eye for ever unless their father set them an example.

Although Vespasian was still somewhat ruffled about Domitian, he was certainly delighted by Titus' loyalty. He told him to keep in good spirits and to glorify his country by war and military exploits: peace and domestic matters would be his own concern. Then he loaded his fastest ships with corn and consigned them to the still stormy seas, for Rome was in such dire straits that not more than ten days' supply was left in the granaries when Vespasian's shipments brought relief.[85]

53. Responsibility for reconstructing the Capitol was entrusted to Lucius Vestinus.[86] Although he was an equestrian, Vestinus' prestige and reputation had won him a place among the leading men of Rome. He summoned the soothsayers, who advised that the rubble of the earlier shrine should be dumped in the marshes and the temple rebuilt on the same foundations, so far as these remained: the gods did not want the ancient plan of the temple to be altered. On 21 June, under a tranquil sky, the whole area that was being dedicated as the site of the temple was wreathed with fillets and garlands, and soldiers with auspicious names entered bearing branches from lucky trees,[87] followed by the Vestal Virgins with boy and girl attendants who had both parents alive. Together they sprinkled the whole site with water drawn from springs and rivers. Then, while the high priest Plautius Aelianus[88] was dictating the formulae, the praetor Helvidius Priscus purified the area by the sacrifice of pig, sheep and ox,[89] and offered up the entrails upon an altar of turf, praying to Jupiter, Juno and Minerva, as the deities who protected the empire, that they would allow the labours now being undertaken to prosper, and that by divine assistance they would raise aloft this building of theirs that had been started by human piety. Then the praetor put his hand on the fillets tied around the foundation stone, to which ropes were secured. At the same time, the other magistrates, the priests, senators, knights and a large number of the common people eagerly and gladly took the strain and hauled the enormous block into place. Everywhere they cast into the foundations offerings of gold and silver nuggets of unrefined metal in the natural state. The soothsayers had instructed that the building should not be desecrated by the use of stone or gold intended for any other purpose. The height of the building was raised, which was the only change that religious feeling permitted and the only respect in which people believed the earlier temple had lacked splendour.

The Rebellion Escalates

54. Meanwhile, news of Vitellius' death had spread throughout the Gallic and German provinces and doubled the scale of the war. Civilis stopped pretending and threw himself headlong at Rome, while the Vitellian legions actually preferred enslavement to a foreign power over acknowledging Vespasian as emperor. The spirits of the Gauls were now high, since they thought that our armies were in the same predicament everywhere. For a rumour had spread that the bases in Moesia and Pannonia were under siege by the Sarmatians and Dacians, and a similar story, though false, was being told about Britain. However, it was above all the burning of the Capitol that spurred them on to believe that the empire's days were numbered.[90] They reflected that the Gauls had captured Rome in the past, but as the house of Jupiter remained untouched the empire had survived. Now, however, the Druids manifested their barren superstition and were singing their prophecies: the gods had signalled their anger by this fateful fire and world dominion was passing to the nations north of the Alps. There was also a rumour abroad about the Gallic leaders who had been sent by Otho to fight Vitellius. Before they separated, it was alleged, they had sworn an oath not to abandon their fight for freedom if Rome crumbled under the impact of continued civil wars and internal disasters.

55. Before the murder of Hordeonius Flaccus,[91] nothing had got out to give any hint of the conspiracy. But after his death, messages were exchanged between Civilis and Classicus, the commander of the Treviran cavalry regiment. Classicus outclassed the others in rank and wealth. He was descended from kings, and members of his family had been prominent in peace and war. He himself used to boast that he counted among his ancestors more enemies of Rome than allies. Also involved were Julius Tutor and Julius Sabinus, the former a Treviran who had been given command of the west bank of the Rhine by Vitellius, the latter a Lingonian. Sabinus, on top of his naturally conceited personality, was inflamed by the distinction of high birth, bogus though this was. He claimed that his great-grandmother's

beauty had captivated the divine Julius Caesar during the Gallic war and that they had become lovers.[92]

These men investigated the mood of other potential rebels in private conversations. Then, after they had involved any individuals they regarded as suitable and shared their plans with them, they met in Colonia Agrippinensium, at a private house. This was because officially the city recoiled from such endeavours, but a few Ubii and Tungri were nevertheless present at the conference. However, the Treviri and Lingones, who carried most weight, would not tolerate lengthy negotiations. They fell over each other to proclaim that the Roman nation was in a fever of disunity, the legions cut to pieces, Italy ravaged, Rome was on the verge of being captured and all her armies were distracted with fighting on their own doorsteps. If the Alps were strongly manned, once the movement for freedom had grown strong, the Gallic provinces would decide the limits of their dominion at will. 56. No sooner were these words spoken than they won instant approval. Dealing with the remaining contingents of the Vitellian army was a more difficult problem. Many thought that they should be put to death as disloyal troublemakers stained with the blood of their generals, but a policy of mercy won the day, so as to avoid sparking desperate resistance by removing all hope of pardon. It was thought better to entice them into an alliance. If the legionary commanders alone were killed, it would be easy to get the common soldiers to join the rebellion, prompted by their guilty consciences and the hope of impunity.

Such, in outline, was their initial plan. Men were sent throughout the Gallic provinces to stir up war, although the conspirators themselves feigned obedience in order to catch Vocula off his guard. There were informants who told Vocula what was afoot, but he lacked the resources to crush the rebellion, as his legions were under strength and disloyal. Caught between an unreliable army and a hidden enemy, he thought that the best course open to him was to engage in deception in his turn, and to attack with the very weapon that threatened him. So he moved downstream to Colonia Agrippinensium. To this same city Claudius Labeo (whose

capture and removal to Frisian territory I have described)[93]
escaped after bribing his gaolers. This man undertook, if given
a bodyguard, to go to the Batavians and get the better part of
the tribe to return to their alliance with Rome. After being given
a small infantry and cavalry force, he made no attempt to carry
out his venture against the Batavians, but induced a few Nervii
and Baetasii to take up arms, and he began to make stealthy
raids against the Canninefates and Marsaci, rather than con-
ducting a regular campaign.

57. Lured on by the treacherous Gauls, Vocula now marched
against the enemy. He was already nearing Vetera when
Classicus and Tutor went ahead, ostensibly to reconnoitre, but
they actually made a firm agreement with the German leaders.
Then, for the first time, they broke away from the legions and
built their own walled camp, although Vocula protested that
Rome was not so racked with civil strife that even the Treviri and
Lingones could afford to despise her. She still had at her disposal
loyal provinces, victorious armies, her imperial destiny and the
avenging gods. That was why Sacrovir and the Aedui long ago,[94]
and in recent times Vindex with the Gallic provinces, had both
been beaten in a single battle. Treaty breakers could expect to
face the same divine forces and the same fate. Julius Caesar and
Augustus had been better judges of the Gallic temper, and it
was Galba and his tax concessions that had prompted them to
adopt an insolent air of hostility. Now the Gauls were enemies
because they bore a light yoke; when they had been plundered
and stripped, they would revert to being friends.

Vocula's words were spirited, but when he saw that Classicus
and Tutor persisted in their treachery, he turned round and
went back to Novaesium. The Gauls set up camp two miles
away on the flat ground. Centurions and soldiers passed to and
fro between the camps, selling their souls to the enemy. The
result was an unparalleled outrage: a Roman army was to swear
allegiance to a foreign power, sealing the monstrous bargain
with a pledge to murder or imprison its generals. Although
many of his staff advised Vocula to flee, he thought that he
must act with daring, and after calling a meeting, he addressed
the troops along the following lines:[95]

58. 'Never have I addressed you when I felt more anxious on your behalf or less concerned for myself. I am glad to hear that there is a plan to kill me and in such a terrible situation I welcome death as the end of all my afflictions. It is for you that I feel ashamed and sorry, for you are facing no ordinary array of battle – that is the proper form of warfare in accordance with the normal rules of enemy engagement. Instead, Classicus wants to use you to wage war with the Roman people, as he dangles before you a Gallic empire and asks you to swear allegiance to it. Even if luck and courage have deserted us for the moment, have things got so bad that we have forgotten the lessons of the past when Roman legions chose to perish rather than abandon their post? Our allies have often endured the sack of their cities and allowed themselves to be burnt to death with wives and children, when their only reward for such a fate was a reputation for loyalty. At this very moment the legions at Vetera are facing hunger and siege,[96] and neither intimidation nor promises can shift them. Our own position is quite different. Apart from weapons, men and excellent defences, we have adequate corn and supplies, however long the campaign. Our financial resources have just allowed the payment of a bounty, and whether you choose to regard this as coming from Vespasian or from Vitellius, you have certainly received it from a Roman emperor. If, after all your victorious campaigns, all the defeats inflicted on the enemy at Gelduba and at Vetera, you are frightened to fight them, this of course does you no credit, but you have a rampart, walls and the skill to hang on until reinforcements and armies gather from neighbouring provinces. To be sure, you may dislike me, but there are other commanders and tribunes or in the last resort a centurion or a common soldier. Do not let this portent be spread around the whole world, that Civilis and Classicus are going to invade Italy assisted by you. Tell me, if the Germans and Gauls lead you to the walls of Rome, will you bear arms against your fatherland? The imagination shudders at the thought of such wickedness. Will Tutor the Treviran make you stand guard for him? Will a Batavian give you the signal for battle? And will you add your strength to the German hordes? What will be the final chapter

in this career of infamy, when Roman legions draw up against you? After deserting the deserters and betraying the traitors, will you hover between your new and old allegiance as an abomination to the gods? I address this prayer and supplication to you, Jupiter Best and Greatest, to whom for 820 years we have paid the tribute of so many triumphs, and to you, Quirinus, father of the city of Rome:[97] if it was not your pleasure to see this camp preserved whole and inviolate, with me in command, please do not let it be polluted and outraged at the hands of Tutor and Classicus. Grant to the soldiers of Rome either innocence or a speedy repentance before it is too late.'

59. The speech was heard with emotions which varied between hope, fear and shame. Vocula withdrew and thought about killing himself, but his freedmen and slaves stopped him from anticipating a most hideous death by suicide. What happened was that Classicus sent Aemilius Longinus, a deserter belonging to the First Legion, and quickly murdered him.[98] As for the legionary commanders Herennius and Numisius, it seemed sufficient to imprison them. Then Classicus dressed himself up in the uniform of a Roman general and entered the camp. Yet, although he was hardened to every kind of criminal act, he found that words failed him and all he could do was to read out the terms of the oath. Those present swore to support the Gallic Empire. He gave Vocula's assassin a glittering promotion, and rewarded the rest according to their villainous services.

Thereafter, Tutor and Classicus assumed separate responsibilities within the command. Tutor surrounded Colonia Agrippinensium with a strong force and compelled its inhabitants and all the troops on the Rhine in Upper Germany to swear the same oath. At Mogontiacum he executed the tribunes and expelled the commander of the camp since they had refused to take the pledge. Classicus selected all the most flawed men from the troops who had surrendered and told them to approach the besieged garrison and offer a pardon if they were prepared to accept the situation.[99] Otherwise there was no hope for them, for they would have to suffer famine, the sword and ultimately death. The messengers reinforced their argument by pointing out the precedent of their own actions.

60. The besieged were torn: their loyalty pulled them towards heroic resistance, but their hunger drew them towards a disgraceful surrender. While they hesitated, all normal and emergency rations ran out. They had by now consumed the mules, horses and other animals which, however unclean and revolting, a desperate plight compels men to use as food. Finally, they were reduced to tearing up shrubs, roots and the blades of grass growing between the stones so that they became a striking example of how to hold out in a wretched situation.[100] However, they finally tarnished their splendid record by a dishonourable finale, sending envoys to Civilis to plead for life – not that their request was considered until they had taken an oath of allegiance to the Gallic confederacy. Then, after Civilis had secured an agreement that the camp should be his to plunder, he appointed guards to secure the money, soldiers' slaves and baggage and to oversee the departing garrison as it marched out empty-handed. About five miles from Vetera, the Germans ambushed the unsuspecting column of men. The toughest fighters fell on the spot, and many others in scattered flight, while the rest retreated to the camp. To be sure, Civilis protested and loudly blamed the Germans for what he described as a criminal breach of faith. However, our sources are unclear whether this was just a pretence or whether Civilis really was incapable of restraining his ferocious allies. After plundering the camp, they threw in torches, and all the survivors of the battle were consumed by the fire.

61. After Civilis had started to fight the Romans, he had sworn a typically barbarian oath to dye his hair red and let it grow until the point when he had annihilated the legions. Now that he had achieved this, he had it cut.[101] He was also alleged to have given some prisoners to his little son to use as targets for his arrows and spears. However, he did not swear allegiance to the Gallic confederacy himself, nor get any other Batavian to do so, since he was relying on the resources of the Germans and his conviction that, if he had to fight against the Gauls for supremacy, his formidable reputation would give him the lead. The legionary commander Munius Lupercus was sent along with other presents to Veleda, an unmarried woman from the

tribe of the Bructeri who enjoyed wide influence.[102] The Germans have a long-standing custom whereby they regard many women as prophets and even (as their superstitious awe grows) as goddesses. At that point, Veleda's influence had reached its peak, for she had foretold the German successes and the extermination of the legions. Lupercus, however, was put to death before he reached her. A few of the centurions and tribunes who were born in Gaul were kept on as hostages to secure the alliance. The winter-quarters of the cohorts, cavalry regiments and legions were dismantled and burnt, apart from those at Mogontiacum and Vindonissa.

62. The Sixteenth Legion and the auxiliary units which had surrendered at the same time received orders to move from Novaesium to Augusta Trevirorum, a time-limit being fixed for their departure from the camp.[103] They spent this whole interval brooding over different concerns. The cowards were quaking as they thought back to the massacre at Vetera, while the better sort were ashamed at the disgrace: what sort of march was this to be and who would lead the way? Besides, they reflected, everything would be done at the whim of the men to whom they had given absolute power over life and death. Others again, totally unconcerned about the disgrace, were busily stowing about them their money or favourite possessions. A few got their equipment ready and armed themselves as if they were going into battle. As the men contemplated such matters, the hour of departure arrived. It was even grimmer than they had anticipated. For inside the rampart, their sorry state had been less obvious, but the open country and broad daylight revealed the full extent of their humiliation. The emperors' portraits had been ripped off and the standards thus dishonoured, while all around them fluttered the gleaming banners of the Gauls. The marching column was silent, like a long funeral procession. Their leader was the one-eyed Claudius Sanctus, a man of fateful appearance, whose character was even more abominable.[104] Their disgrace was doubled when the other legion joined them from the now abandoned camp at Bonna. Besides, the word had gone round that the legions had capitulated. All those who used to tremble at the mere name of Rome

a short time ago now rushed out from their farms and houses and scattered everywhere, gloating over the novel spectacle. The delight of the insolent people proved too much for the Picentian cavalry regiment. Ignoring the promises or threats of Sanctus, they made off to Mogontiacum, and when they happened to come across Vocula's murderer, Longinus, they hurled their weapons at him and thus took the first step upon the road to redemption. The legions, however, stuck to their route and in due course encamped before the walls of Augusta Trevirorum.

63. Elated by success, Civilis and Classicus considered whether they should give their armies licence to plunder Colonia Agrippinensium. By inclination cruel and greedy for booty, they were strongly attracted to the idea of sacking the city, but they were prevented by strategic considerations of war and by the useful possibility of acquiring a name for clemency while they were starting to establish a new state.[105] Civilis was also influenced by his memory of past services, since at the outbreak of hostilities his son had been imprisoned at Colonia Agrippinensium, but they had kept him in honourable custody. The tribes east of the Rhine, however, hated the city for its opulence and rapid growth, and only contemplated ending the war on one of two conditions: either the settlement was to be opened up to all Germans without discrimination or else it would have to be demolished, thereby scattering the Ubii.

64. So the Tencteri, a tribe separated from Colonia Agrippinensium by the Rhine, sent envoys to present their demands to the assembled citizens of the town. The most spirited envoy laid out the arguments roughly as follows: 'We thank the gods whom we all worship, above all Mars,[106] the greatest of our deities, that you have rejoined the German nation and assumed once more the name of Germans. We congratulate you that at last you will be free men belonging to an association of free peoples. For until today, the Romans shut off the rivers, the earth and in a sense the very sky, to prevent conversation and contact between us, or else – and this is a greater insult to natural warriors – they saw to it that we met disarmed and practically defenceless under supervision and only for a price.

However, so as to confirm our friendship and alliance for all time, we call upon you to dismantle those defences that marked your slavery, your city-walls. Even wild beasts forget their fighting spirit if you keep them locked up. We also demand that you put to death all the Romans in your territory, for liberty is incompatible with the presence of tyrants. The property of the executed men should be shared among the community, so that nobody can conceal anything or keep his own interests separate. We and you must have the right to settle on either bank of the Rhine, as our fathers did in the past. Just as nature has permitted all men to enjoy the daylight, so she has opened up all lands to brave men. Go back to your fathers' practices and their way of life, and tear yourselves away from those pleasures which give the Romans more power over their subjects than their weapons do.[107] Then you will become a pure and unimpaired people as you forget about your past enslavement, and you will deal with men as their equals, or as their leaders.'

65. The citizens of Colonia Agrippinensium took their time to think over the matter. Then, as submitting to the terms was impossible for fear of future consequences, but their present plight did not allow the option of outright rejection, they replied along the following lines: 'As soon as we had a chance of freedom, we seized it with greater eagerness than caution, so that we could join with you and the rest of the Germans, our kinsmen. As for our city-walls, at a moment when the armies of Rome are gathering, it is safer to strengthen rather than demolish them. All the foreigners from Italy or the provinces who previously lived among us have become casualties of war, or have fled to their various countries. As for the original settlers who have been united with us through marriage, and their families, this is their homeland. We do not believe that you are so unjust that you want us to kill our parents, brothers and children. We are ready to abolish taxes and charges upon trade, and to allow unsupervised crossing of the Rhine, provided that this happens by day and no weapons are carried, until what are now novel concessions develop into a tradition with the passing of time. Civilis and Veleda will be the arbiters of our proposals, and they shall negotiate and witness the agreement.' This reply

satisfied the Tencteri,[108] and envoys sent to Civilis and Veleda with gifts secured a decision fully satisfactory to Colonia Agrippinensium. They were not, however, permitted to approach Veleda in person or to speak with her. By preventing them from seeing her, they intended to enhance the aura of veneration surrounding the prophetess. She herself lived in a high tower and one of her relatives used to transmit questions and answers as if he were a messenger between a god and his worshippers.

66. The alliance with Colonia Agrippinensium strengthened Civilis' position, so he decided to court the nearby communities or to attack them if they offered opposition. Having taken over the Sunuci and arranged their fighting men in cohorts, he found that he could not advance any further because Claudius Labeo and his hastily conscripted units of Baetasii, Tungri and Nervii barred the way. Labeo relied on his advantageous position after he had anticipated the enemy by seizing a bridge over the River Mosa. The battle fought in this confined space was inconclusive until the Germans swam the river and attacked Labeo in the rear.[109] At the same moment, Civilis showed great daring (or perhaps it was by prior arrangement) when he rode up to the Tungrian lines and exclaimed loudly: 'We have not declared war to allow the Batavians and Treviri to rule over the other tribes. Such arrogant conduct is beneath us. Take up this alliance. I am coming over to your side, whether you want me as general or a common soldier.' This made a great impression on the ordinary soldiers and they were sheathing their swords when two of the Tungrian nobles, Campanus and Juvenalis, offered him the surrender of the whole tribe. Labeo fled before he could be rounded up. Civilis took the Baetasii and Nervii into his service, too, and added them to his own forces. He was now in a strong position, as the communities were demoralized, or else inclined to support him of their own free will.

67. Meanwhile, Julius Sabinus, who had demolished all reminders of the alliance with Rome, claimed the title 'Caesar'.[110] He then hastily led a large and disorganized crowd of his countrymen against the Sequani, a neighbouring state faithful to us. Nor did the Sequani decline the challenge. Fortune

favoured the better side and the Lingones were routed. Sabinus'
rashness in forcing an encounter was matched by the panic with
which he abandoned it. In order to spread a rumour that he
was dead, he set fire to the house where he had taken refuge,
and people believed that he had committed suicide there. I will
relate in the proper place, however, the ingenious ways in which
he hid himself and stayed alive for another nine years, as well
as the unflagging fidelity of his friends, and the remarkable
example set by his wife, Epponina.[111] With this victory won by
the Sequani, the war lost its momentum. Gradually the communities began to recover their senses and honour their obligations and treaties. In this the Remi took the lead and they
sent word throughout Gaul that the tribes should send representatives to a general meeting to decide whether they wanted
independence or peace.

68. At Rome, however, all the pessimistic and exaggerated
rumours made Mucianus anxious. He was worried that, however eminent the generals (for he had already selected Annius
Gallus and Petilius Cerialis[112]), they would not be up to the
burden of such a serious war. Nor could Rome be left without
supervision; and besides that, he was afraid of Domitian's
ungovernable passions and suspected Antonius Primus and
Arrius Varus, as I have said.[113] The praetorian prefect Varus
still had a powerful military force under his command. So
Mucianus removed him from his post and put him in charge of
the corn supply as a consolation prize. To pacify Domitian,
who was well disposed towards Varus, he appointed Arrecinus
Clemens as praetorian prefect. This man was related to
Vespasian by marriage[114] and stood high in Domitian's favour.
Mucianus repeatedly said that Clemens' father had held the
post with distinction during Gaius' principate, that a familiar
name would please the troops, and that, while belonging to the
senatorial order, Clemens was quite competent to discharge
both functions.[115]

The most distinguished men at Rome were selected to assist
in the operations, and others not so distinguished used their
influence. Domitian and Mucianus prepared themselves too,
although their attitudes differed. Domitian was impetuous,

thanks to the optimism of youth, while Mucianus kept on contriving delays to hold back the prince's burning enthusiasm. He feared that if Domitian got his hands on an army, his youthful belligerence and the prompting of bad advisers would result in his jeopardizing what was in the best interests, whether of peace or war. The expeditionary force consisted of the victorious Eighth, Eleventh and Thirteenth Legions, the Twenty-First (which had supported Vitellius) and the Second (one of the recently recruited legions). Most of these were led across the Alps by the Pennine and Cottian Alps, but some crossed by the Graian Alps. The Fourteenth Legion was summoned from Britain and the Sixth and First from Spain.

So the news that this army was approaching, together with the natural inclination of the Gallic communities for a less aggressive policy, prompted them to hold a meeting in the territory of the Remi. Here they found waiting for them a delegation from the Treviri, including the most fervent instigator of war, Julius Valentinus. In a carefully rehearsed speech, he made all the usual criticisms of great empires, and poured out malicious abuse against Rome, for he was a troublemaker who was expert at stirring up rebellions, and his senseless rhetoric won him many admirers. 69. However, Julius Auspex, one of the chieftains of the Remi, spoke expansively about Rome's power and the advantages of peace. Even cowards, he said, found it easy enough to declare war, but it was the most dynamic men who ran the risks of fighting, and already the legions were poised to strike. So he managed to restrain all the most sensible men by stirring respectful feelings of loyalty, and the younger ones by appealing to their sense of danger and their fears. So while applauding Valentinus' spirit, they followed the advice of Auspex. It is clear that the Gallic states looked unfavourably upon the Treviri and Lingones because they had sided with Verginius during the revolt of Vindex. Many were deterred from acting by the mutual jealousy of the provinces. Where would the headquarters for the war be set up? From whom should they seek legal and religious sanctions? If everything went well, which city would they choose as their capital? They had not yet secured victory, but dissension was already upon them. They squabbled with one another, some boasting about their alliances, and others about their wealth and man-power or their ancient origins. They eventually grew so tired of discussing the future that they settled for the current state of affairs. A letter was written to the Treviri in the name of the Gallic provinces, inviting them to refrain from arms, since they could still get a pardon and many were ready to intercede for them if they expressed repentance. However, that same man Valentinus opposed this and blocked the ears of his country-men, although he concentrated not so much on organizing the war effort as on making frequent speeches.

70. Therefore the Treviri, Lingones and other rebellious com-munities did not act in a manner that was appropriate to the huge risks they had undertaken. Even their generals failed to make a common plan. Civilis was scouring remote parts of Belgica in an effort to capture Claudius Labeo or dislodge him. Classicus spent most of his time in idleness as if enjoying an empire that had already been won. Not even Tutor hurried to man the Rhine in Upper Germany and close the Alpine passes. In the meantime, moreover, the Twenty-First Legion invaded from Vindonissa, and Sextilius Felix with some auxiliary cohorts did the same from Raetia. In addition to this there was the mixed cavalry unit of special recruits which had been mobilized by Vitellius and had then gone over to Vespasian's side. It was commanded by Julius Briganticus, the son of Civilis' sister, who, with the intense bitterness typical of family feuds, was loathed by his uncle, and vice versa. Tutor's Treviran contingent had been reinforced by a recent levy of Vangiones, Caeracates and Triboci,[116] and he now strengthened it with veteran infantry and cavalry, after enticing or intimidating some legionaries to join him. At first these troops annihilated a cohort sent on ahead by Sextilius Felix, but when in due course the Roman army and its generals drew near, they returned to their original allegiance by an act of honourable desertion, followed by the Triboci, Vangiones and Caeracates. Tutor, accompanied by the Treviri, avoided Mogontiacum and withdrew to Bingium, relying on an advantageous position after he had cut the bridge over the River Nava. However, some cohorts led by

Sextilius hurried forward and discovered a ford, and Tutor was betrayed and put to flight. This defeat broke the morale of the Treviri, and a great crowd of them threw down their arms and scattered over the countryside. Some of their chieftains, to give the impression that they were the first to cease hostilities, fled to those communities which had not renounced their alliance with Rome. The legions which, as I have already mentioned,[117] had been transferred from Novaesium and Bonna to Augusta Trevirorum took the oath to Vespasian voluntarily. These events occurred in the absence of Valentinus. When he arrived in a frenzied state and was ready to reduce everything to confusion and destruction once more, the legions retired to the friendly Mediomatrici. Valentinus and Tutor forced the Treviri to fight again, murdering the legionary commanders Herennius and Numisius to lessen the chances of pardon and strengthen the bond of crime.

71. This was the military situation when Petilius Cerialis reached Mogontiacum. On his arrival there was a resurgence of hope. Petilius was spoiling for a fight, and his strength lay rather in despising the enemy than in treating them warily. His fiery language set his troops alight, as he promised that he would engage the enemy at close quarters as soon as he could, and would allow nothing to delay the battle. He sent back to their homes the troops levied throughout Gaul, and told them to announce that the legions were enough to defend the empire: the allies might return to their peacetime tasks confident that a war taken in hand by the Romans was as good as over. This made the Gauls more obedient. Now that they had their men back at home, they tolerated the taxes more readily, and the mere fact of being despised made them more prepared to do their duty. Civilis and Classicus, on the other hand, hearing about Tutor's rout, the Treviran disaster and the fact that everything was going the enemy's way, were gripped by panic and scrambled into action. While concentrating their own scattered forces, they sent a succession of messages warning Valentinus not to risk a decisive engagement.

This only made Cerialis act more quickly. After sending officers to the country of the Mediomatrici to lead the legions back against the enemy by the direct route, which was shorter, and after gathering such troops as were available at Mogontia- cum and the force he had brought with him over the Alps, he marched in three days to Rigodulum. Valentinus had already occupied this place with a large contingent of Treviri, since it was protected on one side by mountains and on another by the River Moselle. He had reinforced the position with trenches and rock barricades, but these defences could not frighten a general of Rome. Petilius ordered his infantry to force a way through and sent his cavalry up the rising ground, pouring scorn on such a hastily assembled enemy force: any advantage they derived from their position was more than outweighed by his own men's courage. There was a slight delay while they climbed up, as the cavalry rode past the missiles hurled by the enemy. However, when the hand-to-hand fighting came, the Treviri were dislodged and sent tumbling down the hillside like an avalanche. Moreover, a detachment of the cavalry which had ridden around along the lower contours, captured some chieftains of the Belgae, including their general Valentinus.

72. On the next day Cerialis entered Augusta Trevirorum. His men were bursting to destroy the city: this was the home of Classicus, this was the home of Tutor, the criminals who had encircled and slaughtered Roman legions. What crime had Cremona committed to deserve its fate in comparison? Yet it had been torn from the heart of Italy because it had de- layed the victors for just one night. Here, still standing intact upon the borders of Germany, was a place which was revelling over the plundered armies and murdered generals. By all means let the booty pass to the exchequer. They, the troops, felt that the conflagration and downfall of a rebel town was enough compensation for the destruction of all those camps.[118]

However, Cerialis feared that he might become notorious if people believed that he had given the troops a taste for licence and brutality, so he restrained their angry feelings. What is more, they obeyed, for now that the civil war was concluded their discipline had improved when facing foreign enemies. After that, their attention was seized by the pitiful appearance of the legions brought from the land of the Mediomatrici. The men stood about, miserably conscious of their guilt, their eyes fixed on the ground.[119] No words of greeting were exchanged between the armies as they met, nor would the newcomers respond to consolation or encouragement, but they hid themselves in their tents and avoided the very daylight. What had petrified them was not so much their predicament or fear, but the shame and scandal. Even the victors were astonished. Not daring to articulate a plea, the guilty asked for pardon with tears and in silence until Cerialis reassured them by repeatedly blaming destiny for events actually caused by the feuding troops and their generals or the enemy's low cunning. They should regard this as the first day of their military service and sworn allegiance. Neither the emperor nor he, Cerialis, wanted to dwell upon wrongs committed in the past. Then they were admitted to the same camp, and orders were circulated amongst the various companies that, in the event of an argument or dispute, nobody should taunt a comrade with sedition or defeat.

73. Then, Cerialis assembled the Treviri and Lingones and addressed them as follows:[120] 'I have never been trained in oratory and I have always maintained Rome's reputation for bravery by force of arms. However, since you attach great importance to words, and judge good and evil according to the utterances of agitators rather than by their real nature, I have decided to make a few comments. Now that the fighting is over, it may be more useful for *you* to hear these facts than it will be for me to state them.

'Roman generals and emperors occupied your land and the territory of the other Gauls, not because they were greedy, but because your ancestors invited them. Their quarrels had exhausted them to the point of collapse, while the Germans summoned to help had imposed servitude on allies and enemies alike. It is clear enough to you how many battles we fought against the Cimbri and Teutoni,[121] what great labours our armies endured and what was the outcome of the German campaigns. We planted ourselves on the Rhine not to protect Italy but to stop a second Ariovistus[122] from dominating Gaul. Do you believe that Civilis, the Batavians and the tribes from across the Rhine care any more for you than did their ancestors for your fathers and grandfathers? The Germans always have the same motives for invading Gaul – their lust, greed and roving spirit made them eager to abandon their marshes and deserts and seize possession of this fertile land and of you, too. However, they use "liberty" and other fine phrases as their pretexts. Indeed, nobody has ever desired to enslave others and gain dominance for himself without using this very same language.

74. 'Throughout Gaul there were always despots and wars until you united yourselves with us. We ourselves, despite many provocations, imposed upon you by right of conquest only such additional burdens as were required to preserve peace. Stability between peoples cannot be maintained without armies, nor armies without pay, nor pay without taxation. Everything else is shared equally between us. You yourselves often command our legions, and you yourselves govern these and other provinces.[123] There is no question of segregation or exclusion. Again, although you live far away, you benefit from praiseworthy emperors just as much as we do, whereas the tyrannical ones oppress only those nearest to them. Just as you resign yourselves to natural disasters like bad harvests or excessive rainfall, you must put up with spending and greed on the part of your masters. There will be shortcomings as long as there are men, but these bad governments are not constant, and there are compensations from the better regimes which crop up at intervals.

'You are surely not going to tell me that you expect a milder rule when Tutor and Classicus are in control, or that less taxation than now will be needed to maintain the armies for defending you from the Germans and Britons? For if the Romans are driven out – may the gods prevent that! – the only result can be that all peoples will fight universal wars with one another. The good luck and good discipline of 800 years has consolidated this imperial framework, which cannot be torn down without destroying in turn those who demolish it, but you will be in the most danger, for you have the riches and resources which are the main causes of war. Accordingly, you must learn to love and foster peace and the city of Rome in which all of us, victors and vanquished, enjoy the same rights. Your experience of both alternatives should warn you not to choose wilful disobedience and ruin over obedience and security.' Cerialis' hearers had been fearing harsher treatment, but a speech of this sort reassured and encouraged them.

75. Augusta Trevirorum was still being occupied by the victorious army when Civilis and Classicus sent Cerialis a letter whose substance was as follows: Vespasian was dead, although this news was being suppressed; Rome and Italy were worn out from civil conflict; and Mucianus and Domitian were just empty and powerless ciphers. If Cerialis wanted to take power in the Gallic provinces, Civilis and Classicus would for their part be content with the present boundaries of their two states. If, however, he should prefer a fight, then they were ready for that, too. To this Cerialis gave Civilis and Classicus no answer. The bearer of the offer and the letter itself he sent on to Domitian.

The enemy now advanced on Augusta Trevirorum in several bodies and from every direction. Many blamed Cerialis for allowing them to unite when he could have intercepted the separate contingents. The Roman army dug a ditch and built a rampart round their camp, which previously they had rashly occupied without fortifying it.

76. Among the Germans there were differing opinions and disagreement ensued. Civilis suggested waiting for the tribes from across the Rhine, who would create sufficient terror to crush the shattered Roman forces to pieces. What else were the Gauls but booty for the victorious side?[124] And in any case, their only strength, the Belgae, were openly on his side, or at least sympathized with him. Tutor, however, asserted that delay favoured Rome, since her armies were coming together from all quarters. One legion had been shipped across from Britain, others had been summoned from Spain or were arriving from Italy. Nor were these hastily raised troops, but veterans with experience of war. As for the Germans, on whom they were pinning their hopes, they did not know what orders or obedience meant, but invariably did whatever they wanted. Money and gifts, the only means of bribing such people, were in greater supply on the Roman side. Nobody was so keen on fighting as

not to prefer peace and quiet to danger if the reward was the same. If they clashed with the enemy immediately, Cerialis only had legions made up of the leftovers from the German army, and these were in any case committed to the Gallic alliance. Again, the very fact that the Romans, much to their surprise, had just routed Valentinus' scrappy force would make the soldiers and their general more reckless. They would try another gamble, and this time fall into the hands, not of an inexperienced youth more practised in words and speeches than in fighting and the sword, but of Civilis and Classicus. Seeing them would revive in their imaginations a picture of fear, flight and famine, and the realization that men who had surrendered so often only survived on sufferance. Nor were the Treviri or Lingones restrained by real affection. They would take up arms again when their fear left them.

This conflict of opinion was resolved when Classicus expressed support for Tutor's view, and the plan was immediately put into effect.

77. The centre was assigned to the Ubii and Lingones. On the right wing were the Batavian cohorts, on the left the Bructeri and Tencteri. One division moved up over the hills, a second by the road and a third along the ground between the road and the River Moselle. They attacked the Romans so unexpectedly that Cerialis was still in his quarters in bed (he had not spent the night in camp)[125] when he heard simultaneously that the battle had begun and that his men were being beaten. At first he reprimanded the messengers for their panic, but soon the whole extent of the catastrophe was revealed before his eyes. The legionary camp had been penetrated, the cavalry had fled and the connecting bridge over the Moselle which links the suburbs with the city was held by the enemy. Cerialis tended to remain calm in a crisis. He caught hold of the fugitives and forcibly dragged them back, rushing forwards into the shower of missiles although he was not wearing any protective armour.[126] Thanks to this beneficial recklessness and to the onslaught of his best fighters, he recovered the bridge and strengthened the position with a picked force. Then, returning to the camp, he saw that the companies of the legions captured

at Novaesium and Bonna were wandering aimlessly about, while only a few soldiers were gathered around the standards and the eagles were practically in the hands of the enemy. Exploding with rage, Cerialis exclaimed: 'It is not Hordeonius Flaccus nor Vocula that you are deserting. There is no question of treachery here. The only thing that I must apologize for is that I rashly believed that you had forgotten your alliance with Gaul and remembered your oath to Rome. Will I be added to the tally of Numisiuses and Herenniuses?[127] Are all your commanders destined to die either at the hands of their own soldiers or those of the enemy? Go and tell Vespasian – or Civilis and Classicus, they are nearer – that you have abandoned your general on the battlefield. Other legions will come, and they will not leave me unavenged or you unpunished.'

78. His words were true, and the same taunts were driven home by the tribunes and prefects. The men formed up in their cohorts and companies, since it was impossible to deploy them in an extended battleline while the enemy was pouring in and the tents and baggage were in the way, now that the fighting was in progress inside the camp rampart. At their various command posts, Tutor, Classicus and Civilis were spurring their men to battle, urging the Gauls to fight for freedom, the Batavians for glory and the Germans to gain plunder. Indeed, everything went in the enemy's favour until the Twenty-First Legion, having managed to assemble in a more open space than was available to the others, first sustained the onslaught of their opponents and then drove them back. Then, with the help of the gods, the victors suddenly lost their nerve and retreated. Their own story was that they had been terrified at seeing the Roman auxiliary cohorts, who had been scattered at the opening of the attack; for these had now gathered once more on the top of the ridge, giving the impression that they were a fresh reinforcing army. However, the real obstacle to a rebel victory was their shocking scramble with each other for loot, which distracted them from the Romans. So, although Cerialis had nearly ruined everything by his carelessness, he restored his chances by determination and exploited his success to the full, capturing the enemy camp on the same day and destroying it.

79. Cerialis' troops were not allowed to rest for long. The people of Colonia Agrippinensium were calling for help and offering to hand over Civilis' wife and sister and Classicus' daughter, who had been left there as pledges for the alliance. Moreover, they had in the meantime killed the Germans who had been billeted separately in private houses. As a result, they were afraid and had good cause to appeal for aid before the enemy could recover its strength and get ready to achieve its ambition or take revenge. For Civilis had moved in their direction too. He had considerable striking power, for the most passionate of his cohorts remained intact: made up of Chauci and Frisii, the unit was stationed at Tolbiacum[128] in the territory of Colonia Agrippinensium. However, bad news made Civilis change his plans. It turned out that the cohort had been destroyed by a cunning ruse of the people of Colonia Agrippinensium. They had plied the Germans with lavish food and drink until they were sleepy, then shut the doors, set fire to the building and burnt them to death. Moreover, Cerialis came to the rescue at full speed. Yet Civilis was assailed by a further worry on top of this – the possibility that the Fourteenth Legion, aided by the British fleet, might raid the Batavians who were exposed to attack from the North Sea. However, the legion's commander, Fabius Priscus, marched his men by land against the Nervii and Tungri, who surrendered to him. As for the fleet, the Canninefates took the initiative and attacked it, so that most of the ships were either sunk or captured. These same Canninefates also routed a mob of Nervii who had volunteered to fight on behalf of Rome. Classicus also fought a successful battle against the cavalry sent ahead by Cerialis to Novaesium. These minor but repeated losses were damaging the positive impact of the recent victory.

80. Over this same period Mucianus gave orders for Vitellius' son to be put to death,[129] giving the excuse that discord would continue unless he stamped out the last embers of war. Nor did he allow Antonius Primus to join Domitian's staff, since he was worried by his popularity with the troops and by the conceit of a man who could not tolerate equals, let alone superiors. Antonius left to join Vespasian, and although he was not received as

warmly as he had hoped, the emperor did not rebuff him either. Vespasian was being torn in two different directions. On the one hand he appreciated Antonius' services, since it was his generalship which had undoubtedly finished off the war, but on the other hand there were Mucianus' letters. Besides, other men were denouncing Antonius for his hostile personality and arrogance, throwing in for good measure the earlier scandals of his life. He made matters worse himself, as his haughty airs provoked resentment and he endlessly harped on about his services. He jeered at the other generals for having no fight in them and called Caecina a prisoner who had surrendered unconditionally. As a result, he gradually came to be regarded as relatively unimportant and worthless, although outwardly the emperor remained friendly.

Signs and Wonders

81. During the months which Vespasian spent at Alexandria, waiting for the regular season of summer winds when the sea was reliable,[130] many miracles occurred. These seemed to show that Vespasian enjoyed divine blessing and that the gods were leaning favourably towards him. One day, one of the common people from Alexandria, a man who was well known as being blind, prostrated himself at Vespasian's knees, imploring him with a whimper to heal his blindness. He had been told to do this by Serapis, the favourite god of a nation much addicted to strange beliefs. He asked the emperor if he would deign to anoint his eyelids and eyeballs with the saliva from his mouth.[131] A second man, who suffered from a withered hand, also on the advice of Serapis, asked Caesar if he would tread upon it with the imperial foot. At first Vespasian laughed at them and refused, but when the two men insisted, he hesitated. At one moment he feared gaining a reputation for foolishness, but at the next moment, the urgent appeals of the two men and the flattery of his entourage prompted him to hope that he would succeed. Finally, he told the doctors to give an opinion whether blindness and withering of this sort were curable by human means. The doctors held forth on the various possibilities. The

blind man's sight was not completely destroyed and would return if certain impediments were removed, while the other man's limb had been distorted, but could be put right by effective treatment. Perhaps this was the will of the gods, they added; perhaps the emperor had been chosen to perform a miracle. Anyhow, if a cure were effected, the glory would go to Caesar; if it failed, the poor wretches would have to bear the ridicule. So Vespasian reckoned that his destiny knew no limitations and that nothing now defied belief. With a smiling expression and surrounded by an excited crowd of bystanders, he did what was asked. At once the cripple regained the use of his hand and the light gleamed again in the blind man's eyes. Those who were there still vouch for both these incidents, although they have nothing to gain now from lying.[132]

82. This deepened Vespasian's desire to visit the sacred house of Serapis,[133] for he wished to consult the god on matters of state. He gave orders for everyone else to be excluded from the temple and went in, concentrating on the deity. Happening to glance round, he caught sight of a leading Egyptian named Basilides standing behind him. He was well aware that this man was detained by illness far from Alexandria at a place several days' journey away. He asked the priests whether Basilides had entered the temple that day. He also asked those he met whether he had been seen in the city. Finally, after sending off some horsemen, he ascertained that at that very point in time Basilides had been eighty miles away. Vespasian therefore regarded the vision as divine and guessed that the force of the response lay in the meaning of the name Basilides.[134]

83. The origins of the god Serapis have not yet been made known to the public by Roman writers.[135] The Egyptian priests give the following account: King Ptolemy, the first Macedonian king of Egypt,[136] bolstered the resources of the country, and while he was busy providing the newly founded city of Alexandria with walls, temples and religious cults, he dreamed that he met a young man of remarkable beauty and superhuman stature, who instructed him to send his most trusty friends to Pontus[137] to fetch a statue of himself. This, he said, would make the kingdom prosper, and whichever place received the image

would become great and famous. Thereupon, this same youth appeared to rise up to heaven in a blaze of fire.

Ptolemy, excited by this marvellous omen, revealed his nocturnal vision to the Egyptian priests, who customarily interpret such signs. As they knew little about Pontus and foreign parts, he consulted Timotheus, an Athenian from the clan of the Eumolpidae, whom he had brought over from Eleusis[138] to supervise religious rites, and asked him what sort of cult this was and which divine power was involved. After Timotheus had asked regular travellers to Pontus, he found out from them that there was a city there called Sinope, near which was a temple long famous amongst the locals and dedicated to Jupiter Dis, but what was also relevant was that the image of a female figure stood nearby, referred to as Proserpina by most people.[139] However, Ptolemy had the typical character of a despot: although he was prone to take fright, once the emergency was over he pursued his pleasures rather than his religious duties. So he gradually disregarded the matter and devoted himself to other business until the same vision appeared before him, now more terrifying and overwhelming in appearance, and threatening both king and kingdom with ruin if he did not follow his commands. Then Ptolemy ordered envoys with gifts to be made ready for a visit to King Scydrothemis, who ruled Sinope at that time, and he told them as they were about to set sail that they should visit the shrine of Pythian Apollo.[140] They were granted a favourable voyage and an unambiguous answer from the oracle. They were to go on their way and bring back the image of Apollo's father, but to leave behind the one of his sister.[141]

84. When they reached Sinope, they presented the offerings, requests and instructions of their king to Scydrothemis. He found it hard to make up his mind. At one moment, he was afraid of the divine power, at another he was terrified by the threats of his people, who opposed the arrangement; and often he was tempted by the gifts and promises of the envoys. In this way three years passed, although Ptolemy did not give up making his enthusiastic appeals. He sent in increasingly distinguished ambassadors, more and more ships and greater

quantities of gold. Then a dreadful apparition confronted Scydrothemis in a dream, forbidding him to delay further the god's plans. When he still hesitated, he was assailed by all manner of disasters, including plagues, and the divine anger, which became more oppressive every day, was clear. Then he called his people together and laid before them the orders of the deity, the visions seen by himself and Ptolemy and their ever growing afflictions. The common people were displeased with their king, jealous of Egypt and afraid for themselves, so they blockaded the temple. At this point, the story became even more impressive: apparently the god himself went on board one of the ships which was moored by the coast and (remarkable to report) they completed the long voyage and put in at Alexandria within three days. A temple worthy of a great city was built in the quarter called Rhacotis, where there had long been a shrine dedicated to Serapis and Isis.[142]

This is the most widely circulated version of where Serapis came from and how he reached Egypt. I am aware that some people believe he was brought from the Syrian city of Seleucia during the reign of Ptolemy, the third ruler with that name. Others, again, confirm that it was this same Ptolemy who was involved, but say that the place from which the god crossed over was Memphis, a city once famous as the capital of the Old Kingdom. As for the identity of the god himself, many equate him with Aesculapius because he heals the sick,[143] some speculate that he is Osiris, the oldest deity known to those peoples, many guess that he is Jupiter owing to his all-embracing powers, but the prevailing view identifies Serapis as Father Dis, based either on the distinctive attributes clearly portrayed on his statues,[144] or on an elaborate set of deductions.

85. I return now to the main narrative. Before Domitian and Mucianus approached the Alps, they received the good news of the victory over the Treviri. Striking confirmation of this success was provided by the presence of the enemy commander Valentinus.[145] He was far from downcast and his looks indicated the brave spirit he had shown. His defence was heard, but only so as to get a sense of his character, and he was condemned. At the moment of execution, someone jeered at him that his

country had been conquered, but Valentinus replied that his solace was in death.

Mucianus now made a suggestion which he had long contemplated in secret, although he pretended that it had just occurred to him. He said that since, by the kindness of the gods, the main forces of the enemy had been crushed, it was unseemly for Domitian to stand in the way of other generals who deserved their glory now that the war was virtually finished. If the stability of the empire or the safety of the Gallic provinces were in danger, Caesar's place would have been in the front line. However, the Canninefates and Batavians should be delegated to minor commanders, while Domitian himself should stay at Lyons and display the power and success of the dynasty from close at hand. By steering clear of petty hazards, he would be available to face greater threats.

86. Domitian saw through this sophistry; but Mucianus' posture of deference meant that he could not be caught out. So they reached Lyons. From there it is believed that Domitian sent secret messengers to test the loyalty of Cerialis, and see if he would hand over the army and supreme command to himself when they met. Whether he was toying with the idea of fighting his father or trying to gain support and strength against his brother was uncertain. For Cerialis showed judicious restraint and returned an evasive answer to what he took to be a boy's idle fancy.[146] Domitian realized that his elders despised his youth, and gave up even the trivial official duties which he had previously undertaken. Looking the picture of innocence and restraint, he shrouded himself in profound reserve and posed as an enthusiastic connoisseur of literature and poetry. The idea was to hide his real character and avoid competing with his brother, whose gentler nature, quite unlike his own, he totally misunderstood.

BOOK 5

The Jews

1. At the start of the same year,[1] Titus Caesar, who had been chosen by his father to complete the conquest of Judaea, and who already enjoyed a fine military reputation when he and his father were still private citizens,[2] received added support and recognition, as provinces and armies vied in displaying their enthusiasm. Titus, wanting to acquire a fine reputation notwithstanding his elevation to power, set about presenting himself as an honourable and enterprising soldier. His affable and courteous conversation inspired devotion, and he often mixed with the ordinary soldiers as they did their duties or on the march, but without compromising the respect due to a general.[3]

Awaiting him in Judaea were three legions that had long served under Vespasian – the Fifth, Tenth and Fifteenth. The emperor also allotted him the Twelfth from Syria and the detachments from the Twenty-Second and the Third brought over from Alexandria. He was attended by twenty cohorts of allied infantry and eight regiments of cavalry, as well as by the two kings Agrippa and Sohaemus[4] and the auxiliary forces offered by King Antiochus. Then there were strong contingents of Arabs, who felt for the Jews the hatred common between neighbours, and many individual adventurers who had come from Rome and Italy, each in the hope of ingratiating himself with an emperor who was yet to choose his favourites. Accompanied by these forces, Titus entered enemy territory, advancing in an orderly manner, using scouts to explore the whole area and keeping his troops ready for battle. Not far from Jerusalem, he set up camp.

2. Since I am now about to record the final days of a famous

city, it seems appropriate to shed some light on its origins.[5] The Jews are said to have been refugees from the island of Crete who settled in the remotest parts of Libya at the time when Saturn was violently ejected from his kingdom by Jupiter.[6] This is a deduction from their name: there is a famous mountain in Crete called Ida, whose inhabitants, the Idaei, had their name lengthened into a foreign word, Judaei. Others believe that in the reign of Isis the surplus population of Egypt was evacuated to neighbouring lands under the leadership of Hierosolymus and Juda. Many think that the Jews are descended from those Ethiopians who were driven by fear and hatred to leave their homes during the reign of Cepheus.[7] Some say that a group of Assyrian refugees, lacking their own land, occupied a part of Egypt, and then built cities of their own, inhabiting the lands of the Hebrews and the nearer parts of Syria. Others again posit a famous ancestry for the Jews in the Solymi, a tribe celebrated by Homer in his poems:[8] these people allegedly founded Jerusalem and named it after themselves.[9] 3. Most authorities, however, agree on the following account. Throughout Egypt there arose a wasting disease which caused bodily disfigurement.[10] So King Bocchoris[11] went to the oracle of Hammon[12] to ask for a cure, and was told to purify his kingdom by expelling the victims to other lands, as they were hateful to the gods. Therefore, a crowd of sufferers was rounded up, herded together, and abandoned in the wilderness. While the other exiles were numb and weeping, one man, Moses, urged his companions not to wait passively for help from gods or men, for both had deserted them: they should rely on their own leadership and accept as heaven-sent whatever guidance first helped them to escape from their present sorrows. They agreed, and set off in complete ignorance along a random route. However, nothing tormented them more than their lack of water. They were already close to death and had collapsed all over the plains when a herd of wild asses left their pasture and made for the shade of a wooded crag. Moses followed them and after making a deduction from a grassy patch of ground, he discovered some abundant channels of water. This relieved their thirst. They travelled on for six days without a break, and on the seventh they drove out the natives, took over their lands and there consecrated their city and temple.

4. In order to strengthen the bond with his people in the future, Moses prescribed for them novel religious rites which were quite different from those practised by other mortals. Among the Jews everything that we hold sacred is regarded as sacrilegious; on the other hand, they allow things which we consider immoral. In the innermost part of the Temple, they dedicated an image of the animal who had guided them and ended their wandering and thirst,[13] after sacrificing a ram, apparently to show their contempt for Hammon.[14] They also offer up bulls, because the Egyptians worship that animal as Apis. They abstain from eating pork in memory of their adversities,[15] as they themselves were once infected with the disease to which this creature is subject. They still fast frequently as an acknowledgement of the hunger they once endured for so long, and as a symbol of their hurried meal, Jewish bread is unleavened. People say that the seventh day was set aside for rest because this marked the end of their toils. Later, the charms of idleness made them devote every seventh year to indolence as well.[16] Others say that this is a mark of respect to Saturn, either because they owe the basic principles of their religion to the Idaei, who, we are told, were expelled together with Saturn and became the founders of the Jewish race, or because, among the seven stars that rule mankind, the one that moves in the highest orbit and exerts the greatest influence is Saturn. A further argument is that most of the heavenly bodies complete their path and revolutions in multiples of seven.

5. Whatever their origin, these observances are sanctioned by their antiquity. The other practices of the Jews are sinister and revolting, and have entrenched themselves by their degeneracy. All the worst types abandoned the religious practices of their forefathers and donated tribute and contributions to the Jews in heaps.[17] That is one reason why the resources of the Jews have increased, but it is also because of their stubborn loyalty and ready benevolence towards fellow-Jews. Yet they confront the rest of the world with a hatred reserved for enemies. They will not eat or sleep with gentiles, and despite

being a most lecherous people, they avoid sexual intercourse with non-Jewish women.[18] Among themselves nothing is barred. They have introduced the practice of circumcision to show that they are different from others.[19] Converts to Judaism adopt the same practices, and the very first lesson they learn is to despise the gods, shed all feelings of patriotism and consider parents, children and brothers as readily expendable. However, they take trouble to make sure that their numbers increase. It is a deadly sin to kill any surplus children, and they think that the souls of those who die in battle or by execution are eternal. This explains their passion for having children and their contempt for death. Rather than cremate their dead, they prefer to follow the Egyptian custom and bury them, and they have the same concern and beliefs as the Egyptians about the underworld, although their conception of the divine is quite different. Whereas the Egyptians worship a variety of animals and half-human, half-bestial forms, the Jews believe that there is just one divine power which exists only in spiritual form. They regard it as sinful to make idols of gods in human form from perishable materials:[20] that most lofty and eternal god of theirs cannot be portrayed by human hands and will never pass away. Therefore they do not set up effigies of him even in their cities, still less in their temple, and they do not use statues to flatter their kings nor to honour the Roman emperors. Since, however, their priests used to chant to the sound of flute and drums, and wore wreaths of ivy, and a golden vine was discovered in the Temple, some observers have concluded that the god being worshipped was Father Liber, the conqueror of the East.[21] Yet the two cults are diametrically opposed, for Liber founded a festive and joyous cult, whereas the ritual of the Jews is discordant and degrading.

6. Their country is bordered on the east by Arabia, on the south by Egypt and on the west by Phoenicia and the sea; on the Syrian frontier they have a distant view to the north. The physical health of the Jews is good, and they can endure hard work. A dry climate and a fertile soil enable them to grow all the crops familiar to us, and in addition balsam and palm. While palm groves are tall and imposing, the balsam is a small

tree. From time to time its branches become swollen with sap, but if you apply an iron blade to them, the sap channels contract so the best way of opening them is with a fragment of stone or pottery. This sap is put to medicinal uses.[22] The most imposing of the mountains rising in that land is Lebanon, a shady place which unfalteringly keeps its covering of snow (a remarkable phenomenon in such a hot climate). This same mountain feeds the tumbling waters of the Jordan. This river does not empty itself into the Mediterranean, but flows through two lakes without losing its identity until it is finally absorbed in a third. This third lake has a vast circumference and resembles a sea, but its water is even nastier to the taste and pestilent to the local inhabitants because of its unhealthy smell.[23] It is never ruffled by the wind, and neither fish nor the usual water birds can live there. The sluggish water bears the weight of objects thrown onto it as if it were solid, and swimmers and non-swimmers find it equally buoyant.[24] At a fixed season of the year the lake discharges bitumen. Experience teaches every skill, including how to gather this substance, too. In its natural state a black liquid, it solidifies when sprinkled with vinegar, and floats on the surface of the water. Those who have the job of gathering the bitumen take hold of it with their hands and haul it on deck. Thereupon, with no further help, it streams in and loads up the boat until you stop the flow. However, you cannot sever it with any tool of bronze or iron, although it does shun blood or a cloth stained with a woman's menstrual discharge.[25] This is the story told by ancient writers; but those who know the locality personally say that the floating masses of bitumen are propelled by hand over the water and dragged to shore. Then, after it has dried out on the hot soil or in the blazing sun, it can be cut up with axes and wedges as if it were timber or stone.

7. Not far from here are plains which people say were once fertile and full of large, densely populated cities, but they were then set ablaze by lightning-bolts.[26] It seems that traces of these cities still remain, and that the very earth looks scorched and has lost its fertility. All natural vegetation and all crops sown by humans, whether in leaf, in flower or apparently fully developed, are black and barren growths which virtually shrivel

into dust. Although I am quite prepared to concede that these once-famous cities were consumed by some cataclysmic fire sent by the gods, I still think that it is the exhalation from the lake which infects the ground and poisons the atmosphere above it, and that this is the reason why the young corn and the autumn harvests rot, since both soil and air are unfavourable. Another river which flows into the Jewish Sea is the Belius,[27] around whose mouth are sands which are collected and fused with soda ash to form glass. The beach concerned is small but inexhaustible, however much sand people remove.

8. A large part of Judaea is peppered with villages, but they also have towns. Their capital is Jerusalem. Here stood their Temple with its enormous riches. An external ring of defensive walls surrounded the city, then there was the royal palace, and the Temple was enclosed by its own inner fortifications. Only Jews were allowed to approach the gate of the Temple, but they could not cross the threshold unless they were priests.

While the Assyrian, Median and Persian empires dominated the East, the Jews were considered to be the lowliest element of those enslaved. After the Macedonians became dominant, King Antiochus[28] made efforts to eliminate their superstitious cult and bring in Greek customs, but he was prevented from changing this most abominable people for the better by the outbreak of war with Parthia, for this was the moment when Arsaces rebelled.[29] Then, while Macedonian power was dwindling and the Parthians had not yet developed into a great power (Roman dominance, too, was still far away), the Jews established a dynasty of their own. These kings were expelled by the fickle mob, but they restored their tyrannical regime by force and committed outrageous acts – banishing fellow-citizens, sacking cities, murdering brothers, wives and parents, and committing all the other outrages typical of despots. The kings cultivated the superstitious cult of the Jews, for they assumed the office of High Priest as a way of bolstering their power.

9. Gnaeus Pompey was the first of the Romans to conquer the Jews and to claim the right to enter their Temple as victor.[30] This is how word got out that there was no image of any god, that the shrine was empty and the innermost sanctuary was

vacant. Although the walls of Jerusalem were destroyed,[31] the shrine remained intact. Later, as civil war was raging amongst us and after the eastern provinces had come under the control of Mark Antony, the Parthian king Pacorus seized Judaea, only to be killed by Publius Ventidius.[32] The Parthians were driven back across the Euphrates, while Gaius Sosius curbed the Jews.[33] Antony gave the kingdom to Herod, and it was enlarged by the now victorious Augustus.[34] After Herod's death, without waiting for Caesar's intervention, a man called Simon usurped the title of king.[35] He was punished by the governor of Syria, Quinctilius Varus,[36] while the Jews were disciplined and divided up into three kingdoms ruled by Herod's sons.[37] In Tiberius' principate all was quiet. Then, after being ordered to put up a statue of Gaius Caesar in the Temple, the Jews chose to fight instead, although the rebellion came to nothing since the emperor was assassinated.[38] As for Claudius, since the Jewish kings had either died or had their sphere of influence reduced, he entrusted the government of the province to Roman knights or freedmen. One of these, Antonius Felix, exercised the authority of a king with the spirit of a slave,[39] plunging into all manner of cruelty and lust, and marrying Drusilla, granddaughter of Cleopatra and Antony. This meant that while Claudius was Antony's grandson, Felix was his grandson by marriage. 10. Nevertheless, the Jews patiently endured such harsh treatment until Gessius Florus became governor.[40] It was in his tenure that war broke out. Cestius Gallus, the governor of Syria, tried to repress the movement but this led to indecisive battles and more often to defeats. When Gallus died a natural death (or perhaps he committed suicide), Nero sent out Vespasian. Thanks to good luck, a distinguished record and excellent subordinates, within the space of two summers[41] he was holding all the plains and cities except Jerusalem with his victorious army. The next year was focused on civil war and passed quietly enough as far as the Jews were concerned, but once peace was established in Italy the anxieties about troubles abroad returned. There was increasing anger that by this time only the Jews had failed to submit. It also seemed advisable that Titus should remain in control of the armies to confront all developments affecting the new dynasty, whether these were good or bad.

11. So after encamping, as I have said, before the walls of Jerusalem, Titus displayed his legions in battle formation. The Jews drew up their forces close under their walls, poised to advance further if they were successful, but with a refuge to hand in case of defeat. Titus sent against them cavalry and some lightly armed cohorts, but the encounter was indecisive.[42] Then the enemy gave ground, and during the next few days they engaged in a series of minor clashes just in front of the gates. Finally, repeated losses drove them behind the walls. The Romans then concentrated on an assault. After all, it seemed beneath them to wait for hunger to do its work on the enemy, and the troops were actually courting danger. Some did so from real courage, many from mere bravado and a desire for rewards. As for Titus, a vision of Rome, wealth and pleasures danced before his eyes, but these dreams would be deferred if Jerusalem did not fall in the immediate future.[43]

However, the city occupied a commanding position, and it had been reinforced by engineering works so huge that they might have made even a flat site impregnable. Two extremely lofty hills were enclosed by walls skilfully built with projecting or retreating angles so as to leave the flanks of any attackers exposed. At the edge of the rocky crags was a sharp drop, and there was a series of towers, 60 feet high where the rising ground helped, and 120 feet high on the lower contours. These were a marvellous sight and appeared from a distance to be the same height. There were further walls inside around the palace, and a conspicuous landmark was the lofty castle of Antonia, so named by Herod to honour Mark Antony.[44]

12. The Temple was like a citadel and had its own walls, which had been built even more laboriously and skilfully than the rest. The porticoes around it consituted in themselves an excellent defensive position. In addition, there was a spring of water which flowed all the time, chambers cut in the living rock and tanks and cisterns for the storage of rainwater. Its builders had foreseen only too well that the Jews would face constant wars as a result of their strange practices. Hence everything was

available for a siege, however long. Moreover, after Pompey's capture of Jerusalem, fear and experience taught them many lessons. So, taking advantage of the greedy instincts of the Claudian period, they bought the right to fortify the city, and during peacetime they built walls meant for war. Already the home to a motley crowd, its population had been swollen by the fall of the other Jewish cities, for all the most determined types had fled there, and thereby added to the turmoil. There were three different leaders and three armies. The long outer perimeter of the walls was held by Simon, the central part of the city by John and the Temple by Eleazar. John and Simon could rely on numbers and equipment, Eleazar on his strategic position. However, it was against one another that they directed battles, ambush and fires, and great stocks of corn went up in flames.⁴⁵ Then John sent off a party of men, ostensibly to offer sacrifice, but actually to slaughter Eleazar and his followers, and so he gained control of the Temple. Thus Jerusalem was divided into two factions, until – since the Romans were approaching – the prospect of a war against foreigners made them cooperate.

13. Various prodigies had occurred, but a nation steeped in superstition and hostile to proper religious practices considered it unlawful to atone for them by offering victims or solemn vows.⁴⁶ Clashing battlelines with glittering arms were seen in the sky and a sudden flash of lightning from the clouds lit up the Temple. The doors of the shrine abruptly opened, a superhuman voice was heard to declare that the gods were leaving, and in the same instant came the rushing tumult of their departure. Few people saw this as reason to be afraid. Most were convinced that, according to the ancient writings of their priests, now was the time when the East would triumph and from Judaea would set out men destined to rule the world. This mysterious prophecy really referred to Vespasian and Titus, but the common people, true to the selfish ambitions of mankind, thought that this mighty destiny was reserved for them, and not even their calamities opened their eyes to the truth.

We are told that the number of the besieged, old and young,

men and women, amounted to 600,000. All who could carry weapons did so, and far more were ready to fight than one would expect from their numbers. The women were no less determined than the men, and the thought that they might be forced to leave their homes made them fear life more than death.

This, then, was the city and people which Titus faced. Since the nature of the place made a headlong assault and surprise attacks impossible, he decided to use earthworks and moveable defences. Each legion had its allotted task, and there was a lull in the fighting while they prepared every conceivable device for storming cities, whether invented long ago or by modern ingenuity.

The Collapse of Civilis

14. After his disastrous battle at Augusta Trevirorum,[47] Civilis gathered reinforcements throughout Germany, and took up position by the camp at Vetera. This was a safe site, intended to bolster the barbarians' spirits with the memory of their successful battles there. Cerialis followed him to the same spot, with his forces doubled by the arrival of the Second, Sixth and Fourteenth Legions. Besides, the cohorts and cavalry regiments summoned long before had come hurrying after news of the victory. Neither commander was a slowcoach, but they were separated by a vast expanse of swampy ground. This was its natural state, but Civilis had also built a dam at an angle into the Rhine to hold up the river and make it flood into the adjacent fields. Such, then, was the terrain. With its unreliable shallows, it was treacherous and did not favour our men, for while the Roman legionaries were weighed down with weapons and frightened of swimming, the Germans were familiar with rivers and could rely upon their tall stature and light arms to raise them above the level of the waters.[48]

15. In answer to the Batavian provocation, therefore, battle was commenced by the most spirited of our troops, but they were struck by panic when their weapons and horses began to sink into the very deep marshes. The Germans, knowing where

the shallows were, galloped through them, usually avoiding our front-line and surrounding the men in the flanks and rear. It was impossible to engage at close quarters, as in a normal infantry battle. Instead, it resembled a naval engagement, as the men floundered about everywhere in the flood waters or grappled hand and foot on any patch of firm ground where they could stand. Wounded and unwounded, swimmers and non-swimmers, they were locked in mutual destruction. However, despite the chaos, losses were comparatively light, for the Germans did not venture beyond the marsh and returned to their camp. The result of this encounter prompted both generals, for different motives, to force a final decision without delay. Civilis wanted to exploit his success, and Cerialis to eradicate his disgrace. While the Germans were elated by victory, a sense of shame stimulated the Romans. The barbarians passed the night singing or shouting, while our troops sullenly muttered threats.[49]

16. At dawn on the next day, Cerialis formed up his cavalry and auxiliary cohorts at the front and posted the legions behind them, keeping a picked force under his personal command in case of emergencies. Civilis avoided extending his line and marshalled his men in wedge formations. The Batavians and Cugerni were on his right, while his left flank nearer the river was held by the Germans from across the Rhine. The two generals did not make the usual speech to their troops at large, but addressed each formation as they rode up to it. Cerialis dwelt on the ancient renown of Rome and alluded to past and present victories, calling for the total annihilation of a treacherous, cowardly and conquered enemy. What was wanted, he said, was revenge, not battle. They had just fought a battle in which they were themselves outnumbered; yet the pick of the Germans had been routed, and the survivors were fugitives at heart and bore scars upon their backs. Then he found appropriate arguments to spur the courage of the various legions, calling the men of the Fourteenth the conquerors of Britain.[50] Galba, he added, had been made emperor by the influence of the Sixth,[51] and in the coming battle the men of the Second[52] would dedicate their new standards and new eagle.

Riding further along the ranks towards the army of Germany, he stretched out his hands and appealed to them to shed the enemy's blood and recover the river bank and camp that were rightfully theirs. They all cheered with mounting enthusiasm. Some were eager for battle after a long peace, others were tired of war and longed for peace, while for the future they hoped for rewards and a quiet life.

17. Nor was there silence among Civilis' troops as he got them into position. He called upon the very site of the battle as a witness to their courage, telling the Germans and Batavians that they were standing upon remains of a glorious victory and trampling the ashes and bones of legions.[53] Wherever the Romans cast their eyes, he said, they only saw captivity, defeat and doom. They must not be alarmed by the fluctuating fortunes of the battle at Augusta Trevirorum when the Germans' own victory had got in their way, making them drop their weapons and fill their hands with loot. Afterwards, however, everything had gone their way and turned against the Romans. Whatever advantages tactical skill could provide had been provided, including a sodden plain which they knew well and marshes which hampered the enemy. The Rhine and the gods of Germany were within sight. Under their divine protection they should take up the battle, remembering their wives, parents and fatherland. This day would either win them a glory unparalleled in their past history, or humiliate them in the eyes of posterity.

When they had expressed their approval of his words with dances and clashing of arms (that was their custom),[54] the battle commenced with showers of stones, slingshots and other missiles. Our troops did not enter the marsh, although the Germans taunted them in an attempt to make them do so.

18. When the missiles ran out and the fight was growing hotter, the enemy charged forward with greater fury. Since their stature was huge and they had very long spears, they could thrust from a distance at our soldiers, who were floundering and slithering around. At the same time, a squadron of Bructeri managed to swim across the river from the mole which, as I have mentioned, was built out into the Rhine.[55] There was a

confused scene here, and the front-line, consisting of allied cohorts, was in the process of being driven back when the legions took up the fight and restrained the fierce charge of the enemy, which put the battle back on an even keel. While this was happening, a Batavian deserter[56] approached Cerialis, promising that he could take the enemy from behind if some cavalry were sent round the far end of the marsh, where the ground was firm and the Cugerni entrusted with guarding the area were not concentrating on the job. Two cavalry regiments were sent off with the deserter and surrounded the unsuspecting enemy. When a burst of shouting revealed what had happened, the legions pressed forward on the main front, and the Germans turned and fled to the Rhine. On that day the war could have been brought to a conclusion if the Roman fleet had been quick enough to follow it up.[57] Not even the cavalry pressed their advantage, as there was a sudden downpour and night was setting in.

19. On the next day, the Fourteenth Legion was sent off to join Annius Gallus in the upper province, and the Tenth Legion from Spain filled its place in Cerialis' army. As for Civilis, he received reinforcements from the Chauci, but not daring to hold the Batavian capital,[58] he hastily gathered up anything that was portable, set fire to the rest and retreated to the Island. He knew that the Romans had no ships for building a bridge, and that their army was not going to cross the river in any other way. What is more, he dismantled the mole constructed by Drusus Germanicus,[59] and so the Rhine, whose course tends to flow into the Gallic branch of the river in any case, poured down in spate when the barrier was removed. This was tantamount to diverting the course of the river, for a shallow bed was all that now separated the Island from Germany, presenting an apparently uninterrupted landscape. Others who crossed the Rhine were Tutor and Classicus and 113 Treviran senators, amongst whom was Alpinius Montanus. This was the man who had been sent into the Gallic provinces, as I mentioned above.[60] He was accompanied by his brother Decimus Alpinius. The other leaders, too, by angling for sympathy and offering bribes, were gathering recruits among tribes who were hungry for danger.

20. In fact, the rebels had plenty of fight left in them, so much so that on a single day Civilis mounted a fourfold assault on the positions occupied by the cohorts, cavalry regiments and legions. His targets were the Tenth Legion at Arenacum and the Second at Batavodurum, together with Grinnes and Vada, where the cohorts and cavalry regiments were encamped. Civilis divided his troops so that he himself, his sister's son Verax, Classicus and Tutor each led a contingent. He was not confident about achieving success everywhere, but the gamble might well come off at one of these points. Besides, Cerialis was a reckless commander, and might be intercepted on the way as he rushed to and fro in response to the various alarms. The force detailed to attack the camp of the Tenth thought that storming the place would be too difficult. So when the Roman troops had gone out and were busy felling timber, they caused chaos by a surprise attack, killing the camp commander, five senior centurions and a few other soldiers. The rest took refuge behind their defences. Meanwhile, a band of Germans tried to break down the bridge being built at Batavodurum, but night put a stop to the battle before it could be resolved.

21. The situation was more dangerous at Grinnes and Vada. Vada was attacked by Civilis, and Grinnes by Classicus. They were unstoppable and our best men were killed, including the cavalry commander Briganticus, who, as I have said, was faithful to Rome and hated his uncle Civilis.[61] However, when Cerialis came to the rescue with a picked body of cavalry, our luck changed, and the Germans were driven headlong into the river. Civilis tried to stop the rout, but he was recognized and targeted by weapons, so that he was forced to abandon his horse and swim across the Rhine. Verax escaped in the same way, while Tutor and Classicus were taken off in some small boats which had landed. Even now the Roman fleet did not participate in the fight. Although ordered to intervene, it was hampered by fear and the dispersal of the crews on other military duties. To be sure, Cerialis did not allow enough time for the execution of his orders. He was a man who made plans on the spur of the moment although he often got dazzling results, since luck made up for any deficiency in his strategy.

As a result, neither he nor his army worried too much about discipline.

Indeed, a few days later there was an incident in which Cerialis managed to escape the danger of being captured, but could not avoid bringing himself into disrepute. 22. He had gone to Novaesium and Bonna to inspect the camps which were being put up to accommodate the legions for the winter, and was returning with the fleet. Discipline on the march was poor, and his sentries were not paying attention. The Germans noticed this and arranged a surprise attack. Choosing a dark and cloudy night, they swept downstream and got into the camp without interference. The massacre was initiated by a productive trick. They cut the guy-ropes and killed the Romans while they were enveloped by their own tents. Another column threw the naval force into disarray, attached chains to the ships and towed them off by the sterns. Although silence had enhanced the element of surprise, once the killing had started the attackers filled the whole area with shouts in a bid to create more terror. As wounds were being inflicted, the Romans woke up, looked for their weapons and scuttled down the passages between the tents. Only a few had their proper equipment on. Most of them rolled their sleeves up their forearms and drew their swords. Their commander, half-asleep and practically defenceless, was saved by a mistake on the part of the enemy. For they carried off the flagship, which was conspicuous, since they thought that the commander was aboard. Cerialis had in fact spent the night elsewhere, as most people believed, because of some sexual dalliance with an Ubian woman called Claudia Sacrata. His guards tried to make excuses for their dereliction of duty by pointing to their commander's scandalous behaviour and alleging that they had been ordered to keep quiet to avoid disturbing his rest: that meant they had neglected to exchange signals and calls and had dropped off to sleep themselves. It was broad daylight when the enemy sailed away in the captured ships and towed the Roman flagship up the River Lippe as a present for Veleda.[62]

23. Civilis was now seized by a desire to stage a naval demonstration. He manned all the biremes[63] and single-banked vessels

he had, and to these he added a large number of small craft carrying thirty to forty men each and fitted out like Liburnians.[64] Moreover, there were the small boats he had captured, enhanced by improvised sails made from multi-coloured coats and presenting a fine sight. He chose a site which was spacious like a miniature sea, the place where the waters of the Rhine come pouring down into the North Sea at the mouth of the River Mosa. His reason for drawing up the fleet, quite apart from his typical native vanity, was so that the convoys sailing from Gaul would be diverted by the terrifying sight. Cerialis, astonished rather than afraid, mustered his fleet. Although it was outnumbered, it had the advantage of experienced rowers, skilful helmsmen and ships of greater size. The Romans moved with the current, but the wind was with the Germans. So the two fleets sailed past each other in opposite directions, only having time for a tentative discharge of light weapons before they lost touch.

Civilis did not risk any further offensive, but withdrew across the Rhine. Cerialis ravaged the Island of the Batavians aggressively, deploying the well-known stratagem of leaving Civilis' houses and farms untouched.[65] By this time summer was becoming autumn, and repeated rainstorms at the equinox made the river inundate the waterlogged, low-lying Island until it looked like a marsh. There was no sign of the Roman fleet or convoys, and the camps on the flat ground were being washed away by the violence of the river.

24. Civilis later maintained that at this point the legions could have been crushed and he claimed credit for deflecting the Germans by trickery when they wanted to act. This may well be true, since his surrender followed a few days later. For Cerialis had been sending secret messages and offering the Batavians peace and Civilis a pardon, as well as urging Veleda and her people to bring about a change in the fortune of a war, which had dealt them many heavy blows, by performing a timely service to Rome. The Treviri had been massacred, the Ubii recovered, the Batavians robbed of their homeland. The friendship of Civilis had only brought them wounds, defeat and grief. As an exile and outlaw, he was a burden to those who

harboured him, and the Germans had incriminated themselves quite enough by crossing the Rhine so often. If they pushed the struggle any further, wrongdoing and guilt on their part would encounter the avenging gods on the Roman side.

25. Cerialis alleviated the threats with promises. The loyalty of the Germans across the Rhine was thus undermined, and there was murmuring among the Batavians, too. It was no use putting off the evil day any longer, they reflected. A single tribe could not shake off a yoke that was common to the whole world. Slaughtering and burning the Roman legions had merely resulted in more numerous and stronger forces being summoned. If they had pursued the war on Vespasian's behalf, then Vespasian was now emperor; but if they were challenging the Roman people by these battles, what a tiny fraction of the human race the Batavians represented! They should look to the burdens borne by Raetia, Noricum and the other provincials. In contrast, the Romans levied from themselves not taxes, but brave fighting men. Such a status was the next best thing to independence, and if they were to have a choice of masters, it was more honourable to tolerate Roman emperors than German women.

This was how the ordinary people felt, but their chieftains spoke more aggressively. It was Civilis' madness,[66] they complained, that had plunged them into war. In a bid to ward off family troubles, he had destroyed his people. The gods had turned against the Batavians at the point when they besieged the legions, killed their commanders and shouldered a war which, however vital for one man, was fatal to themselves. The situation had reached a desperate point, unless they came to their senses and demonstrated their repentance by punishing the individual who was guilty.

26. It did not escape Civilis' notice that people's feelings were changing, so he made up his mind to act first. He was tired of troubles, but he also hoped to escape with his life – a prospect which often undermines the resolve of ambitious characters. He asked for a meeting. There was a shattered bridge over the River Nabalia, and the two generals advanced to the broken edges of the gap. Civilis began to speak as follows:[67] 'If I were

pleading my defence before one of Vitellius' officers, I would not deserve that my actions should be pardoned, nor that my words should be trusted. Our relationship was entirely driven by hate, and Vitellius began the hostilities, which I extended. Yet for Vespasian I have long felt respect, and while he was still a subject, people used to call us friends. Antonius Primus knew this and it was his letters that drove me into a war intended to stop the German legions and the Gallic warriors from crossing the Alps.[68] What Antonius said in his letters Hordeonius Flaccus reinforced in person. I set in motion the war in Germany, but it was the same one that the others were fighting, Mucianus in Syria, Aponius in Moesia and Flavianus in Pannonia . . .'[69]

Notes

All dates are AD unless stated otherwise. Where citations from Tacitus are given without the work being identified, the references are to the *Histories*.

BOOK 1

1. This second consulship is in 69. His first consulship had been in 33 under Tiberius, who allegedly predicted Galba's principate (Tacitus, *Annals* 6.20).

2. Augustus (then Octavian) defeated Antony and Cleopatra at the battle of Actium in 31 BC, which ended a long series of civil wars and left the way open for Augustus to become emperor.

3. Vespasian (69–79), Titus (79–81) and Domitian (81–96) constitute the dynasty of emperors known as the Flavians. Tacitus was in fact hostile to Domitian, as the opening and closing chapters of his first work, the *Agricola*, show.

4. Tacitus famously never produced this work, turning instead to Augustus' successors, the Julio-Claudian emperors (14–68).

5. Galba on 15 January 69, Otho on the morning of (probably) 16 April 69, Vitellius on 20 December 69 and Domitian on 18 September 96.

6. Tacitus probably means Vitellius vs. Otho (69); Vespasian vs. Vitellius (69); and Saturninus vs. Domitian (January 89). The fighting in the civil war between Galba and Otho (69) was restricted to Rome.

7. Tacitus means the Batavian revolt, led by Julius Civilis and narrated at 4.12–37, 54–79 and 5.14–26.

8. This reference is to the advance into Scotland during Domitian's principate led by Tacitus' father-in-law Agricola, followed by a degree of disengagement. It is exuberant rather than exact.

9. Tacitus is thinking above all of the eruption of Vesuvius in 79.

Pliny the Younger wrote two letters to Tacitus offering raw material describing these events (*Epistles* 6.16, 20), but the relevant section of the *Histories* has not survived.

10. See 3.71–2.

11. This probably indicates the final years (93–6) of Domitian's principate.

12. Nero committed suicide on 9 or 11 June 68.

13. As Nymphidius Sabinus was the son of Martianus, a gladiator, and Nymphidia, a freedwoman (Plutarch, *Galba* 9.2), he was not an obvious imperial candidate, although in a bid to raise his status, he claimed that the emperor Caligula was his real father (Tacitus, *Annals* 15.72). He had been commander of the praetorian guard in Rome since 65. After deserting Nero and persuading the praetorians to declare for Galba, Nymphidius was replaced as praetorian prefect by Galba's associate Cornelius Laco. This prompted him to attempt his own imperial coup.

14. The epigram also features at Plutarch, *Galba* 18.2, Suetonius, *Galba* 16.1 and Cassius Dio 64.3.3.

15. See 1.48 for the consul's obituary.

16. See 1.46 for the death of this equestrian.

17. Galba had marched from his province in Spain to Rome during the late summer and early autumn of 68. Cingonius Varro, a senator and consul-designate, had written a speech for Nymphidius Sabinus to deliver before the praetorians during his bid for power (Plutarch, *Galba* 14). Petronius Turpilianus had been consul in 61 and served as governor of Britain. He commanded some of the troops raised by Nero when Galba revolted, but the soldiers switched their allegiance to Nero.

18. The Seventh (Galbiana) Legion, recruited by Galba in Spain in June 68 shortly after arriving in Rome, was posted to Carnutum in Pannonia under the command of Antonius Primus.

19. Vindex, praetorian governor of the province of Lugdunese Gaul, had challenged Nero in early March 68 and eventually mustered a force of nearly 20,000 men (Plutarch, *Galba* 6.3). In mid-May, he was defeated at Vesontio by Verginius Rufus, the governor of Upper Germany, and committed suicide.

20. Despite Galba being proclaimed emperor in Spain, Clodius Macer, the legate in charge of a legion in Africa, decided in April 68 to initiate his own rebellion and issued coins bearing his own name and image. He was put to death in the late summer or early autumn of 68 by the procurator of Africa, Trebonius Garutianus, on Galba's orders. See further 2.97.

21. Fonteius Capito, governor of Lower Germany from mid-67 to 68, had acted promptly to address the threat of a Batavian revolt (4.13), but he had been plotted against by his subordinates (1.58).

22. Nero was thirty-one when he died; Galba was now seventy-two: Plutarch mentions his baldness and wrinkles (*Galba* 13) and Suetonius says that he had a hooked nose and hands and feet deformed by arthritis (*Galba* 21).

23. The ex-consul Cluvius Rufus, Galba's successor as governor of Spain, had accompanied Nero on his singing tours and survived the civil wars to write history under Vespasian. Tacitus presents him as defensive (2.65) and cautious (4.43).

24. Hordeonius Flaccus had succeeded Verginius Rufus as governor of Upper Germany. His efforts subsequently to contain the Batavian revolt were ineffectual (4.18–19) and he was eventually killed by his soldiers (4.36).

25. There were in fact only three legions to hand, since the Third (Gallica) Legion had been sent to Moesia by Nero.

26. This war had broken out in 66 and would last until 73. The main problem now facing the Romans was the capture of Jerusalem.

27. See 2.1, where Titus' trip is not presented quite so straightforwardly.

28. Tiberius Alexander was born in Alexandria and was a member of a prominent Jewish family. He was the first significant figure to endorse Vespasian's imperial challenge by getting his troops to swear an oath of loyalty to him on 1 July 69 (2.79).

29. Tacitus here deploys ring-composition, picking up on the opening words at 1.1 and rounding off the opening section before embarking on his main narrative.

30. Pompeius Propinquus was loyal to Galba and was subsequently murdered (1.58).

31. Tacitus' contemporary readers would no doubt have compared Galba's plans for adopting a successor in 69 with the elderly emperor Nerva's adoption of Trajan in 97.

32. Icelus had travelled from Rome to Clunia with extraordinary speed (the journey took seven days) in order to tell Galba about Nero's suicide, and his promotion to equestrian status was part of his reward, although Tacitus is generally scornful about the promotion of freedmen. The substitution of the respectable Roman name Marcianus for Icelus is a measure designed to obliterate evidence of Icelus' servile past.

33. There are four other versions of this story (Tacitus, *Annals* 13.45–46, Plutarch, *Galba* 19–20, Suetonius, *Otho* 3, Cassius

Dio 61.11) and they all manifest differences in points of detail, reflecting the diverging narrative concerns of each author.

34. Marius Celsus was a military man, who subsequently became governor of Syria in 73. He wrote a monograph on military tactics and Tacitus may well have used his writings as a source.

35. Piso Licinianus came from a lofty but unlucky family. His father, mother and eldest brother were put to death during Claudius' principate; another brother was prosecuted and executed towards the end of Nero's principate, and his last brother, Scribonianus, was approached to make a bid to become emperor in 70 (4.39). Although he refused, he appears to have been executed (1.48). Piso's wife, Verania, survived, but was later victimized by the informer Regulus, who sought a legacy from her (Pliny, *Epistle* 2.20).

36. Rubellius Plautus, a great-grandson of the emperor Tiberius and an aristocrat with strong Stoic sensibilities, was put to death in 62 (Tacitus, *Annals* 14.57–9).

37. Aulus Gellius, *Attic Nights* 5.19 discusses the formal procedures for adoption, including preliminary investigation by the pontiffs and ratification by the curiate assembly. Augustus used a *lex curiata* to adopt Tiberius (Suetonius, *Augustus* 65), as did Claudius in adopting Nero (Tacitus, *Annals* 12.26). Galba's procedure here seems rather less formal.

38. Galba's illustrious ancestry was rooted in these two prominent republican families.

39. Galba means Crassus Scribonianus (see note 35 above).

40. Tacitus means the Fourth (Macedonica) Legion and the Twenty-Second (Primigenia) Legion in Upper Germany.

41. The reality of staging the adoption before the army (the source of power) undercuts many of the plausible and lofty sentiments just expressed by Galba in his speech.

42. Galba refers to an ancient Italian method of levying troops, which is anachronistic in the current context, but is designed to play up his reputation as a man who adheres to standards associated with the Roman republic.

43. This theme recurs in the description of Galba's murder at 1.41.

44. The *sestertius* was a unit of Roman currency. For further details, see S. Hornblower and A. Spawforth (eds.), *Oxford Classical Dictionary* (3rd edn, Oxford 1996), 'coinage, Roman'.

45. Plutarch (*Galba* 23) and Suetonius (*Galba* 16) imply that these men were discharged by Galba because they had been involved in Nymphidius Sabinus' plot, which may mean that Tacitus has

postponed a detail which could have been related earlier. Pacensis and Fronto feature subsequently in the narrative as supporters of Otho.

46. This thought seems to prepare the way for Otho's altruistic and impressive suicide narrated at 2.46–51.

47. Tiberius was the first emperor to keep an astrologer openly at court (Tacitus, *Annals* 6.21), but they were frequently banished (*Annals* 2.32, 12.52). Even an emperor such as Vespasian, who himself habitually consulted astrologers, was prepared to banish them publicly (Cassius Dio 65.9). See further *Histories* 2.78.

48. Tacitus is the only author to name Maevius Pudens, but this coheres with his general practice of naming minor characters in order to bolster his authority as a historian. For Tigellinus see 1.72.

49. The Temple of Apollo, dedicated in 28 BC, was on the Palatine Hill next to the imperial palace and it had a magnificent library attached to it, but its precise site is disputed.

50. Julius Martialis appears only here and at 1.82.

51. Galba had warned Piso about the dangers of flattery at 1.15, so this comment is pointedly ironic.

52. As C. Damon notes (*Tacitus Histories Book I*, 2003), Tacitus' formulation in the Latin here echoes words used by Caesar at *Civil War* 2.32.8 about Nero's great-great-grandfather, L. Domitius Ahenobarbus.

53. Otho makes a point of raising the issue of the unpaid bonus in his speech at 1.37.

54. This colonnade in the north of Rome was completed by Augustus and housed the general Agrippa's map of the world (Pliny, *Natural History* 3.17).

55. This building housed the censors' archives and lay near the senate house, so the German troops were within easy reach of the Palatine and the Forum.

56. This rebuke also features at Plutarch, *Galba* 26, Suetonius, *Galba* 19 and Cassius Dio 64.6.

57. See 1.6.

58. The warping of language in troubled times is a theme in Thucydides (3.82–3). Tacitus returns to it at 2.101.

59. Polyclitus was a freedman of Nero, and Vatinius, a cobbler from Beneventum, was one of his lower-class favourites, described memorably by Tacitus at *Annals* 15.34. Aegialus is otherwise unknown.

60. The Arsacidae, named after the tribal chieftain Arsaces, were the rulers of Parthia *c.* 250 BC–AD 224. Vologaeses I, who spent

much of his reign fighting Rome, was the king of Parthia in 69, and Pacorus was his brother. This comparison does not feature in the parallel tradition.

61. The military standards bore the image of the current emperor. The same powerfully symbolic act occurs when Caecina abandons Vitellius (3.13).

62. The Pool of Curtius was a hallowed spot in the Forum which had emotive associations. It was here that Marcus Curtius sacrificed himself to preserve the well-being of the state in obedience to an oracle in 364 BC (Livy 7.1–6), and subsequently this was where annual vows to preserve the emperor's safety were sworn.

63. Plutarch and Cassius Dio both claim that Densus was protecting Galba, not Piso. In Tacitus, the emperor is completely abandoned.

64. The insincere kisses here recall Otho's kisses for the crowd at 1.36, but once he is dead the praetorians will shower his corpse with kisses which reflect their genuine affection for the man (2.49).

65. Vespasian's elder brother, Flavius Sabinus, was removed from his post as city prefect in 68 by Galba. See 3.75 for his obituary.

66. The freedman Icelus died by crucifixion, which was the standard method of execution for slaves (and thus 'demotes' him in death).

67. Modern critics generally argue for emending this figure to forty-seven, on the grounds that fifty-seven implies that Vinius would have been twenty-six or twenty-seven when he first began his military service (i.e. suspiciously old).

68. Tacitus may have meant to say 'paternal grandfather'. The 'proscriptions' were lists of Roman citizens who were declared outlaws and often hunted down and executed: Sulla, Antony and Octavian (Augustus) all resorted to this brutal means of eliminating personal and political enemies. There was a Titus Vinius on the proscription lists of 43 BC.

69. The emperor Caligula, who held power between 37 and 41.

70. These were all battles which took place during the civil wars of the late republic. At Pharsalus in northern Greece, Julius Caesar defeated Pompey in 48 BC; at Philippi (also in northern Greece), Antony and Octavian defeated Brutus and Cassius in 42 BC; in 41 BC Octavian sacked the town of Perusia (north of Rome), and in 43 BC Antony was defeated at Mutina in northern Italy by Octavian and the consuls Hirtius and Pansa.

71. Tacitus' ambivalent attitude towards Vespasian in some sense

reflects his independence as a historian: since the Flavians won the civil war, the available sources were likely to have cast them in a good light.

72. Tacitus means the boundary between Upper and Lower Germany, formed by the Vinxtbach near Niederbreisig, between Remagen and Andernach.

73. See 1.8.

74. Lyons had suffered a serious fire in 65, but Nero had intervened financially to help (Tacitus, *Annals* 16.13) and the city had stayed loyal to him during the revolt of Vindex.

75. I.e. 68.

76. Vitellius' father had been consul in 34, 43 and 47 (the last two with the emperor Claudius as his colleague). He is the only person other than the emperor to hold a third consulship between Augustus' associate Marcus Agrippa in 27 BC and the accession of Vespasian.

77. Plutarch, *Otho* 6 also offers a description of Caecina in which he stresses his outlandish appearance and tendency to wear Gallic trousers.

78. These clasped hands of bronze or silver (also at 2.8) served as tokens of alliance or hospitality.

79. A similar miscalculation occurs at 1.80 (where exploiting the cover of darkness only increases suspicion).

80. These two legions were based at the same winter camp in Mogontiacum. This sort of 'double occupancy' was later banned by Domitian (Suetonius, *Domitian* 7).

81. This incidental detail about Vitellius' dining (also at Plutarch, *Galba* 22, Suetonius, *Vitellius* 8) introduces an important motif in the characterization of Vitellius (elaborated at 1.62).

82. The base was at Bonna.

83. The Batavian auxiliary leader Civilis will go on to stir up trouble in the form of the Batavian revolt (4.12–37, 54–79, 5.14–26).

84. See 1.56.

85. Trebellius Maximus, the son of a legionary commander and an enthusiastic supporter of Vitellius, governed Britain from 63 to 69. Tacitus gives an alternative version of his governorship at *Agricola* 16, but one which is equally discreditable to Trebellius Maximus. Nevertheless, he survived the civil wars to become one of the Arval Brethren in 72.

86. Vitellius will not arrive in Rome until mid-July 69 (2.89).

87. The troops are themselves playing the role of an ideal general by spurring themselves to action. The lack of involvement

of the supreme commander Vitellius thus becomes even more conspicuous.

88. Tacitus here uses the Latin word *sagina* for food (also associated with Vitellius at 2.71, 88), which has degrading associations with feeding up gladiators.

89. Vitellius continues to shy away from the title of Caesar after he has defeated Otho (2.62), but he does eventually accept it when his position as emperor is under threat (3.58).

90. There is another important bird omen (this time associated with Otho) at 2.50. Vespasian was apparently influenced by omens in formulating his own imperial challenge (2.78).

91. Although the two towns were indeed located on opposite banks of the River Rhône, Vienne on the east bank was 20 miles downstream from Lyons on its west bank. Tacitus has come up with a description which heightens the drama of the rivalry.

92. This was because Lyons was a garrison town through which supplies and reinforcements passed and where retired veterans tended to settle.

93. This was a considerable sum, amounting to one third of a legionary's annual salary.

94. The German armies supported Vitellius but the Pannonian armies subsequently backed Otho (1.76, 2.11). The dispatch was presumably trying to persuade the Pannonian legions to support Vitellius.

95. Claudius Severus is otherwise unknown.

96. Vespasian later established a colony of veterans at Aventicum, possibly a reflection of his gratitude for the Helvetii's attempt to resist Vitellius' forces.

97. This cavalry unit perhaps got its name from Gaius Silius, a governor of Upper Germany under Tiberius.

98. These towns (mod. Milan, Novara, Ivrea and Vercelli) were all located north of the River Po.

99. The reason for this cavalry unit's name is disputed.

100. Tacitus presents the quest for military glory as a crucial motivation for Caecina (cf. 2.24).

101. Tacitus' version of this incident does Otho much less credit than the parallel scene at Plutarch, *Otho* 1 (placed prominently right at the start of the biography), where Otho is cast as kind and sincere in his offer of *clementia*.

102. This plan is curiously similar to Vespasian's strategy for winning the civil war (3.8), but his corn blockade was superseded by the actions of the pro-Flavian general Antonius Primus.

103. There is exaggeration here: Vitellius had been acclaimed emperor in Germany over the course of 2 and 3 January, while Otho had been declared *princeps* in Rome on 15 January. Both men had made their challenge against Galba.

104. In fact the praetorians will remain so loyal to Otho that some of them will commit suicide beside his funeral pyre (2.49). Vespasian shrewdly exploits this loyalty by setting himself up as Otho's avenger (Suetonius, *Vespasian* 6).

105. The text here is uncertain and the name is a conjecture.

106. This was a statue of the general in the costume associated with a triumph. Full triumphal processions in Rome could now only be held by members of the imperial family.

107. The right (enjoyed by a consul) to use a special ceremonial chair (*sella curulis*) inlaid with ivory, and to wear a special bordered toga. These *ornamenta* were awarded to the commanders of all three legions even though only one legion had participated in the fighting.

108. The mutiny is mentioned more briefly in the parallel tradition (Plutarch, *Otho* 3, Suetonius, *Otho* 8, Cassius Dio 64.9). The juxtaposition of this sequence and the easily won victory against the Rhoxolani maintains tension: despite that victory, this is no time for complacency as internal troubles continue to escalate.

109. The cohort's arms, or some of them, were evidently stored in the armoury of the praetorian barracks. It looks as if the unit had been ordered to move northwards to the front.

110. Plutarch, *Otho* 3 says that there were eighty guests.

111. The picture of a captured city (*urbs capta*) was a familiar rhetorical set-piece (cf. Quintilian 8.67–71) so this shorthand would have enabled Tacitus' readers to summon up their own vision of the troubled city.

112. This extraordinarily generous sum represents 20 months' pay for a legionary (and seems excessive given that order has now been restored). Plutarch, *Otho* 3 gives the same figure.

113. Plutarch's abridged version of this speech at *Otho* 3 has a different emphasis.

114. Otho takes the opportunity to appeal to his soldiers' xenophobia by aligning Vitellius' men in exaggerated terms with German barbarians.

115. Otho here appears to exaggerate the scope for upward social mobility in a bid to forge a bond between the senate and the soldiers.

116. Some Vitellians do appear to have been sent to Rome already (1.75).

117. Lists of prodigies regularly appeared in traditional republican annalistic history (especially Livy), but here there is a tension between the 'traditional' subject matter and the unconventional context – civil war.

118. Plutarch, *Otho* 4 and Suetonius, *Vespasian* 5 imply that this portent indicates the challenge of Vespasian, based in the East, but Tacitus avoids making this reading explicit.

119. This ancient wooden bridge, famously defended during the early republic by Horatius Cocles against the invading army of Lars Porsenna, was considered sacred. It was therefore maintained by priests. Augustus took special pride in the fact that he had restored it (*Res Gestae* 20.5).

120. This was the main road for travel between Rome and the Po valley in the north. It ran through the Tiber valley, across the Apennines to Ariminum on the Adriatic coast. Suetonius, *Otho* 8 locates the obstruction at a point on the road 20 miles out of the city.

121. This was a purification ritual to propitiate the gods – the presiding priest progresses around the city boundary three times and then sacrifices a pig, a sheep and an ox. Otho's respectful attitude towards omens and the gods here contrasts with Galba (1.18) and Vitellius (2.91).

122. This campaign will be described at 2.12–15 and 28.

123. The ex-consul Suetonius Paulinus was the most famous of the three generals, particularly after his exploits in Britain where he put down the revolt of Boudicca (60–61). In Otho's council-of-war he argued for a delay before engaging with the Vitellians, but he was ignored, despite his experience (2.32).

124. Aquinum was the hometown of the poet Juvenal.

125. Dolabella's luck would not last. See 2.63–4 for his death at the hands of Vitellius.

126. Scribonianus was a governor of Dalmatia, who led a short-lived revolt against Claudius in 42, but he was abandoned by his troops and soon met his death. Tacitus would have given an account of these events in one of the lost sections of the *Annals*.

127. The original sacred shield had been a present from Jupiter to Numa, but then eleven copies were made to safeguard the original (Ovid, *Fasti* 3.365–86). Special priests called the Salii would carry them around Rome from 1 until 23 March. For Otho to have waited until this ceremony was complete would have involved lingering in Rome for another eight days. Otho's desire for speedy action is here presented in positive terms, but it will prove fatal to him in the first battle of Bedriacum (2.39–45).

128. The eminent and charismatic orator Galerius Trachalus had been consul in 68 with Silius Italicus and then became Otho's spin-doctor (despite being related to Vitellius' wife, Galeria). He was apparently very good looking and had an extraordinary speaking voice (Quintilian 10.1.119, 12.5.5).

BOOK 2

1. Titus (born 30 December 39) was currently twenty-nine years old and was probably seeking a praetorship.

2. Suetonius, *Titus* 3 gives a description of Titus, emphasizing his strength, small stature, pot belly and excellent memory.

3. Tacitus makes a point of stressing that the Flavian challenge emerged at a relatively early stage in the year 69, whereas Josephus (reflecting pro-Flavian propaganda) locates the first moves to the principate of Vitellius. The emphasis on Titus here, rather than Vespasian, hints at a possible fault-line in the Flavian camp, with Titus as the potential emperor rather than Vespasian himself.

4. Berenice, great-granddaughter of Herod the Great of Judaea, was a prominent and fabulously wealthy eastern queen, who had the potential to assist the Flavians financially, but she could also evoke memories of dubious predecessors, such as Cleopatra, from the civil wars of the late republic. After the civil war, she came to Rome in 75 to live with Titus, but she was eventually dismissed, despite the help she had provided.

5. The temple of Venus on Cyprus in Old Paphos overlooked the wealthy city of New Paphos, which contained the Roman pro-consul's residence and the main port for those en route to Syria and Egypt. It was a backdrop aptly reflecting the character of the hedonistic young Titus.

6. Aerias (also featuring at *Annals* 3.62) is not mentioned outside Tacitus. Alternative versions of the story suggest that Agapenor, leader of the Arcadian forces who fought with Agamemnon at Troy, founded the temple.

7. A legendary king of Cyprus, who was supposed to have invented tiles and copper mining (Pliny, *Natural History* 7.195).

8. Tacitus' readers could have seen this conical representation of Venus on coins.

9. The Jewish revolt began in May 66 and was eventually sup-pressed on 2 September 70 when Titus overran Jerusalem and destroyed the Temple. Masada, the final fortress to hold out after the fall of Jerusalem, capitulated in April 73, but Vespasian and

Titus still held their joint triumph in Rome in 71. Tacitus would have narrated all of this in the lost books of the *Histories*.

10. Tacitus also implies that Mucianus commanded four legions at 1.10, 2.6 and 76, but the Third (Gallica) Legion had been transferred to Moesia by Nero.

11. This understatement downplays the campaigns of Nero's general Corbulo, who fought a number of campaigns to recover Armenia from Parthia.

12. The Latin text here is problematic and different editors have suggested different readings. See R. Ash, *Tacitus Histories II* (2007), p. 94 for discussion.

13. The appearance of a false Nero, suggestively juxtaposed with Tacitus' account of the incipient Flavian challenge, neatly captures the uncertainty of the times. At least one, and more probably two other men, would claim to be Nero. One pretender appeared during the principate of Titus (Cassius Dio 66.19) and another surfaced in 88 or 89 under Domitian (Suetonius, *Nero* 57). The chaotic circumstances of Nero's suicide left room for belief that the emperor had not actually died.

14. These references would have featured in the missing books of the *Histories*.

15. This was a small island in the Cyclades, famous for its cheeses and hot springs.

16. Calpurnius Asprenas, a member of a distinguished consular family, was a relative of Galba's adopted son, Piso. He became suffect consul at some point between 70 and 74 and proconsul of Africa in 83.

17. The journey of the severed head back to Rome marks a neat, if gruesome, narrative transition. Tacitus liked this touch sufficiently to deploy it again almost at once (2.16).

18. At *Dialogue* 8.1, Tacitus' Aper cites Vibius Crispus as the model of a successful speaker, while Quintilian calls him 'smooth, agreeable, born to please' (10.1.119). He flourished under Nero and became a notorious informer, but he still went on to become a friend and adviser to Vespasian. Crispus allegedly survived to the age of eighty by not speaking his mind (Juvenal 4.89–93), or by doing so only when it was safe. He was dead by 93.

19. This Neronian equestrian informer appears only here in Tacitus, despite the emphasis on his notoriety.

20. Boudicca's revolt had broken out in the late summer of 60, but it was suppressed by Suetonius Paulinus in 61 (Tacitus, *Agricola* 15–16, *Annals* 14.29–39, Cassius Dio 62.1–12).

21. Tacitus is our only source to preserve an account of this Othonian expedition (2.12–15).

22. This pleasant Ligurian town features in the *Histories* only here.

23. The mother of Tacitus' father-in-law Agricola was also killed in this very attack (Tacitus, *Agricola* 7).

24. Julius Classicus was a wealthy and high-ranking noble from Augusta Trevirorum, who will later join the rebellion of Julius Civilis.

25. *Histories* 1.70.

26. Those recruited to the Roman army were trained to swim, but the Batavians were renowned as naturally talented swimmers (2.35, 4.12).

27. The multicoloured cloak and trousers were seen as archetypal Gallic clothing. The locals are right to be wary of Caecina, but this should not be because of his clothing.

28. Plutarch, *Otho* 6 has onlookers criticize Caecina, but in Tacitus he puts pressure on himself.

29. The village of Bedriacum, notorious, yet obscure, provided the name for the two central battles of the civil wars of 69, although the fighting actually took place closer to Cremona, 20 miles to the east.

30. Plutarch, *Otho* 7 also relates this military action, but his primary interest is in the hostile reaction of the Othonian soldiers to Suetonius Paulinus. Tacitus instead uses it as a marker of Caecina's deteriorating morale.

31. Castores was named after the twin gods Castor and Pollux, who probably had a shrine here.

32. The capable and warlike Epiphanes, son of the wealthy king of Commagene, Antiochus IV, survived his injuries and is seen leading auxiliary troops to Judaea for his father in May or June 70 (Josephus, *Jewish War* 5.460–65).

33. This mutiny has been strikingly displaced within the narrative. It broke out before the Vitellians reached Ticinum on *c.* 6 April, but perhaps after they had crossed the Alps and reached Augusta Taurinorum (*c.* 30 March). The decision not to place it before the narrative of the skirmish at Castores (the logical position) enables Tacitus to avoid interrupting the sequence of Caecina's military setbacks and hints at the general's self-absorption, as he appears to know nothing about the problems being faced by his colleague Valens.

34. Ancient authors liked to use the metaphor of the body for the army (cf. Dionysius of Halicarnassus 1.48, Plutarch, *Galba* 4,

Curtius Rufus 6.9.28, Silius Italicus 10.309–11), but here, while the auxiliaries are the 'limbs' and the legionaries the 'trunk', the 'head', usually representing the general, is completely (and expressively) ignored by the soldiers.

35. This assertion seems to contradict Tacitus' observation at 2.27 that it was Caecina's defeat that prompted Valens' men to obey their general, but it is not necessarily inconsistent: here we have a momentary disciplinary 'blip', which the soldiers resolve themselves.

36. Tacitus here refines the earlier public assessment of Otho and Vitellius at 1.50, which had tended to elide the differences between the two men. The impressive conduct of Otho during the narrative of his suicide (2.46–50) will undercut the opinion here and demonstrates how quickly reputations can fluctuate.

37. There are a number of council-of-war scenes in the *Histories* (extensive ones at 1.32–3, 3.1–2; abridged ones at 2.1, 2.16, 2.81). Often it is the personalities of the speakers rather than the specific nature of the advice in which Tacitus seems most interested. Here it is suggestive that Suetonius Paulinus' unsuccessful set of arguments is given in full, whereas there is only one sentence devoted to the winning proposition that they should fight at once (outlined in more detail by Plutarch at *Otho* 8).

38. The notion of a dramatic reversal on a single day derives from ancient epic, but Tacitus' focus on the 'first' day sets up a painful reversal in slow motion. There is a poignant contrast, too, between the knowledgeable narrator and readers on the one hand and the protagonists in the text on the other, who have no idea of the impending disaster.

39. This sequence of the battle on the River Po narrated at 2.34–6 has led some critics to see Tacitus as a bad military historian, since it is unclear what the strategic purpose of Caecina and Valens is (or indeed whether the crossing really was a bluff). The aim was presumably either to divert some Othonian troops from preparing for battle or to maintain pressure on the Othonian generals: in these two respects the venture certainly succeeds. Plutarch's brief version of the same events (*Otho* 10) gives no hint that the Vitellians are bluffing.

40. This was not Vespasian's brother, the city prefect, but probably that man's son, Vespasian's nephew.

41. Tacitus implies diligent consultation of multiple sources. Plutarch at *Otho* 9 cites Otho's secretary Secundus for one explanation

of the decision to fight immediately, but if Tacitus used Secundus, this must have been supplementary to his main source.

42. Plutarch at *Otho* 9 offers a very different version, in that he speculates that the flawed characters of Otho and Vitellius make it plausible that the soldiers conferred in this way.

43. This digression, written in such a style as to evoke the republican historian Sallust (cf. *Catiline* 10–13, *Jugurtha* 41–2, *Histories* 1.11–12), locates the latest power struggle in a dark moralizing framework and opens up a broad sweep of history for comparison. It also delays for dramatic impact the description of the final battle.

44. The general and statesman Gaius Marius (157–86 BC), who was consul seven times, famously abolished the practice of enrolling soldiers from the propertied classes and enrolled a large army of volunteers from the people. With such a force he was able in 101 BC successfully to confront a German invasion by the Cimbri. In 88 BC, tensions came to a head with his rival Cornelius Sulla (138–78 BC), who had been elected to command the war against Mithridates VI, but who now marched on Rome and drove Marius to flee to Africa. Sulla was voted in as dictator for the purpose of reforming the constitution in 82 BC, after which he dominated Rome.

45. At Pharsalus in northern Greece, Julius Caesar defeated Pompey in 48 BC; at Philippi (also in northern Greece), Antony and Octavian defeated Brutus and Cassius in 42 BC.

46. There is a notorious problem in the Latin text here. See R. Ash, *Tacitus Histories II* (2007), p. 186 for discussion.

47. 14 April 69.

48. Caecina and Valens will refer to this incident during Vitellius' subsequent tour of the battlefield (2.70).

49. For Suetonius, *Otho* 9, this rumour directly causes Otho's defeat. The notion of the deception was useful afterwards as it allowed the Othonian soldiers to save face and to cast their enemies as underhand. By asserting that the rumour could have started by chance, Tacitus is laying claim to his independence as a historian.

50. The notion that it was difficult to sell captives during civil war features again (3.34), but the reason highlighted there is the unanimous feeling of the people of Italy, determined not to buy such slaves, rather than any lack of effort from the Flavian soldiers.

51. The lack of burial is shockingly expressive about the moral

deterioration unleashed by civil war and also prepares the way for Vitellius' gruesome visit to the battlefield almost forty days later (2.70).

52. Otho's suicide at Brixellum early in the morning of 16 April is a focal point in all our accounts (Plutarch, *Otho* 15–17, Suetonius, *Otho* 9–12, Cassius Dio 64.11–15). Tacitus employs various techniques to ennoble and add pathos to the death scene. His emphasis on calmness here imbues Otho with Stoic traits, further pointed up by the rising hysteria of everyone around him. Tacitus' readers would have compared Otho's conduct with famous scenes of suicide by Cato the Younger and Seneca the Younger.

53. Versions of Otho's speech to his soldiers also feature in the parallel tradition (Plutarch, *Otho* 15, Cassius Dio 64.13).

54. Otho's effort to lay the blame firmly on Vitellius for starting the war is put into perspective and undermined by an earlier observation that nobody attributed the start of the war to Vitellius (2.31).

55. Otho's grandiloquent use of his name to refer to himself in the third-person suggests emotional detachment and pride.

56. The Latin word *nouus* here (*in familiam nouam*) is used in the same sense as in the phrase *nouus homo*: i.e. 'new' in the sense of being the first to attain the office of consul.

57. Tacitus (and his readers) were well aware that Cocceianus would later be executed by the emperor Domitian for celebrating the birthday of his uncle Otho (Suetonius, *Domitian* 10.3).

58. Plutarch, *Otho* 17 reports that Otho slept so soundly his attendants outside the room heard him snoring. Tacitus may have toned down this prosaic detail in accordance with the dignity of his genre.

59. Otho knew all about such dangers from the treatment accorded to Galba, Piso and Vinius by his own troops in Rome. It is a pointed reminder of his more dubious characteristics just when he is at his most impressive. Severed heads could be a focus for particularly scornful treatment, as when Nero looked at Rubellius Plautus' severed head and said 'I didn't know that he had such a big nose!' (Cassius Dio 62.14).

60. The prodigy of the strange bird is part of a structuring diptych which picks up on the earlier incident of the eagle leading Valens' army south from Germany (1.62).

61. Rubrius Gallus was sent by Nero to confront Galba (Cassius Dio 63.27), but promptly changed sides. He switched his loyalty first to Otho, then to Vitellius, and perhaps served as Flavius Sabinus' agent in securing the betrayal of Caecina (2.99). He became

governor of Moesia in 70 and conducted a punitive campaign against the Sarmatians.

62. The Latin term *patres conscripti* (literally, 'enrolled fathers') is an honorific title designating the members of the Roman senate.

63. Licinius Caecina, a new man in the senate and clearly ambitious, has chosen a formidable target. Eprius Marcellus was a notorious informer under Nero. His most famous victim was Thrasea Paetus in 66 and for prosecuting him he earned a staggering 5 million sesterces (Tacitus, *Annals* 16.33). Eprius Marcellus will feature again scrapping with Thrasea Paetus' son-in-law, Helvidius Priscus, during the same senatorial meeting at which Vespasian was voted imperial powers (4.7–8).

64. These travel warrants (*diplomata*) were folding tablets bearing the emperor's name and seal and entitling the bearer to use the administrative infrastructure of the imperial communication network (posting-stations, transport and provisions).

65. Wellesley emends the text here to make it clear that Lucius Vitellius, not the new emperor, is meant. Lucius was at Bononia (*c.* 200 miles from Rome) while Vitellius was at Andematunnum in Gaul (*c.* 600 miles from Rome), and as only days passed before the order reached Rome it is much more likely that the brother who was closer to the capital gave the order.

66. The festival of Ceres was celebrated between 12 and 19 April with shows and games. On the final day of the festival, foxes were set on fire and released onto the track as an offering to Ceres (Ovid, *Fasti* 4.681–2). The holiday atmosphere of the festival of Ceres, a goddess associated with productivity and growth, seems alarmingly out of place after the self-destructive sequence of the battle and Otho's suicide.

67. Military commanders were normally deputies of the emperor, and as such reported to him, and not directly to the senate via the consuls. In the morally debased world of the *Histories*, even the absence of a vice can be taken as a virtue.

68. Suetonius, *Vitellius* 12 accentuates the sensational, casting Asiaticus as Vitellius' lover, whom he sold in a fit of temper to a travelling trainer of gladiators, but then he retrieved him and set him free. Suetonius does not mention anything about the request to reward Asiaticus coming from the soldiers.

69. Albinus had been a particularly corrupt governor of Judaea between 62 and 64.

70. Juba was the illustrious king who ruled Mauretania from 25 BC to AD 23. He was a cultured man and a prolific writer of works

(now lost) in Greek on history, ethnography, geography, zoology, painting and drama.

71. Albinus' unnamed wife dies beside her husband in exemplary Roman fashion and indeed trumps Albinus by her bravery (cf. the unnamed Ligurian woman at 2.13).

72. Vitellius will later secure the death of Junius Blaesus by poisoning (3.38–9).

73. The boy, now about six years old, will be put to death by Vespasian's general Mucianus (4.80). Try as he might, Vitellius, in projecting a message of a robust dynasty for the future, cannot compete with Vespasian's two grown-up sons.

74. Vitellius' edict that all astrologers should leave Italy by 1 October apparently met with a sharp and witty response. The astrologers countered with their own notice that 'a great good will have been done if Vitellius is no more by the same date' (Suetonius, *Vitellius* 14, Cassius Dio 65.1).

75. See 1.88.

76. Given that Dolabella is about to be murdered, it is grimly appropriate that the first part of the Flaminian Way was flanked by tombs (Juvenal 1.170–71).

77. The ex-consul Lucius Arruntius, famously considered capable of being an emperor by Augustus (Tacitus, *Annals* 1.13), was appointed governor of Hispania Tarraconensis, but Tiberius then kept him in Rome for ten years (*Annals* 6.27). He killed himself shortly before Tiberius' death.

78. See 2.43.

79. The violent escalation is pointed up by the focus on *two soldiers* fighting to *two cohorts* being annihilated.

80. Tacitus means the Batavian revolt (4.12–37, 54–79, 5.14–26), seen variously as a continuation of the civil war or as a foreign conflict.

81. Warped spectatorship is an increasingly insistent aspect of Tacitus' portrayal of Vitellius (cf. 2.61), but in the end he himself will become a 'revolting spectacle' (3.84). Victorious generals are seen surveying battlefields elsewhere in Roman literature (Caesar at Pharsalus, Lucan 7.786–96; Hannibal at Cannae, Livy 22.51, Silius Italicus 10.449–53), but usually they themselves have participated in the battle and there is not such a long interval between the fighting and the visit.

82. The generals pointedly 'rewrite' the account of the battle, suggesting that the start of the fighting was much more organized than it really was (cf. 2.42).

83. Even Hannibal after Cannae buried the Roman dead (Livy 22.52, Silius Italicus 10.558–75), so Vitellius' callous treatment of his fellow-citizens is especially shocking.

84. The implicit point of comparison is Vespasian (Tacitus, *Annals* 16.5, Suetonius, *Vespasian* 4), but Tacitus here omits the name, perhaps in a bid to distance himself from pro-Flavian propaganda.

85. The man's identity is not completely certain, but he was probably the nephew of Galba's adopted heir Piso Licinianus and thus came from an illustrious family.

86. That is, he was crucified.

87. Tacitus now returns to the Flavian challenge, last considered extensively at 2.1–7. This current section has the effect of 'decelerating' Vitellius' march to Rome by splitting it into two sections (2.57–73, 87–9) and it also undercuts pro-Flavian accounts of the challenge, which emphasized the spontaneity of the rising and suggest that it was triggered by a popular movement from the soldiers (Josephus, *Jewish War* 4.588–604). Tacitus' Vespasian is much more calculating.

88. See Book 1, note 28 for Tiberius Alexander.

89. Tacitus will narrate the pro-Flavian uprising of the Third (Gallica) Legion at 2.85.

90. Mucianus' speech recalls but trumps Fabius Valens' self-interested address to Vitellius to persuade him to become an imperial challenger (1.52; cf. the speeches to the wavering Flavius Sabinus at 3.64, and to Gnaeus Piso at Tacitus, *Annals* 15.59). The *suasoria*, 'speech of advice', was a familiar feature of the declamation schools, but Mucianus' speech is much more than a rhetorical exercise. It serves to introduce a central figure in the Flavian campaign in his own voice, where previously he had only been characterized by Tacitus as narrator.

91. Corbulo was an able but arrogant general under Claudius and Nero and had campaigned in Germany and Parthia. Nero forced him to commit suicide late in 66 or early in 67. His daughter, Domitia Longina, will marry Domitian, perhaps as early as 70.

92. Mucianus' point is that although he and Vespasian were unlikely to have worried Nero, Vitellius, not coming from such a lofty background, was far more likely to feel threatened.

93. Mucianus is effusive about the unnamed Titus, but expressively silent about Domitian, with whom he may have had a tense relationship (4.85–6).

94. Compared with the range of examples listed at Suetonius,

Vespasian 5 and Cassius Dio 66.1, Tacitus is pointedly selective, passing over other early omens from the tradition.

95. Carmel was the eponymous god of a mountain situated near the coast on the borders of Syria and Judaea. The place had long been associated with divine activity. The story of Vespasian's consultation of Carmel's oracle also features in Suetonius (*Vespasian* 5), but it is much less detailed there than the version in Tacitus.

96. This detail is also in the parallel tradition (Suetonius, *Vespasian* 6), although there only the German legions are earmarked for transfer to the East and Mucianus is not identified as the originator of the emotive statement.

97. Sohaemus became king of Emesa on the Syrian river Orontes in northern Syria in 54 and consistently helped the Romans, especially the Flavians. Antiochus IV was made king of Commagene by Caligula in 38. Despite the fact that he promptly aided Vespasian in both the civil and the Jewish wars, the emperor annexed his kingdom in 72 after the governor of Syria had accused him of planning an alliance with Parthia.

98. Agrippa II, who had accompanied Titus on his journey to Rome, was the brother of Berenice, with whom he ruled a large area of eastern Palestine.

99. Tacitus means the coastal region of Egypt, especially the area around the cities of Alexandria and Pelusium.

100. Mucianus has already staked his claim to the role of Vespasian's *socius*, 'colleague' (2.77). It was a term which recalled the relationship between the elderly emperor Nerva and his adopted son, Trajan (Pliny, *Panegyricus* 9), as well as more dubious precedents such as the emperor Tiberius' partner in power, Sejanus (Tacitus, *Annals* 4.2).

101. The formulation that Vespasian's plans were accelerated, not prompted, by the enthusiastic Illyrian army pulls against pro-Flavian accounts of the civil war which suggested that the soldiers rather than Vespasian triggered this phase of the civil war (Josephus, *Jewish War* 4.588–604).

102. This self-selected Flavian general (nicknamed 'Beaky', Suetonius, *Vitellius* 18) is perhaps the most influential figure on the outcome of the whole civil war. The ambivalent character sketch which follows has been criticized as being inconsistent with the more positive portrait in *Histories* 3, but nothing in Tacitus' subsequent narrative will detract from the opening assessment, which acknowledges the general's talents, but warns of a distinctively amoral personality.

103. Cornelius Fuscus went on to become prefect of the praetorian guard under Domitian and so he would have featured prominently in the lost books of the *Histories*. He was killed on active service in 86 or 87 while fighting the Dacians.

104. See 2.68–9.

105. By this bridge (which was the inauspicious site of Galba's massacre of the marines as he entered the city), the Flaminian Way crossed the Tiber two miles north of Rome.

106. In 477 BC the Romans were defeated on the River Cremera by Etruscan soldiers from Veii, and in 390 BC or 387 BC, they were beaten by the Gauls on the River Allia, after which Rome was sacked. Such anniversaries were deemed *religiosi*, that is, days when sacrifices should not be offered, nor any public business be conducted.

107. See 4.5 for Tacitus' character sketch of this man.

108. Thrasea Paetus, a man of consular rank and a famous Stoic, engaged in increasingly frequent clashes with his fellow-senators and the emperor Nero (Tacitus, *Annals* 13.49, 14.48–9, 15.20, 15.23) and eventually withdrew from public life. He was prosecuted by Eprius Marcellus and Cossutianus Capito in 66, and this prompted his suicide (*Annals* 16.35), which was carried out in front of Helvidius Priscus, his son-in-law.

109. Promotion from commanding an auxiliary cohort to become one of the prefects of the praetorian guard is a meteoric rise. Vitellius will later imprison Sabinus because of his friendship with the treacherous general Caecina (3.36).

110. Now that the former masters of these freedmen had been reinstated, they could expect to be supported by them financially in a time of need and also to claim inheritances from them. In reinstating these rights, Vitellius is passing on to the former slaves a cost which he might potentially have had to bear himself.

111. Under Tiberius there were nine pretorian cohorts of 500 or 1,000 men each (Tacitus, *Annals* 4.5), but Sejanus added a further three cohorts. Vitellius' increase to sixteen cohorts of 1,000 men was unprecedented.

112. Vitellius' birthday was either 7 or 24 September (Suetonius, *Vitellius* 3).

113. Tacitus later corrects himself, saying that Tatius, not Romulus, had instituted the Titian priesthood (*Annals* 1.54). Tatius was a Sabine king who was supposed to have ruled jointly with Romulus for a time, but was eventually murdered.

114. Vettius Bolanus' task was not made any easier by the fact

that Vitellius had removed 8,000 troops from the island (2.57).

115. Suetonius, *Vespasian* 4 gives a different picture of Vespasian's proconsulship, stressing his integrity and honesty (despite once getting pelted with turnips during a riot).

116. The Etesian winds blow in the Mediterranean during July and August from a north-westerly direction, making it easier to travel from west to east than vice versa.

117. It is probably now mid-September. Valens will set off in a few days (3.36), but Tacitus expressively and proleptically inserts his entire account of the Vitellian defeat at the second battle of Bedriacum (24–25 October; *Histories* 3.16–35) before narrating Valens' departure.

118. The shifty former cavalry commander Lucilius Bassus was promoted by Vitellius to the prefecture of the fleets at Ravenna and Misenum (an unprecedented dual command), which makes his bitterness at lack of promotion seem rather unreasonable, although this is a conventional motive for treachery. Caecina's motives for betraying Vitellius are much harder to pin down. Bassus was later adlected to the senate and made governor of Judaea in 71. He died in 72 or 73.

119. The warping of language during times of civil strife is a motif from the Greek historian Thucydides (*Peloponnesian War* 3.82). We have already seen the phenomenon when Otho appeals to his riotous soldiers to check their 'valour' (1.83).

BOOK 3

1. Antonius Primus' point is endorsed by Tacitus' own description of the soldiers in the narrative at 2.93 and 99.

2. The soldiers had earlier complained that they had been beaten by deception (2.44). The Pannonian legions in question are the Seventh (Galbiana), of which Antonius Primus himself is the legate, and the Thirteenth (Gemina/Twin), while those from Moesia are the Third (Gallica), the Seventh (Claudia) and the Eighth (Augusta).

3. This version of events does not tally with the narrative at 2.41 (and cf. 2.70 for another version).

4. See Book 2, note 103 for Cornelius Fuscus.

5. This was a nomadic Sarmatian tribe who occupied the area between the Danube and Tisza rivers. Domitian led at least one campaign against them in 89.

6. Sido and Italicus ruled the Suebian tribes, the Marcomanni and

Quadi, in mod. Bohemia–Moravia. J. B. Rives, *Tacitus Germania* (Oxford 1999), pp. 298–300, has a helpful note.

7. See Book 2, note 91 for Corbulo. Varus will be rewarded for his role in the Flavian campaign with the post of prefect of the praetorian guards, but Mucianus was clearly wary of his military talents and demoted him, although he puts him in charge of the corn supply as a compensation (4.68). Nothing is heard about him after this point.

8. The defection will be described at 3.12, but the writing is already on the wall at 2.100–101.

9. The exact location of Forum Alieni is unknown.

10. The strategy of a corn blockade would also have a devastating impact on Italy, as well as on Vitellius' soldiers, so the military intervention of Antonius Primus can, in some sense, be cast in a positive light. The plan is mentioned again at 3.48, and by February 70 Rome is presented as having only enough grain left to last her populace for ten more days (4.52).

11. There appears to be a short lacuna in the Latin text here.

12. The Po.

13. The military tribune Vipstanus Messalla, the temporary commander of the Seventh (Claudia) Legion at the second battle of Bedriacum, is twice named by Tacitus as one of his sources (3.25, 28). He also features as a protagonist in Tacitus' *Dialogue*, and later defends his half-brother, the informer Aquilius Regulus (4.42).

14. The military standards were decorated with medallions bearing the images of Jupiter, Victory and Mars.

15. Vespasian must have summoned or complimented Flavianus, who was therefore allowed to go on his way without further trouble.

16. This pleasant accommodation is hardly the ideal place for a commander on campaign to be staying, accentuating as it does the contrast with the living situation of the common soldiers.

17. Editors are divided over whether the Latin text here should read Memmius or Vibennius Rufinus. Either way, this commander features only here in the *Histories*.

18. The idea that intermediate officers in the military hierarchy are unreliable and that the bond between the emperor and the soldiers takes precedence recurs in the *Histories*. We have seen it before in the response of the soldiers to the Othonian defeat after the first battle of Bedriacum and their protestations of loyalty to their emperor (2.46).

19. This was a bridge across the Po which the soldiers destroyed in a bid to protect their rear as they marched westwards.

20. Anticipating problems and taking action in advance to prevent them is a mark of the ideal general in Classical literature. Antonius Primus is highly competent as a general, if morally flawed as a man.

21. 24 October 69.

22. The description here recalls the conduct of the republican rebel Catiline in his final battle narrated by Sallust, *Catiline* 60. Catiline, talented but morally flawed, was an eloquent figure for Tacitus to evoke in his portrait of Antonius Primus. He will conjure him up again in his character sketch of Sejanus at *Annals* 4.1.

23. This is another instance where the Latin text is uncertain. Editors have suggested different readings for the first two words of the Latin of this sentence.

24. Otho had used a similar argument at 1.84 in his speech to the mutinous praetorians. In both instances, the emphasis on the proper military hierarchy is problematic in the mouths of men who have been prepared to subvert it in order to get what they want.

25. Weapons and uniforms were normally a way to distinguish two sides, but this differentiation evaporates in civil war: cf. Livy 8.6.15, Virgil, *Georgics* 1.489, Lucan, *Civil War* 1.6–7, Cassius Dio 41.58.

26. The Latin text specifies the Fifteenth Legion, which was not involved in the fighting, so the Sixteenth is an emendation.

27. Cassius Dio 64.13.1 also mentions the moon as a factor in the battle, but casts it as a dramatic effect, rather than a strategic one, as Tacitus does. Soldiers are portrayed elsewhere as having a superstitious regard for the moon, as in the description of the lunar eclipse at Tacitus, *Annals* 1.28.

28. The Third (Gallica) Legion had served in Syria from the time of Mark Antony until 68, so it was well attuned to local customs.

29. The father is fighting for the Vitellians and the son is a soldier with the Flavians. This story is trumped by *Histories* 3.51, an incident of fratricide where a Flavian soldier kills his brother on the opposing side and then shockingly seeks a reward for his actions. The notion of family members who kill their relatives on the enemy side is an expressive motif in the context of civil war (and may even make us think of the fratricide of Romulus and Remus, which lies at the heart of the Roman foundational

myth). See also [Caesar] *De Bello Hispaniensi* 27.6 and Silius
Italicus, *Punica* 9.66–177.

30. A testudo (Latin for 'tortoise') was a military formation, a closely
    bunched party of men interlocking their semi-cylindrical shields
    above their heads to form a screen against missiles.

31. This sort of disreputable incentive was usually portrayed as being
    offered by foreign commanders to their troops, as when Juba
    gives the town of Vaga to his men to plunder ([Caesar] *De Bello
    Africo* 74.2); or if a Roman commander did make such an offer,
    it would ideally be in the context of a foreign war. There is
    something surreptitious and underhand about pointing to
    Cremona without giving clear and explicit orders.

32. Pliny the Elder, whose *Natural History* survives, also wrote a
    continuation of the history of Aufidius Bassus (cited by his
    nephew Pliny the Younger in *Epistle* 3.5.4). It covered some or
    all of Nero's principate, the civil wars and at least some of
    Vespasian's principate, perhaps culminating in the Jewish
    triumph of 71.

33. Priestly headbands (*infulae*) were woollen headbands adorned
    with ribbons worn by priests and used as symbols of surrender
    (cf. 1.66). They were also worn by sacrificial victims.

34. The Vitellians capture some Othonian forces at Cremona (2.17)
    to which Caecina advances after his defeat at Placentia (2.22–3).
    The Cremonese may have capitulated relatively quickly to the
    Vitellians after that, but the level of Cremonese collaboration
    with the Vitellians during this phase of the war is left open by
    Tacitus. For the building of the amphitheatre, see 2.67.

35. Descriptions of the sack of a city were a conventional aspect in
    Roman historical narratives and epic, with a familiar set of rhetori-
    cal motifs (cf. Sallust, *Catiline* 51.9, Livy 21.15.1, 29.17.15 and
    indeed the whole of Virgil, *Aeneid* 2). The fact that this sack
    takes place during a civil war deepens the sense of horror.

36. Mefitis was the goddess of sulphurous vapours emanating from
    the ground who was worshipped in Italy for her power to avert
    such pestilential exhalations and to protect the fields and flocks.
    The reference to her here is pointed, given that the bloody battle-
    field full of stinking unburied corpses was likely to generate
    disease.

37. 218 BC.

38. This is a gentle dig at the parsimonious Vespasian, who appar-
    ently refused to offer financial help to restore Cremona, even
    though it had been destroyed by troops fighting in his name.

39. Caecina's departure was described at 2.100, and the narrative now moves back to relate events in Rome from that point onwards. Tacitus' decision to place this material after his account of the Vitellian defeat at Bedriacum accentuates the sense of futility associated with all of Vitellius' actions during this period.

40. Caecina had beaten them to it by betraying Vitellius and currying favour with the new regime.

41. It may seem odd, but although under the principate the Roman people no longer elected their magistrates (including the consuls), such appointments were still formally terminated by popular legislation, not by the senate. So by offering the one-day consulship to Rosius Regulus, the emperor was insulting the Roman people, with the collaboration of the senate.

42. See Book 2, note 72 for Blaesus. Romans had developed a taste for so-called *exitus* literature, involving descriptions of the death scenes of famous men and women. It is possible that Blaesus' death featured in such a work written by Titinius Capito, a friend of Pliny the Younger, who mentions the work (*Epistle* 8.12).

43. In Roman literature, there were often piquant connections between dining and death. Models of skeletons featured at Roman dinner-parties in a bid to remind guests to enjoy themselves (life being short). Here, however, the association is rendered all too literal.

44. Suetonius also records the grisly aphorism (*Vitellius* 14), although he attaches it to a different murder. It recalls the emotive language of Cicero (*In Verrem* 2.5.65, *Orationes Philippicae*. 11.8). We have already seen Vitellius' grisly spectatorship of the aftermath of the first battle of Bedriacum (2.70).

45. The accusation of sleeping with other men's wives is a good device to blacken character: Cicero memorably uses it to denigrate the corrupt governor of Sicily, Verres (*In Verrem* 2.5.81). Tacitus reinforces his earlier portrait of Valens at 1.66.

46. We last saw him in action at 2.12, resisting an Othonian incursion, albeit ineffectually. His loyalty would not last for long (3.43).

47. Claudius had appointed him to the post in 43 (Tacitus, *Agricola* 13). See Suetonius, *Vespasian* 4 and Cassius Dio 60.20 for Vespasian and the campaigns in Britain.

48. Caratacus was king of the Catuvellauni, a powerful tribe in southern Britain. He led an armed revolt against the Romans, but after his defeat he was handed over to the Romans by Cartimandua, queen of the Brigantes with whom he had sought refuge. Claudius spared his life (Tacitus, *Annals* 12.33–8).

49. Julius Civilis had been preparing his revolt between August and November 69. Tacitus will narrate these events at 4.12–37, 54–79 and 5.14–26.

50. Tacitus has already narrated the short-lived incursion of the Rhoxolani into Moesia (1.79). Tacitus' contemporaries would have been reminded of Domitian's defeats when campaigning against the Dacians in 86 and 88 (which he would have narrated in the missing books of the *Histories*), and Trajan's more success-ful campaigns against them in 101 and 102.

51. The former consul Fonteius Agrippa was killed in Moesia late in 69 or early in 70 (Josephus, *Jewish War* 7.90–91). Rubrius Gallus (2.51, 99) was sent out to replace him and engaged in a series of punitive campaigns.

52. Polemo II was the last king (38–63) of independent Pontus before it became a Roman province. He apparently continued to rule parts of Cilicia.

53. This digression on Pontic shipbuilding exemplifies a standard technique of Roman historians, who liked to add colour to their narratives by supplying ethnographical details (cf. Tacitus, *Annals* 2.6 for a similar digression about special boats). Here, however, the potential enjoyment for Roman readers would have been tinged with concern that the digression is set in the context of barbarians threatening the stability of the Roman Empire.

54. See Book 3, note 10 on the plan for a corn blockade.

55. Mucianus will successfully deflate Antonius' power-base by re-moving his most loyal soldiers to their winter-quarters, leaving the general isolated (4.39), and by writing critical letters to Vespasian (4.80).

56. Legionary pay and terms of service were better than what was on offer to those who served in the fleet.

57. Roman soldiers were made to pay for their kit by stoppages against their pay, and excessive marching wore out their hob-nailed boots more quickly. It is interesting that Tacitus' readers should need the term glossed, but this must reflect the increasing professionalization of the Roman army.

58. In what survives of the *Histories*, Tacitus names only two sources directly, Vipstanus Messalla (3.25, 28) and Pliny the Elder (3.28), but the identity of Tacitus' main source remains elusive.

59. See note 29 above.

60. This battle took place in 87 BC, when the Marian army under Cinna captured Rome, which was being defended by Pompeius Strabo (father of Pompey the Great).

61. L. Cornelius Sisenna, praetor in 78 BC and legate to Pompey, died in 67 BC. He wrote a (now fragmentary) history of the Social war and the Sullan civil war, covering the period 91 to 78 BC. The work was consulted by Sallust (*Jugurtha* 95) and admired by Cicero (*Brutus* 228, *On the Laws* 1.7).

62. Tacitus apparently took a story (the centurion's suicide), which other sources (Suetonius, *Otho* 10, Cassius Dio 64.11, Plutarch, *Otho* 15) locate in the run-up to Otho's suicide, and attached it to Vitellius. This reflects Tacitus' narrative agenda in two respects: he did not want to detract from the heroism of Otho's suicide by having a soldier show him the way, but instead he saw the potential of switching the tale to Vitellius in order to accentuate the emperor's passivity and his stubborn denial that the Flavians were winning.

63. The Latin right awarded (among other things) Roman citizenship to those who had held office as magistrates in their own communities, and legal privileges (without full Roman citizenship) to the inhabitants of such towns.

64. Cassius Dio 64.16.1 says that they were vultures. For other suggestive omens involving birds, see 1.62 and 2.50.

65. Tacitus likes to draw attention to cases where long-standing local rivalries flare up in the context of civil war (Lugdunum (mod. Lyons) and Vienna (mod. Vienne), see 1.65; Placentia and her neighbouring colonies, 2.21; Lepcis and Oea, 4.50). At 5.1, Tacitus refers generally to 'the hatred common between neighbours'.

66. See 1.62 and 2.62.

67. Tacitus accentuates Flavian good fortune at 2.1, but he makes it clear here that this was partly due to inadequate leadership on the Vitellian side.

68. The dashing but careless Petilius Cerialis had been commander of the Ninth Legion in Britain in 61, where he had suffered a humiliating defeat against Boudicca (Tacitus, *Annals* 14.32–3). He would go on to be consul and commander in the Rhineland in 70, where he was put in charge of quelling the revolt of Civilis, and he became governor of Britain over 71–74 (and consul again in the year 74).

69. Urvinum is usually taken to be mod. Urbino, but Wellesley suggests that Tacitus refers to Urvinum Hortense (mod. Collemancio). The date is *c.* 10 December 69.

70. Tacitus is probably thinking here primarily of Caecina and Bassus (2.100).

71. See Book 1, note 65 for Flavius Sabinus.

72. See Book 1, note 23 for Cluvius Rufus. Silius Italicus, consul in 68 and later governor of Asia, was an orator and poet whose epic on the Punic wars, the *Punica*, is still extant. Both men were dead by the time that Tacitus wrote the *Histories*.

73. Strictly speaking, neither Julius Caesar nor Augustus had the opportunity to display clemency: Pompey had been murdered in Egypt without Caesar's knowledge, and Antony committed suicide after his defeat in the battle of Actium.

74. Vitellius, the emperor's father, had been consul in 34, 43 and 47 (the last two with Claudius). The emperor Vitellius had been consul in 48, but Claudius was not his colleague.

75. Vitellius' wife is Galeria Fundana, cast by Tacitus at 2.64 as a woman of exemplary moderation. She was the mother of his two children, a boy (Germanicus, about six years old) and a girl (Vitellia? Suetonius, *Vitellius* 6). The daughter became a political pawn, being betrothed first to Valerius Asiaticus, who soon died (1.59); then she was requested as a wife by Otho (Suetonius, *Otho* 8) and was offered to the Flavian general Antonius Primus as a wife (3.78). Vespasian later arranged her marriage, though the identity of her husband is not known (Suetonius, *Vespasian* 14). Vitellius' mother is Sextilia (2.64, 89).

76. Suetonius, *Vitellius* 15 presents this as a ruse, which stirs the crowd to declare that Vitellius himself was Concord, after which the emperor defiantly lays claim to the surname Concordia. The Temple of Concord, founded by the republican general Camillus in 367 BC, was where the fate of the Catilinarian conspirators had been discussed in 63 BC. Lucius Vitellius' house was presumably close to it, overlooking the north-western end of the Forum. Cassius Dio 65.16 actually has Vitellius successfully reaching his brother's house.

77. The Sacred Way led from the south-eastern end of the Forum to the Velia (a hill between the Palatine and Oppian hills), which therefore gave access to the imperial palace.

78. The house of Flavius Sabinus was located on the Quirinal Hill in the north-eastern quarter of Rome.

79. The Pool of Fundanus was somewhere along the route which led down from the Quirinal towards the Forum.

80. Tacitus does not mean that her children and relatives were Vitellian sympathizers, but that as a woman she had duties to her family which she dropped in order to support Sabinus. She is named here partly to accentuate her bravery in doing so, but she does not feature again in Tacitus' narrative. She was married

to the Stoic Arulenus Rusticus (3.80) and was exiled after his execution in 93.

81. The Aventine Hill in the south of the city was historically associated with the *plebs*, but by this point it was the location of elite housing. In the end, Vitellius will indeed flee to his wife's house shortly before his death (3.84).

82. The Grove of Refuge and Tarpeian Rock were both ancient sites with suggestively ironic associations, given the self-destruction and criminality of the protagonists. Romulus established the Grove of Refuge, located in a dip between the two peaks of the Capitoline Hill, as a way of expanding the citizenship and strengthening the state (Livy 1.8). The Tarpeian Rock, now the route for carrying out a criminal act, was the place from where criminals and traitors were thrown to their deaths (Livy 1.11).

83. By suggesting that public opinion at the time pointed to the besieged as having set fire to the houses, Tacitus here is asserting his independence from pro-Flavian accounts (Josephus, *Jewish War* 4.649, Suetonius, *Vitellius* 15, Cassius Dio 64.17), which categorically laid the blame for setting fire to the Capitol on the Vitellians (the besiegers) rather than on the Flavians (the besieged).

84. I.e. the Temple of Jupiter Best and Greatest.

85. Tacitus refers here to two events. First, the Etruscan king Lars Porsenna laid siege to Rome (*c.* 507 BC) in order to try to reinstate the exiled king Tarquinius Superbus. The usual version of the story is that he was so impressed by Roman heroes such as Horatius Cocles and Mucius Scaevola that he abandoned his efforts and made peace with the Romans. Tacitus, in saying that the city surrendered, apparently follows a different version. Second, after defeating the Romans at a battle on the River Allia, the Gauls in either 390 or 387 BC captured and sacked the city of Rome (but according to many accounts, not the Capitol).

86. This was in 83 BC during the civil war which Sulla won (Appian, *Civil War* 1.86, Plutarch, *Sulla* 27).

87. Tarquinius Priscus, Servius Tullius and Tarquinius Superbus were the fifth (trad. 616–579 BC), sixth (trad. 578–535 BC) and seventh – and last (534–510 BC) – kings of Rome. Suessa Pometia, the capital of the Volsci in Latium, was captured by the Romans and its spoils were used to help pay for the building of the Capitoline Temple (Livy 1.53).

88. Horatius Pulvillus' second consulship is usually dated to 507 BC.

89. I.e. 83 BC.

90. Sulla's associate Lutatius Catulus (consul in 78 BC) had dedicated the rebuilt temple in 69 BC.

91. The Velabrum, a low-lying and congested commercial area of Rome, was located between the Capitol and the Palatine Hill.

92. Unsurprisingly, Domitian's activities during the siege of the Capitol later became the focus of flattery (Josephus, *Jewish War* 4.649, Martial, *Epigrams* 9.101, Statius, *Thebaid* 1.21, *Silvae* 1.1.79, Silius Italicus, *Punica* 3.609). In contrast, Tacitus accentuates Domitian's cowardice on the day (Suetonius, *Domitian* 1 is more neutral).

93. At the Gemonian Steps ('Stairs of Groaning') leading from the Capitol to the Forum, near the Mamertine prison, the bodies of criminals were exposed for final humiliation before being thrown into the River Tiber, so the place encapsulates the extremity of Flavius Sabinus' fall from power. They will feature dramatically in Vitellius' own death scene (3.85, Suetonius, *Vitellius* 17).

94. This figure of a twelve-year tenure (not necessarily in consecutive years) has been questioned. It is possible that Tacitus has made a mistake, or a scribal error has crept in.

95. This ploy of Atticus taking the blame did not succeed in the longer term: see note 83 above.

96. The shrine of Feronia, an Italian goddess often associated with freedmen, was about three miles from Tarracina in the direction of Rome.

97. See 3.57.

98. Vergilius Capito had been governor of Egypt between 47 and 52. He came from Capua but seems to have owned property near Tarracina. His slave will later be executed for his treachery (4.3).

99. Lucius Vitellius shares the vice of warped spectatorship with his brother the emperor: see Book 2, note 81 and Book 3, note 44.

100. The city was probably captured during the night/early morning of 17/18 December.

101. The Flavians had left Narnia on 16 December (Ocriculum was about 45 miles from Rome). The fact that they stop here to celebrate the festival of Saturnalia, which began on 17 December and lasted for several days, is highly inappropriate. If they had hurried to Rome, then they might have drawn trouble away from the Capitol and its temple, which was destroyed on 19 December.

102. This was the night of 19/20 December. The Saxa Ruba lay between Rome and Veii on the Flaminian Way, about 5 five miles north of Rome. The name was derived from the red volcanic rocks of the area (Vitruvius 2.7.1), but suggests a blood colour

appropriate in the context of imminent slaughter in the city. The rocks were visible from the Janiculum (Martial, *Epigrams* 4.64.15).

103. Arulenus Rusticus, tribune in 66, praetor in 69 and suffect consul in 92, was a member of the Stoic group whose most prominent representatives were Thrasea Paetus and Helvidius Priscus. He published an account of Thrasea Paetus' death (*Agricola* 2), which Tacitus may have used as a source in *Annals* 16. He was put to death by Domitian in 93. See note 80 above for his wife, Verulana Gratilla.

104. Musonius Rufus was a Stoic philosopher exiled by Nero in 65 (Tacitus, *Annals* 15.71). He had only recently returned to Rome after being recalled by Galba. Vespasian exiled him again, but he was recalled by Titus. Here Tacitus makes him seem especially unworldly in the face of the menacing soldiers.

105. I.e. 21 December. Antonius' meeting with the legions took place on 20 December.

106. At 3.80, Tacitus had depicted the city populace as arming enthusiastically for Vitellius, and their glinting arms in the hills have just been seen by the Flavians (3.82). Here, however, Tacitus elaborates a general rhetorical theme of the work, which often casts the people of Rome as fickle and mercurial in the face of imperial challengers.

107. Sulla's troops won victories in Rome in 88 BC and 82 BC (although on the latter occasion, strictly speaking, the fighting itself took place just outside the city); Cinna's men did the same in 87 BC.

108. This was located just outside the Colline Gate to the north.

109. Suetonius specifies that it was a doorkeeper's cubbyhole made to look inconspicuous by a dog tethered outside it (*Vitellius* 16) while Cassius Dio says that it was a dog kennel (64.20). Tacitus avoids such details, either because he regarded them as being inconsistent with the grandeur of historiography, or because he wanted to allow his audience some scope for pitying Vitellius in his final moments (or both).

110. Near the Pool of Curtius: see Book 1, note 62. The place is also a focus of attention at Vitellius' accession (2.55).

111. See note 93 above.

112. The Latin text here has a short gap, but it obviously contained some basic information about Vitellius' father which editors have supplied.

113. Tacitus sets up an apt closural device to the book (day becoming

evening), but his focus on Domitian (who only emerges when it is safe to do so) points forward to the future; and the same device ends Book 4. In the absence of Vespasian and Titus, Domitian becomes a natural focus for the soldiers' attention.

BOOK 4

1. This is a familiar motif from accounts of the proscriptions which took place under the late republic (e.g. Appian, *Civil Wars* 4.26, a passage which also offers examples of loyal slaves).

2. Capua had been loyal to Vitellius (3.57), but the Flavians had used Tarracina as a base, which was then captured by the Vitellians (3.76–7). So one might have anticipated that Tarracina would be treated especially well by the victors, but this did not happen.

3. See 3.77.

4. The combination of consular power with the praetorship (also specified at Suetonius, *Domitian* 1) is unparalleled. In the absence of Vespasian and Titus, Domitian is a convenient focus for the senate's expression of support for the new regime.

5. A triumph could only be celebrated for a victory over a foreign enemy (not over fellow-Romans). At 3.46 Tacitus records Mucianus quelling trouble which had broken out among the Dacians (rather than Sarmatians).

6. Religious business usually took precedence over secular on the agenda of the senate, so Tacitus is being cutting here.

7. Valerius Asiaticus, governor of Belgica, was Vitellius' son-in-law (1.59), but he apparently died at some point very soon, leaving Vitellius' daughter available for marriage again.

8. His first appearance is at 2.91, but Tacitus postpones his character sketch until now in order to accentuate Helvidius Priscus' role as a major opponent of the Flavians (Vespasian exiles him in 75 and he was subsequently executed).

9. There are problems with the Latin text at this point.

10. That is, Stoicism.

11. See Book 2, note 63.

12. Barea Soranus had been condemned in 66 under Nero (Tacitus, *Annals* 16.23, 30–33). The other man mentioned here may be Sentius Saturninus (the consul in 41 who had taken part in Claudius' invasion of Britain), but this identification is far from secure.

13. The references here are to Lucius Junius Brutus, who expelled

Tarquinius Superbus, the last king of Rome, and instituted the republic, and to Marcus Junius Brutus, the 'tyrannicide' who was one of the leaders of the group which assassinated Julius Caesar in 44 BC. The austere Marcus Porcius Cato (234–149 BC), the 'Censor', was a byword for upright behaviour, as was his great-grandson of the same name (95–46 BC), who opposed Julius Caesar.

14. During the republic, tribunes of the people could use their 'veto' to intervene and stop particular motions being passed by the senate. It was an office which therefore originally had revolutionary and popular associations, but by the time of the principate tribunician power was subsumed under the emperor's personal powers. This is the last known example of a veto being imposed by a tribune, but the fact that it is being used to bolster imperial power (rather than as an expression of independence) is striking and ironic.

15. Publius Egnatius Celer was a Stoic from either Berytus or Tarsus, whose treacherous involvement in the downfall of Barea Soranus in 66 is described emotively by Tacitus at *Annals* 16.32 (cf. Juvenal, *Satires* 3.117). His subsequent conviction is narrated by Tacitus at 4.40.

16. Calpurnius Galerianus had been exiled by the emperor Caligula, but was restored and given the consulship by Claudius. He was the cousin and son-in-law of the unlucky Piso who was proconsul of Africa (4.49) and son of the famous Piso who became the figurehead of the unsuccessful conspiracy against Nero in 65.

17. This scene inauspiciously recalls Vitellius' elimination of Dolabella narrated at 2.64.

18. He was crucified (the usual mode of executing slaves). Tacitus accentuates that the freedman Asiaticus was 'demoted' in his manner of death.

19. Civilis was preparing his revolt over the months August to November 69, but the really serious trouble only broke out in December (4.36 and 55).

20. Tacitus also describes the Batavians at *Germania* 29. Their island (formed by the split of the lower Rhine in the Netherlands) is first mentioned by Julius Caesar (*Gallic War* 4.10). They had served as auxiliaries in the Roman army since the time of Augustus, and their knowledge of Roman fighting techniques potentially made them dangerous enemies.

21. This land mass in the Netherlands is located between the mouths of the rivers Rhine and Waal. Tacitus describes it at *Annals* 2.6.

22. Either in 43 when the invasion of Britain took place, or in 60–61 during the rebellion of Boudicca.

23. The text here is contested: the name may be Julius Paulus.

24. I.e. Civilis had lost an eye; Hannibal lost an eye while crossing the Alps during the invasion of Italy. Sertorius was a distinguished adherent of Marius and as governor of Spain was in rebellion against the Sullan regime during the years 80–72 BC. His liminal position between Roman and foreign makes him an especially apt point of comparison with Civilis, and Tacitus' language here directly recalls Sallust's description of Sertorius in a fragment of his (now fragmentary) *Histories*.

25. This reflects the traditional ethnographic motif that northern barbarians had a large frame (e.g. Caesar, *Gallic War* 1.39, 4.1, Velleius Paterculus 2.106, Tacitus, *Germania* 4).

26. Pro-Flavian accounts cast this revolt unambiguously as a foreign movement, but Tacitus persistently emphasizes the way in which it evolved from the civil wars (1.2, 2.69, 4.22).

27. See 2.69 for the Batavians being sent to Germany.

28. Gaius (Caligula) had gone to Germany in 39–40 and tried to engineer a 'triumph' by getting some Gauls to dye their hair red and pretend to be German prisoners (Suetonius, *Caligula* 47).

29. Tacitus has Civilis use another ethnographical stereotype, namely submissive easterners passively acquiescing in kingship. Yet it will become clear by 4.17 that Civilis himself is aiming at kingship (4.17), so he is using the emotive language of liberty for ulterior motives. The Roman general Petilius Cerialis formulates this as a general point in his speech to the Treviri and Lingones: 'However, they [the Germans] use "liberty" and other fine phrases as their pretexts. Indeed, nobody has ever desired to enslave others and gain dominance for himself without using this very same language' (4.73).

30. Since the collection of tribute was imposed in 27 BC, Civilis is clearly exaggerating for dramatic impact.

31. In 9, the German rebel leader Arminius had famously ambushed the troops of Quinctilius Varus in the Teutoberg forest and massacred three legions. Varus subsequently committed suicide.

32. The camp was at Vetera, and the two legions were the Fifth (Alauda) and the Fifteenth (Primigenia). Both legions were operating at a reduced strength since a proportion of each force had been sent to Italy (2.100, 3.14).

33. Civilis appears to have read his ethnographical handbooks. This practice of stationing women and children behind the battleline

for inspiration is described elsewhere as a stereotypical aspect of German warfare (Caesar, *Gallic War* 1.51, Plutarch, *Marius* 19 and 27, Tacitus, *Germania* 7).

34. The auxiliary cavalry enjoyed more pay and prestige than the auxiliary infantry.

35. I.e. the First (Adiutrix) Legion.

36. The common soldiers are being much more decisive and robust in their denunciation of Civilis than their hesitant and ineffectual generals (whose potential status as traitors Tacitus leaves open as a possibility). At 4.24, they will direct their angry feelings towards Hordeonius Flaccus and openly accuse him of treachery.

37. The serious consequences of this basic error become clear at 4.60.

38. See also Tacitus, *Germania* 7.

39. There is further ethnographical stereotyping at work here: short-lived ferocity at the start of a battle and greed for booty are common attributes of German fighters in Roman texts.

40. Notice of the continuing siege is given at 4.28, 34 and 36; its grim finale is described at 4.59–60.

41. Cf. here a related but different omen involving a river, the sudden flooding of the Tiber (1.86).

42. In a related passage, Tacitus sceptically highlights the tendency for appropriate omens to be supplied only after events have happened (1.10).

43. There are some words missing from the Latin text at this point (possibly indicating the distance of Novaesium from Gelduba), but the general sense is clear.

44. For a similar instance of the common soldiers' loyalty to Vitellius (and support for Vespasian amongst the officers), see 3.61.

45. The official name Colonia Agrippinensium (mod. Cologne) reflects the settlement of a Roman colony of veterans there in 50 at the request of Agrippina the Younger (wife of Claudius), who had been born there.

46. I.e. the camp at Vetera.

47. Further ethnographical colouring: fondness for alcohol and pointless recklessness in battle were stock elements in the portrayal of northern barbarians.

48. That is, until the point when news of the battle (24–25 October) reached Germany on about 7 November 69.

49. Civilis may have appealed to Montanus in an opportunistic way, but the bond between the two men proved enduring: see 5.19.

50. I.e. the Fifth and Fifteenth legions at Vetera.

51. Vitellius had been killed in Rome on 20 December 69 (3.82–5).
52. Tacitus will supply the details of these events at 4.48–50. The groundless fear of supposed trouble in Africa is particularly ironic given the apparent lack of reaction to the much more serious chain of events in Germany.
53. Cf. Juvenal *Satires* 10.81 (the famous snub about the Roman people only being concerned with bread and circuses).
54. The competent Julius Frontinus would go on to hold three consulships after serving as a legionary commander in Germany in 70 and governing Britain (*c.* 73–7). He wrote *About the Aqueducts of the City of Rome* (Nerva had appointed him superintendent of the aqueducts in 97) and *Stratagems* (both extant). He died in 103 or 104.
55. For Tettius Julianus see 1.79 and 2.85.
56. For Plotius Grypus see 3.52.
57. Crassus Scribonianus was the brother of Galba's adopted son, Piso. See Book 1, note 35.
58. I.e. the Seventh (Galbiana) Legion, raised by Galba in Spain and brought to Rome (1.6). Its winter camp was at Carnutum in Pannonia.
59. Suetonius, *Domitian* 18 refers to Domitian's ruddy complexion. Tacitus at *Agricola* 45 claims that Domitian's natural flush was a screen against showing any potential shame at his callous acts (also Pliny, *Panegyricus* 48). Blushing was normally associated with modesty (Pliny, *Epistle* 1.14, Seneca, *Moral Epistles* 11).
60. The calendar was highly susceptible to proposals involving changing the names of months in a bid to flatter the emperor. So, the senate proposed that the month of April should be named after Nero (Tacitus, *Annals* 15.74), and May and June should be named after Claudius and Germanicus (*Annals* 16.12).
61. See 4.10.
62. The famous Cynic philosopher Demetrius, independent and outspoken, was later banished by Vespasian in 71 for criticizing the regime (Cassius Dio 66.13). He features regularly in the writings of Seneca the Younger, who appears to have been fond of him, and he is seen advising Thrasea Paetus about the nature of the soul in the run-up to his death (Tacitus, *Annals* 16.34). Cynics abided by the principle that they should live according to nature and often lived a simple, primitive lifestyle. They frequently found themselves at odds with the Roman authorities.
63. Junius Mauricus, the brother of Arulenus Rusticus (3.80 and Book 3, note 103), was exiled by Domitian after his brother's

execution. Nerva recalled him and he became one of Trajan's advisers. Pliny the Younger speaks highly of him in *Epistle* 4.22.

64. Despite Tacitus' emphasis on the notoriety of these three informers, nothing further is known about them.

65. In 67 (the year in which Paccius Africanus was consul), Scribonius Rufus and Scribonius Proculus were summoned to Greece and forced to commit suicide by Nero (Cassius Dio 63.17).

66. For Vibius Crispus, see 2.10.

67. The normal minimum age for a senator was twenty-five.

68. Aquilius Regulus was a notorious informer under Nero and in 67 he had accused Marcus Licinius Crassus Frugi (brother of Galba's adopted son, Piso), as well as his father-in-law Quintus Sulpicius Camerinus Pythicus. Salvidienus Orfitus had been consul in 51 and was executed in 66 by Nero thanks to Regulus' prosecution. No doubt these events would have featured in the lost final books of the *Annals*.

69. Tacitus relates the colourful case of Octavius Sagitta, condemned in 58 for killing his lover Pontia, in more detail at *Annals* 13.44. Antistius Sosianus had been condemned in 62 for writing slanderous poems against Nero (*Annals* 14.48).

70. The mock funeral is curiously reminiscent of the grand finale of Trimalchio's dinner-party, narrated by Petronius at *Satyricon* 78.

71. See 2.67 for their original discharge by Vitellius.

72. See 4.2 for the surrender at Bovillae.

73. The hunting down in Rome of individuals who were distinctively tall and young (4.1) already implies a particular vindictiveness against German troops (traditionally cast as being unusually tall, according to the ethnographic stereotype).

74. See 2.71 and 91 for Vitellius' distribution of consulships.

75. Marcus Junius Silanus, who had been consul in 19 and had married Augustus' great-granddaughter Aemilia Lepida, had been governor of Africa in 36–9 (although the dates have been contested). All four of their children suffered because of their illustrious parentage.

76. The legates were appointed by the emperor, who personally decided when to bring them back, which often meant that they were in post for a long time, but the proconsular governors of senatorial (public) provinces rotated in office much more regularly so had less time to become entrenched.

77. Valerius Festus, legate of the Third (Augustan) Legion, was a new man from Arretium. Despite being Vitellius' relative (probably by marriage), he secretly switched his loyalty to Vespasian (2.98)

and concocted a sound scheme to prove his loyalty by securing Lucius Piso's death and winning gratitude from the Flavians. He was later granted triumphal ornaments for defeating the Garamantes, became suffect consul in 71 with Domitian and served as curator of the Tiber in 72–3. He afterwards served as legate of Pannonia in 73 and legate of Hispania Tarraconensis in perhaps 78–81.

78. The reason for this cavalry unit's name is disputed.

79. See 4.11 and note 16 above for Galerianus.

80. Baebius Massa became a notorious informer under Domitian and was later condemned for extortion in the province of Baetica in 93. Pliny the Younger writes to Tacitus about this case in *Epistle* 7.33 (also 3.4, 6.29), in a bid to ensure its inclusion in the *Histories*. Tacitus' reference here suggests that Pliny would have found him receptive to such information.

81. The Garamantes, from the interior, south of Oea and Lepcis, were a troublesome tribe who had helped the rebel Tacfarinas during Tiberius' principate (Tacitus, *Annals* 3.74). Pliny the Elder talks about their irritating habit of filling up the wells with sand to prevent inroads being made into their terrain (*Natural History* 5.38).

82. Vologaeses I was king of Parthia from 51 to 79.

83. Tacitus will pick up this narrative at 5.1–13.

84. Tacitus' portrait of Vitellius' mother, Sextilia, is an illustration of this point (2.63).

85. See Book 3, note 10 on Vespasian's original plan for blockading the corn supply. Tacitus uses the focus on the corn-ships as a neat transitional device to shift his narrative back to Rome.

86. Lucius Vestinus, a knight from Vienna (mod. Vienne, in Gaul) had been prefect of Egypt (59–62) under Claudius.

87. Certain types of tree were considered to bring good luck (Macrobius, *Saturnalia* 3.20 lists fourteen varieties).

88. Plautius Silvanus Aelianus had been suffect consul in 45 (again in 74), and after military service in Germany (39–40) and Britain (43–44) he became proconsul of Asia in perhaps 53/4 and, later, legate of Moesia (60–66 or 67). Under the Flavians he served as governor of Hispania Tarraconensis and became prefect of Rome. Vespasian belatedly awarded him triumphal ornaments for his military achievements on the Danube during Nero's principate.

89. This triple sacrifice was a standard part of Roman rituals of purification. The sacrificial victims were led in procession around

the object to be purified and then sacrificed to Mars, as the god who was supposed to ward off plague and pollution.

90. The juxtaposition of this point with the narrative in the previous chapter about the restoration of the Capitol is pointed. The Flavians may have embarked on a physical restoration of the temple, but it will take more than that to reinstate respect for Rome after the civil wars.

91. See 4.36.

92. Julius Caesar apparently had many casual affairs: see Suetonius, *Divine Julius* 50–52, including some choice verses about his philandering in Gaul.

93. See 4.18.

94. Julius Sacrovir was an Aeduan chieftain who was one of the ringleaders of a Gallic revolt against Rome in 21 (Tacitus, *Annals* 3.40–47). He committed suicide after a decisive defeat and so offers Vocula an apt historical precedent.

95. In terms of style, Vocula's speech can be seen at many points to evoke Livy's version of Scipio's speech to his mutinous soldiers at 28.27–9.

96. At 4.22, we can see that this lack of supplies is partly down to a basic mistake made by the Roman generals.

97. Quirinus is the name that was taken by the deified Romulus, founder of Rome.

98. The tables will soon be turned on Aemilius Longinus (a minor character named for impact): see 4.62.

99. The early stages of the siege at Vetera are described at 4.21–3; and details of its continuation are given at 4.28, 34 and 36.

100. See note 96 above.

101. Tacitus at *Germania* 31 attributes a similar practice to the Chatti.

102. Tacitus also mentions at *Germania* 8 the veneration in which Veleda was held. She also features briefly in a poem of Statius (*Silvae* 1.4.90), indicating her capture in 77 or 78 by the Roman general Rutilius Gallicus, after which she was taken to Rome.

103. Tacitus has added significant Livian echoes in what follows. Livy had recorded in a vivid and memorable scene (9.4–6) the humiliating surrender of the Romans to the Samnites in 321 BC, after their defeat at the battle of the Caudine Forks. Further echoes are added at 4.72 in the description of the formerly rebellious legions.

104. Claudius Sanctus' physical affliction recalls the one-eyed Civilis (4.13).

105. For the odium which could attach to an individual general for

allowing the sacking of a city, we can compare Antonius Primus and the bad reputation which he gained after the destruction of Cremona (3.34). That incident becomes a point of comparison for the Roman soldiers in expressing their desire to sack Augusta Trevirorum (4.72); and a deterrent for their general Petilius Cerialis, who restrains his men for fear of gaining a bad reputation.

106. Tacitus allocates a Roman name (Mars) to the native god (Tiu), a ubiquitous technique among Roman authors, even if to a modern reader it seems a little odd in the immediate context of the envoy asserting German independence.

107. See especially Tacitus, *Agricola* 21.

108. This civilized vignette of the Tencteri and the people of Colonia Agrippinensium resolving their internal differences by speech rather than by resorting to warfare offers a pointed contrast to the conduct of the Romans during the recent sequence of civil wars.

109. See 4.12 for the talents of the Batavians at swimming.

110. He was building, perhaps, on his earlier claims of descent from Julius Caesar (4.55), but he seems not to have any of the military talents associated with his 'ancestor'.

111. Sabinus and his wife successfully hid out for many years in an underground tomb and they even managed to have two sons during this time. Plutarch tells the story of their execution (*Moralia* 770d).

112. See Book 3, note 68 for Petilius Cerialis.

113. See 4.39.

114. His sister Tertulla had been married to Titus before her death (Suetonius, *Titus* 4). Clemens went on to become consul in 73 (and again at some point under Domitian) and governor of Spain in 81–3. Domitian eventually put him to death (Suetonius, *Domitian* 11).

115. The prefect of the praetorian guard was normally a knight, not a senator.

116. These are tribes from the west bank of the Rhine. The Vangiones had provided the Roman general Pomponius Secundus with auxiliary troops to combat raids made by the Chatti (Tacitus, *Annals* 12.27); and the current defection of all three tribes from Rome is very short-lived.

117. See 4.62.

118. The Roman troops here are represented in relatively positive terms by Tacitus: they are motivated not by a desire for booty, but by desire for revenge for the slaughter of their colleagues. Yet how far Tutor and Classicus were directly responsible for

slaughtering the legions who had been besieged at Vetera is an open question. We see again how easy it is for individuals to be blamed for events set in motion by large groups of people.

119. See note 103 above for the Livian echoes in play here.

120. Although the Lingones are represented as having been defeated in battle (4.67), there is no indication that they had surrendered and hence they are an appropriate component for the audience of Cerialis' speech defending Roman imperialism (cf. 4.14 for Civilis' denunciation of it). The defeat of the Treviri under Valentinus is narrated at 4.71.

121. In the time of Marius, the Teutoni had invaded Narbonese Gaul and the Cimbri had marched into northern Italy, but the former were defeated in 102 BC at Aquae Sextiae and the latter were repulsed in 101 BC at Vercellae. These invasions had, nonetheless, caused huge anxiety at Rome.

122. Ariovistus, king of the Suebi, had invaded Gaul in about 71 BC. He defeated the Aedui and resisted all attempts of the Gauls to oust him. In 58 BC, however, Julius Caesar intervened and routed him (Caesar, *Gallic War* 1.31–53).

123. This assertion is an exaggeration: the one prominent example is Julius Vindex, governor of Lugdunese Gaul. Cf. Tacitus' version of the debate in 48 about whether Gauls should be allowed to become senators (*Annals* 11.23–5).

124. This cynical observation endorses the point made by Petilius Cerialis in his speech at 4.74.

125. The reason for his absence is unclear. At 5.22, he is away from the camp because (people thought) he was having an affair with an Ubian woman named Claudia Sacrata.

126. This rash move is indicative of bravery, but could have been fatal: when the African rebel leader Tacfarinas did the same thing, he was promptly killed (Tacitus, *Annals* 4.25). Civilis tries something similar during battle and the plan backfires (5.21).

127. See 4.70 for their execution.

128. Tolbiacum was an important road junction.

129. Vitellius' six-year-old son, Germanicus, had featured at 2.59, when the army had met him at Lyons. He apparently had such a bad stammer that he was almost dumb (Suetonius, *Vitellius* 6) and he is a poignant figure in the history of these civil wars.

130. Vespasian left Alexandria in late August or early September 70. His absence from Rome was convenient, in that he left Mucianus to handle the most distasteful aspects of the immediate aftermath of the civil war (such as the execution of Vitellius' son).

131. Tacitus here uses a grand periphrasis for saliva (*oris excrementum*, 'refuse of the mouth'), perhaps in order to avoid a term which he deemed incompatible with the grandeur of his genre. The most famous example is at *Annals* 1.65, when he refers to a spade as 'the implement with which earth is removed'.

132. The two healings are also reported by Cassius Dio 66.8 and Suetonius, *Vespasian* 7, but in the latter version, they are preceded by the incident involving Basilides, which Tacitus places subsequently (4.82). The cynical coda about the witnesses who no longer have an incentive to lie is a Tacitean addition.

133. The oracular god Serapis (whose name is a blend of the Egyptian god Osiris and the Egyptian sacred bull Apis) was associated with the underworld. His most magnificent temple, the Serapeum, was in Alexandria. Vespasian's visit reminds us of Titus' earlier visit to the shrine of Aphrodite at Paphos (2.4) and Vespasian's other visit to the altar of the god of Mount Carmel (2.78).

134. The name Basilides means 'prince' which (despite the fact that Vespasian regards the incident as confirmation of his own power) should draw our attention to his sons Domitian and Titus. Tacitus appears to have moved this story from a point before Vespasian was aware that he had won (cf. Suetonius, *Vespasian* 7). Here it points forward in a suggestive way to the problematic son Domitian at the end of the book.

135. There is also an account at Plutarch, *On Isis and Osiris* 28, but Tacitus' claim to originality is one of a range of techniques he uses to bolster his authority as an author.

136. Ptolemy I Soter (*c.* 367–283 BC) was one of Alexander the Great's generals. Following the struggles in the aftermath of Alexander's death, Ptolemy made himself king of Egypt and instituted a Greek-speaking administration of Egypt (with Alexandria as his capital). He wrote a comprehensive and eulogistic history of Alexander the Great, which is no longer extant.

137. A mountainous and fertile region in Asia Minor which included the south coast of the Black Sea and extended southwards to Cappadocia.

138. Eleusis was a town near Athens, which contained a sanctuary of Demeter and held the annual festival of the Eleusinian Mysteries (an initiation cult associated with Demeter).

139. Jupiter Dis indicates Pluto (= Greek Hades), god of the underworld. Proserpina, daughter of Jupiter and Ceres (= Greek Demeter), was queen of the underworld, after being abducted by Pluto.

140. This was the famous oracle at Delphi.
141. Apollo's father is Jupiter (here to be identified with Jupiter Dis, strictly speaking Pluto, Apollo's uncle) and his sister is Proserpina.
142. This temple, the Serapeum, was actually built in the reign of Ptolemy I's grandson, Ptolemy III Euergetes (reigned 246–221 BC).
143. Aesculapius was the Roman god of healing.
144. These common attributes of Pluto's statues which could allow this identification with Serapis include the depiction of the dog Cerberus and a snake, suggesting the underworld, and a corn-measure, associated with Ceres (Demeter).
145. Julius Valentinus had been captured at Rigodulum (4.71).
146. Suetonius, *Domitian* 2 links Domitian's role in the aborted expedition to Gaul and Germany to his desire to compete with Titus. He also notes that Domitian was reprimanded for his ambition (a point which may reflect Cerialis' snub here).

BOOK 5

1. In the year 70.
2. See Suetonius, *Titus* 4 for his exploits in Germany (also mentioned by Mucianus in his speech at 2.77) and Britain.
3. Cf. the praise of Vespasian at 2.5.
4. See Book 2, notes 97 and 98 for Sohaemus and Agrippa.
5. The ethnographical digression which follows is highly controversial and contains various errors, but, in narrative terms, the formally demarcated excursus stands as a marker of the transition from self-destructive internal civil conflict to more laudable foreign campaigning.
6. According to myth, Jupiter ejected his father Saturn and became ruler of the gods: Tacitus' point about the Jews being refugees from Crete is not found in other sources. The use of Saturn's deposition as a chronological marker will be picked up at 5.4 when Tacitus offers explanations for the Jewish institution of the Sabbath.
7. In Greek myth, Cepheus was king of Ethiopia and father of Andromeda, who was famously rescued by Perseus.
8. See Homer, *Iliad* 6.184 and 204, where they appear to come from Lycia (Herodotus 1.173 notes that they were displaced by arrivals from Crete).
9. The connection is between the Solymi and Hierosolyma (the Latin name for Jerusalem).

10. Leprosy.

11. Bocchoris was king of Egypt during the eighth century BC (*c.* 721–715), but the exodus is thought to have taken place at some point in the thirteenth century BC.

12. The oracle of Hammon was located at the oasis of Siwa in the Libyan desert. Alexander paid a visit here in 331 BC which subsequently led to stories that the general was the son of the god (commonly identified with Zeus).

13. Tacitus means that they dedicated the image of an ass, but this is inconsistent with what he says at 5.5 and 9. Josephus, *Against Apion* 2.248 expresses his disapproval of the belief (held by others before Tacitus) that the head of an ass was to be found in the innermost part of the Temple.

14. Hammon was frequently depicted as having horns and the Egyptians regarded the ram as sacred to him.

15. This practice apparently prompted the emperor Augustus to joke: 'I would rather be Herod's pig than Herod's son' (Macrobius, *Saturnalia* 2.4.11; the original version in Greek would have contained a pun involving 'pig' and 'son').

16. This pejorative comment reflects the Jewish observance of the Sabbatical year, when every seventh year the land is left to lie fallow and debts are remitted.

17. All Jews made annual contributions (whether financial or otherwise) to the Temple. Josephus, *Jewish Antiquities* 7.2 says: 'Let nobody wonder at the wealth of our Temple, seeing that all the Jews in the world had long been contributing to it' (cf. Cicero, *On Behalf of Flaccus* 28, 66–9). After the Temple was destroyed, the Romans required that the Jews send their tribute to Rome. Tacitus refers to the wealth of the Temple specifically at 5.8.

18. In Classical texts, in accordance with general theories of environmental determinism, lack of sexual restraint was often attributed to those living in hot southern climates (Hippocrates, *Airs, Waters, Places* 20–22), whereas those living in the chilly north were usually portrayed as chaste (cf. *Germania* 18.1). Here Tacitus ingeniously condemns the Jews for being sexually loose and exclusive at the same time.

19. However, the Egyptians also practised circumcision. Petronius makes Giton refer with comic exaggeration to circumcision as an extreme way to disguise oneself as a Jew (*Satyricon* 102). Juvenal also points to circumcision as a typically Jewish practice (*Satire* 14.99).

20. Juvenal alludes to the lack of physical images of the gods

when he says that the Jews worship only the 'clouds and the divine spirit of the sky' (*Satire* 14.97). The absence of images of the gods in other cultures tends to provoke comment and becomes something of an ethnographical commonplace: Persians (Herodotus 1.131), Gauls (Diodorus Siculus 22.9) and Germans (Tacitus, *Germania* 9) are described in this way. Yet the Roman King Numa, inspired by Pythagoras, apparently forbade cult-images of the gods (Plutarch, *Numa* 8).

21. I.e. Bacchus, the god of wine.

22. Pliny, *Natural History* 16.135 says that balsam can only grow successfully in Judaea. Josephus, *Jewish War* 4.469 identifies it as the most valuable local crop.

23. Tacitus is describing the Dead Sea.

24. Josephus, *Jewish War* 4.477 says that Vespasian threw in some non-swimmers with their hands tied behind their backs to test this quality: luckily, they floated.

25. This same method of gathering bitumen is also related by Josephus, *Jewish War* 4.478–81.

26. This is a reference to the destruction of Sodom and Gomorrah (Genesis 18–19).

27. Tacitus appears to jump rather suddenly from the south-east of the country to the north-west: the River Belius flows into the Mediterranean near Ptolemais (Pliny, *Natural History* 36.190).

28. King Antiochus IV Epiphanes of Syria (ruled 176–164 BC) banned Jewish religious practices in 167 BC, but then faced a revolt (described by Josephus at *Jewish Antiquities* 12.265ff.) which forced him to annul his legislation.

29. Something has gone wrong here. The revolt of Arsaces I took place in 247 BC under Antiochus II (ruled 261–246), whereas Antiochus IV campaigned against Parthia in 165 BC.

30. This took place in 63 BC after Pompey had been invited to decide between rival candidates – Hyrcanus and his brother Aristoboulus – for the throne. Pompey opted for Hyrcanus.

31. Julius Caesar granted permission for the walls to be rebuilt soon afterwards.

32. Antony controlled the East between 42 and 31 BC. Pacorus (the son of King Orodes rather than king himself) captured Jerusalem in 40 BC, only to be killed by Antony's associate Ventidius in 38 BC.

33. The general Gaius Sosius was appointed by Antony as governor of Syria and Cilicia in 38 BC, after which he captured Jerusalem and helped to set up Herod as king in 37 BC (celebrating a triumph for his achievements in 34 BC).

34. Herod the Great (c. 73–4 BC) became governor of Galilee in 47
    BC. Despite being made king of Judaea by Antony in 37 BC, he
    supported Octavian at Actium. In 23 BC he was given various
    territories north-east of Galilee, including Trachonitis, Batanea
    and Auranitis.

35. Simon had been one of Herod's slaves (Josephus, *Jewish War*
    2.57–9). He was one of a number of rival claimants, but Tacitus
    has simplified the story.

36. Quinctilius Varus was governor of Syria from 6 to 4 BC. See
    further Book 4, note 31.

37. The three sons were Archelaus, Antipas and Philip. In fact, the
    eldest son, Archelaus, was deposed in 6 and Judaea was placed
    under the control of Roman prefects.

38. The assassination took place on 24 January 41.

39. Antonius Felix, brother of another imperial freedman, Pallas,
    governed Judaea between 52 and 60. Tacitus gives further details
    about his troubled tenure as governor at *Annals* 12.54.

40. Gessius Florus, a Greek from Clazomenae, was governor of
    Judaea between 64 and 66.

41. I.e. the years 67 and 68.

42. Josephus, *Jewish War* 5.52–63 says that Titus narrowly missed
    being killed at this point after getting separated from the main
    force with only a few men.

43. The sources generally portray Titus as a hedonist, particularly
    before Vespasian became emperor (2.2, Suetonius, *Titus* 7). His
    motivation for conquering Judaea highlighted here does him little
    credit.

44. Josephus, *Jewish War* 5.136–75 offers a lavish description of
    Jerusalem and its defensive walls. Tacitus' version is concise in
    comparison, but it still accentuates the imposing nature of the
    city and points forward to the impressive achievement of Titus
    in finally conquering it.

45. Tacitus here casts the factions in Jerusalem as enacting a civil
    war in miniature, despite the pressing threat now facing them
    from the Romans. Josephus, *Jewish War* 5.25 observes that the
    corn which was lost would have lasted the besieged for many
    years and that famine played a significant part in the fall of the
    city. This is curiously reminiscent of the self-inflicted problems
    resulting from lack of food that were faced by the legionaries
    besieged at Vetera (4.22).

46. Josephus, *Jewish War* 6.288–98 also lists some of these portents
    (a star over the city and a comet lasting for a whole year; a bright

light around the altar in the middle of the night lasting half an hour; a cow giving birth to a lamb in the Temple; the spontaneous opening of the eastern gate of the Temple's inner sanctuary; chariots and soldiers in the sky; words apparently spoken by the divine spirit leaving the Temple). In comparison with Josephus, Tacitus is selective and relatively brief about the portents which he reports.

47. See 4.76–8.

48. The unambiguous polarization of 'Romans' and 'Germans' offers a refreshing change from the murky allegiances of the civil war and hints at a gradual recovery of Roman identity. Tacitus' emphasis on the potential strategic impact of the terrain on the two sides is a technique he will redeploy at *Annals* 1.65–69 in describing the German ambush of the Romans in 15 on the site of the massacre of Roman legions by Arminius in 9.

49. Tacitus offers a similar contrast at *Annals* 1.65.

50. The Fourteenth (Gemina/Twin) Legion had been based in Britain since the conquest of 43 and it had been the main Roman force at the battle in which Boudicca's revolt was suppressed in 61 (Tacitus, *Annals* 14.34).

51. The Sixth (Victrix) Legion in Spain had taken the initiative in hailing Galba as emperor.

52. The Second (Adiutrix) Legion was a new formation, possibly consisting of former sailors (cf. 3.55).

53. Civilis here seems to be self-consciously playing the role of the rebel Arminius (see note 48 above; Tacitus, *Annals* 1.65), hoping that history will repeat itself, but the original victory of Civilis on this site is hardly an equivalent to Arminius' devastating massacre of Varus' legions in 9.

54. See Tacitus, *Germania* 11 for the German practice of clashing arms as an indication of approval after a speech. Caesar represents the Gauls as doing the same thing (*Gallic War* 7.21). The explicit pointing up of the ethnographical detail here enhances the sense of polarization between the two sides and accentuates the difference.

55. See 5.14.

56. There is a certain appropriate symbolism in the fact that it is a Batavian deserter whose actions determine the final outcome of the battle between Cerialis and Civilis, since Civilis himself is a slippery figure and has already been denounced by the Roman legionaries as a 'Batavian deserter' (4.21).

57. The Roman fleet (from Britain) was last seen in action at 4.79, when it suffered significant losses at the hands of the Canninefates.

58. Batavodurum. Its precise location has been debated by modern scholars.

59. Nero Claudius Drusus Germanicus (38–9 BC), the brother of the emperor Tiberius, was a popular figure, famous as a republican sympathizer. He died in Germany during a campaign against the Chatti and the Cherusci after falling from his horse. The speedy journey which Tiberius made from Italy to see him before he died was seen as a reflection of fraternal devotion. Tacitus records modification to Drusus' mole made in 58 (*Annals* 13.53).

60. See 4.32.

61. See 4.70.

62. See Book 4, note 102.

63. These were ships built with two banks of oars.

64. The Liburnian was a type of fast galley, named after an Illyrian people, the Liburni, who were famous as seafarers and pirates. Octavian had made good use of Liburnian ships at the battle of Actium.

65. This was a standard trick to make people think that the person whose property was spared was in cahoots with the enemy (cf. Thucydides 2.13), but given the uncertainty running through the narrative about the slippery Civilis' true allegiance, it was particularly sensible to use it here.

66. The Latin word used for Civilis' madness (*rabies*) is the same one used at 2.38 as a causal factor in generating civil war. This is a suggestive echo, given the debate surrounding the status of the Batavian revolt and to what extent it was a continuation of the Roman civil war.

67. Civilis' speech of defence completely contradicts what he wrote in his letter to Petilius Cerialis (4.75). The scene of two enemies confronting each other from opposite banks of a river is replayed at *Annals* 2.9, where the rebel leader Arminius talks to his brother Flavus (a Roman auxiliary) across a river.

68. Tacitus refers to Antonius Primus' letter to Julius Civilis right at the start of the narrative of the revolt (4.13). When one letter from Antonius to Civilis is read out to the Roman troops in Germany, it makes them angry because Civilis seems to be addressed as an ally of the Flavian party (4.32).

69. Unfortunately, this is where the manuscript breaks off. The narrative went on to cover the completion of the Jewish war by Titus and the subsequent triumph in 71 (even though the fortress of Masada held out until 73). As we know from Tacitus' outline at 1.1–3, in the remaining books (possibly seven further books,

making twelve in total), Tacitus dealt with the principates of Vespasian (70–79), Titus (79–81) and Domitian (81–96). Highlights would have included the exile and death of Helvidius Priscus in about 74 for his opposition to Vespasian, the spectacular eruption of Mount Vesuvius in 79 (Pliny the Younger had written Tacitus two letters about this extraordinary event), Domitian's Dacian campaigns in the 80s, the execution of Vestal Virgins in 83 and 89 or 90, Domitian's affair with his niece Julia and the assassination of Domitian in 96.

MAPS

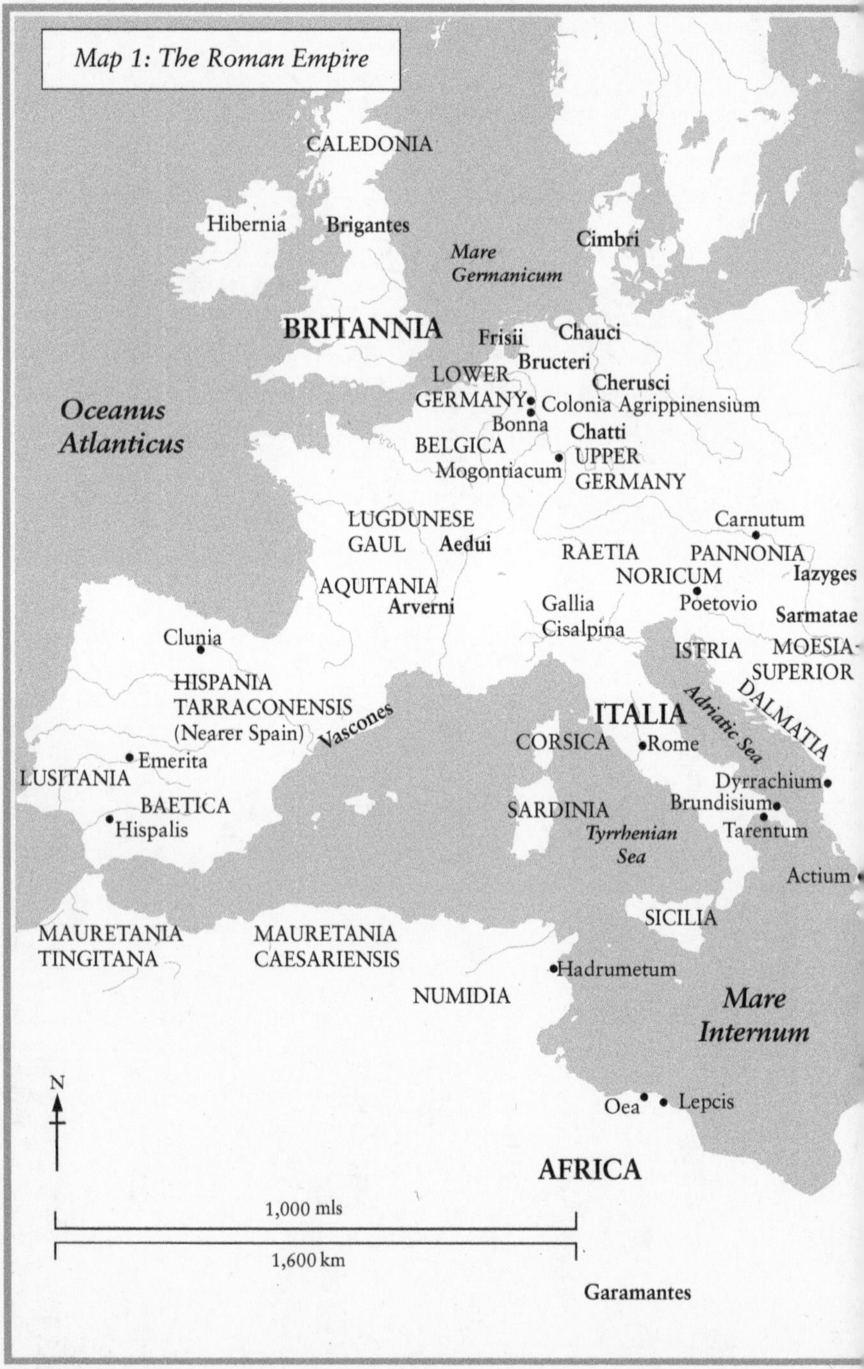
Map 1: The Roman Empire
CALEDONIA
Hibernia
Brigantes
Mare Germanicum
Cimbri
BRITANNIA
Frisii
Chauci
Bructeri
LOWER GERMANY
Cherusci
Colonia Agrippinensium
Bonna
Chatti
Oceanus Atlanticus
BELGICA
UPPER GERMANY
Mogontiacum
LUGDUNESE GAUL
Aedui
Carnutum
RAETIA
PANNONIA
NORICUM
Iazyges
AQUITANIA
Arverni
Gallia Cisalpina
Poetovio
Sarmatae
Clunia
ISTRIA
MOESIA SUPERIOR
HISPANIA TARRACONENSIS (Nearer Spain)
Vascones
ITALIA
Adriatic Sea
DALMATIA
CORSICA
Rome
Emerita
LUSITANIA
Dyrrachium
BAETICA
SARDINIA
Brundisium
Hispalis
Tyrrhenian Sea
Tarentum
Actium
SICILIA
MAURETANIA TINGITANA
MAURETANIA CAESARIENSIS
Hadrumetum
NUMIDIA
Mare Internum
N
Oea
Lepcis
AFRICA
1,000 mls
1,600 km
Garamantes

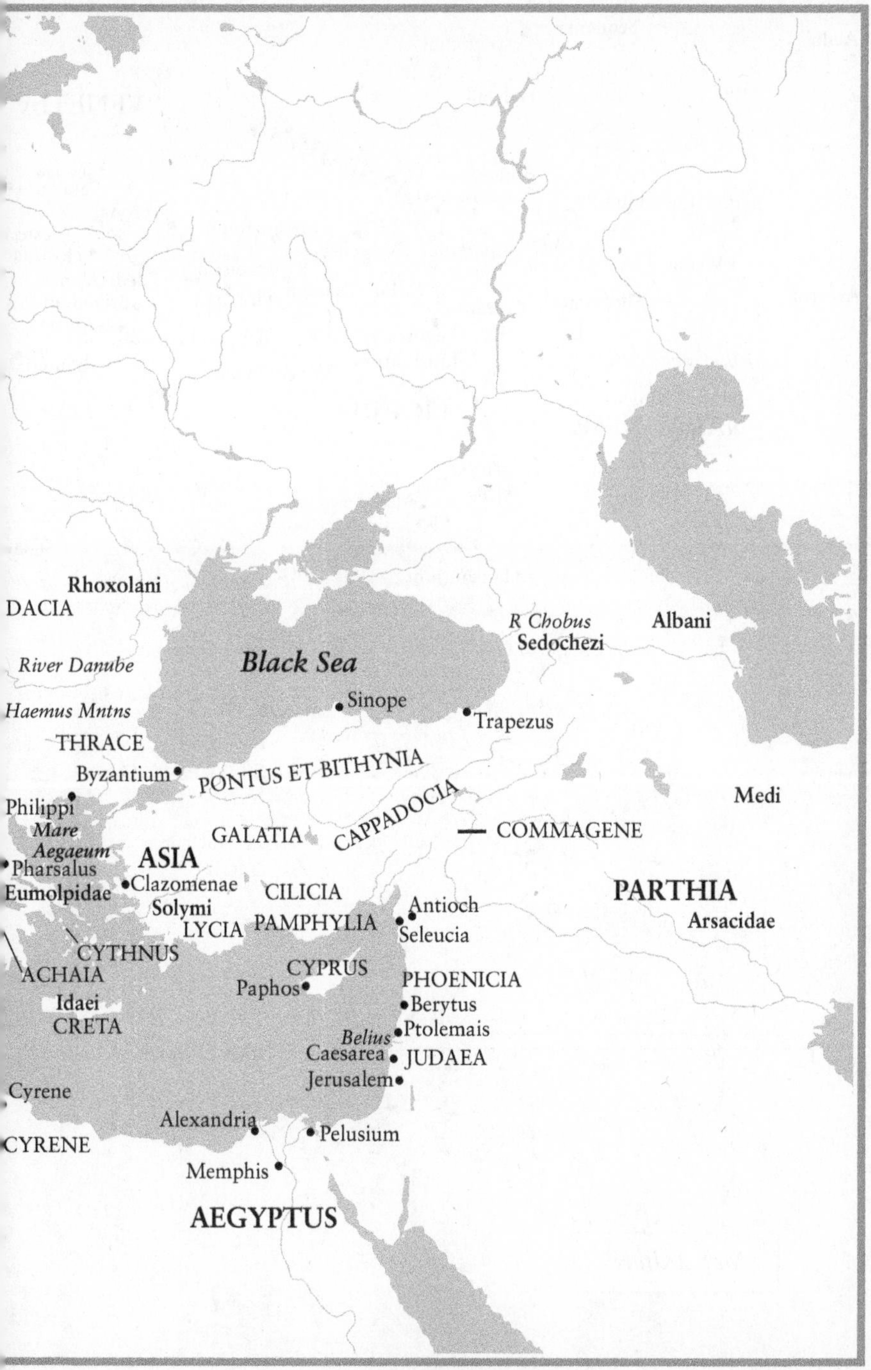

Rhoxolani
DACIA
River Danube
Haemus Mntns
THRACE
Byzantium
Philippi
Mare Aegaeum
Pharsalus
Eumolpidae
Clazomenae
ASIA
Solymi
LYCIA
CYTHNUS
ACHAIA
Idaei
CRETA
Cyrene
CYRENE
Black Sea
Sinope
Trapezus
R Chobus
Sedochezi
Albani
PONTUS ET BITHYNIA
CAPPADOCIA
GALATIA
COMMAGENE
Medi
CILICIA
PAMPHYLIA
Antioch
Seleucia
PARTHIA
Arsacidae
CYPRUS
Paphos
PHOENICIA
Berytus
Ptolemais
Belius
Caesarea
JUDAEA
Jerusalem
Alexandria
Pelusium
Memphis
AEGYPTUS

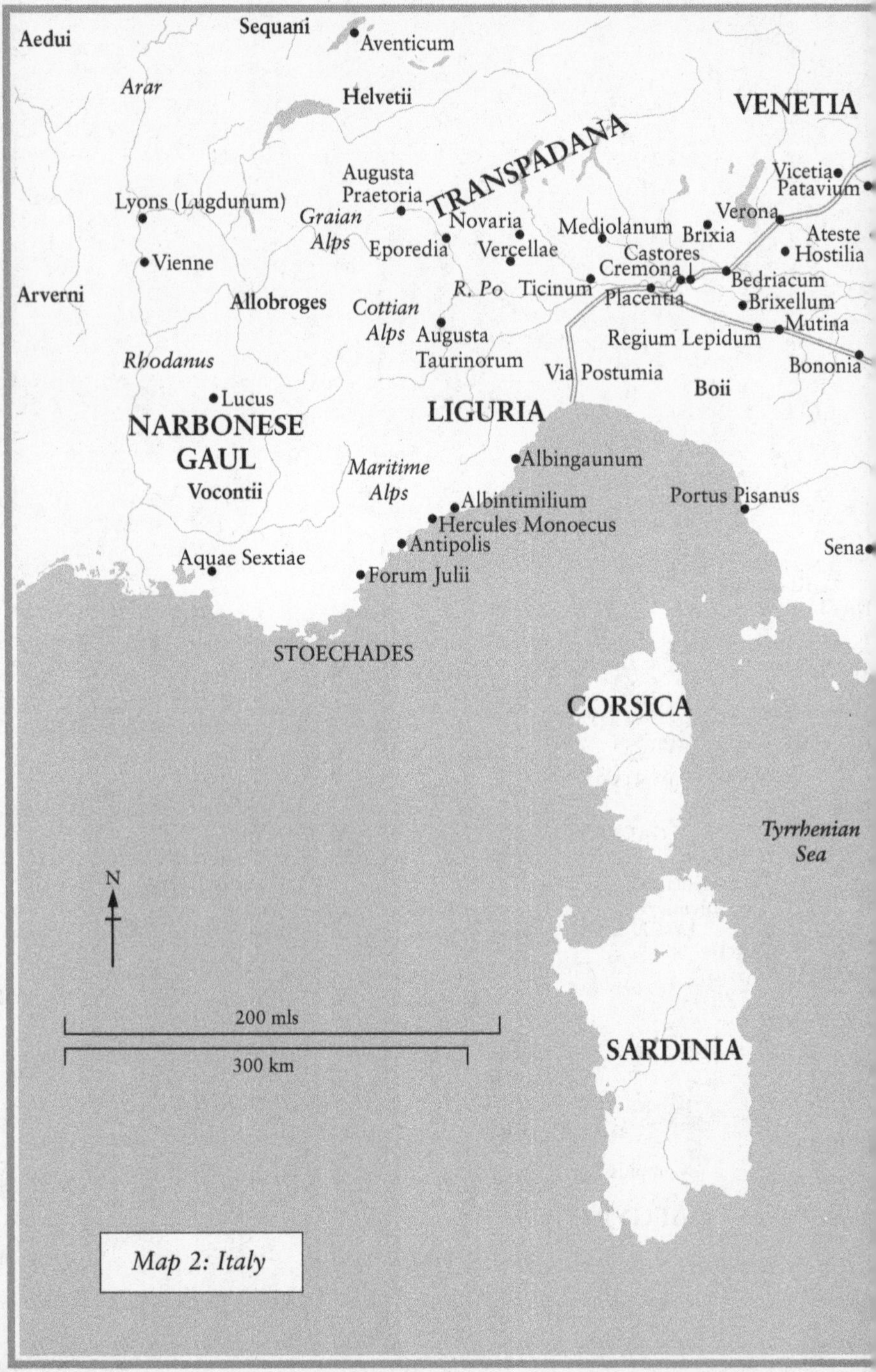

Aedui

Sequani •Aventicum

Arar

Helvetii

VENETIA

Lyons (Lugdunum) •

Graian Alps

Augusta Praetoria

TRANSPADANA

Vicetia•
Patavium•

Eporedia

Novaria

Mediolanum

Verona

Brixia

Ateste•

•Vienne

Vercellae

Castores

Hostilia•

Arverni

Allobroges

R. Po Ticinum

Cremona

Bedriacum

Placentia

Brixellum

Cottian Alps

Augusta Taurinorum

Via Postumia

Regium Lepidum

Mutina

Bononia

Rhodanus

•Lucus

LIGURIA

Boii

NARBONESE GAUL

Vocontii

Maritime Alps

•Albingaunum

Portus Pisanus •

•Albintimilium

•Hercules Monoecus

Sena•

Aquae Sextiae

•Antipolis

•Forum Julii

STOECHADES

CORSICA

Tyrrhenian Sea

N

200 mls

300 km

SARDINIA

Map 2: Italy

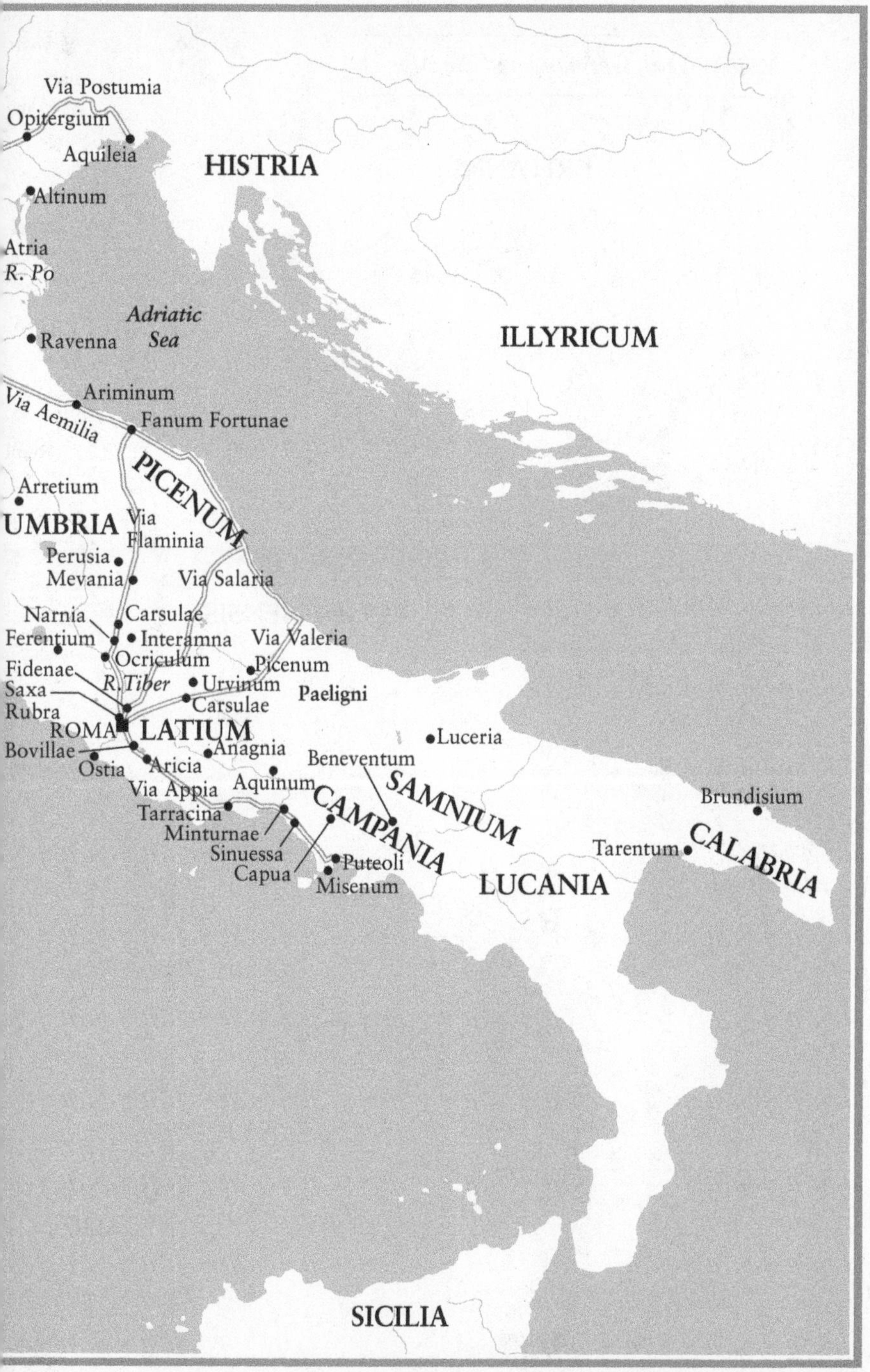

Via Postumia
Opitergium
Aquileia
HISTRIA
Altinum
Atria
R. Po
Adriatic Sea
Ravenna
ILLYRICUM
Ariminum
Via Aemilia
Fanum Fortunae
PICENUM
Arretium
UMBRIA
Via Flaminia
Perusia
Mevania
Via Salaria
Narnia
Carsulae
Ferentium
Interamna
Via Valeria
Ocriculum
Picenum
Fidenae
R. Tiber
Urvinum
Saxa Rubra
Carsulae
Paeligni
ROMA
LATIUM
Luceria
Bovillae
Anagnia
Ostia
Aricia
Beneventum
Via Appia
Aquinum
SAMNIUM
Tarracina
CAMPANIA
Brundisium
Minturnae
Sinuessa
Capua
Puteoli
Misenum
Tarentum
CALABRIA
LUCANIA
SICILIA

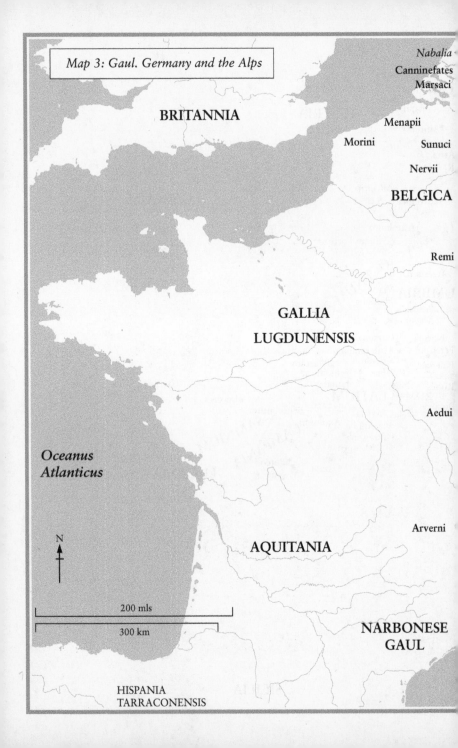

Map 3: Gaul. Germany and the Alps

BRITANNIA

Nabalia
Canninefates
Marsaci

Menapii

Morini   Sunuci

Nervii

BELGICA

Remi

GALLIA
LUGDUNENSIS

Aedui

*Oceanus
Atlanticus*

N

Arverni

AQUITANIA

200 mls

300 km

NARBONESE
GAUL

HISPANIA
TARRACONENSIS

Frisii

Batavi Batavodurum   Cherusci
Grinnes   • Arenacum   Bructeri
Vada Cugerni • Castra Vetera   Marsi
             • Asciburgium
LOWER   • Gelduba   GERMANIA
        Baetasii • Novaesium
GERMANY
Marcodurum • Ubii • Colonia Agrippinensium
Sunuci   Tolbiacum • Bonna
Tungri   Usipi   Chatti

             Mattiaci

     Treviri
Rigodulum •   Bingium   • Mogontiacum
       Augusta   Nava
       Treverorum Vangiones   Suebians
Mosa

Divodurum •

     Mediomatrici

       Moselle   Danube
             Triboci
   Leuci
        UPPER
Andematunnum GERMANY
                      RAETIA   Aenus
Lingones   Vindonissa •
        ▲ Mount Vocetius   NORICUM
Vesontio •
   Sequani
        • Aventicum

Arar
       Helvetii   TRANSPADANE
                        GAUL   Opitergium
                              Vicetia • • Patavium   Aquilae
Lyons   Augusta
(Lugdunum) Graian Praetoria   Brixia
      Alps   • Novaria Mediolanum •   Verona
      Eporedia Vercellae Cremona Bedriacum
• Vienne   Po (Padus) Adriatic
   Allobroges Cottian   Ticinum Brixellum   Sea
        Alps   Placentia • Mutina
Rhodanus   Augusta   Regium Lepidum   • Ravenna
  • Lucus   Taurinorum   Bononia
NARBONESE
GAUL   Maritime   • Albingaunum
  Vocontii   Alps   Portus Pisanus   ITALIA
              • Hercules Monoecus
Aquae Sextiae • Antipolis
          • Forum Julii

   STOECHADES   CORSICA Tyrrhenian
                              Sea

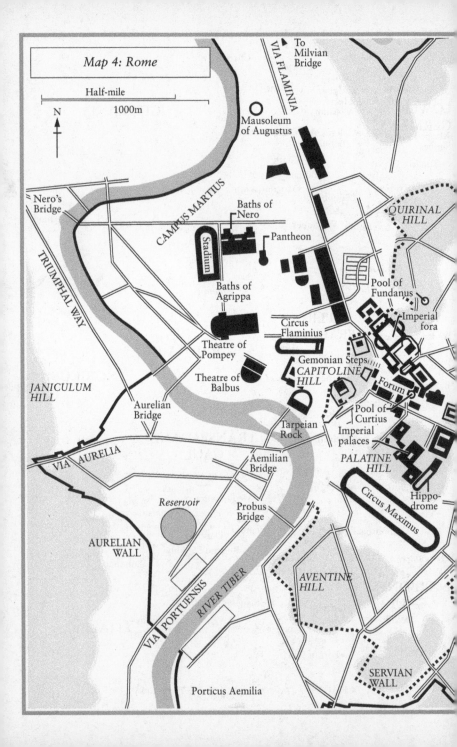

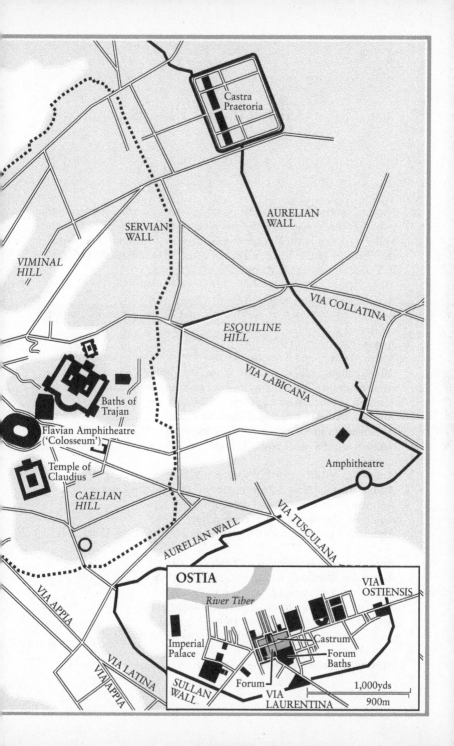

Glossary of Places

For each entry, if the ancient name is listed, then the modern name (where known) and country are given. Some places (e.g. 'Aventine Hill') are given in their modern English form. The first appearance in the *Histories* is also listed, except in cases where names do not feature in Tacitus' text but are mentioned in the Notes.

Achaia (central and southern Greece) 1.23
Actium (promontory at the mouth of Gulf of Amvrakia, western Greece) 1.1
Aenus (River Inn, in the Alps) 3.5
Africa (Tunisia and Tripolitania) 1.7
Albingaunum (Albenga, town of northern Italy) 2.15
Albintimilium (Ventimiglia, town of northern Italy) 2.13
Altinum (Altino, town of north-east Italy) 3.6
Anagnia (Anagni, town of central Italy) 3.62
Andematunnum (Langres, town of eastern France)
Antioch (Antiochia (Latin), Antakya (mod.), city of southern Turkey) 2.78
Antipolis (Antibes, town of southern France) 2.15
Aquae Sextiae (Aix-en-Provence, town of southern France)
Aquileia (Aquileia, town of northern Italy) 2.46
Aquinum (Aquino, town of central Italy) 1.88
Aquitania (province located south-west of the River Loire, France) 1.76
Arar (River Saône, south-east France) 2.59
Arenacum (Rindern, village in Germany) 5.20
Aricia (Ariccia, town of central Italy) 3.36
Ariminum (Rimini, town of northern Italy) 3.41
Arretium (Arezzo, north-west Italy)
Asciburgium (Asberg, town of northern Germany) 4.33
Asia (western Turkey) 1.10
Ateste (Este, town of northern Italy) 3.6

Atria (Adria, town of northern Italy) 3.12
Augusta Praetoria (Aosta, north-west Italy)
Augusta Taurinorum (Turin, north-west Italy)
Augusta Trevirorum (Trier, on the Moselle, central-southern Germany) 4.62
Aventine Hill (Rome) 3.70
Aventicum (Avenches, town of Switzerland) 1.68

Baetica (Andalucia, region of southern Spain) 1.53
Batavodurum (north-eastern suburbs of Nijmegen, Netherlands) 5.20
Bedriacum (probably Tornata, west of Bózzolo, town of northern Italy) 2.23
Belgica (region of north-eastern France/Belgium) 1.12
Belius (River Nahal Naaman, in Israel) 5.7
Beneventum (Benevento, southern Italy)
Berytus (Beirut, Lebanon) 2.81
Bingium (Bingen, city of northern Germany) 4.70
Bithynia (country in north-west Asia Minor, organized into a province with Pontus by Pompey in 63 BC)
Bonna (Bonn, northern Germany) 4.19
Bononia (Bologna, northern Italy) 2.53
Bovillae (near Frattochie, town of central Italy) 4.2
Britannia (the province of Britain)
Brixellum (Brescello, town of northern Italy) 2.33
Brixia (Brescia, town of northern Italy) 3.27
Brundisium (Brindisi, town of southern Italy) 2.83
Byzantium (Istanbul, Turkey) 2.83

Caesarea (town between Tel Aviv and Haifa, Israel) 2.78
Calabria (province of Lecce, southern Italy) 2.83
Campania (Lazio and Campania, central Italy)1.2
Campus Martius (Field of Mars, Rome) 1.86
Capitoline Hill (Capitolium, Rome) 1.2
Cappadocia (eastern Turkey) 1.78
Capua (Santa Maria di Capua Vetere, southern Italy) 3.57
Carnutum (town on the Danube between Petronell and Deutsch-Altenburg, Austria)
Carsulae (close to Sangémini, central Italy) 3.60
Caspian Gates (Dariel Pass in the Caucasus Mountains between Tblisi and Vladikavkas) 1.6.
Castores (near Cremona, northern Italy) 2.24
Chobus (River Khobi or Inguri, Caucasus, Georgia) 3.48

Cilicia (coastal area in southern Asia Minor (now in Turkey)
Clazomenae (town on the coast of Ionia, Turkey)
Clunia (town in northern Spain, 25 miles north-west of Osma)
Cluviae (exact location uncertain, central Italy) 4.5
Colonia Agrippinensium (Cologne, Germany) 1.56
Commagene (kingdom located between the River Euphrates and the
    Taurus mountains)
Cottian Alps (mountain range west of Turin covering northern Italy
    and southern Switzerland) 1.61
Cremona (Cremona, northern Italy) 2.17
Cyrene (Shahhat, Libya) 4.45
Cythnus (island of Kythnos, Aegean, Greece) 2.8

Dacia (Romania) 3.53
Dalmatia (Croatia, Bosnia, Serbia) 1.76
Divodurum (Metz, central-eastern France) 1.63
Dyrrachium (Durazzo, Albania) 2.83

Emerita (Merida, central-southern Spain) 1.78
Eporedia (Ivrea, northern Italy) 1.70
Etruria (Tuscany, central Italy) 1.86

Fanum Fortunae (Fano, central-northern Italy) 3.50
Ferentium (Ferento, central Italy) 2.50
Fidenae (Castel Giubileo, central Italy) 3.79
Forum Alieni (perhaps Legnago, northern Italy) 3.6
Forum Julii (Fréjus, southern France) 2.14

Galatia (central Anatolia) 2.9
Gelduba (Gellep, near Krefeld, western Germany) 4.26
Gemonian Steps (Rome) 3.74
Graian Alps (area round the Little St Bernard Pass) 2.66
Grinnes (perhaps Rossum, Netherlands) 5.20
Grove of Refuge (Rome) 3.71

Hadrumetum (Sousse, Tunisia) 4.50
Haemus (mountain range of Stara Planina and Rodolpi Planina,
    Bulgaria) 2.85
Hercules Monoecus (Monaco, southern France) 3.42
Hispalis (Seville, southern Spain) 1.78
Hispania Tarraconensis (province covering north and east Spain)
Histria (Istria, Croatia) 2.72

Hostilia (Ostiglia, northern Italy) 2.100

Ida, mountain (Psiloriti range, Crete, Greece) 5.2
Illyricum (an area covering the Balkan peninsula, divided by the
    Romans into two provinces, Dalmatia and Pannonia) 1.6
Interamna (Terni, central Italy) 2.64

Janiculum (Rome) 3.51
Julian Alps (also known as the Pannonian Alps; located between the
    north-east of Italy and north-west of Slovenia) 3.8

Latium (region of central Italy)
Lepcis (near al Khums, Libya) 4.50
Liguria (Liguria with parts of Piedmont, northern Italy) 2.15
Lower Germany (province on the left bank of the Rhine consisting
    of southern and western Netherlands, parts of Flanders and the
    Nordrhein-Westfalen region) 1.9
Lucania (Lucania and southern Campania, Italy) 2.83
Luceria (Lucera, town of Apulia, southern Italy) 3.86
Lucus (Luc-en-Diois, south-eastern France) 1.66
Lugdunese Gaul (a Roman province created by Augustus and covering
    the central region of France) 1.59
Lusitania (province in central-western Spain and Portugal) 1.13
Lycia (country in south-west Asia Minor)
Lyons (Lugdunum (Latin), France) 1.51

Marcodurum (perhaps Merken, near Düren, western Germany)
    4.28
Maritime Alps (small coastal province created by Augustus 14 BC and
    forming a buffer zone between Italy and Narbonese Gaul)
Mauretania Caesariensis (eastern Morocco and western Algeria)
    2.58
Mauretania Tingitana (Morocco west of River Moulouya) 2.58
Mediolanum (Milan, northern Italy) 1.70
Memphis (near Bedrashen, south of Cairo, Egypt) 4.84
Mevania (Bevagna, central Italy) 3.55
Milvian Bridge (a Tiber crossing on the Via Flaminia just north of
    Rome) 1.87
Minturnae (near mouth of River Garigliano, western-central Italy)
    3.57
Misenum (Miseno, western-central Italy) 2.9
Moesia (area south of River Danube) 1.76

Mogontiacum (Mainz, central-western Germany) 4.15

Mosa (River Meuse or Maas, rising in France, then flowing through Belgium and the Netherlands until it reaches the North Sea) 4.28

Mount Vocetius (perhaps Wöschnau, Switzerland) 1.68

Mutina (Modena, northern Italy) 1.50

Nabalia (river, perhaps Ijssel or Vecht, Netherlands) 5.26

Narbonese Gaul (Provence and Languedoc, southern France) 1.76

Narnia (Narni, central Italy) 3.58

Nava (River Nahe, rising in the area of Nohfelden (Saarland), flowing through the Rhineland-Palatinate and joining the River Rhine at Bingen) 4.70

Nearer Spain (Hispania Citerior (Latin), which designates the eastern area of Spain, later to be reorganized to become the province of Hispania Tarraconensis) 1.49

Noricum (province in eastern Austria) 1.11

Novaesium (Neuss, western Germany) 4.26

Novaria (Novara, northern Italy) 1.70

Numidia (eastern Algeria, western Tunisia)

Ocriculum (Otricoli, central Italy) 3.78

Oea (Tripoli, Libya) 4.50

Opitergium (Oderzo, north-east Italy) 3.6

Ostia (Ostia-Scavi, central Italy) 1.80

Palatine Hill (Rome) 1.39

Pamphylia (southern Anatolia) 2.9

Pannonia (western Hungary and northern Croatia and Serbia) 1.76

Pannonian Alps (also known as the Julian Alps; located between the north-east of Italy and north-west of Slovenia) 2.98

Paphos (Cyprus) 2.2

Parthia (country extending between the Caspian Sea and the Persian Gulf, incorporating Iran, and parts of Iraq, Turkey, Armenia, Azarbaijan, Turkmenistan, Afghanistan and Pakistan) 1.2

Patavium (Padua, northern Italy) 3.6

Pelusium (Tell el-Farama, the city at the easternmost end of the Nile in Egypt)

Pennine Alps (Great St Bernard Pass through the western Alps on the Swiss-Italian border) 1.87

Perusia (Perugia, central Italy) 1.50

Pharsalus (Farsala, central Greece) 1.50

Philippi (near Kavalla, Greece) 1.50

Phoenicia (coastal land extending from Syria to southern Lebanon and Galilee) 5.6
Picenum (Abruzzi, central Italy) 3.42
Placentia (Piacenza, northern Italy) 2.17
Po (river, Padus (Latin), in northern Italy, running from the Alps to the Adriatic Sea) 1.70
Poetovio (Ptuj, eastern Slovenia) 3.1
Pontus (northern Turkey) 2.6
Pool of Curtius (Rome) 1.41
Pool of Fundanus (Rome) 3.69
Portus Pisanus (San Stefano, near Livorno, northern Italy) 3.42
Ptolemais (Acre, coastal town of northern Israel)
Puteoli (Pozzuoli, western-central Italy) 3.57

Quirinal Hill (Rome)

Raetia (east Switzerland, west Tirol and Germany within the Danube and Inn rivers) 1.11
Ravenna (Ravenna, north-eastern Italy, but used to designate the port of Classis, 8 km to the south-east of the city) 2.100
Regium Lepidum (Reggio Emilia, northern Italy) 2.50
Rhacotis (south-west quarter of Alexandria, Egypt) 4.84
Rigodulum (Riol, near Trier, western Germany) 4.71

Samnium (region of southern Italy)
Saxa Rubra (a few miles north of Rome) 3.79
Seleucia (Samandağ, western Turkey) 4.84
Sena (Siena, central Italy) 4.45
Sinope (Sinop, western Turkey) 4.83
Sinuessa Spa (Terme di San Ricco, near Mondragone, western-central Italy) 1.72
Stoechades Islands (Îles d'Hyères, off the southern coast of France) 3.43
Suessa Pometia (town about 20 miles south of Rome, which no longer existed in Tacitus' time) 3.72

Tarentum (Taranto, southern Italy) 2.83
Tarpeian Rock (Rome) 3.71
Tarracina (Terracina, western-central Italy) 3.57
Thrace (Bulgaria) 1.11
Ticinum (Pavia, northern Italy) 2.17
Tolbiacum (Zülpich, near Cologne, western Germany) 4.79

Glossary of Peoples

Wherever possible, the locations of these peoples and tribes have been given in terms of the equivalent modern country or region. The first appearance in the *Histories* is also listed, except if a name does not feature in Tacitus' text but is mentioned in the Notes.

Aedui (Gallic tribe based in Burgundy, France, whose capital was Augustodunum (Autun)) 1.51
Albani (people of Azerbaijan) 1.6
Allobroges (tribe from around the River Rhône and Lake Geneva, Switzerland) 1.66
Arsacidae (rulers of Parthia from the third century BC to the third century AD) 1.40
Arverni (tribe from the Auvergne, south-east France) 4.17

Baetasii (tribe from around Louvain and St Truiden, central Belgium) 4.56
Batavi (tribe from between the rivers Rhine and Waal, central Netherlands) 1.59
Belgae (people from northern Gaul, with individual tribes located in Belgium and northern France) 4.17
Boii (tribe from between the rivers Adda and Po, northern Italy) 2.61
Brigantes (tribe from between Hadrian's Wall and the River Trent, northern Britain) 3.45
Bructeri (tribe from between the rivers Lippe and Ems, western Germany) 4.21

Caeracates (German tribe based on the west bank of the Rhine) 4.70
Canninefates (tribe from around The Hague, Netherlands) 4.15
Chatti (tribe from around the upper Weser River, western Germany) 4.12
Chauci (tribe from between the rivers Elbe and Ems, northern Germany) 4.79

Cherusci (tribe from north-western Germany)
Cimbri (tribe from northern Jutland, Denmark) 4.73
Cugerni (tribe from around Krefeld, western Germany) 4.26

Dacians (a Thracian people inhabiting the area in and around the Carpathian mountains, Romania) 1.2

Eumolpidae (clan from Eleusis, an ancient city of Attica, and hereditary priests of the Eleusian Mysteries) 4.83

Frisii (tribe from the northern Netherlands and Friesland) 4.15

Garamantes (tribe from north Africa) 4.50

Helvetii (tribe of western Switzerland) 1.67

Iazyges (tribe occupying area between Danube and Tisza rivers, Hungary) 3.5
Idaei (inhabitants of Mount Ida, Crete) 5.2

Leuci (tribe from around Toul, north-east France) 1.64
Lingones (tribe from around Langres, north-east France) 1.53

Marsaci (tribe from the Netherlands) 4.56
Marsi (tribe from south of upper Lippe River, western Germany) 3.59
Mattiaci (tribe from around Wiesbaden, central-western Germany) 4.37
Medi (people from northern Iran) 5.8
Mediomatrici (tribe from around Divodurum (Metz), north-eastern France) 1.63
Menapii (Belgic tribe inhabiting northern Belgium) 4.28
Morini (tribe from around the west Pas-de-Calais, north-western France) 4.28

Nervii (tribe from between the rivers Schelde and Meuse, Belgium) 4.15

Paeligni (tribe from Abruzzi, central Italy) 3.59
Parthi (people of Iraq and Iran) 1.2

Remi (Gallic tribe from around Rheims, northern France) 4.67
Rhoxolani (a tribal sub-set of the Sarmatians, living around the Danube) 1.79

Samnites (tribe from the southern Apennines, central-southern Italy) 3.59

Sarmatians (tribe from around the lower Danube, Hungary and Slovakia) 1.2

Sedochezi (tribe from the Caucasus, Georgia) 3.48

Sequani (tribe from eastern France and western Switzerland) 1.51

Solymi (originally a people from south-west Turkey and supposedly the founders of Jerusalem) 5.2

Suebians (tribe from the Elbe valley, southern Germany) 1.2

Sunuci (tribe from southern Netherlands and western Germany) 4.66

Tencteri (tribe from south of the River Lippe, western Germany) 4.21

Teutoni (Germanic tribe, originally from the Baltic region) 4.73

Treviri (Gallic tribe, whose capital was Augusta Trevirorum (Trier), central-southern Germany) 1.53

Triboci (tribe from Alsace, eastern France) 4.70

Tungri (tribe from near the Ardennes, north-eastern France) 2.14

Ubii (tribe from around Cologne, western Germany) 4.18

Usipi (tribe from between the rivers Sieg and Lahn, western Germany) 4.37

Vangiones (tribe from around Worms, south-western Germany) 4.70

Vascones (tribe from north-eastern Spain) 4.33

Vienne (Vienna (Latin), central-southern France) 1.65

Vocontii (Gallic tribe from south-east France, who occupied the western foothills of the Alps) 1.66

Index of Personal Names